Endorsements for *Against the Corporate Media*

"With a glorious collection of writers—many of them former insiders—*Against the Corporate Media* is the single best dissection of the major media I've ever seen. Read it and share a copy with a journalist friend. Highly recommended."

–Peter Schweizer, Author of #1 *New York Times*
bestsellers *Blood Money* and *Red Handed*

"No matter how much you hate the media, it's never enough. And if you really hate the media, *Against the Corporate Media* is a no-holds barred takedown of a corrupt media establishment that lies, cheats and destroys good people by some of the best in the business."

–Daniel Greenfield, VP David Horowitz Freedom Center, Author
of *Domestic Enemies: The Founding Fathers' Fight Against the Left*

"Twenty years ago, the Internet and the rise of thoughtful 'citizen journalists' in the blogosphere seemed to herald the promise of an accountable media industry and greater focus on objectivity. Instead, Big Tech has combined with activist media organizations, Marxist Academia, and the bureaucratic state to stamp out dissent and debate, in the US and around the world. *Against the Corporate Media*'s all-star symposium demonstrates that the market cannot defeat that political/cultural Marxist consortium without a sustained effort to deconstruct it—and provides a sobering look at just how daunting that mission will be."

–Ed Morrissey, Managing Editor of HotAir.
com and Author of Going Red

Also by Michael Walsh

Nonfiction

Fiction

AGAINST THE CORPORATE MEDIA

FORTY-TWO WAYS THE PRESS HATES YOU

Edited and with an Introduction by
Michael Walsh

BOMBARDIER
BOOKS

Published by Bombardier Books
An Imprint of Post Hill Press
ISBN: 979-8-88845-421-3
ISBN (eBook): 979-8-88845-422-0

Against the Corporate Media:
Forty-two Ways the Press Hates You
© 2024 by the-Pipeline.org
All Rights Reserved

Cover Design by Jim Villaflores
Cover Illustration by Michael Ramirez

This is a work of nonfiction. All people, locations, events, and situations are portrayed to the best of the author's memory.

Post Hill Press
New York • Nashville
posthillpress.com

Published in the United States of America
1 2 3 4 5 6 7 8 9 10

For Mark Steyn, free-speech warrior.

CONTENTS

PART THREE: THE PAST AS PROLOGUE

PART FOUR: THE MEDIA VS. AMERICA

PART EIGHT: THE RISE—AND FALL—OF THE INTERNET

INTRODUCTION: A "HIGHER LOYALTY"

BY MICHAEL WALSH

In the first chapter of his magnum opus, *Public Opinion* (1922), the journalist and public intellectual Walter Lippmann makes this statement about the role of a free and independent press in the United States of America:

> I argue that representative government, either in what is ordinarily called politics, or in industry, cannot be worked successfully, no matter what the basis of election, unless there is an independent, expert organization for making the unseen facts intelligible to those who have to make the decisions...
>
> The newspapers are regarded by democrats as a panacea for their own defects, whereas analysis of the nature of news and of the economic basis of journalism seems to show that the newspapers necessarily and inevitably reflect, and therefore, in greater or lesser measure, intensify, the defective organization of public opinion. My conclusion is that public opinions must be organized for the press if they are to be sound, not by the press as is the case today.

Given the time and place of publication, Lippmann's sentiments were hardly extraordinary. His book appeared the same year as Sinclair

Lewis's resentful excoriation of middle-class America, *Babbitt*, in the direct aftermath of World War I and, more important, of the presidency of Woodrow Wilson, who was greatly influenced by Lippmann; indeed, the journalist briefly held a position in the Wilson administration in 1917, as an assistant to the Secretary of War Newton D. Baker. Lippmann's real calling, however, was as a member of the press: He was one of the founders of *The New Republic* magazine; a lead writer for and later editor of the partisan-Democratic *New York World*; and, in 1931, the editor of the moderate-Republican *New York Herald-Tribune* and a syndicated columnist, a column which he wrote until 1967. He died in 1974 at the age of 85. Throughout his long life, he moved from socialism to big-government, save-the-world Republicanism—which, given the signal events of his lifetime, his Reform Jewish upbringing on Manhattan's toney Upper East Side, and his Harvard education, is hardly surprising.

Today, after more than a century of argument and disputation, it appears that Lippmann's argument has won out. His posthumous victory, however, is recent. Throughout most of the twentieth century, his premise that public opinion should be shaped by a committee of Wise Men may have been accepted by Madison Avenue and the public-relations spawn of Edward Bernays (Freud's nephew, who wrote *Crystallizing Public Opinion* a year later, in 1923), but it was, in fact, roundly rejected by actual journalists; having the opinions of what evolved into the modern media subject to external influence and control was anathema to a trade that prized its working-class roots. Instead, the primacy of independent objectivity was upheld—or at last paid lip service to—by the press and, later, by the national television networks. No matter what the individual reporter's or editor's opinion was, the thinking went, it should be kept out of a news story to the greatest extent possible. Just the facts, ma'am.

No longer. The fracturing of the Republic into red and blue states, into pro- and anti-American/anti-Western constituencies has cast "objectivity" in a repressive light. Like most other traditions of vanishing America, it is increasingly seen as a tool of the "patriarchy." When I

2

began my career in journalism at the Rochester *Democrat & Chronicle*
in February 1972, there were still two (or more) sides to every story,
and the conscientious reporter—we didn't call ourselves "journalists"
back then—made sure he or she got all of them, or at least made the
effort. Despite the partisan origins of most of the newspapers at that
time—often reflected in their very names—the postwar consensus
was to strive for fairness and even-handedness.

That year coincided with the heyday of the "Women's Lib" movement and the concomitant wave of women entering the American
work force, and so a concerted effort was made (Gannett, which
owned the *D&C*, was one of the leaders) to get more female reporters
into the field, and more female bylines into the paper. In reaction to
the racial unrest that had broken out across the country from Harlem
and Rochester in 1964, through Watts the following year, to the widespread turmoil of 1967–1978 in Newark, Detroit, Washington, D.C.,
and elsewhere, there had been a similar drive to get more black voices
into the local and national media.

Still, "objectivity" largely remained the journalist's goal. With
the arrival of Donald Trump on the American political scene, however, that consensus shattered along ideological lines. *The New York
Times* signaled the new standard in an August 7, 2016, piece by Jim
Rutenberg:

> If you're a working journalist and you believe that
> Donald J. Trump is a demagogue playing to the
> nation's worst racist and nationalistic tendencies, that
> he cozies up to anti-American dictators and that he
> would be dangerous with control of the United States
> nuclear codes, how the heck are you supposed to cover
> him? Journalism shouldn't measure itself against any
> one campaign's definition of fairness. It is journalism's
> job to be true to the readers and viewers, and true
> to the facts, in a way that will stand up to history's
> judgment. To do anything less would be untenable.

Call it a "higher loyalty." Today's journalists now openly celebrate the death of objectivity, arguing that reporters have biases like everybody else, so why pretend that they don't? In clear violation of their own—and now very much outmoded—Society of Professional Journalists' Code of Ethics, they happily ignore such tenets as:

* *Identify sources clearly.*
* *Consider sources' motives before promising anonymity.*
* *Avoid conflicts of interest, real or perceived.*
* *Expose unethical conduct in journalism, including within their organizations.*

Thus, after nearly a century's consensus about journalistic best practices, we have come full circle to the days of naked partisanship that marked the earliest American newspapers. Gossip has become news, journalistic crusades are fabricated out of whole cloth and attributed to anonymous sources as justification. It's noteworthy that the word "objectivity" nowhere appears in the current SPJ code, which was revised in 2014. Why would it? Objectivity has become the mortal enemy of the current vogue for "explanatory" or "advocacy" journalism—otherwise generally known as propaganda.

The transformation of journalism from rank advocacy to lukewarm "objectivity" and back to even ranker political propaganda (nearly all news stories today are couched in political terms, including those about pop music and sports) is one of the principal subjects of this book. Accordingly we have assembled a corps of forty-two journalists—some grizzled veterans, some newcomers, some of whose primary occupations lie in the wider fields of book publishing, fiction, non-fiction, television, and even Hollywood—to analyze the startling changes that have come over the profession in our lifetimes.

Even greater than the abandonment of "objectivity" as a pernicious influence on journalism is the internet, the great destroyer of printed periodicals, which has laid waste to the newspaper and magazine industry and has fallen under the control of the social-media giants, such as X (formerly Twitter) and Facebook, and is now subject to favoritism and even censorship by near-monopolies like Google, a search engine that also now controls visual media via its ownership of YouTube. Whether the patrician Lippmann would have admired his wishful handiwork now that it is a reality is open to question, but surely he would celebrate the intrusion of the American federal government, along with governments around the world, into both *de facto* and *de jure* informational control of cyberspace. In many countries around the world, the press and attendant broadcast media are now directly and unabashedly controlled by government entities which, in many cases, openly fund and censor them.

Even in a work of this length, it is of course impossible to touch upon every aspect of the current state of the media. From the point of view of one who has labored in it, off and on, for more than half a century, it is parlous and getting worse. Ask someone with less than ten years' experience in the field and you may well—very likely will—get a different answer: that it's liberated, responsive, unfettered. Still, my work as a historian has convinced me of the truth of Jean-Baptiste Alphonse Karr's famous axiom, *plus ça change, plus c'est la même chose.* (The Paris-born Karr, who lived from 1808 to 1890, was, of course, a journalist himself, in addition to being a critic, novelist, and flora-culturalist. But that was back in the day when "journalists" were men of accomplishment in other fields.) That is to say, the fundamental things apply in all walks of human endeavor, and among these things is mankind's innate desire to convince others of the rightness of his position on any given subject. The question always has been: What's the best way to go about it?

The forebears of modern pundits are essayists, such as Montaigne, Bacon, Pascal, and Emerson, while reporters easily can trace their lineage to the eighteenth century and, if you want to go all the way back, to Pheidippides, who announced the Greek victory at Marathon in 490 B.C., with a terse, one-word report, *nikomen*, and then, mission accomplished, promptly dropped dead. From the start, news was not just news, but the interpretation of news; the Persians probably got a very different report when they heard the outcome of the battle. And so it remains today; Claud Cockburn's famous if perhaps apocryphal 1930s account of an earthquake in the *Times* of London was headlined, "Small Earthquake in Chile, Not Many Dead." The affected Chileans, if any, might have begged to differ.

A profession as idiosyncratic as journalism necessarily attracts certain types of individuals: In my experience, shy loners who found in reporting—not simply pontificating; the internet is currently rife with juveniles who have opinions on every subject but have never in their lives covered a town meeting, reported from federal court, worked the cop shop, seen a dead body at the site of a murder, experienced the stench of a fire scene, and been dragged away by a state security service in a communist country (all of which I have), or broken a single story—a license to come out of their shells, belly up to the bar of life, and ask the most personal and intrusive questions imaginable in order to do the job. Reporting gave you a license to do something you never might have done on your own otherwise: to get personal details about the dearly, recently departed; boldly walk into a crime scene and view a fresh murder victim; grab your notebook and interpose yourself in an ongoing riot or even a war zone. Somehow, because you were a neutral—"objective"—observer, you felt immune to embarrassment, revulsion, or even physical danger. In fact, you found that you *liked* it.

You also had to be able to type (sometimes with just two fingers, and, man, were those old-timers fast), rapidly synthesize information, get it into narrative form as accurately and interestingly as possible— it's no wonder that the early ranks of screenwriters were comprised of former journalists themselves—produce copy amidst the chaos of a newsroom and on ironclad deadlines, field the editor's queries (generally delivered in a shout, as rudely as possible), watch as the pasted-together stream of copy disappeared into the composing room where proofs were struck (proofreading was part of the job), and cast into lead on the Linotype machines, pounded in plates, and affixed to the presses. Then came the most thrilling moment of all as the whole building shook with the roar of the presses and the newspapers came flying off, were assembled and bundled, delivered to the docks to be loaded onto trucks and finally delivered to homes and newspaper boxes all over the circulation area. At which point, reporters were at the bar, having a weary but celebratory shot before (on morning newspapers like the one I started on) returning home in the wee hours to sleep away most of the next day and then do it all over again.

Another element, vanishing today, is the notion of the newsroom itself, and its socializing and morale function. Reporters on the staff of even a medium-sized urban daily felt part of a larger team dedicated to a noble and very competitive enterprise. Newsrooms took their leads from the managing editor and his top editors: Their loyalty to the publication was not dependent on the corporation that owned it, but to the boss who ran it. Very often, this boss had hired you personally and, accordingly, you would follow him or her anywhere. I was lucky to work for two such men: Reg Murphy at the *San Francisco Examiner*, and Ray Cave at *Time*. In those days, in media companies big and powerful (Hearst and Time, Inc.), the best editors stood by their hires, always took their sides during reader controversies, and if they had criticism of your work, relayed it to you privately but often in no uncertain terms.

In other words, there was camaraderie and a shared sense of purpose. You weren't going to get rich in journalism, but you had a mission. You could make a difference, every day. It wasn't a profession the way that being a doctor or a lawyer was, it was a craft—which was why the newspaper union was called the Newspaper Guild, now the NewsGuild-CWA (Communications Workers of America)—a craft that could be learned from the ground up while on the job. One did not need to major in journalism at a college or university; in fact, for most of journalism's existence one didn't need a college degree at all. Newspapermen (and they were almost always men) came from the streets, not the campuses. They had been educated at the school of hard knocks, not at a School of Communication. By 1972, that was already changing. When I was hired at the *Democrat* after contributing a few music reviews as a stringer, the only question the editor asked me was whether I had a college degree of any kind. That mine was a Bachelor of Music made no difference to them at all. After short stints writing the weather story and reporting on suburban town meetings, I soon found myself on the police beat, and loving it. That was the quickest, and best, education in human nature I could possibly have had.

Today, as the lesser newspapers have vanished and the principal ones—*The New York Times* and a handful of others—have survived the digital transformation into 24/7 operations with national and international audiences, they have increasingly become monochromatic in background or outlook, no matter how "diverse" they may appear to be in artfully assembled group photographs. Most top journalists today went to the same Ivy League schools, live in the same urban neighborhoods, clump together when they buy summer houses—beach or country?—date the same people while having discreet affairs with each other and, if and when they have children— often their wives or husbands are also journalists—send them to the same schools. What was once a profession of hustling hardscrabble "ink-stained wretches" is now the circumscribed province of carefully manicured New Yorkers and Washingtonians who themselves often rotate in and out of the governments they cover at the highest levels.

Most disconcerting is the uniformity of outlook and political affiliation. Among the ranks of elite reporters today there is near-universal agreement on all the political and social issues that matter, which is to say, to those issues that matter to them. In the early days of conservative talk radio and the blogosphere, men like the late Rush Limbaugh and the late Andrew Breitbart rose up in direct reaction to the menacing media monolith they were both then experiencing and which they saw evolving even further. Neither of them lived to see the full, joyous abandonment of "objectivity," the gleeful embrace of political and ideological partisanship, and the annihilation of the old media infrastructure by the internet that has resulted today in what has been called the Mainstream Media, but which we have here termed the Corporate Media.

Far from embracing genuine diversity or harkening back to the contentious, multi-voiced press environment of the nation's founding, today's Corporate Media brooks no demurrals or disdain, celebrates uniformity of opinion, scourges dissent from the prevailing political orthodoxy, and has utterly forsaken the First Amendment protections of freedom of religion, speech, and assembly that once protected it during its post-Cold War incubation, and to which it once paid such crocodilian lip service. Instead, the media in nearly all Western countries now link up in a kind of multi-headed monster much like the monopolies once feared by such muckraking American authors as Upton Sinclair in *The Jungle* and Frank Norris in his uncompleted trilogy, *The Epic of the Wheat*, of which he only finished *The Octopus: A Story of California* before his premature death at age thirty-two in 1902. (That book described the frontier battles between ranchers and unscrupulous agents of the Southern Pacific Railroad.) The internet, which once promised to let a thousand flowers bloom, to quote Chairman Mao, has instead become the voice of the powerful—which, given the multi-billionaire status of many of its founders, is perhaps not surprising.

In short, the Narrative—increasingly hard Left—has become everything. And where once reporters dreamed of becoming screenwriters, today they don't even have to bother. Every day, they push a narrative far more politically potent than anything Ben Hecht or Charlie MacArthur ever dreamed of.

And so: The old gatekeepers are gone; long live the new gatekeepers. Or, to put it another way: Meet the new boss, even worse than the old boss. In his 1979 book *The Right Stuff*, author and iconoclastic journalist Tom Wolfe referred to the press as the "Victorian Gentleman," a Pecksniffian scold out of Dickens always on the alert for moral failings in the objects of his attention: "the constant hypocrite, who insisted on public manifestations of morality that he would never insist upon privately in his own life," as Wolfe later explained in a 1980 interview with *Rolling Stone*. Today, the new Gents tend more toward the sybaritic than the stuffed shirts of midcentury last, but their determination to root out apostasy and heresy is every bit as great, just as long as their media colleagues don't include themselves in the coverage.

The effect of all this has been to move the Overton Window of acceptable thought and behavior increasingly to the left: irresponsible and libertinistic when it comes to personal comportment, and progressive, proscriptive Stalinist when it comes to politics. Today's media is not so much informational as a kind of institutional opposition research bureau, forever ready to hunt down and punish heresy—even if has to reach back years, decades, and even if the wrong-think wasn't objectional at the time.

The internet wag who goes by the name of Iowahawk once summed up the modern journalist's primary duty as "covering important stories. With a pillow, until they stop moving." Like Ray Bradbury's firemen in *Fahrenheit 451*, modern journalists have stepped in to incinerate journalism's anarchic background. Having picked the side of the "progressive" billionaires, they have gleefully abjured not only their former ethics but also their profession's entire legacy of working-class backgrounds and state-university (or less) educations in order to take their proper places at the courts of Bezos, Gates, Zuckerberg, and the Googleplexers, stenographers of the Brave New World to come: a noxious paradise of malignant anonymity in the service of rigorous dogma, with nary a hint of dis- or mis-information to mar the rosy skies of Unanimity.

Our field of fire, therefore, is wide. For argumentative clarity and thematic unity, I have grouped the essays into the following sections: After opening under "General Principles" with Lance Morrow's evocation of what the old newsrooms felt like, "Journalism Was a Rascal," a brief excerpt from his 2023 book *The Noise of Typewriters*, the first section considers journalism in general, and features essays on the nature of journalism and journalists by Andrew Klavan, Peter Berkowitz, David Reaboi, John O'Sullivan, Charlie Kirk, and Jon Gabriel.

The second section, "On *The New York Times*," is devoted to the *fons et origo* of twenty-first century's journalism problems, once the most prestigious institution of center-left news reporting but latterly the house organ not simply of its beloved Democratic Party but of "progressivism" itself. Both Ashley Rindsberg and J. Peder Zane are longtime *Times* watchers—Zane worked for the paper for a few years—and herewith chart its descent into often embarrassing partisanship. Indeed, the *Times* has become the arbiter of political and social thought, instructing the politicians in the fine points of ever-changing Leftist orthodoxy on a daily basis, right down to the proper use of plural pronouns for single-entity transgender non-binaries still with their original sex characteristics assigned at birth.

Break the *Times*, break the Left.

Section three, "The Past as Prologue," contains seven essays on the history and background of American journalism, beginning with "The Founders and the Press" by Arthur Milikh of the Claremont Institute, and continuing with pieces on the overall decline of journalistic standards by former Gannett top executive Peter Prichard; the media's abandonment of "objectivity," by John Fund, for many years a writer at *The Wall Street Journal*; and some thoughts on the foundational nature of partisanship by *National Review* and Hillsdale College's John J. Miller. Mark Hemingway of *The Federalist* looks askance at the current mania for "fact-checking" by the Corporate Media, while Clarice Feldman, a former attorney with the Department of Justice Office of Special Investigations and a columnist for *The Pipeline*, conducts a withering cross-examination of the Supreme Court's notorious *Sullivan* decision, which has effectively made impossible libel suits against the media. Finally, Kyle Shideler of the Center for Security Policy in Washington, D.C., examines the extremely cozy relationship between the media and members of the intelligence community.

Part four, "The Media vs. America," is the heart of our *j'accuse*. Its ten essays treat politics, the "Russian collusion" hoax, the January 6, 2021, protests, wokism, race relations, immigration, the military, guns, the energy industry, and the police. Contributors include

Monica Crowley, Steven Hayward, Nick Searcy, Sebastian Gorka, Roger Simon, Mark Krikorian, Kurt Schlichter, Elizabeth Sheld, *The Pipeline*'s Tom Finnerty, and Jack Dunphy. Several of these names will be instantly familiar to regular readers of the political blogosphere: Crowley, a familiar figure on Fox News, began her career as an assistant to Richard Nixon, Gorka served as a special assistant to President Donald J. Trump, while Searcy, an actor, is well known for his appearances in the TV series *Justified*, as well as performances in two recently Oscar-nominated films, *The Shape of Water* and *Three Billboards Outside Ebbing, Missouri.*

Part five, "Foreign Affairs," consists of five essays about the media abroad. Ian Gregory tackles the once-beloved Beeb in "Inside the Woke BBC"; Canadians David Solway and Elizabeth Nickson cast a gimlet eye on their native land and its compliant media, especially the CBC. Ireland's disgraceful one-party mediaverse, personified by the national broadcaster Raidió Teilifís Éireann (RTE), gets a hiding from Ben Scallan, one of the bright young stars in the country's counter-media, while Australia's monolithic ABC is dismantled by Brit-turned-Aussie Peter Smith, also a *Pipeline* contributor.

Arts criticism is a disappearing discipline in culturally egalitarian cyberspace, but it has a long and distinguished history in such areas as motion pictures, literature, and music. Armond White, the best film critic in America, and the pseudonymous George MF Washington, a Hollywood insider, both have a go at film critics, while veteran book-publishing executive Thomas Lipscomb bemoans the death of the industry he long served. And I have a few words to say on the vanishing of serious "high" cultural commentary in the American media as well. This section is part six, "Criticism and Its Discontents."

No examination of the media would be complete without considering the expanded role of "Women and Sexuality" (part seven) in a once nearly all-male craft, and Priscilla Turner—a former Berkeley leftist, movie executive, writer for network television, the author of seven children's books, and at the dawn of the blogosphere the voice of *Priscilla's Daily News*—treats the fairer sex with no mercy. *The Pipeline's* very own lifestyle columnist, Jenny Kennedy, displays her devotion to saving the planet while traveling in style all over the world by taking some readers' questions, and Catholic commentator and activist Austin Ruse explains "how the media went gay."

We conclude with part eight, "The Rise of the Internet," now the standard medium for the dissemination of news and opinion. Veterans of the early, Wild West, days of cyberspace join us. Glenn Reynolds, the "blogfather" of the influential *Instapundit* site, still going strong, takes us back to the earliest days of blogging; Hannah Giles, the young woman in the series of videos that demolished the leftist activist group ACORN in 2009 when they appeared on the late Andrew Breitbart's *Big Government* website, returns us to that tumultuous period and her role in it, while radio talk-show host Larry O'Connor—who was also there at the beginning, writing for *Big Hollywood* under the name "Larry Stage"—reminds us of what a force of nature Andrew was.

Finally, Bill Whittle—whom you know from his *Afterburner* videos but who first came to my attention as the host of the *Eject! Eject! Eject!* site in those early days, ties the bow on our package with some concluding words on the biggest threat now facing journalism: explicit, unconstitutional, censorship from an unholy, fascistic alliance between governments and Big Tech to bring political conformity to the unruly craft of journalism.

True, journalism was always a rascal, as Lance Morrow notes. And over the years, decades, and centuries, the trick was to tame the rascal without turning him into a dreary Victorian Gent. Journalism has produced, worldwide, some of the greatest men and women of letters since practically the invention of the printing press. From it have sprung novelists, poets, playwrights, scenarists, scriptwriters, and movie directors (Stanley Kubrick, the Beethoven of cinema, began as a photojournalist). Journalists have succeeded in just about every discipline that involves telling stories by means of concentration, bravery, a facility with languages, an organizational brain, unbounded curiosity about the world, an ability to conceive and write in long forms, and inspiration. The more pedestrian—the vast majority to be sure— have remained journalists.

To what further end, however? Lippmann's dream has come true: Opinions are now organized *for* the press but *by* the press itself. We have bought into Lippmann's statement that a journalist's

> version of the truth is only his version...the more he understands his own weaknesses, the more ready he is to admit that where there is no objective test, his own opinion is in some vital measure constructed out of his own stereotypes, according to his own code, and by the urgency of his own interest. He knows that he is seeing the world through subjective lenses.

Lippmann's quarrel, however, was not simply with journalism, but with the very nature of American democracy; he was, after all, a Wilsonian:

> For the troubles of the press, like the troubles of representative government, be it territorial or functional, like the troubles of industry, be it capitalist, cooperative, or communist, go back to a common source: to the failure of self-governing people to transcend their casual experience and their prejudice, by inventing, creating, and organizing a machinery of knowledge. It is because they are compelled to act without a reliable picture of the world, that governments, schools, newspapers and churches make such small headway against the more obvious failings of democracy, against violent prejudice, apathy, preference for the curious trivial as against the dull important, and the hunger for sideshows and three legged calves. This is the primary defect of popular

government, a defect inherent in its traditions, and all
its other defects can, I believe, be traced to this one.

It's taken a century since *Public Opinion* was first published for
Lippmann's ideas to finally have become mainstream—indeed, corporate. Few read Sinclair Lewis anymore, his Pulitzers and Nobel Prizes
notwithstanding, but Lippmann's insistence that the media's manifest
imperfections must be disqualifying in a properly run modern state
have now found wide favor across the political spectrum. The "penny
dreadfuls" that once posed such a serious threat to American morals
may have been replaced by social media, but the instinct to strangle
them remains the same.

What's different today is that this time, the Corporate Media has
joined the crusade. It gatekeeps, cheerleads, and openly indulges in
and celebrates censorship—the most recent and memorable example of which was the deliberate throttling of the Hunter Biden "laptop from hell" story, the suppression of which clearly influenced the
results of the 2020 election in the service of a frankly partisan cause.
Indeed, the Corporate Media barely bats an eye when the governments of any Western nations establish anti-"disinformation" bureaus
to surveil protected speech in the specious name of "safety," such as
the late, unlamented Disinformation Governance Board, mercifully
smothered in its cradle shortly after its birth during the Biden administration in 2022 but undoubtedly still lurking in the bowels of the
national-security state. And it seems entirely untroubled by such
bureaucratic excrescences as the U.S. government's Cybersecurity and
Infrastructure Security Agency, a three-billion-dollar-a-year arm of
the post-9/11 Department of Homeland Security, one of George W.
Bush's dubious gifts to the nation.

Largely controlled by a handful of immensely wealthy men, many
of whom have made their fortunes—which put those of William
Randolph Hearst and Joseph Pulitzer to shame—from the institutional
destruction wrought by the internet on the news business, the media
monolith no longer even pretends to welcome a multiplicity of voices,

but instead has allied itself with the prevailing transnational narrative of "progressive" liberalism. How this state of affairs came about, what have been its consequences, and what it portends for the future of both freedom of speech and democracy we now address in these pages.

PART ONE: GENERAL PRINCIPLES

JOURNALISM WAS A RASCAL
AN EXCERPT FROM *THE NOISE OF TYPEWRITERS*

BY LANCE MORROW

Journalism was a rascal—a smoker and a drinker—and the life was picaresque: hectic, improvised, although at times as dull as a clerk's. The pay was bad. You were broke half the time, and often hung over. But you were young enough to enjoy the scruffy mystique and a winking intimacy with big shots—with history itself (which, up close, was apt to look like a bit of a fraud). Did it add up to anything? I wondered. Henry Luce insisted that it did, but Henry Luce—with his money and power and the influence of his Presbyterian conscience upon the middle-class American mind—was a Big Picture man. (Luce believed in capitalizing Big Ideas and once sent a memo to his editors encouraging the practice.) He was certain that everything that fell beneath his gaze must mean something important.

People have forgotten Henry Luce. But he is, in some ways, the key to understanding journalism in the twentieth century. His career raised essential questions—about the nature of journalism, about the politics of storytelling, about the morals of power. Luce was a brilliant American success story—and a cautionary tale.

The journalism I am speaking of owed a lot to the atmosphere of the Great Depression, which was a generation before my time but nonetheless lingered on as folklore—a kind of warning and a moral framework: a lifestyle, an aesthetic.

During the Depression, the reporters were mostly New Dealers, while their publishers were overwhelmingly Republicans. Capra framed his stories around Americans' anxiety about whether they are Good; they imagined that if they were not Good, they must be Evil. Or anyway, they must be Pretty Bad. At the same time, it became a complicated lesson of the twentieth century, starting in the 1930s, that when people try to be perfect, they turn into fanatics. That was the story in foreign countries—in Russia, in Germany, around the time of *It Happened One Night*, which got the Oscar for Best Picture in 1934. Could it happen here? Capra liked to show Americans being tempted by an evil genius (often played by Edward Arnold)—a newspaper publisher with a fascist agenda—but, at the end, returning safely to the arms of their sweet democracy, like Dorothy restored to the farm in Kansas. I sometimes think that the leftist tendencies of twenty-first-century media have their origin in the myths of Frank Capra's movies.

There was a certain amount of decaying theology at work in all of this. In time, the country's Calvinism—the founding religion— had settled for democratizing itself as a cult of emotions. Feelings— like money—give the country a least common denominator: a lingua franca in which people in a diverse society might communicate with one another and affirm their humanity and their citizenship as Americans. Now, instead of hard theological thoughts, the country moralized its feelings. Almost from the start, the need to justify the American enterprise had produced an elaborately sentimental self-image. The Frank Capra movies (for example, *Meet John Doe* and *Mr. Smith Goes to Washington*) were a twentieth-century advance in that art—and so were Norman Rockwell's anecdotal paintings, the glowing American allegories that illustrated covers of *The Saturday Evening Post* in the days when it was a great and influential magazine; my father was an editor at the *Post* in those flush times, after the war. The self-confident and sometimes preacherly and overbearing narratives of Henry Luce's *Time* magazine had an immense moral and cultural influence on Americans. As a child, Luce, a China missionary's son, learned storytelling from the New Testament, from Christ's parables—each of which teaches a moral lesson. Stories in his magazines would similarly instruct. Hotchkiss and then Yale exposed him to the moralizing Greeks and Romans, especially Plutarch, who sought the truth of things in the lives of great men.

In any case, mass-circulation American journalism (especially Luce's) joined American politics and American religion and American movies in the restless project of making and remaking—or, eventually, unmaking—the national myth.

Journalism in the twentieth century proceeded on the assumption that there was such a thing as objective reality. The task of journalism, said Carl Bernstein—a companion of my youth when we were picaresque rascals side by side on the dictation bank at the *Washington Evening Star* back in the mid-1960s—was to obtain "the best available version of the truth." But in the writing and editing, objective reality tended to become subjective reality; facts were well enough, but important facts needed to be evaluated, judged—characterized. Which was the priority of a mythmaker like Luce: the hard facts of the case, or the storyteller's interpretation of them—the narrative line? Is journalism inevitably engaged in the working up of myths, whatever its pretensions to objectivity? A journalist needs a disciplined reverence for the facts, because the temptations of storytelling are strong and seductive.

I don't mean that mythmaking is necessarily perfidious; in any case, it is inevitable. It's a problem of storytelling and, so to speak, of entertainment. Where journalism is concerned, as I discovered over the years, the narrative line is not only a chronic problem of ethics but the key to culture itself—and even the glue that holds a society together.

But in the era that I am writing about, questions like that were above our pay grade. We took it for granted that there was something called the truth and that it could be discovered. Start at the level of the cop's truth: The victim was either white or black, male or female.

The murder weapon was of a certain caliber. Someone had pulled the trigger. Who? I'm talking about hard facts that are beneath the radar of controversy, of politics. Such facts did not invite abstract speculation. Woodward and Bernstein approached Watergate as a crime story, not a political one; they would knock on doors like police detectives and find things out. Woodward and Bernstein were like the boy in the story of the emperor's new clothes. In *Citizen Kane*, that great fable of journalism and American truth, an obscure clue like "Rosebud" might mean something. Find out what he meant by that, the editor told his boys in the smoky projection room at the start of the movie.

In the twenty-first century, on the other hand, journalism would find itself plunged into the metaverse. Politics and culture would migrate into the country of myth, with its hallucinations and hysterias—the floating world of a trillion screens. There might come to be no agreed reality at all. You did not dignify journalism by referring to it as "journalism" (a word that is even now a little too grand, too self-important) unless you put the word "yellow" in front of it. You called yourself a reporter or a newspaperman. News ceases to be news the minute that people know about it. Newspapers were for wrapping the fish or swatting the dog or else announcing, in big, black headlines, a sudden turn in the movie's plot (KANE CAUGHT IN LOVE NEST). The journalist and historian Eric Alterman went overboard in order to make the point: "Reporting was seen as a job for winos, perverts, and those without sufficient imagination to become gangsters."

Contempt for reporters had a long history. General William Tecumseh Sherman hated them (and he had reason, for they sometimes made things up or, worse, they aided the enemy by publishing entirely accurate information about his army's movements), and one day when he learned that Confederate guns had sunk a barge-load of Yankee reporters in the Mississippi River near Vicksburg, he laughed and cheered. The journalists swam ashore and survived, but at least they had gotten their notebooks wet.

When Janet Malcolm died in 2021, obituaries remembered the famous rant with which she opened her 1989 *New Yorker* magazine piece, later to become a book called *The Journalist and the Murderer* (about Jeffrey MacDonald, convicted of killing his wife and daughters, and Joe McGinniss, who wrote a book about the case). "Every journalist who is not too stupid or too full of himself to notice what is going on knows that what he does is morally indefensible," she wrote. "He is a kind of confidence man, preying on people's vanity, ignorance, or loneliness, gaining their trust and betraying them without remorse."

We have all been there at one time or another—gaining the source's trust, smiling, and then betraying that trust. Any reporter, reading Malcolm's rant, experiences a shudder of recognition and shame. But her indictment is too savage, and it belongs to the category of irrelevant generalization. What mattered, ultimately, was not whether you treated a source shabbily but whether you got the story and—who knows—wrote the truth. A (so to speak) secondary betrayal might be the price of getting the story right.

LETTER TO A YOUNG JOURNALIST

BY ANDREW KLAVAN

My Dear Friend:

It does my old heart good to address a young person of such talent, honesty and integrity. I am only sorry you are going into the field of journalism, where none of those qualities will be of any use to you. To enter American journalism today in search of honest work is like entering an Episcopal church in search of Christianity. If you find any, you probably brought it with you and, once you're there, you're going to have to fight to hold onto it.

Over the past decade or so, the largest and most respected American news outlets have sunk to once-unimaginable depths of mendacity. They have repeatedly spread disinformation to protect the power of the powerful and have demonized and attempted to silence those who tried to tell the simple truth. Let me give a few recent examples.

In 2020, *The New York Times* won a Pulitzer Prize for the 1619 Project, which claimed the American Revolution was fought primarily to preserve slavery—a lie. During the 2020 Covid pandemic, various outlets decried the "racist" idea that the virus originated in a Chinese lab—as it most likely did.

When a felonious drug addict named George Floyd died in Minneapolis police custody in May 2020, journalists elevated the story as representative of widespread police racism against blacks. Repeated studies have cast doubt on whether such widespread racism exists, and it is unclear even now whether Floyd died of a cop's sloppy manhandling or a drug overdose. But the media version helped to inspire nationwide race riots that caused a record $2 billion in damage and left somewhere between twenty and forty people dead. Some TV reporters declared these riots "mostly peaceful" and "not generally unruly," even as their cameras captured buildings burning down behind them.

During the 2020 presidential election, the *New York Post* unearthed an abandoned laptop belonging to Democrat candidate Joe Biden's son Hunter. The laptop contained evidence of extensive Biden family corruption, possibly reaching to the candidate himself. The Biden camp, led by soon-to-be Secretary of State Antony Blinken, orchestrated a letter signed by fifty-one former high-level intelligence officials claiming that the laptop had "all the classic earmarks of a Russian information operation." This nonsense allegation was taken up by journalists at all the major outlets, and went unchallenged when it was repeated by the candidate himself. The *Post*'s reporting was suppressed on social media outlets without protest from the journalistic community. Indeed, Terence Samuel, National Public Radio's managing editor for news, refused to allow NPR to report on the laptop at all, saying, "We don't want to waste the listeners' and readers' time on stories that are just pure distractions." He was then promoted to vice president of newsgathering and executive editor.

A cranky old conservative like myself may be forgiven for suspecting that this habitual dishonesty is an effort to support the age-old leftist cause of larger government and less individual freedom. In a 2013 poll, about 13 percent of journalists said they leaned right, while three times as many, about 39 percent, said they leaned left. This means that a whopping 48 percent of journalists lean left and lie about it. Perhaps more to the point, a recent Gallup poll showed that only 7 percent of the public have a great deal of trust in the news media, while 70 percent of Democrats trust them. In a nation where the people are sovereign, and where that sovereignty is equally divided between the two political parties, a media trusted by one party alone is almost surely reporting with its mind closed.

It is easy to believe that American journalism was always a liar's game. In his screenplay for the film *Nothing Sacred*, newspaperman Ben Hecht wrote: "I'll tell you briefly what I think about newspapermen: the hand of God, reaching down into the mire, couldn't elevate one of them to the depths of degradation." That was in 1937.

He had a point, too. Just a few years earlier, *New York Times* Moscow bureau chief Walter Duranty actively covered up Soviet tyrant Joseph Stalin's systematic starvation of nearly 4 million Ukrainians. Why? "To put it brutally, you can't make an omelet without breaking eggs," the communist-loving Duranty said. The *Times* has never returned Duranty's Pulitzer.

Yet for all the bias, distortion, and deception of the past, I feel obligated to warn you that, over the past fifty years, American journalism has changed very much for the worse.

I saw some of this change unfold live and in person. In the 1980s, I was a radio news writer. I worked at a station in Manhattan that was reputed to have one of the best newsrooms in the country. We prided ourselves on longish—say, forty-five-second—stories that sought to give the audience a clear idea of the issues of the day. If we got a fact wrong, or treated a politician unfairly, we heard about it from the higher-ups. We policed ourselves and each other for accuracy and bias.

That all changed when a new boss was installed. He wasn't a bad man, just an emissary of the age. With competition from cable news on the rise, broadcasting executives who once considered reporting the news a public service had now begun to wonder whether their news divisions could be transformed into profit centers.

In meeting after meeting, the new boss coached us on how to be "relatable." Twelve-second stories focusing on sex, violence, disasters, and flashy scandals were the key. The AIDS crisis was a perfect opportunity to discuss bizarre sexual practices with an air of gravitas. "Scare people," I was told more than once. "That's what makes them tune in."

I was young then, as you are now. I had a naïve idea that the work of a man's hands ought to have a purpose, and that that purpose ought to govern how he does his job. The purpose of writing news seemed obvious to me: to inform a free people of the facts and fairly report the positions of at least the two major parties so that the people could decide what they believed and whom they supported.

As it happens, I am a man of even temper. Once, after thirty-five years of marriage, my wife heard me shout at someone over the phone, and literally hid under the bedcovers because she'd never before heard me raise my voice in anger. But when the new regime purposely set out to cheapen the work it paid me to do, I repeatedly flew off the handle. I remember one hellacious fight in which my boss and I shouted at each other nose to nose. I really thought we were about to start swinging. When the boss abruptly quit, I flattered myself that it was at least in part because I had made his life so miserable. I thought I had defeated the evil forces of relatability.

A few years later, during the first surge of political correctness, I became so weary of American culture I decided to leave the country. I lived overseas for many years. During one return visit, I went to see my old boss to mend fences. He was now a top executive at one of the largest news networks in the country. As we shook hands, it occurred to me: I was a cultural exile, and Mr. Relatable was a prince of the news industry. I had thought myself a living firewall against the destruction of a once-noble profession. In fact, I'd been a pebble on the beach, and he had been the tidal wave of the future.

With the news business now wholly governed by the profit motive, costs were cut and reporters were fired in droves. I remember coming to work several different times at several different venues to find the newsroom like a battlefield, with women weeping and men in despair after mass layoffs had cost them their jobs. What's more, media companies began to consolidate so that once-independent newsrooms became a small part of much larger corporations.

Such corporations historically align themselves with Big Government because Big Government discourages small competitors who can't afford the lawyers, lobbyists, and bribes that the corporations can.

The death of smaller news outlets also meant that news jobs were increasingly located on the coasts and in big cities, liberal Democrat enclaves. The coming of the internet only worsened the trend until, by 2016, around 70 percent of all journalists worked and lived among people who agreed with their leftwing politics. How did they miss the coming election of Donald Trump to the presidency that year? Simple. They didn't live where the voters were, and it didn't occur to them to go there.

To show you the practical effect of these pernicious developments, let me give you one more example of how the media distorted a major story.

In theory, the so-called #MeToo movement was an attempt to expose the mistreatment of women by powerful men in the workplace. A valid enterprise. But how was it covered in practice?

Let's start with Bill Clinton, president of the United States from 1993 to 2001. During his first presidential campaign, Clinton was repeatedly accused of harassing, committing adultery with and, in one instance, raping women who came within his reach. But whenever Clinton's victims tried to go public, Clinton campaign aide George Stephanopoulos would help squelch what the Clinton team called "bimbo eruptions."

It worked. When Arkansas state employee Paula Jones accused Clinton of exposing himself to her, Stephanopoulos called top brass at NBC, CNN, and other outlets, and convinced them to keep Jones's news conference off the air. Clinton was later impeached for committing perjury while defending himself against Jones's sexual harassment suit. He ultimately settled with her for $850,000.

When Stephanopoulos left the White House, he was hired as a political analyst at ABC News and rapidly rose through the ranks despite having no journalistic experience. By 2010, Stephanopoulos was a host of ABC mainstay *Good Morning America*. That year, he attended a party given by Jeffrey Epstein, a financier who procured underage women and shared them with his upscale pals. At the time of the party, Epstein had recently finished a prison term in Florida for procuring an underage girl for prostitution.

According to White House logs, Epstein visited the White House seventeen times during Clinton's first term in office. According to a Fox News analysis, Clinton flew on Epstein's plane at least twenty-six times in the two years after he left the presidency. The plane was dubbed the "Lolita Express" because it was used to transport underage girls to Epstein's various locations.

In a video obtained by guerilla journalists at Project Veritas, ABC News host Amy Robach claimed she had the Epstein story as early as 2016, when Hillary Clinton was running for president against Donald Trump. "It was unbelievable what we had. Clinton. We had everything," Robach said. But, she went on, ABC spiked the story. An ABC spokesperson told Fox News that Stephanopoulos had "no involvement" in that decision. Stephanopoulos was then ABC's chief anchor and political correspondent.

ABC alleged to CBS that one of its staffers, an Emmy-winning 25-year-old named Ashley Bianco, had leaked the Robach tape to Project Veritas while working for ABC, her previous employer. CBS fired Bianco in 2019 for reporting the news while a journalist, though Bianco claimed she was innocent. Meanwhile, CBS anchor and PBS talk-show host Charlie Rose, an associate of Jeffrey Epstein who sometimes consulted Epstein when hiring female employees, was harassing many of the women he worked with. He was fired in 2017 after multiple allegations of sexual harassment appeared in *The Washington Post*.

Also meanwhile, according to journalist Ronan Farrow, NBC spiked his story of how film producer and Clinton donor Harvey Weinstein repeatedly raped and harassed various Hollywood hopefuls who stumbled into his clutches. In his book *Catch and Kill*, Farrow claims NBC came under heavy pressure from its parent organization NBC-Universal, which has multiple Hollywood interests. This occurred at the same time NBC was allegedly covering up the sexual predations of its star anchorman Matt Lauer. Lauer is accused of assaulting one young staffer until she passed out, and of sodomizing a co-worker while she cried and begged him to stop. Lauer was fired in November 2017.

Now, at the same time the Epstein story and the Weinstein story and the Lauer story and the Rose story were being covered up by ABC, NBC, and CBS, NBC released a tape of Donald Trump making ugly remarks about women. The tape was released in October of Trump's 2016 election campaign. NBC had been in possession of the tape since 2005.

Like Hunter Biden's laptop, the Trump tape was real. But there were no former intelligence officials to cast doubts on its reality, no corporate news outlets to denounce it, and no social media to silence those who promoted it. Instead, feminists poured into the streets *en masse* to protest Donald Trump's lewd remarks. The #MeToo movement had begun!

Cut to 2018. The movement continued. Feminists stormed the Supreme Court in protest after Christine Blasey Ford accused fifty-three-year-old conservative Supreme Court nominee Brett Kavanaugh of having drunkenly climbed on top of her in 1982 at a party when they were teenagers. Kavanaugh vigorously and emotionally denied the charges and Ford could produce no one to back her story. Nonetheless, most news outlets reported Blasey Ford's version as the truth. They piled other unsubstantiated charges on Kavanaugh, including accusations that he'd attended parties where there were gang rapes. These stories collapsed when examined.

Leading the anti-Kavanaugh charge, *The New York Times* ran a story headlined "'As a Rape Survivor, I was Shaking in my Chair' as Christine Blasey Ford Testified," in which readers explained "how their experiences with sexual assault and trauma affected their viewing" of Ford's testimony. To my knowledge, there were no stories about men who had been falsely accused of sexual assault and how they, too, were shaking in their chairs.

Now compare the case of Tara Reade, who worked for Joe Biden as a congressional aide in the 1990s. During Biden's 2020 presidential campaign against Donald Trump, Reade claimed that Joe Biden once pushed her against a wall, kissed her, put his hand under her skirt and penetrated her with his fingers. *The New York Times* did not cover Reade's accusations for nineteen days. It then ran a piece on page twenty of the Easter Sunday edition, dismissing the accusations.

When asked about the disparity between the treatment of Kavanaugh and Biden, *Times* executive editor Dean Baquet explained, "Kavanaugh was already in a public forum in a large way. Kavanaugh's status as a Supreme Court justice was in question because of a very serious allegation. And when I say in a public way, I don't mean in the public way of Tara Reade's. If you ask the average person in America, they [sic] didn't know about the Tara Reade case." In other words, the *Times* didn't cover the allegation against a presidential candidate because no one knew about Reade's allegation because the *Times* didn't cover it.

In 2022, Universal, which, as you remember, owns NBC, released the film *She Said*, detailing the heroic struggle of two female *Times* reporters to expose the trail of rapes left by Harvey Weinstein. So the *Times*'s reputation remains intact.

I tell you all this so you will understand: As a young person entering the field of journalism, you are not entering a profession afflicted with bias. You are joining a business riddled with wickedness and corruption. Keep your mouth shut and toe the line, and you will soon be sharing morally polluted Pulitzers with some of the best-dressed and best-educated scum of the earth.

It is my sincere hope that this letter will encourage you to seek out more wholesome work, like prostitution or organized crime. But if you insist on your current career path, you should know that you are in for the fight of your life. Seek truth and speak truth as a journalist, and you will be thwarted like Ronan Farrow, silenced like Amy Robach, and forced off social media like the *New York Post*.

But there is an honorable way forward. Much of the hysteria and panic mainstream journalists exhibit in the presence of honesty is enflamed by the proliferating opportunities to speak truth through independent venues that could render them obsolete. Reporters expelled from the corrupt high places—as Bari Weiss was from *The New York Times*—may create fresh vehicles for genuine journalism, as she did on Substack.

Myself, through a lifetime as a writer of both fiction and non-fiction, I have tried my best to speak honestly. I can't prove my articles denouncing Hollywood leftism caused me to be blacklisted as a screenwriter, I can only point out that my annual income from screen work went from six and seven figures to nothing in a year. I can't be sure that *Empire of Lies*, my novel about the War on Terror, damaged my publishing career, but my award-winning and sometimes bestselling novels went from receiving dozens of positive mainstream reviews to receiving one, in which I was called a "right wing crackpot."

Yet here I am, a commentator on *The Daily Wire*, with both novels and non-fiction on the bestseller lists. My work has a large audience and wins praise on an internet that did not exist when I was, like you, setting out.

Perhaps more important, I have enjoyed every moment of the fight. My young friend, I tell you truly: There is nothing more delightful, more energizing, more inspiring, or more fun than doing battle with a sinister gang of corrupt rat bastards when you have the truth on your side.

With that in mind, welcome to American journalism. An empire of lies indeed, it marches against liberty in lockstep, much like the empire that came to Lexington and Concord in 1775, thinking to seize the guns of the upstart colonists.

For the rebel media now, as for the rebels back then, there is nothing for it but to take cover where you must and fire back when you can. Now, as then, it is a fight the rebels can't possibly win.

Go to it.

THE PRESS, THE PROFESSORS, AND POSTMODERN PROGRESSIVISM

BY PETER BERKOWITZ

Postmodern progressivism occupies the commanding heights of contemporary American culture. It combines a commitment to rule by credentialed elites, an ever more expansive egalitarianism conceived in terms of group identities, and a repudiation of traditional moral principles. Progressive elites draw from these clashing convictions a license to do whatever is necessary to make Americans conform to their prescriptions for diversity understood as intellectual conformity; equity understood as differential treatment based on race, ethnicity, and sex; and inclusion understood as silencing or excluding those who disagree with the progressive agenda. Oscillating opportunistically between a moral relativism that haughtily disdains to judge and a dogmatic moralism that judges haughtily, this incoherent sensibility fortifies self-righteousness and induces ideological blindness. It drives the mainstream media's and the elite academy's efforts to banish opposition, stigmatize debate, control the flow of information, supervise public discussion, and establish authoritative and unchallengeable progressive narratives.

Postmodern progressivism undercuts liberal democracy in America. Freedom and democracy depend on a knowledgeable citizenry, which requires a self-aware press that reports the facts accurately and analyzes the issues fairly, and an educational system devoted to the transmission of knowledge and the cultivation of independent minds. However, the prestige press and the elite academy collaborate to cocoon citizens within a set of purportedly final and uncontestable progressive assumptions and conclusions. This drastic narrowing of moral and political perspectives erodes the conditions for public discussion and reasoned deliberation essential to responsible self-government.

Seldom does the onrush of events provide a real-time laboratory for testing claims about culture, politics, and society. But the mainstream media's starkly contrasting coverage of two grave accusations—the Russia-collusion accusation directed at candidate and then President Donald Trump, and the influence-peddling-scheme accusation directed at candidate and then President Joe Biden, his son, and other family members—demonstrates the lengths to which the mainstream media is willing to go to twist, suppress, or invent facts to advance progressive moral judgments and political interests.

From the 2016 presidential campaign through 2019, the mainstream media championed the falsehood that Donald Trump colluded with Russia to steal the 2016 presidential election. However, the "Report on the Investigation Into Russian Interference in the 2016 Presidential Election" Volume I and Volume II, submitted by special prosecutor Robert Mueller in March 2019 after nearly two years of work, failed to find evidence to establish that the Trump campaign engaged in a criminal conspiracy with Russia. Meanwhile, investigations by Department of Justice Inspector General Michael Horowitz—"A Report of Investigation of Certain Allegations Relating to Former FBI Deputy Director Andrew McCabe" (February 2018) and "Review of Four FISA Applications and Other Aspects of the FBI's Crossfire Hurricane Investigation" (December 2019)—along with the "Report on Matters Related to Intelligence Activities and Investigations Arising Out of the 2016 Presidential Campaigns" (May 2023) issued by Special Prosecutor John Durham found abundant evidence of serious wrongdoing by law enforcement officials.

According to these reports, the Obama administration's FBI and Department of Justice flouted standard operating procedures and abused their formidable law-enforcement powers in their investigations of candidate Trump. In no small measure driven by Obama administration holdovers, the FBI and Department of Justice continued to defy regular practices and protocols in investigations of Trump after he entered the White House. The mainstream media has tended to dismiss the significance of the Horowitz reports and the Durham report on the grounds that they did not uncover substantial prosecutable conduct, as if serious wrongdoing in politics is limited to crimes that can be proven in a court of law.

From the 2020 campaign to 2023, the same mainstream media ignored or suppressed the abundant evidence that Joe Biden's son Hunter and other Biden family members conducted lucrative influence-peddling schemes while Biden was vice president. In October 2020, the *New York Post* reported that a laptop abandoned by Hunter Biden in a Delaware computer store and turned over to the FBI by the store's owner contained on its hard drive—among sordid photos and extensive electronic communications—an email to Hunter Biden from Vadym Pozharskyi, "a top executive at a Ukrainian energy firm," thanking the son for the introduction to his father, who was then vice president. The meeting took place "less than a year before the elder Biden pressured government officials in Ukraine into firing a prosecutor who was investigating the company."

The mainstream media largely declined to cover the story, based in part on an open letter that was ginned up by then-Biden campaign advisor Antony Blinken and signed by fifty-one former intelligence officials. With reckless disregard for the truth, the open letter dismissed the laptop and its contents as "Russian disinformation." The mainstream media's insistence that the story was of little public interest was buttressed by collaboration between federal law enforcement and social media: With the FBIs encouragement, Twitter and Facebook censored the laptop story. The stubborn facts remained. Ample evidence indicated that Hunter Biden, who has been under federal investigation since 2018 for, among other things, improper business dealings, received millions of dollars from Ukrainian natural-gas giant Burisma while his father was vice president and Obama's point man on Ukraine despite Hunter's lack of expertise on Ukraine and the natural gas industry. Meanwhile, other family members as well as Hunter received millions of dollars from companies connected to the Chinese Communist Party. Yet the mainstream media found few, if any, leads it regarded as worth pursuing about family members' efforts to cash in on Joe Biden's service as vice president.

These overlapping case studies throw into sharp relief an egregious journalistic double standard. In the case of the manufactured Russia-collusion false narrative, *The New York Times*, *The Washington Post*, the major broadcast networks, and cable-news outlets CNN and MSNBC—along with the local editors around the country who take their cues from these industry leaders—rushed to condemn Trump. Despite flimsy evidence and the steady unraveling of the case against him, the mainstream media persisted for years in fanning the flames of outrage against Trump's supposed Russia collusion, promulgating deceptive story lines to hamstring and delegitimize his presidency.

In contrast, the same media outlets concocted far-fetched justifications for ignoring or denying credible allegations of Biden family malfeasance while hushing up the *New York Post*'s accurate reporting. Not even a video of former Vice President Biden boasting at a Council on Foreign Relations event that, by threatening to withhold $1 billion of U.S. foreign aid, he compelled Ukrainian authorities to fire a prosecutor investigating his son's employer Burisma was enough to prompt the mainstream media to swing into action. Finally, in March 2022, leading news organizations began to belatedly acknowledge the provenance of Hunter's laptop. However, they continued to ignore, or slow-walk, reporting of the influence-peddling revealed by his emails and corroborated by the eye-witness testimony of Hunter's former business partner Tony Bobulinski.

While priding themselves on serving as the nation's watchdogs, America's prestige news and opinion organizations have demonstrated little recognition of, and offered scarcely a word of apology for, their opposite derelictions of duty in the cases of Trump and Biden. The likely explanation for the absence of public expressions of remorse is absence of private pangs of remorse. Publishers, editors, reporters, and columnists appear to believe, all things considered, that no apology is owed.

The starkly contrasting approaches to reporting the allegations against Trump and Biden followed a familiar pattern. Consider the mainstream media's coverage of several high-profile stories since Trump was elected: the never-substantiated charges of sexual assault slung at judge Brett Kavanaugh during his 2018 Senate Judiciary confirmation hearings; the false accusation advanced by the press in January 2019 that boys from Covington Catholic High School mocked a Native American on the steps of the Lincoln Memorial; the Jussie Smollet "MAGA" hoax a few weeks later; the much-derided hypothesis during the early months of the pandemic, now widely viewed as more likely than not, that Covid originated in a lab in Wuhan, China; the soft-pedalling of the George Floyd protests, at many points lawless and destructive, during the spring and summer of 2020; and the sedulous portrayal of the January 6, 2021, Capitol Hill riots, involving three hours of criminal trespassing, as insurrection, which in common parlance means the effort to overturn a regime. In each case, the mainstream media promulgated a sensationalized version of events consistent with progressive prejudices and aims. As it became increasingly difficult to suppress the facts, the mainstream media lost interest and moved on. Nevertheless, its one-sided characterizations continued to echo through news accounts and op-ed pages and burrow into the progressive imagination and memory.

The temptation should be resisted to attribute the mainstream media's two-tiered system of reporting to ordinary bias or to the hastiness bound up with producing the first draft of history. Elite news organizations' acts of commission and omission are not haphazard; they consistently advance progressive interests and goals, simultaneously demonizing the Right and running interference for the Left.

PART ONE: GENERAL PRINCIPLES

Rank partisanship cloaked as morally righteous truth-telling has become a regular feature of the mainstream media's work product.

Another error is to view the mainstream media's subordination of accurate reporting to activism as a return to the past. It's true that for much of American history, newspapers frankly served one party's interests or another's. It's also true that in the twentieth century, the media establishment resolved to professionalize its operations and to make objective reporting its mission. And it's true that thanks to the internet, which places abundant partisan content to fit nearly every taste and style within easy reach of a few clicks or taps, the days are gone in which a handful of newspapers and networks controlled the nation's access to news and opinion. Nevertheless, the twenty-first-century mainstream media retains a substantial influence on the nation's elites and popular discourse. That influence, however, does not stem from a return to the frank partisanship of early American newspapers or from a doubling down on the professional commitment to objectivity that marked mid-twentieth-century reporting. Instead, the mainstream media contradictorily combines covert partisanship with pious attestations to its own dispassionate professionalism. While riding roughshod over the truth to advance progressive ends, it persists in claiming that it reports reliably on the world as it really is.

To the extent that they own up to a change in their political coverage, members of the mainstream media tend to blame Trump. For example, in the summer of 2016 in "Trump Is Testing the Norms of Objectivity in Journalism," *New York Times* journalist Jim Rutenberg brought to the public's attention a question echoing through the media: "If you're a working journalist and you believe that Donald J. Trump is a demagogue playing to the nation's worst racist and nationalistic tendencies, that he cozies up to anti-American dictators and that he would be dangerous with control of the United States nuclear codes, how the heck are you supposed to cover him?" The obvious answer was that journalists should recommit themselves to getting the story right, scrupulously reporting the bumptious billionaire's wild rhetoric and erratic conduct, the better to equip voters to make an informed decision on his qualifications for the highest office in the land.

Instead, the mainstream media proceeded in the opposite direction. Rutenberg suggested that it was "unavoidable" for reporters to cover Trump as an "abnormal" eruption into the political system: "No living journalist has ever seen a major party nominee put financial conditions on the United States defense of NATO allies, openly fight with the family of a fallen American soldier, or entice Russia to meddle in a United States presidential election by hacking his opponent (a joke, Mr. Trump later said, that the news media failed to get)," the *Times* journalist wrote. "And while coded appeals to racism or nationalism aren't new—two words: Southern strategy—overt calls to temporarily bar Muslims from entry to the United States or questioning a federal judge's impartiality based on his Mexican heritage are new."

There is, however, a world of difference between covering Trump's abnormalities and covering Trump abnormally. It is one thing to unsparingly report Trump's deviations from the norm. It's quite another to conclude that Trump's deviations compelled journalists to deviate from traditional reportorial standards.

How would the public have been harmed or journalism betrayed if the mainstream media had accurately reported that Trump wanted to put financial conditions on NATO allies because he recognized that they were not paying their fair share for the collective defense; that it was indecent for Trump to mock a fallen soldier; that in context it sounds like Trump is speaking facetiously when, at a large political rally, he invites the Russians to hack Hillary Clinton's email; that a temporary ban on Muslims' entering the United States was a crude response to plausible threats (President Trump issued a ban on nationals from seven Muslim-majority countries to the United States on the grounds that they posed a terror risk); and that vulgar as it is to question a federal judge's impartiality based on his or her heritage, Trump's accusation reflects the practice all-but institutionalized among progressive elites of ascribing opinions to individuals based on their ethnic and racial identity (a sitting Supreme Court justice appointed by

President Obama stated that her Latina ethnicity gave her an advantage in adjudicating cases and controversies, and elite law-school professors, overwhelmingly progressive, routinely disparage white judges as implacably racist)?

The answer, toward which Rutenberg gestured but never forthrightly stated, is that the mainstream media felt obliged to use all means, fair and foul, to besmirch Trump because its members saw him as an unprecedented threat to their political convictions and priorities. Although they flirted in print with the need to renounce objectivity in their treatment of Trump, they believed that he objectively menaced all they held dear. Therefore, they refrained from reporting facts or considering opinions that might lend support to Trump's campaign and validate his voters' views while hastening to publish wild accusations and flimsy speculations to damage Trump. Since the objective truth in their eyes was that a Trump presidency would overthrow progressivism's righteous hegemony in America, the corporate media considered itself duty bound to spare no effort in using its extensive powers to shape the narrative to defeat Trump and, if he were elected, to straitjacket his presidency.

In "The Press Versus the President," a deep dive into the Russian-collusion narrative that appeared in the *Columbia Journalism Review* in early 2023, veteran journalist Jeff Gerth dispassionately analyzed the extraordinary extent to which the mainstream media abandoned dispassionate analysis to construct the false Trump collusion narrative. The prestige press, he demonstrated, published stories riddled with inaccuracies, uncritically reported mendacious statements by FBI Director James Comey and California's Democratic Representative Adam Schiff, hyped accounts that contained false claims "without any attribution or sourcing" and "significant omissions," greatly increased their reliance on anonymous sources, excluded exculpatory evidence and explicit denials by key actors while presenting statements out of context to make them seem incriminatory, and stood by error-riddled reporting for months despite mounting evidence of erroneous details and misrepresentation of the larger picture. In 2018, the Pulitzer Prize

Board awarded journalism's most prestigious honor jointly to the *Times* and the *Post* in the face of coverage that systematically betrayed traditional journalistic standards. Its judgment and conduct in convicting Trump in the court of public opinion having been spectacularly rewarded, the mainstream media proceeded to bury the Biden influence-peddling scheme, the better to exonerate its party's leader.

"My main conclusion is that journalism's primary missions, informing the public and holding powerful interests accountable, have been undermined by the erosion of journalistic norms and the media's own lack of transparency about its work," wrote Gerth. "This combination adds to people's distrust about the media and exacerbates frayed political and social differences." Accordingly, Walter Lippmann was right to worry in his 1920 book *Liberty and the News* "that when journalists 'arrogate to themselves the right to determine by their own consciences what shall be reported and for what purpose, democracy is unworkable.'" But Gerth offered no explanation as to why, a century later, our prestigiously credentialed and highly educated journalists believe that their job is to determine what the public needs to know, what it should feel, and what it is better off not knowing.

One crucial factor inspiring journalism's abandoning of its primary mission to inform the public and impartially hold powerful interests accountable is the postmodern progressivism inculcated by higher education in America. Since at least the late 1940s, colleges and universities have been reshaping the curriculum by putting it in the service of progressive priorities. Since the 1970s, colleges and universities have come to function as the indispensable credentialing institution for journalism's higher echelons. And since roughly the 1980s, they have injected into the curriculum the postmodern demotion of reason and repudiation of authoritative norms and standards. Eventually, the progressivism and the postmodernism coalesced into a single sensibility, committed to empowering government to emancipate individuals from traditional moral virtues and judgments. Few are the members of the mainstream media who, during their passage through the credentialling institutions of American higher education, have not imbibed the spirit of postmodern progressivism.

Thanks to instructive writings by predominantly—but by no means exclusively—conservative authors, four stages stand out in the establishment of postmodern progressivism as higher education's governing ethos.

The process began in the soft dogmatism that then-recent-Yale-University-graduate William F. Buckley documented in 1951 in his book *God and Man at Yale.* Buckley's examination of course syllabi from the social sciences, particularly economics and political science, demonstrated the faculty's determination to portray what Buckley called collectivism—a preference for larger government staffed by supposedly disinterested technocrats seeking the people's good often contrary to the people's expressed interests—as preferable to individualism, or the traditional American view of individual liberty and limited government. At the same time, Buckley's review of syllabi from Yale's humanities curriculum as well as from the Yale Divinity School's course offerings, disclosed readings and assignments that did not merely teach the arguments and influences of atheism but consistently advocated a secular point of view. While assuming basic principles of objectivity and academic freedom, Yale's overall curriculum gently eroded them by presenting the faculty's preferences for collectivism and atheism as objectively correct and the alternatives, by their silent omission, as unworthy of serious exploration.

In his 1988 bestseller *The Closing of the American Mind*, University of Chicago professor Allan Bloom illuminated the soft relativism that, with the cultural upheavals of the 1960s, had conquered the campuses. This relativism—which derived in part from Nietzsche's assertion that morality expresses the desire for power, and in part from the neo-Marxist doctrine that morality reflects institutionalized structures of power—was soft because of its transparent insincerity and inconsistency. Students and professors invoked moral relativism to disarm the claims of inherited authority and to disparage the achievements of Western civilization. But students and professors maintained firm convictions about the falseness and harmfulness of biblical faith, the irrelevance of classical political philosophy, the goodness of the liberation of sexual mores from the tyranny of traditional norms and practices, and the evilness of Ronald Reagan's presidency.

In the 1990s, campus dogmatism turned hard. In their 1998 work *The Shadow University: The Betrayal of Liberty on America's Campuses*, University of Pennsylvania history professor Alan Charles Kors and Boston lawyer Harvey Silverglate explored an outbreak of cases across the country in which university administrations, often joined by faculty, conspired to deprive students of rights basic to a liberal education: liberty of thought and discussion, and the right to due process in the adjudication of allegations of misconduct, particularly sexual misconduct. Underwritten by the emancipation from the standard norms of free societies thought to be conferred by Nietzsche and the neo-Marxists, administrators and professors justified crude infringements on liberty by dubious progressive interpretations of social reality. Speech codes sought to protect historically discriminated-against minorities and women from supposedly hateful opinions and ideas. The curtailment of due process for males accused in cases involving women's allegations of sexual misconduct was intended to compensate for the pervasive inequalities that, it was said, society had imposed on women.

In practice, as Kors and Silverglate exhaustively showed, university administrations rode roughshod over the facts to censor speech that deviated from orthodox progressivism and to convict students accused of sexual assault on the grounds that the achievement of equality for women demanded belief in whatever they said. Students internalized the implicit lesson: Objectively true progressive ends justified authoritarian means, including the promulgation of gross falsehoods. Despite their hope that the Foundation for Individual Rights in Education (FIRE)—established in 1999 by Kors and Silverglate to combat the assault on rights on university campuses—would complete its work within a decade, the organization's case load has only grown and now extends beyond the world of higher education. To reflect the proliferation of challenges to free speech and due process that it has been compelled to address, FIRE has recently changed its name to The Foundation for Individual Rights and Expression.

Over the past twenty years, political correctness has metastasized into "wokeness," in which dogmatism has become militant. Wokeness combines an idiosyncratic interpretation of postmodernism according to which only the West's grand historical narrative has been thoroughly discredited with a dogmatic grand historical narrative of its own. According to woke doctrine, America's political ideas and institutions—and indeed those of the Western civilization from which they emerged—serve white people's interests in domination, are permeated by racism and sexism, ineluctably usher in colonialism and imperialism, and must be overcome by all means necessary. Wokism builds on identity politics, which teaches, on the one hand, that truth is relative to racial, ethnic, cultural, sexual, and gender backgrounds and, on the other hand, that some racial, ethnic, cultural, sexual and gender backgrounds—those that embody progressively endorsed accounts of oppression—bestow moral superiority. No book has done more to expose the woke spirit's militant dogmatism than *Woke Racism: How a New Religion Has Betrayed Black America*. In that 2021 work, Columbia University professor of linguistics John McWhorter explained how elites' redefinition of "truth" as that which serves the empowerment of socially approved oppressed groups harms those it purports to benefit, poisons the public square, and undermines the quest for knowledge.

The declension of higher education in America over the past seventy-five years make it a great irony that the mainstream media blamed Donald Trump for undertaking a war on the very notion of truth. In fact, the prestige media are exemplary products of a system of higher education that—through the partisan content of its curriculum, the tendentiousness of its teaching, the slant of its scholarship, and the canons of illiberal conduct on its campuses—has for decades self-righteously subordinated the search for truth to politics.

Progressive opinions deserve a respectful hearing in a liberal democracy. However, the indoctrination of students to use the press to indoctrinate citizens in progressive opinions is anathema to liberal democracy. To overcome the postmodern progressivism that has corrupted the mainstream media by institutionalizing a two-tier system of news coverage and opining—one for the progressive party that the mainstream media serves and one for the conservative opposition—the nation must reform higher education.

THE VAN JONES RULE

BY DAVID REABOI

The state of American disunion is well advanced. It feels like we are coming apart, because we are. The nation is, for the first time, less divided by the race, religion, or class distinctions that have consumed humanity for most of civilization than by political ideology and the partisan labels that are its rough shorthand. Americans have increasingly segregated voluntarily into geographic regions, where we find ourselves in more like-minded political environments and prepare to push federalism to its limits. The small and large things we consume have been shot through with partisan meaning, as corporations take on the operational attitudes of political campaigns aimed not at rival products, but at their consumers themselves. And every four years, we struggle over the precarious and contentious balance of the presidency, as the old saw about "the most important election in our lifetime" is now *always* true—at least as long as the republic remains intact.

The tenor of our political and cultural discourse seems to be contempt, laced through with rhetoric that can only be described as pre-genocidal. It has laid waste to families, relationships, and jobs. Even as the conflict rarely spills into real violence, the mainstream Left has begun to see the very existence of the Right as a potential kinetic threat, and has responded accordingly. Firmly in control of the government and media, it has turned the awesome post-9/11 powers that Americans have given to the national security and law enforcement bureaucracy to keep us safe from terrorists against its domestic political adversaries. The Right, feeling helpless in combating it, rages against its tormentors while retreating into conspiracy theories and rewarding opportunistic grifters who articulate their frustration and anger.

Of course, all this hasn't come out of nowhere. The Right and Left aren't merely separated by personality and temperament, lifestyle preferences, and visions of the Good Life; they hold different, entirely incompatible worldviews. The old, inherited labels emerge from very real differences about how Americans understand the most consequential things—most especially culture and justice—and now even reality itself. Our ways of life are an affront to one another, and we find the world that our opposites have created to be monstrous. These are legitimate sources of acrimony that the ancients would have recognized as causes of war or pitiless, apocalyptic conflict. As it all comes to a boil, a growing number of Americans now see this period as a kind of Late Republic, and realize that an uneasy coexistence within the confines of the same political project cannot last forever.

The Corporate Media serves as an amplifier for this struggle, and a constant instigator of its everyday battles and skirmishes. The press has always been able to change attitudes through clever narrative framing, constant repetition, and social pressure. But since the cultural revolution of the 1960s, its world view has bent hard toward the Left; the subsequent decades have seen Baby Boomer politics transform broadcast and print journalism into a ceaseless, didactic celebration of that generation's ethos and real or imagined virtues. Both news and entertainment have been packaged as a commercial for "social justice," the never-ending quest for individual- and group-identity fulfillment and grievance, and the destruction of the American Founding and its common culture. The mainstream media has been self-congratulatory about the many victories for "progress" it has affected—but, naturally, it is triumphalist only in retrospect.

Twenty years ago, technology exploded the monopolistic grip that the Corporate Media once had on the dissemination of information. While channels such as Fox News and talk radio had allowed the Right to bypass the major newspapers, magazines, and television networks that comprise the mainstream media and get their message to millions of Americans, these mediums were a one-way broadcast for passive reception. Securing the means of communication in a conflict is essential to affect change from above, but it is no longer sufficient to create a mass movement for long-term political success in a democracy; successful outlets need to make constructive use of their supporters' enthusiasm. On the Right, the internet and the explosion of social media created armies of activists that encouraged involvement and energy, including, crucially, an ecosystem of reputational and financial incentives.

Conservatives celebrated, cheering the democratizing force of social media just as they'd celebrated the power of blogs, cable news, and talk radio years before. It seemed for a while that the mainstream media's monopoly on the flow of information and its ability to dominate political and cultural narratives had ended. Consequently, over the past three decades, the Right's alternative media infrastructure has ballooned from a handful of monthly magazines (so modest, most were run as non-profits) into a billion-dollar industry of shareable, politically driven entertainment to be consumed on our ubiquitous smartphones.

The mere existence and continued proliferation of these right-leaning voices led many on the Right to believe that they had the wind at their backs: As more Americans became active online, millions would soon leave the cocoon of the leftwing mainstream media forever. Conservative media would expose the worst excesses and failures of the Left's worldview and serve as a voice for that half of the country alienated from the dominant leftwing culture. By reaching enough people to win elections, the people-powered movement the Right was building on the fly could finally allow it to do battle with the institutions in the Left's control, like entertainment, education, Big Business, and journalism.

Conservatives envisioned something like media parity, with the Left reacting to its media the way the Right had reacted to the mainstream media for decades: with a lot of yelling, argumentative fact checking, but ultimately, a kind of contentious dialogue. This was the case during what was arguably the high point of conservative media, at least in terms of what it was able to accomplish on a shared political battlefield.

In January 1998, when the internet was in its early days, Matt Drudge had made his reputation as an adversary—and competitor—of the mainstream media by publishing a giant newsworthy scoop about President Bill Clinton that Beltway reporters and editors had spiked merely for partisan reasons. Drudge's story suddenly flashed on newspapers and television screens across America and the world: The sitting president's affair with a young White House intern consumed headlines for the next year and a half. Even as the leftwing mainstream media tried to protect a Democratic president, making the scandal disappear was impossible. It was a morality tale, a detective story, and a courtroom drama, and it ended, finally, in a cliffhanger of an impeachment vote that nearly brought Clinton down.

A decade later, in early 2009, recently inaugurated President Barack Obama had appointed little-known leftwing radical activist Van Jones as his "Green Jobs Czar." Even as most Republican politicians feared opposing the new president and exposing themselves to accusations of racism, the reaction from the conservative press was swift and impassioned. On his nightly Fox News show, Glenn Beck railed against Jones's appointment, pointing to a disqualifying 9/11 conspiracy petition he'd signed several years before. It began to look like a feeding frenzy, as the mainstream media began reporting on the growing backlash on the Right.

And then Obama blinked. Under pressure from other cable news and talk radio voices on the Right, the White House felt the heat from the hostile media coverage and hastily withdrew Jones's name. Obama instinctively did what nearly every politician had done before: When heat came down on one of his people, he looked to stop the bleeding and move on by cutting him loose.

Almost immediately, though, the White House realized that it had made a tactical mistake by caving—or even reacting—to its critics in conservative media. The people fuming about Van Jones in rightwing media, it had realized, were already sworn enemies. Tossing one of its own to the wolves wouldn't halt or slow down the enemy's advance; it would do the opposite and encourage more. From then on, not only would the Obama administration refuse to bend to pressure on appointments, nominations, or criticism from adversarial media, it treated right-leaning media itself—and, by extension, its audience of millions—as illegitimate.

Even as the White House clung to the "Van Jones Rule" and refused to give the Right an inch, conservative media remained potent. While Drudge had put the media on notice as gatekeepers of information, he was less a reporter than an editor; together with his then-unknown sidekick, Andrew Breitbart, *The Drudge Report* took the raw materials provided by the traditional media and presented the news in a provocative way by collating links to existing reporting—and, crucially, re-contextualizing it based on catching essential details buried deep in the middle paragraphs. And, as websites proliferated, the internet allowed everyone with a blog to become an instant media critic, fact-checking, debunking, and commenting on the media's daily reporting.

Striking out on his own several years later, Breitbart masterfully recruited the mainstream media as an unwitting accomplice in providing exposure for his campaigns. This time, he and his team did their own investigative journalism and, like the Left, his muckraking always had a precise policy goal in mind. An expert student of the incentives and workings of the mainstream media, Breitbart sought to replicate what it was able to do: Create pointed and dramatic events that unfolded episodically into information campaigns. Defining the energy of the Tea Party movement, his efforts would focus on pressuring Republican officeholders to take action against the administrative state: proposing legislation, defunding corrupt organizations on the government dole, or opposing Democrats' nominations.

This was possible because the media, then, took a kind of debate-oriented approach; like malevolent and pedantic fact checkers, it attempted to undermine Breitbart's journalism by making increasingly strident and convoluted excuses for a story's leftwing villains. Anticipating their moves, he allowed the Left and its media to walk out confidently on rhetorical limb after limb just before he sawed them off. Breitbart realized that convincing the media (or even the entirety of the American people) was a fool's errand. He would focus, rather, on hijacking the power of the mainstream media to reach an audience that was predisposed to be supportive of his efforts—or, at least, those open to giving them a fair hearing. In such a politically polarized environment, the media's fevered attempts to debunk his reporting and destroy him would only amplify the story; the exposure would make him enemies, but he'd win enthusiastic converts, too. It worked for a while, as Breitbart's own sense of humor, energy, and outsized personality made him the perfect face of the Right's alternative media world.

These halcyon days wouldn't last long. It took a few years for the Van Jones Rule toward the conservative press to bleed over, whether by design or not, to the media. Editors slowly realized that the newspapers and broadcast networks of the mainstream media themselves played the decisive role in the Van Jones firestorm by legitimizing the Right's criticism, and they wouldn't allow these narratives, controversies, and stories emerging from conservative media to penetrate their news cycles again. No longer would it be possible for the Right's media to push a story into national news as Andrew Breitbart or Matt Drudge had done. In the subsequent years and decades, facts emerging from conservative media would be ignored and embargoed, not only by Democratic politicians, but by the mainstream press, as well. The Van Jones Rule has been in effect since; and, because it works so well for the Left, it is unlikely to change.

Of course, the Left's delegitimization of opposing views in a free society isn't new. Frankfurt School Marxist Herbert Marcuse's "Repressive Tolerance"—in which he repudiated the classical liberal ideal free expression, arguing for limiting the Right's speech in accord with the aims of social justice—had been influential on the New Left and its academic descendants since it was first published in 1966. But the Van Jones Rule was a significant milestone in bringing this radical position out of the universities, coming at a time when the old-school liberals who occupied newsrooms were being replaced by younger, more ideologically committed reporters and editors.

Over the next decade, Marcuse's position went mainstream, with massive downstream repercussions. Its logic is the foundation of the Left's current fixation with de-platforming and crackdowns on what it considers "disinformation" or "misinformation." If, as it believes, the reporting of facts—true or not—has the ability to destabilize and imperil society, the tight grip on the flow of information encouraged by the Van Jones Rule becomes something like a national security imperative. It didn't take long, then, for the Left and Right to divert into disparate realities as they retreated into media ecosystems that would seldom overlap. The effects of this dynamic took its toll on our discourse: a near-infinite swelling of partisanship, the disappearance of a culture common to all Americans, and the dissolution of social cohesion that comes with it.

Looking back, though, even as the corporate media's monopolistic grip on the flow of information has been shattered, there hasn't been anything resembling parity. The power imbalance between the Left's and Right's media infrastructures remains stark. Though it's often been pronounced dead or debilitated, the leftwing Corporate Media remains the most powerful political and cultural force in America, capable of steamrolling the Right and quickly moving public opinion into spasms of hysteria, fear, self-righteousness, or near-ubiquitous virtue signaling. Its ability to create and solidify narratives across the population was in evidence throughout the presidency of Donald Trump.

Perhaps nothing in modern American history caused a greater erosion of social cohesion than the years-long false narrative about the elected president being an agent of a foreign enemy power. "Russiagate" was an epic tale, with a cast of hundreds or even thousands of players; it was a *bona fide* information campaign, unfolding and rising with daily intensity, like the most potent scripted drama.

From the start, the Left and its media allies were in control. Democrats were able to employ institutional assets that were—and will likely remain—unavailable to the Right: Both serving and retired agents in the national security bureaucracy generated leaks, leads, and stories to be reported breathlessly in the press, while members of Congress used the media coverage to justify their own investigations, which then became fodder for yet more Russiagate content. All the while, the Left's hired commentariat was increasingly apocalyptic and braying for blood and long prison sentences. By the conclusion of the Trump administration, this information campaign had been able to convince nearly half of Americans that they'd just endured four years of a hostile, foreign-occupied—and, for good measure, *fascist*—government.

For those who read or watched any type of media, the waves of Russiagate content were inescapable and unrelenting; for four years, conservative media was consumed by little else but refuting the intricate, daily micro-narratives from the mainstream media. The drama was rich and consistent enough for countless conspiracy theorists, amateur sleuths, and newly minted pundits to develop cult, fiercely partisan followings on both sides.

Of course, the Van Jones Rule had become second nature by then, and none of the fact-checking and evidence-assessing analysis from conservative media penetrated through the gatekeepers into the mainstream media and influenced the trajectory of the story. Americans were watching different movies about the same subject—but, as ever, that subject was chosen by the Left, and it remained relevant until the Left decided its usefulness had reached its end.

Once the drama had sufficiently saturated American politics—and the media frenzy had converted enough undecided voters into Democrats or poisoned them against Trump and the Republicans—Russiagate ceased to be useful and wound down with less than a whimper. Around the corner was an election year, and new dramas would be required for voter turnout in the media's constant and unrelenting partisan blitzkrieg. Over the next twelve months, the Covid pandemic and Black Lives Matter protests (and subsequent riots) monopolized the airwaves and attention of the Right and Left (BLM). Unlike Russiagate, though, both were moral crusades with intense peer-pressure enforcing behaviors and signaling virtuous, even visible (in the form of masks and T-shirts) ideological commitment from every citizen.

Months of compelled participation finally caused a backlash. On both issues, the Right was able, after a while, to claw back and offer its own narratives to combat the Left's. The existence of conservative media enabled millions of Americans to stand defiantly against enforced virtue signaling. For many of them, these experiences irreparably shattered the credibility of the mainstream media, reinforcing their decision to seek alternative sources of news. But these skirmishes over BLM or Covid narratives took place exclusively in conservative media or on social media feeds; readers of *The Washington Post* only encountered the Right's arguments as dangerous or ridiculous caricatures worthy of debunking or silencing. The Van Jones Rule assured that reporting from conservative media organs existed only to be mocked and discredited.

For the Left, the millions who abandoned their programming in favor of right-leaning news, commentary, and entertainment signaled nothing less than "the end of democracy" or the "rise of fascism in America." The large audiences for conservative media have so terrified the Left in government, academia, and media, they have come to justify censorship and social and economic sanction against both creators and their audiences. Unfortunately, the Right allowed itself to be persuaded—and certainly, for those of us in conservative media, flattered—by the Corporate Media's hysteria about its loss of monopolistic control over the information that Americans received.

Even as it's been beneficial, that success in drawing audiences has disfigured conservative media, as well. Owing to its history with talk radio—and because professionalizing and cadre-building institutions have long been controlled by the Left—conservative media is, as it has always been, reliant on personalities and a strong entertainment component. Even considering the Right's often-contentious relationship with Fox News, the cable network remains the largest single communications node in the conservative media ecosystem. The Right's younger cohort, however, is splintered across a constellation of social media personalities, podcasts, and websites.

Whether by natural inclination or lack of imagination, those looking to break into media on the Left most often aspire to be muckrakers; on the Right, they aim to be public intellectuals or talking heads. Unfortunately for conservatives, not only are the muckrakers more effective in creating their desired policy outcomes, but the economics of the media ecosystem can sustain far more of them than it can thousands of aspiring pundits, jockeying for views or sponsorships.

Coupled with the shortened attention spans that social media encourages, these incentives lend themselves to indulgence in a kind of nihilist sensationalism, less concerned with truth than with chasing the clicks and eyeballs by which advertising is both measured and rewarded. Those with large followings are enticed to monetize their social media accounts through shady and undisclosed backdoor payments from political action committees or consulting firms, leaving their viewers or readers unaware of any transactional motivations. For an audience that has pointedly—and reasonably—rejected the mainstream media as manipulative and deceitful, its reliance on these well-paid social media "influencers" merely trades one cynical source of news for another. On the Left and the Right, the bifurcated nature of the modern media environment ensures that those who've traded veracity for viral sloganeering will profit, regardless of political outcome.

Certainly, much of that cynicism and its sloganeering is baked into the virality of the social media medium. Even aside from the new ubiquity of video and audio content, addictive timeline scrolling devalues serious journalism—or, really, any complex idea or narrative that can't be explained in a sentence or two. Throughout the history of the two most popular social media networks, Twitter (now X) and Facebook, impressions have rarely translated into clicks or page views; since so much content is simply shared without being read, the underlying piece might as well be no more than a provocative headline. It didn't take long, then, for links to become merely credibility-establishing rather than edifying, like a mountain of unread footnotes in a book. This dearth of clicks (and readers) led to a collapse in advertising revenue for websites, consolidating the conservative media ecosystem into fewer media outlets that often prioritize fodder for quick bursts of social media buzz rather than the complex investigative reporting that is essential to the kinds of robust and involving information campaigns that the Left is able to construct.

The evidence of failure is all around us. Relying so heavily on social media and infotainment, the media infrastructure that the Right has built cannot replicate the drama or involvement that the mainstream media can generate for campaigns such as Russiagate, BLM, or Covid. And it's not for lack of trying or lack of substantive material: The shocking contents of Hunter Biden's laptop, for example, revealed evidence of a mountain of personal vice and a sitting vice president's clandestine influence-peddling to foreign nations. Even more, the pre-election attempt to throttle the story was a corruption of the national security bureaucracy and the mainstream media. And yet, despite some excellent and detailed investigative reporting—and attempts by members of Congress to generate media interest via televised hearings—the Right has been unable to capitalize on it politically.

While the tight gatekeeping of the Van Jones Rule prevents even the best, most professional efforts of conservative media from crossing into the mainstream, its insurgent, antagonistic posture toward the Corporate Media leaves it without the tools to offer a vision of a complete, aspirational lifestyle to compete with the Left's. Conservative media doesn't aspire to build its own *New York Times*, which sets the bar for smaller outlets through its resources and reporting; its own taste-making cultural bible like *Vogue*; or its own home for profiles and feature writing, like *The New Yorker*. These outlets are essential communications nodes, and the Left understands that their influence is greater than its number of clicks, and treats them like the vital loss leaders they are.

Many of these outlets have been saved from the collapse of advertising revenue by massive corporations or by becoming the playthings of leftwing billionaires. Rather than transform them into non-profits, the Left's financiers are content to lose tens of millions of dollars annually, as they understand that the value of these institutions are derived elsewhere. Even as it has been responsive to its activists' intensity online, the Left's success in its information campaigns illustrated how it has been able to leverage social media largely as a megaphone for messages emanating from either its mainstream media or its political or professional institutions. Its forces in government and media are steering the ship, instituting policy with implications in the real world.

Because the Right's media universe was created in order to demystify and delegitimize the Left, it has ignored the imperative of building institutions and communications nodes. Donors who bankroll the Right's projects have thus far been uninterested in creating their own professional cadre of outlets, journalists, and editors; "what's my return on investment?" they whine. These credentialing mechanisms, like journalism schools or robust media networks, create the raw material from which these information campaigns—and the policy changes that result—are made. Perhaps even more important, these institutions provided viable career paths for professionals outside that of the cable news contributor or the social media influencer that currently circumscribe conservative intellectuals.

Sadly, it's not just a media problem. The Right needs to stand up its own robust institutions and its own parallel economy: from corporations to small businesses, from universities to education centers, from guilds to professional associations. These efforts take work, seriousness of purpose, and money. If it continues neglecting these tasks, the future for the American Right looks bleak—even as its media grows in popularity, and the economics benefit the wallets of its biggest stars and social media influencers.

It would be simplistic to say that the media has brought us to this place, mostly as it would give us false hope: The roots of our current political situation can be found in the contradictions of modernity and are merely finding expression in all the ways we human beings communicate. As a perfect outlet for rage and discontent, social media makes it easy to destroy institutions rather than to build them. Even with its potential to transcend location and create virtual communities based on ideology or interest, the hard work of making things—businesses, creative endeavors, organizations, schools, churches, neighborhoods, or retail politics—remains a real-word pursuit; it requires those who undertake the effort to unplug and focus on tangible things.

THROUGH THE REVOLVING DOOR: HOW THE FOURTH ESTATE VANISHED

BY JOHN O'SULLIVAN

Journalism as a profession has an inferiority complex. In the old vaudeville joke, a patient seeking treatment for this condition is told by his analyst that psychologically speaking he's perfectly healthy, even unusually perceptive. He simply happens to be inferior. He gets up from the couch and leaves with a spring in his step.

Journalism, too, is inferior, and the clue to recovering the spring in its step lies in demystifying the words "as a profession" in the opening sentence above. Journalists often tell themselves that they are professionals—it lets them feel the equals of lawyers and doctors—but the truth is that journalism is a trade with none of the traditional marks of a profession. It does not require the mastering of a recognized body of knowledge; it does not regulate the entry of newcomers; it has neither governing institutions nor legal powers to prohibit non-journalists from practice; and it can have no provision for expelling those of its members who break its rules (few of which exist, and those vary from place to place.)

These disadvantages, however, are not accidental. They are inherent in the journalism of a free society in which anyone who can write—that is, physically scribble, type, or speak into a recorder of some kind—for publication is free to do so. It is the act of writing multiplied by the fact of publication that makes its practitioner a journalist of any kind—reporter, editor, columnist, or commentator. And since more people can write than can read—as Ferenc Molnar once remarked mordantly about reviewers of his collected plays—almost anyone who feels like it can be a journalist in good standing. That's too many people to confine inside a professional cage of skills, rules, and disciplinary procedures. And it's a living proof that men and ideas can be genuinely free.

That freedom, however, is threatened by the envy of journalists for the professional status of doctors and lawyers, which has tipped the balance between two different kinds of journalism and two different kinds of people in the journalistic trade. To oversimplify greatly: The difference is that between rebels and governors, between pirates and admirals, between outsiders and insiders, between the entrepreneur and the organization man, between poets and critics, between tacticians and strategists, between radicals and conservatives, between Protestants and Catholics, and in short between those who want to right the wrongs they see and those who want to avoid creating new wrongs by hasty reforms that overthrow an essentially decent order.

Human beings are not, of course, stereotypes. The dividing line between rebel and governor, pirate and admiral, and so on, runs in reality through every human heart. We are all partly rebel and partly governor, but some rebels are rebellious 24/7, and some governors prefer velvet gloves to iron fists. And when we move from individual temperament to the mood of a crowd, social prediction becomes much easier. A roomful of journalists who secretly want to be lawyers—or at least be *like* lawyers socially—would be very different from a meeting of either the National Union of Journalists or a gathering at the Groucho Club in London. And the more journalists with lawyerly ambitions who join an actual media enterprise, the more they are likely to dilute its combative journalistic energies and to narrow its sympathies.

For most of my lifetime the balance of temperaments in newsrooms, both in America and the U.K., has been weighted—this is plainly not a scientific judgment—strongly toward the bohemian, rebellious, and creative, and away from the respectable, conformist, and administrative on something like 70 lines to 30 lines. That division strikes me today as a pretty good corporate personality mix if you want to produce a lively, controversial, and unpredictable newspaper, magazine, television, or internet current affairs program. It didn't track too well with partisan political divides between liberals and conservatives—which was a good thing because it meant that the common journalistic mission could and sometimes did override politics and ideology. Most newsrooms had a liberal majority but relaxed ideological attitudes. Bohemian Tories were more popular than liberal ideologues, for instance, and the most significant question you could ask about any newsroom was "Does it have an *esprit de corps*?"

That had less to do with the administrative virtues—important though getting expenses paid on time is to basic morale—than with bold and courageous editorial leadership shown by people as different as Arnaud de Borchgrave in *The Washington Times*, Roger Wood on the *New York Post*, Andrew Neil on the London *Sunday Times*, and Colin Welch as deputy editor of the *Daily Telegraph*. All of them had the necessary buccaneering self-confidence to drive their papers to excel in challenging not only governments but also all the respectable people, institutions, opinions, and causes mired in groupthink and self-congratulation—whom the Brits summarize ironically as "the Great and the Good"—who exercise enormous social and cultural power but too often get a pass when criticisms are being handed out.

Though we didn't all realize it at the time, the era from the early 1980s to the start of the century was a golden age of journalism financially, technically, and creatively. And that produced freer countries and better governments. Those active in the press of those days drew a high card in the lottery of life.

Opening the Door to...What?

So, what went wrong? Many things, as we'll see, but one unnoticed cause was that even in those glory days, journalism wasn't a particularly good launching pad for a career in high society (in which, incidentally, there are many mansions, not only on Park Avenue but also in Harvard, Yale, Princeton, Stanford, Washington, Los Angeles, and London). That didn't sit well with the growing number of lawyerly minded and socially ambitious journalists who were entering the trade not as copy boys but as former editors of Ivy League papers on special entry programs. They wanted more, better, and earlier avenues to the top than were offered by the relatively few senior positions in major media corporations.

That was hard to fashion directly but what they found was a sidedoor—a revolving door in fact between government and the media and vice versa. Opening it allowed reporters, editors, and columnists to leave the media to serve in government, and politicians to exchange jobs on Capitol Hill for jobs in the newsroom, and a few especially ambidextrous people to go back and forth through it several times as their talents permitted, or the voters insisted.

Opening that door was an important moment in the decline of American journalism, after which the door's locks were permanently removed and the traffic through it increased exponentially. And it happened publicly at a 1988 dinner at the Washington Press Club in honor of David Broder, *The Washington Post*'s political correspondent, who was well-regarded by all as a good man and a scrupulous reporter but neither a revolutionary nor a reactionary.

Broder seems to have surprised his audience by the force of his criticism of those who went in both directions through the door as "androgynous insiders"—politicians one day, journalists the next, and on the third "slipping into a phone booth from which they emerged in their original guise." He argued that the press should make it clear that the job of journalists was to criticize and check government, not to become interchangeable members of an insiders' clique in

Washington. If journalists were to lose their distinctive role as independent critics of government, he said, "it will not be long before we lose our freedom."

These were fighting words to those of his fellow journalists who had gone between press and government and back, and they hit back. William Safire, Carl Rowan, Chris Matthews, and Pat Buchanan all wrote columns defending themselves, Pat Buchanan calling Broder "a sermonizing, sanctimonious prig." And it stimulated debate about the propriety of "line-crossing" on the op-ed pages and professional press journals. The debate died down after a while, but it never really stopped altogether.

And three years later it produced a short but highly informative academic study of the speech and its echoes—*Through the Revolving Door: Blurring the Line between the Press and Government*—written by Lewis W. Wolfson, professor of communications at American University, and published by the Jean Shorenstein Barone Center at Harvard's JFK School of Government. Professor Wolfson interviewed all those involved in the debate on both sides (except for a handful who refused); he asked all the relevant questions an interested person would ask; he provides innumerable quotations from the answers his subjects give; and overall, he gives a full and fair-minded overview of the controversy. His little twenty-four-page report is an excellent starting point for anyone who wants to understand what the revolving door means and why it remains controversial.

His closing judgment accepts that many of the line-crossers make good arguments for their decisions—they get greater knowledge of how government works, for instance—but overall, he thinks it's a bad practice that will over time erode the independence of the press and weaken its power to check government. In short, he reaches the same conclusion as David Broder when he launched the controversy:

> Every able journalist who thinks of going into government inevitably erodes the press's unique role. Journalists should be outsiders and skeptics, challenging the conventional wisdom, searching for political

vision and new approaches to policy, pushing for reform of government even if the odds are long.

And a paragraph later: "Newspeople do not have to be monks or ascetics; but, more than ever, we need a watchdog who is truly independent, and seen to be so. It is still a special privilege to be a journalist in America, and the press should earn, and get, the respect it deserves."

For what it's worth, the Society of Professional Journalists reaches exactly the same conclusion today in a position paper on ethics: "The simplest answer is 'No.' Don't do it. Don't get involved. Don't contribute money, don't work in a campaign, don't lobby, and especially, don't run for office yourself."

Illusions of a Lost Liberalism

But isn't this doctrine too austere to be observed fully? For, as a practical matter, it was hardly observed at all in the years following Wolfson's report. Some reasons for this failure may lie in the attitudes demonstrated by Wolfson's interviewees, and by Wolfson himself, which are very much of their time. They are also both high-minded and self-deceiving—or in terms then still allowed, they demonstrate a League of Women Voters approach to journalism. They are too goo-goo-goody for words. Their central notion of the journalist as uniquely equipped to challenge the conventional wisdom, search for political vision and new approaches to policy, and push for reform of government is dubious on two grounds.

First, in a democracy these are the concerns of everyone. A writer may certainly enjoy the privilege of being paid to pursue them, but he has no special authority to recommend paths to their solution. His conclusions are as good as the facts and arguments he brings to their support, and he must then engage others in intellectual combat on equal terms. His opponents may include other journalists; indeed, except on purely technical matters, they will almost certainly include columnists, commentators, and other "journalists of opinion."

But none of them is likely to be advancing some special social balm unknown outside the Press Club.

Second, politics is a struggle for power, between not only parties but also economic interests, NGOs and other pressure groups, and social philosophies. An underlying assumption of many journalists in Wolfson's report—hidden, I suspect, from themselves as much as their readers—was that the press is a bastion of disinterested truth from which light can be shone on the night-time clashes of ignorant armies. I wouldn't rule that out completely; some clashes can be clarified by reporters and columnists who bring a detached outlook to remote or eccentric quarrels. And among leading Washington editors of that time, some in Wolfson's survey, there was something of a fetish of formal political neutrality. It was said of the *Post's* Leonard Downie, Jr., that he never voted, in case it influenced him. That probably had some effect in softening their own and others' partisan prejudices, but it didn't justify a liberal information monopoly.

Most senior Washington journalists in 1988 were pleasantly swimming together in a warm ambience of kinder, gentler liberalism while occasionally enjoying challenging cold showers of radicalism from the Left. A series of academic studies of media bias were showing that in their newsrooms, liberal reporters were massively over-represented and provided poor coverage of the America they didn't know. One *Post* story described evangelical Protestants as poor, uneducated, and easy to lead, when, in reality, they have above-average levels of wealth, high levels of postgraduate education, and are notorious for splitting into new denominations after religious disputes. In short, media elites were dispensing not wisdom to society but news and commentary that was technically accurate, slanted slightly toward a tepid liberalism, and expressed in carefully neutral language.

Judged from outside the Beltway, however, they were liberals and seen therefore as being earnestly on one side of most political issues rather than a helpful umpire between the two. That became evident as the 1980s and 1990s wore on and they were challenged by newspapers, talk radio, and new broadcasting stations with different commercial and political values. Rupert Murdoch's 1976 purchase of the *New York Post* revolutionized the coverage of Albany and City Hall, forcing *The New York Times* to shake up its own people. The joke that the *Times* had appointed a new foreign correspondent who would be arriving in the Bronx shortly had real bite. Competition worked well for Murdoch, advertisers, *Post* readers, and even for the *Times*, which became much livelier, but it put paid to the concept of the journalist as social leader. In response to that, the punters would simply move on to the next tent.

Besides, even if they had wanted to close the revolving door, there was no way of doing so. Broder, Wolfson, and all those in the 1988 debate were able to propose only informal discouragements, which would usually be worth swallowing for the sake of, say, a White House policy job that would sweeten their CV. As a result, traffic through the revolving door in both directions rose steadily through the 1990s and well into the next century. And it demonstrated that Broder had been entirely correct—indeed, that he had underestimated the damage it would do to the press, the government, the conduct of public life in America, and the way that Americans think of themselves.

Admittedly, not all examples of the revolving door are awful warnings. The distinction between reporters and columnists—or journalists of fact and those of opinion—is an important and legitimate one. A journalist of opinion is someone who earns his bread by making the case for the opinions he holds. Neither William Safire nor Pat Buchanan were betraying their own opinions when they went to work for Richard Nixon. In fact, it would be truer to say that they were getting a better megaphone for their views and rhetorical abilities than their own unaided voices could provide. And when they went back into journalism, they were hired to speak in their own voices for the kind of politics they favored in signed columns. Both of them performed these tasks well, indeed brilliantly, writing regular columns and books and appearing on television to discuss matters on which they had different but well-formed views—politics, language, culture, history, and religion. Of course, they were denounced violently by hostile partisans because having been aides to Richard Nixon, they inherited the unhinged hatred for the former president that gives meaning to so many leftwing lives. Buchanan was denounced less violently than Safire—a rare experience for the former—because Safire was felt to be desecrating the sacred pages of *The New York Times*. (His later Pulitzer will have soothed their hurt feelings there.) Nothing in either of their histories was a betrayal of any duty they had to journalism. Quite the reverse; they were ornaments to it.

George Stephanopoulos illustrates the opposite point. He had little or no experience in journalism when he left the Clinton White House for a career not as an opinion journalist but as an "objective" one. All his working life he had been a political apparatchik, and by reputation a ruthless one, and he lacked the full range of journalist skills. He duly fell at the first fence. As *Investor's Business Daily* pointed out, he gave donations of $75,000 to the Clinton Foundation, which objective journalists are not allowed to do. That wouldn't be a mortal sin if it hadn't reflected the cozy chumminess between the political and media elites, especially on the Democratic side of the aisle that the revolving door symbolizes.

That relationship was warm, if "correct," under George W. Bush, but it became almost incestuous under Barack Obama. Here's Erick Erickson in *Real Clear Politics* describing the "symbiotic relationship" between Washington's political Left and the media:

> Jay Carney went from *Time* to the White House press secretary's office. Shailagh Murray went from the *Washington Post* to the Veep's office while married to Neil King at the *Wall Street Journal*. Neil King has left the *Wall Street Journal* to work for Fusion GPS. Linda Douglass went from ABC News to the White House and then the *Atlantic*. Jill Zuckman went from the *Chicago Tribune* to the Obama Administration's Transportation Department. Douglas Frantz went from the *Washington Post* to the State Department and Stephen Barr went from the *Post* to the Labor Department.

Ruth Marcus, who heads the *Washington Post* Editorial Board, is married to the Obama Administration's former Federal Trade Commission Chairman. Jonathan Allen had been at *Politico* before going to work for Debbie Wasserman Schultz, then back to *Politico* before going to the left leaning *Vox*. Now he is at NBC News. Andy Barr worked for the *Politico* before leaving for Democrat politics. Michael Scherer was at both *Salon* and *Mother Jones* before going to *Time*. Laura Rozen was at *Mother Jones* and *The American Prospect* before *Foreign Policy* magazine. Even Nate Silver had started out at *Daily Kos*. Then, of course, there is Matthew Dowd, who worked for scores of Democrats before working for George Bush. That, though he later washed his hands of Bush, bought him street credibility with ABC News to become its senior political analyst alongside George Stephanopoulos, formerly of the Clinton Administration.

All very innocent, no doubt—a post-partisan elite enjoying itself—and yet it reminds me of David Broder's melodramatic warning that if journalists were to lose their distinctive role as independent critics of government, "it will not be long before we lose our freedom."

Could It Happen Here?

Once we might have dismissed such anxieties as "alarmist" in societies such as Britain and America with traditions of a free press going back to John Wilkes (1725–1797) and John Peter Zenger (1697–1746), respectively. But if we go back to read or watch the media coverage of both countries over the past decade without rose-colored spectacles, we have to admit that it *has* happened here—and it has happened not in low scandal sheets and tabloids (or at least less there) but in the most respected, professional, and well-edited media institutions.

In their coverage of the COVID-19 pandemic, the lockdown, the "Russiagate" scandal, Brexit, the 2020 election, and much else, the elite corporate media have inflicted a corrupt, partisan, ideological, and (as is increasingly clear) evidence-free coverage upon their readers.

Nor have they shrunk from imposing a joint censorship of "sensitive" topics in alliance with the Big Tech companies and the U.S. and other Western governments. These private-sector bodies did so, moreover, in what looks increasingly like a secret relationship with the Biden administration and its intelligence agencies. Together they have constructed a vast unconstitutional apparatus of state and private surveillance and agitprop in which the old vices of government censorship and McCarthyite slander have returned in the fashionably progressive guises of "countering disinformation," "fact-checking," and a "whole of society" approach to "security." It's a big story, and one might have thought, a juicy one. But it's still struggling to get attention in the public square. If you don't know the meaning of the phrases in quotation marks in the last sentence, it won't be much use turning to the *Times* or the *Post*.

While this was all happening, moreover, most people in the "working press," far from safeguarding accuracy and honesty, acted as cheerleaders for official viewpoints and supported the exclusion of dissenting voices from the media. Still more ominously, they were abetted in this by the institutions of journalistic standards and collective self-congratulation. Thus, the staffs of both *The Washington Post* and *The New York Times* received Pulitzer Prizes for their coverage of the imaginary Russiagate contretemps that afflicted the Trump administration from its very beginning. In retrospect, they look like prizes for giving credibility to a completely false conspiracy theory while furthering an actual conspiracy to cripple the Trump presidency.

Likewise, the *Times* got another Pulitzer for its coverage of the Covid pandemic which, among other things, amounted to a prize for supporting the official narratives of the dangers of the pandemic, the efficacy of vaccines (and other CDC-approved remedies to it), and the need to suppress other remedies or cancel viewpoints labelled either misinformation or disinformation by scientific officialdom. Much of the official narrative has since been abandoned, some alternative remedies have since been approved, individual critics have since been judged correct, and not one of the prizes has been returned. Indeed, the Pulitzer board itself has declared that they should *not* be returned. That leaves hanging in the air the question of, What, exactly, were the prizes awarded *for*?

One result of this mass professional suicide, however, is that the general reader—in order to be reasonably well-informed on an expanding range of sensitive topics from immigration policy to vaccine efficacy—has to turn to rebellious writers, such as Toby Young, Jason Siegel, Matt Taibbi, Michael Shellenberger, and Glenn Greenwald, in small independent journals or websites. Otherwise, he will be in unknowing thrall to forms of censorship that masquerade as fact-checking, as countering disinformation, and—what is astonishing for a country with the First Amendment—as prohibitions on news reports that contradict official information.

As for the journalists who both endorse official disinformation and then accept prizes for doing so, they seem to have turned themselves quite voluntarily into unofficial press spokesmen for government and official agencies without being directly paid for their services. That would have astonished and humiliated almost any American press-man during, say, the Watergate scandal, and for a long time afterwards. It's worth pointing out that my criticism of the consequences of Washington's revolving door in no way relies on anything resembling a conspiracy theory. Its deleterious effects occurred because that is how people in groups behave. And if that sounds a little too abstract, let me hang the explanation on a personal anecdote.

In 1972, the London *Daily Telegraph* appointed me to be its parliamentary sketch-writer. This is an almost unique British journalistic institution that combines a report of yesterday's events in Parliament, a drama critic's review of them, and a satirical take on them in which partisan bias is perfectly acceptable. It's a dream job, much sought after, and oddly powerful. MPs care more about how they are depicted in a light-hearted sketch than in a full-length serious parliamentary report.

On my first day, a rival sketch-writer who happened to be an old friend took me aside to give me some advice. Don't, he said, socialize with MPs. Reporters have to do so because it's how they get stories, especially scoops. But sketch-writing is about what's already public, namely debates and clashes between MPs on the floor of the House. If you socialize with politicians, who as a class are good company and personally likeable, you'll find it hard to skewer them on the many occasions when they screw up.

It was advice which I ignored, but he was right. It was hard to be unforgivingly witty at the expense of someone you liked or generally agreed with or who had become a friend. Mostly I was kept honest by the fact that other sketch-writers with different opinions and different friendships were also writing. A mixture of competition and partisanship kept us all honest. But there were probably occasions when I pulled my punches. Like MPs, we're all human.

That's why the revolving door is always a temptation to bias, and in some circumstances a mortal danger to honest reporting. Washington's press corps and its counterpart in government all share a common interest in politics. Both have many of the same social habits—notably drinking, eating, and not sleeping too much—and thrown together, they tend to become friends. As long as they lived in different social worlds outside of working hours, there was a limit to the influence of their camaraderie. Reporters were below the salt and largely happy to be there. But the advent of the Ivy League correspondent pushed their social worlds closer; the joint impact of Watergate and Vietnam convinced many reporters that journalism had—or even was—an ideological mission; and the revolving door reduced the suspicion of government that had driven much American reporting, and was weakened and in some cases replaced by an ideological sympathy for the natural party of government which since FDR had been the Democrats.

It was at that point that David Broder rose to address the Press Club. His conclusion seemed unduly gloomy—for a long time I thought so—but maybe he saw something the rest of us missed. All these different trends were moving in the same direction; unless they encountered obstacles, they would continue doing so; and the revolving door removed the most obvious obstacle. Broder's nightmare came true in the period 2016 to 2020 when the mainstream media, Big Tech, and the U.S. government merged to defeat Covid, Disinformation, and Donald Trump by any means necessary and with perfectly clear consciences.

THE FALLING HALF-LIFE OF A LIE

BY CHARLIE KIRK

What is the half-life of a lie?

Sixty years ago, a lie with enough backers could last a very, very long time. President Johnson said the troops in Vietnam were making excellent progress and the war would be won soon, while his generals knew the opposite to be true. President Kennedy and the Rev. Martin Luther King, Jr., presented themselves as loyal family men when they were anything but. The small gaggle of elite press with access in Washington, who reported for a handful of magazines, newspapers, and TV networks, nodded along, repeated the lies, and called it the "news."

The truth about Vietnam took years to bubble up as the war dragged on. The full truth about JFK took decades. The truth of MLK's dalliances is still not fully known, thanks to FBI files kept classified to this day.

How would Hunter Biden's laptop story have worked half a century ago (besides the fact it all wouldn't be on a laptop)? There wouldn't need to be any "tech censorship" a half-century ago. All that would be needed is a few major newspapers and the major news networks to refuse to cover it. Besides those outlets, no publication would have the reach to make sure that the story reached the whole country, and few reporters would have the resources to chase down the story's difficult and far-flung details. Just as in 2020, the press could have kept a lid on things long enough to help a flagrantly corrupt, near-senile candidate eke out a narrow election in.

But then, the con would have continued, for years. The press would dutifully avoid covering the story, and editors would dutifully avoid publishing any of the truth about Hunter Biden. They might entirely conceal the fact that the president's son was addicted to drugs and prostitutes, offering instead the same completely fake "family man" image that the Biden clan itself wanted to project.

Sure, the truth might have gotten into some conservative magazine or local paper here and there, but what then? There would be no internet to make sure that the whole nation and the whole world could see it.

Perhaps after ten years, or twenty, or fifty, some journalist would finally publish a book exposing the "real" Hunter Biden. It would be a topic of interest to history buffs and political die-hards, but nobody else. Its impact on history would be nil. For the average news consumer, it would be almost impossible to track. After years and years, how would he even remember which reporters were reliable, and which ones had lied repeatedly? Simply checking what the same writers were saying a couple of years ago would have required a labor-intensive trip to a library to read old newspapers on microfiche. And, even if you did notice a lie or deceptive narrative, what could you do about it? At most, you could complain to a friend, or write a letter to the editor of some magazine or newsletter, or get in contact with some national reporter, and beg him or her to actually report it.

It was an impossible task for any normal citizen. So instead, Americans mostly just trusted their national media—and since America was at its peak, trust was easy.

Why are so many Americans, including young Americans, so much more distrustful and outright disdainful of the mainstream, elite, corporate media? It's not just that America itself is clearly not what it once was, and it's not just that the press lies more often (though it does). It's also that the half-life of its lies has collapsed.

Today, it's still possible for the media to lie, distort, downplay, and deflect. But the lifespan of the lies is measured in days, hours, and minutes instead of in years and decades. The number of alternative outlets has exploded. A handful of national papers and magazines has turned into thousands and thousands of websites, and unlike in 1960, there is a credible, potent conservative alternative media with its own separate power to make a story go viral.

But it's not just that more news outlets lead to more accountability. It's that the Corporate Media has lost the readers' trust, especially that of young people. The Corporate Media disdains the contemporary media because its members can intuit that they are in fact now the equals of the "professional journalists," who feel entitled to boss them around.

Every high schooler has the tools he needs—Twitter/X access and a search engine are enough—to debunk institutional media narratives that change almost moment to moment. For any aspiring amateur journalist, there is no need to be tied to any kind of publication at all. There is no longer such a thing as a "professional" reporter class.

An upstart reporter can simply self-publish, and still have immediate access to the entire planet as an audience. A single intrepid or observant Twitter/X account can break a national news story. A lone blogger on Substack can outcompete the politics desk of *The Washington Post* or the national security reporting of *The New York Times*. A clever twenty-five-year-old with no degree of any kind can debunk the work of a double-Ivy grad pushing some sham like the Russiagate hoax. Today, any person with a smartphone and an internet connection has resources and access greater than even the world's best-funded reporter did decades ago.

But there is another reason that young people have learned not to trust or be overawed by press elites who boss them around: Today, it is laughably simple to see their real (and unimpressive) nature.

Journalists of the past either lurked in the shadows, or towered above their audience, cloaked by the prestige of their outlets, and were otherwise distant and unknowable. "I have a prestigious byline," they could say, in spirit if not in fact. "What do *you* have?"

As they say, never meet your heroes. And never read their tweets, either. Today, we can gaze behind the veil and see the media high priests for what they are—and the sight is ugly.

In 2019, a George Washington University media professor, David Karpf, made a mild joke by calling *New York Times* columnist Bret Stephens a "bedbug." The tweet received almost zero views, and Stephens wasn't tagged in it; pretty much the only way Stephens could have known about it was that he compulsively searched his own name on Twitter, just to see what people were saying about him. And when he did see it, Stephens went berserk, sending an angry email not just to Karpf but to his boss, GW's provost, in an obvious bid to get him fired. Instead, Karpf was fine, while Stephens looked ridiculous. Forty years ago, it's hard to imagine such an incident. Today, it's possible for anyone with an internet connection to pick a fight with a member of the journalist class—and win easily. This sort of thing happens all the time.

When the elite University of Chicago–educated voices on *The New York Times* opinion page so publicly act like bratty children, why is it any surprise that young people don't view them with awe? Why trust people who routinely act like the dumbest and most repugnant people in your high school; do you trust *them*? Of course not. The curtain has been rent asunder. And for the journalist class, there is no going back.

We know who you are.

JOURNALISTS: HEROES IN THEIR OWN MINDS

BY JON GABRIEL

Sometimes, a selfie is worth a thousand words. CNN White House reporter Jim Acosta, the definition of journalistic self-regard, posted a photo to Twitter midway through the Trump presidency. Taken just before his 2018 appearance on *The Late Show with Stephen Colbert*, Acosta stares longingly into his Broadway-style lighted mirror, grasping a director's chair emblazoned with the show's logo. His reflection gazes into the camera's eye revealing his bottomless well of self-satisfaction, insolence, and unearned pride. An open box of Zantac sits on the vanity.

The image was widely mocked across social media, much to the shock of the D.C. press corps. That picture revealed far more than the flaws of one spotlight-hogging reporter. It laid the soul of modern political journalism bare: the media's supercilious id and ego, perfectly framed in an ignorant instant. Acosta quickly turned into a lightning rod, getting banished from the White House after a set of tedious stunts and histrionic hatred for the president of the United States. Yet he is far from the only Narcissus on the Potomac. The legacy media's love for itself is topped only by its contempt for its audience.

It's difficult to describe how awful modern journalism has become. It is preening, biased, ignorant, vainglorious, arrogant, unfair, corrupt, vindictive, smug, anti-science, and stupid beyond measure. It hasn't always been this way. Vintage news hawks reveled in their role as a yellow rabble of ill-educated, over-intoxicated, ink-stained wretches. Today's reporters, inconceivably, consider themselves our betters.

Their pretension to status is puzzling. Perhaps, they could have been lawyers but lacked the intelligence or study skills. Or politicians, but they're too socially awkward. Engineering is out of the question; they don't know math. Science, too, as it requires critical thinking. Not good-looking enough to be Hollywood celebrities, not entrepreneurial enough to create businesses, not courageous enough to be out-of-the-closet activists, let alone out-of-the-box artists. The only requirement for modern journalism is a rudimentary ability to stitch sentences together at forty words per minute. For on-camera talent, not even that. Contrary to recruitment pitches from the Columbia School of Journalism, reporting is a trade, not a profession.

For better or worse, I "earned" a J-school degree, the last seven semesters of which I learned nothing about the career. Following a stint in the U.S. Navy, I took a community college night class titled "How to Create a Small Newsletter" to help to produce my fledgling indie music 'zine. The class met once per week, each night featuring a new subject. Reporting, photography, layout, editing, and the like. All that higher education had to teach me on the subject was provided that first semester in a classroom full of church secretaries, office managers, and a couple of self-styled hipsters like myself.

Like reporters of old, journalists learn by doing. It's a trained skill, not high art. Nevertheless, after accumulating loads of student debt for an undergraduate degree, you can pay the Columbia School of Journalism (CSJ) more than $126,000 for the nine-month master's program. I advise you to stick with your local community college. Graduating *summa cum laude* in journalism is one of the slightest accomplishments of my life. It pales in comparison to the Navy nuclear-power program that prepared me to be a submarine reactor operator. (That actually required math.) Your local welder, carpenter, or mechanic provides far more to society than the average CNN talking head or *New York Times* scribbler. These essential tradesmen are likely smarter and more knowledgeable as well. Deep down, a reflective journo realizes this—and resents it deeply.

Average CSJ graduates watched their fellow undergrad students go on to wealth in finance, innovation in technology, or power in politics. Meanwhile, the high Masters of Journalism are struggling to avoid replacement by college interns and to out-write AI software. After years in expensive schools cozying up to the right people, they believe that an equal professional respect is due. The trouble is, they've done little to earn it.

The media follows a socialism of status, demanding cultural equity with the newsmakers they cover. The members of the media don't realize that the elites consider them with as little regard as does their dwindling audience. Striving for acceptance into the right social circles makes them all the more desperate to parrot the conventional wisdom of the ruling class. *See, I'm on your team*, the reporter thinks, as the Vice Undersecretary for the Department of Agriculture (Tropical Fruit Division) glances across the room to find someone worthy of his notice.

To please their corporate masters and retain their at-risk jobs, today's media staffers must generate clicks. Sober analysis and accurate reporting never stir the blood as much as cheap emotionalism. Combine that with the old newspaper maxim of "if it bleeds, it leads," and modern journalists are paid to catastrophize everything. Journalists love a crisis, even if they have to invent one. At least labeling anything they dislike a "crisis." Each day's headlines warn of a climate crisis, housing crisis, refugee crisis, energy crisis, and financial crisis—and that's just on page A1. There are also crises of food insecurity, racial disparity, income inequality, and mental health equity.

Perhaps journalists could improve that last item by not catastrophizing every issue that has plagued humanity since ancient Sumer. But one crisis left unnoticed has doomed journalism to dwindling audiences, rising irrelevance, and public contempt. Newsrooms from Washington to San Francisco, New York to London, suffer from a humility crisis. What makes this odd is that journalists have so much to be humble about.

Gossip sites highlight celebrity arrogance, sharing juicy tidbits about leading politicians, Big Tech executives, sports heroes, and Hollywood stars. At least the stars have a reason to be arrogant, however inadvisable. Possessing great power, wealth, ability, beauty, or intelligence understandably can lead to a big head. Journalists have no such excuse. In general, the press ranks low in all these categories, excelling only in unpaid student debt, personal grievance, and self-regard.

Every reader or cable-news watcher has suffered from Gell-Mann Amnesia. A citizen reads a story covering a topic with which he is intimately familiar. He quickly realizes that the reporter has mangled the basic facts and drawn wildly incorrect conclusions. Upon turning the page, however, the reader accepts whatever nonsense the same publication reports about foreign policy or energy security. This effect was common in 2002 when author Michael Crichton coined the term, but among vast swathes of the public, that acute amnesia has faded away. After more than two decades of false story after false story, they've learned to consider all of it suspect.

The numbers prove it. In 2022, the Pew Research Center surveyed nearly 12,000 American journalists on a variety of concerns. The press proved as utterly out-of-step with its readers as one would expect. When asked if news organizations do a very, or somewhat good, job reporting the news accurately, 65 percent of journalists agreed. When the same question was posed to U.S. adults, just 35 percent agreed. A plurality—43 percent—of these civilians said that journalists do a bad job of this.

This disconnect was mirrored in questions about the other core functions of journalism: covering the most important stories of the day, serving as a watchdog over elected leaders, giving voice to the underrepresented, and managing or correcting misinformation. Members of the press gave themselves high marks, while the public thought they failed at every one of them. Just 29 percent of the audience claimed to have at least a fair amount of trust in the news, while 44 percent had little to none.

On a deeper level, journalists recognize the public's distrust. When asked which one word they think the public would use to describe the news industry, the respondents overwhelmingly offered negative options, such as "inaccurate," "untrustworthy," "biased," or "partisan." They accept that the audience is unhappy with their work. But instead of improving their industry, journos angrily blame their readers and viewers.

Individual examples of journalistic arrogance are legion. While still a managing editor at Fox News, Shepard Smith regularly made himself the story, as well as the arbiter of what viewers should and should not see. During a speech by President Donald Trump, Smith shut down the feed. "We're interrupting this because what the President of the United States is saying, in large part, is absolutely untrue," Smith said with a sneer. The breaking news anchor's overweening ego was long evident in his private life as well. In 2000, he was charged with aggravated battery with a motor vehicle after ramming his car into a journalist in a fight over a parking space. In 2013, a waitress claimed that Smith screamed obscenities at her for not refilling his specially mixed cocktail quickly enough.

Chris Matthews and Matt Lauer both lost their roles with NBC News during the #MeToo era over multiple allegations of sexual harassment and worse. NBC put fabulist Brian Williams on ice for six months after it had been proved that he regularly lied about his experiences on the front lines in Iraq. "The helicopter we were traveling in was forced down after being hit by an RPG," Williams said while anchoring the nightly news, backed by images of a battered helicopter. "Our traveling NBC News team was rescued, surrounded, and kept alive by an armor mechanized platoon from the U.S. Army 3rd Infantry." That never happened. Neither did his yarns about seeing a dead body float past his window during Hurricane Katrina or dodging gunfire during the Israeli-Hezbollah war.

For a symbol even more telling than Jim Acosta's selfie, consider the emptied and shuttered remnants of the Newseum. Just months before the 2008 financial collapse, *USA Today* founder Al Neuharth opened this ultimate tribute to journalistic hubris. The 250,000-square-foot glass and steel monolith featured fifteen theaters, and 131 interactive video monitors. Finally, a chance for D.C. tourists to see White House reporter Helen Thomas's red dress, long-time *Meet the Press* host Tim Russert's workspace, and former Wonkette blogger Ana Marie Cox's house slippers. All for just $25 a head.

At the Newseum's debut, Neuharth gushed over his "glamorous glass house" while museum chief executive Charles Overby declared that the news museum was "laying down a marker right here on Pennsylvania Avenue that the First Amendment is the cornerstone of our democracy." The press palace was ostentatiously situated on Pennsylvania Avenue between the White House and Capitol Hill. In its first year, the Newseum hosted a gala for incoming President Barack Obama, where Jesse Jackson schmoozed with Sting while Marisa Tomei hobnobbed with Gloria Borger.

Over the institute's eleven-year history, however, the media's views on the presidency altered somewhat. One study measured the tone of reporting produced during the Obama and Trump eras. During the first, major news organizations showed President Obama in a positive light 59 percent of the time. For President Trump, only 20 percent was positive.

Former *Fox News Sunday* host Chris Wallace was one of the Newseum's final speakers. "I believe that President Trump is engaged in the most direct, sustained assault on freedom of the press in our history," he said at this final gala event. (Marisa Tomei did not attend.) Wallace then praised himself by saying, "Ours is a great profession. Maybe the best that anybody ever thought of as a way to make a living. Think of it! We get paid to tell the truth. How many people can say that?" Hubris invites Nemesis. A few weeks after the December 2019 speech, the Newseum shut its doors for good.

National Public Radio lamented its end, calling it an "almost unavoidable metaphor of a museum dedicated to the free press shutting down right in the middle of what some call a crisis period for journalism...the line between unbiased reporting and fake news is getting murkier by the minute." Belatedly, the Newseum followed the maxim offered in one of its exhibits that "a free press could be used to challenge the government should it grow too powerful or abusive." Right up until a Republican administration was replaced with a Democratic one.

The late David Broder, "dean of the Washington press corps," presciently warned his colleagues two decades ago: "The besetting sin of big-time journalism is arrogance—the belief in our own omniscience, that we know so much that we don't have to listen to criticism." His advice wasn't heeded then, and there's no sign it will be in the future.

PART TWO: ON THE NEW YORK TIMES

THE SINS OF THE GRAY LADY

BY J. PEDER ZANE

Readers of *The New York Times* know that while the news may change the message is always the same in the paper of record. It will play up every Republican kerfuffle and downplay Democratic scandals while presenting the choice between the two parties as a Manichean struggle between good and evil. Now clad in rainbow colors, the Gray Lady will, in the name of inclusion, celebrate a wide-range of heretofore marginal behaviors—homosexuality, polyamory and transgender-ism—while sowing divisions by separating Americans into warring camps based on race, gender, and ethnicity.

The transformation of the *Times*, and much of American journal-ism, during the past decade from a traditional newspaper that largely reports the news into the daily call sheet for the "woke" revolution that seeks to undermine the traditional pillars of American society is now so complete that it may seem unremarkable. Both its defenders and critics know exactly what to expect when they open its pages. Such acceptance, or resignation, is dangerous because it normalizes the great sin of *The New York Times*: the betrayal of hitherto bedrock jour-nalistic principles of fairness, objectivity, and pluralism that made the Fourth Estate a pillar of American democracy during the 20th century.

The paper's radical reinvention of itself into a results-oriented tool serving leftwing social change has happened quickly—the *Times* of 2010 bears little resemblance to the paper published today. But enough time has passed so that we can identify both the key incidents and the dynamic political, cultural, and economic forces that have transformed America's most influential newspaper, and thus the nation itself.

That story began to come into focus on August 7, 2016—the day on which American journalism crossed the Rubicon. That's when *The New York Times* published a front-page article arguing that Donald Trump was such an "abnormal" candidate that "normal standards" of reporting on him were henceforth "untenable." From now on, the paper made clear, the news columns of the *Times* would be taking sides. "If you view a Trump presidency as something that's potentially dangerous," Jim Rutenberg wrote, "then your reporting is going to reflect that. You would move closer than you've ever been to being oppositional."

Rutenberg never explained why the normal standards of objectivity were insufficient. If Trump were truly a danger to the republic, wouldn't an honest accounting of his behavior be enough to expose him? As would become clear in the years that followed, the true danger to the nation would come from the license that Rutenberg's piece gave to reporters at the *Times* and the many news outlets that follow its lead to betray the core tenets of modern journalism not just in covering Trump, but on a wide array of issues. "All the news that's fit to print" became redefined as all the news that advances the Left's narrative on race and crime, climate change and gender, capitalism, and even the history of the United States.

The breadth of this effort was suggested by researcher Zach Goldberg whose keyword searches of the *Times*'s archive revealed the newspaper's politically correct embrace of hot-button terms associated with the Black Lives Matter movement. In 2010, Goldberg found that fewer than two hundred articles per year mentioned the term "social justice"; by 2018, the recorded total had more than quadrupled. He found similar increases in the number of articles that mentioned "diversity and inclusion," "whiteness," "white privilege," "white supremacy," "systemic racism" "discrimination," "critical race theory," "unconscious bias," and "implicit bias." In 2010, Goldberg found about four hundred *Times* articles which included the word "racism"; by 2018, the total had risen six-fold.

The *Times* did not just radically change what it covered, but also how it covered it. Views on race and other issues that conflicted with the progressive narrative were increasingly seen through the anti-Trumpian lens as "abnormal" and "potentially dangerous." As Rutenberg suggested, journalism's time-honored commitment to "objectivity" fell before the argument that respectfully airing a range of views on consequential issues was to fall prey to the sin of "both-siderism," "whataboutism," or "moral equivalence"—giving people deemed to be liars (conservatives) the same space as truth-tellers (progressives).

Echoing language once restricted to discussion of the Holocaust, the *Times* brands anyone who questions global warming orthodoxy or the results of the 2020 presidential election as "climate-change deniers" and "election-deniers." Those who challenge the wisdom of allowing young children claiming gender dysphoria to receive irreversible "medical treatment" or who assert that America has, in fact, removed racial impediments to advancement, are cast as bigots.

Yes, the *Times* has always had a liberal bias, and its history is filled with egregious examples of distorted coverage. As Ashley Rindsberg documented in his 2021 book, *The Gray Lady Winked: How* The New York Times's *Misreporting, Distortions and Fabrications Radically Alter History*, these include the downplaying of Stalin's crimes during the 1930s, largely ignoring the Holocaust during World War II, romanticizing Fidel Castro during the 1950s, and retailing a long history of anti-Israel coverage.

But its recent turn is different thanks to its aggressive ambition and scope. Rather than serving as an honest broker whose mission is to provide readers with the information needed to make decisions about important issues, the paper insistently put its thumb on the scale, both in terms of the stories it covered and those it ignored. By replacing skepticism with ideology, the *Times* seeks not to inform, but to persuade. Its aim is not to reflect society but to transform it, and views to the contrary are *verboten*, beyond the pale of acceptable discourse.

Because the *Times* is, by far, the most influential news outlet in the United States, its embrace of progressive ideology has had a cascade effect, transforming the coverage and sensibility of thousands of newspapers and websites, TV and radio stations, entertainment companies, and corporations that follow its lead. Deliberately, it has legitimized and mainstreamed far-left views.

As Goldberg demonstrated, the *Times*'s commitment to the ongoing cultural revolution is deeply embedded in the sensibility and assumptions of almost every article it publishes. These include unnuanced celebrations of polyamory and drag queens and mainstreaming gender confusion among children in its *"New York Times* for Kids" special section. But two especially significant failures—the 1619 Project and the paper's coverage of the Trump-and-Russia conspiracy theory—capture the extreme, dangerous path the paper of record now follows.

In August 2019, the newspaper devoted an entire issue of its *New York Times Magazine* to "The 1619 Project." The project's stated goal was "to reframe American history by considering what it would mean to regard 1619 [the year enslaved sub-Saharan Africans first landed in North America] as our nation's 'real' birth year. Doing so," the magazine's editor Jake Silverstein wrote in an introduction, "requires us to place the consequences of slavery and the contributions of black Americans at the very center of the story we tell ourselves about who we are as a country." Through eighteen articles and fifteen artistic contributions that spanned the length of American history, the project abandoned journalism's traditional mission of presenting the complexity of consequential issues in order to make the argument that the nation's past, present, and future have been and forever will be defined by anti-black racism. There were no dissenting views, and few countervailing facts.

The vast ambition of the 1619 Project underscores the *Times*'s transformation into a tool of the cultural revolution whose aim is to disrupt traditional understandings and beliefs about almost every aspect of American life. The hubris is astonishing. While newspapers have often revisited episodes of the past in response to scholars having unearthed new information, the 1619 Project started with an ideological position about the sweep of American history which it then set out to demonstrate through tendentious pieces. The lead essay was not written by a scholar, but an activist black journalist, Nikole Hannah-Jones.

The backlash was immediate, as many leading historians wrote lengthy critiques of nearly every article. This included a letter to the *Times* signed by five prominent scholars—including James M. McPherson and Sean Wilentz of Princeton University, and Gordon Wood of Brown University—which challenged two of Hannah-Jones's most sweeping assertions about the Revolutionary War and Abraham Lincoln:

> On the American Revolution, pivotal to any account of our history, the project asserts that the founders declared the colonies' independence of Britain "in order to ensure slavery would continue." This is not true.... The project criticizes Abraham Lincoln's views on racial equality but ignores his conviction that the Declaration of Independence proclaimed universal equality, for blacks as well as whites, a view he upheld repeatedly against powerful white supremacists who opposed him.

The historians explained that, "These errors, which concern major events, cannot be described as interpretation or 'framing.' They are matters of verifiable fact, which are the foundation of both honest scholarship and honest journalism. They suggest a displacement of historical understanding by ideology."

Rather than engage these prominent scholars, Hannah-Jones dismissed them as "white historians." A few months later, their interpretation of the project's ideological spirit was underscored by Leslie M. Harris, a black historian at Northwestern University who helped to fact-check Hannah-Jones's essay. She wrote in *Politico* that she was stunned by Hannah-Jones's assertion "that the patriots fought the American Revolution in large part to preserve slavery in North America," because "I had vigorously argued against [it] with her fact-checker."

> In response to a letter from the five historians, Silverstein admitted that we disagree with their claim that our project contains significant factual errors and is driven by ideology rather than historical understanding....
> We can hardly claim to have studied the Revolutionary period as long as some of the signatories, nor do we presume to tell them anything they don't already know...

Instead of directly engaging the historians' scholarship built on decades of professional experience and research, Silverstein advanced the postmodern view that there is no truth. "As the five letter writers well know, there are often debates, even among subject-area experts, about how to see the past. Historical understanding is not fixed; it is constantly being adjusted by new scholarship and new voices."

Scholarship and journalism, however, are not supposed to be echo chambers for any current view; they are professional disciplines because they employ multiple processes of verification. They compare interpretations and opinions against the known body of facts—which can change—to determine the most accurate version of reality. Silverstein rejected that standard because he and his team didn't want to search for the truth, they wanted to make an argument: "The very premise of The 1619 Project, in fact, is that many of the inequalities that continue to afflict the nation are a direct result of the unhealed wound created by 250 years of slavery and an additional century of second-class citizenship and white-supremacist terrorism inflicted on black people."

This helps to explain why the *Times* ignored most leading scholars of the period when preparing its sweeping reframing of American history. In interviews after publication, Hannah-Jones was even more explicit in the results-oriented structure of the 1619 Project when she stated that her goal "is that there'll be a reparations bill passed" compensating black Americans for past mistreatment. In another sign of the power of the *Times*, the call for an African-American reparations movement, long a fringe idea, became a mainstream issue in the wake of publication as many communities and states openly considered the idea, including California, which assembled a commission that called for more than $800 billion in payments.

The *Times*'s influence and power was also apparent when Hannah-Jones was awarded a Pulitzer Prize for her lead essay despite her profound errors.

The *Times* shared another Pulitzer Prize with *The Washington Post* in 2018 for coverage of the Trump-Russia conspiracy theory. Although reports from two special counsels, Robert Mueller and John Durham, rejected the claim that Donald Trump had conspired with Russia's Vladimir Putin to steal the 2016 election, the two papers earned journalism's top prize for what the Pulitzer board described as their "deeply sourced, relentlessly reported coverage in the public interest that dramatically furthered the nation's understanding of Russian interference in the 2016 presidential election and its connections to the Trump campaign, the President-elect's transition team and his eventual administration."

As with the 1619 Project, the *Times*'s Russiagate coverage was so one-sided, so driven by the goal of making the case against Trump, that the news that Mueller cleared Trump of the major claims against him came as a shock to many *Times* readers. Still, its corruption is easy to see in its refusal to address failures and to correct clear errors.

For one thing, the newspaper often relied on anonymous sources for its assertions On February 14, 2017, it published one of the foundational articles of the conspiracy theory, reporting that, "Phone records and intercepted calls show that members of Donald J. Trump's 2016 presidential campaign and other Trump associates had repeated contacts with senior Russian intelligence officials in the year before the election, according to four current and former American officials."

Four months later, then-FBI Director James B. Comey, told Congress that "in the main," the *Times* report "was not true." Documents declassified in 2020 show that Peter Strzok, the top FBI counterintelligence agent who opened the Trump-Russia probe, described the article at the time as "misleading and inaccurate."

Similarly, on December 30, 2017, the *Times* published another article based on anonymous sources that purported to describe the event that led the FBI to open the probe that Strzok headed. It began:

> During a night of heavy drinking at an upscale London bar in May 2016, George Papadopoulos, a young foreign policy adviser to the Trump campaign, made a startling revelation to Australia's top diplomat in Britain: Russia had political dirt on Hillary Clinton. About three weeks earlier, Mr. Papadopoulos had been told that Moscow had thousands of emails that would embarrass Mrs. Clinton, apparently stolen in an effort to try to damage her campaign.

The Australian diplomat Alexander Downer directly contradicted these details in subsequent interviews. He said that he and Papadopoulos each had one early evening drink at the London bar, during which Papadopoulos never mentioned "dirt" or "thousands of emails," just that "the Russians might use material that they have on Hillary Clinton in the lead-up to the election, which may be damaging." The electronic communication that the FBI used to officially open the probe on July 31, 2016, was even less precise. It stated that Papadopoulos had

> suggested the Trump team had received some kind of suggestion from Russia that it could assist with the anonymous release of information during the campaign that would be damaging to Mrs. Clinton (and President Obama). It was unclear whether he or the Russians were referring to material acquired publicly or through other means.

In fairness to the *Times*, the Russiagate hoax was advanced by current and former officials at the highest reaches of government—including the CIA and the FBI—which almost certainly served as anonymous sources for the newspapers. Because reporters rely on others for information, they can be duped. But, once such manipulation is clear, all promises of confidentiality are off and journalists are under no obligation to protect sources who intentionally use and mislead them. Indeed, they have a public duty to identify the source for many reasons. The first is to make their first draft of history as accurate as possible. In the case of the Russiagate hoax, this meant identifying those who perpetrated the fraud. What did they seek to gain? What weaknesses in current systems did they exploit? There are also journalistic concerns: To keep faith with their audience, news organizations must explain why they transmitted false information. They also have a professional interest in exposing liars to deter other sources from misleading them. Not only has the *Times* never revealed its deceitful sources, but, years later, the newspaper has still not corrected these and other identified errors in its reporting.

This willful refusal to set the record straight is a stark illustration of the newspaper's ideological transformation. The *Times*, of course, famously runs a column of corrections each day. During its long history it has also, on several occasions, reinvestigated and owned up to lapses in its own work, including a very public reassessment of its reporting on whether a Taiwanese-American atomic scientist named Wen Ho Lee had spied for the Chinese communists, and a 7,000-word front-page story about how a troubled affirmative-action reporter named Jayson Blair had produced a number of fabricated and plagiarized stories. That led to his forced resignation in May 2003.

The *Times*, however, engaged in no such soul-searching about Russiagate—even after one of its former star reporters, Jeff Gerth, wrote a 24,000-word piece in the *Columbia Journalism Review* that took the newspaper and other news outlets to task for their Trump-Russia coverage that "includes serious flaws." It appears that the story was too big to correct. Nevertheless, the problems with the Russiagate coverage were so apparent that the Pulitzer board took the highly unusual step of commissioning what it called two "independent reviews" of prize-winning articles submitted by the *Times* and *The Washington Post*. However, in yet another sign of how the *Times*'s corruption has become standard operating procedure at the highest levels of American journalism, the board refused to release the reports or to identify their writers. It simply issued a brief statement declaring that "no passages or headlines, contentions or assertions in any of the winning submissions were discredited by facts that emerged subsequent to the conferral of the prizes."

The Pulitzer board's cover-up for the *Times* shows why the newspaper's sins are especially grave and consequential. As journalism's pied piper, the *Times* plays the tune—sets the narrative, normalizes the practices—that others follow. If the *Times* had simply not rejected the "normal standards" of journalism—if it had accepted that its primary role is to inform, not to persuade—the national conversation would be far less angry. Instead, Americans are being gaslighted at the highest level, as the *Times* embraces the Rutenberg approach while at the same time invoking the traditional values it violates at every turn. For even as the *Times* twists the news, its authority still depends on being seen as an honest broker of the news—which is yet another reason why it is so loath to admit serious errors. As it betrays that trust, it must double down on claims of being trustworthy. In his 2023 State of The Times address, the paper's chairman and publisher A.G. Sulzberger, declared:

> The information ecosystem has been overtaken by misinformation, propaganda, punditry and clickbait, making it harder than ever to sort fact from fiction. And in this increasingly polarized era, fewer institutions are engaged in the difficult work of searching for the truth with an open mind and a first order commitment to independence, fairness and accuracy.

Sulzberger, however, diagnosed the illness, without any suggestion of how the *Times* is spreading the disease. Instead of responding to legitimate critiques of its coverage, the newspaper continues to dismiss them as rightwing talking points. That said, it would be wrong to blame the *Times* for all these ills. Despite its enormous influence as a thought leader, it is also a fragile follower, trying to remain profitable at a time when the news business continues to suffer significant financial losses during a period of social and technological change.

The *Times* did not invent the postmodern critiques of objectivity. It did not create the social media platforms that have empowered radical activists. It did not corrupt America's education system—from K-12 to most colleges and universities—which have become factories of leftwing indoctrination. It did not spark the "Great Awokening," that culture of identity and tribal politics, of grievance and guilt, which increasingly defines the worldview of its readers. It has, instead, capitulated to and facilitated the mainstreaming of these dangerous and dishonest forces.

Part of this is a business decision. As the *Times* has transformed itself into a digital operation, it is now far more dependent on revenues from partisan subscribers than on advertisers who have long balked at controversy. These readers increasingly demand that the paper present news that confirms their views. Former opinion editor Bari Weiss described how the *Times* has changed in her 2020 resignation letter to Sulzberger:

> Twitter has become its [the newspaper's] ultimate editor. As the ethics and mores of that platform have become those of the paper, the paper itself has increasingly become a kind of performance space. Stories are chosen and told in a way to satisfy the narrowest of audiences, rather than to allow a curious public to read about the world and then draw their own conclusions. I was always taught that journalists were charged with writing the first rough draft of history. Now, history itself is one more ephemeral thing molded to fit the needs of a predetermined narrative.

Weiss noted that the newspaper's staff—which, like the paper's readers, increasingly sees journalism as an instrument of social change—also have pressured the newspaper to abandon traditional values. On June 3, 2020, for example, the newspaper asked GOP Senator Tom Cotton of Arkansas to write a piece responding to the riots then spreading across the country following the death of a black man, George Floyd, at the hands of a white police officer in Minneapolis. Cotton opined that "these rioters, if not subdued, not only will destroy the livelihoods of law-abiding citizens but will also take more innocent lives.… One thing above all else will restore order to our streets: an overwhelming show of force to disperse, detain and ultimately deter lawbreakers."

The backlash inside the newsroom was immediate. Dozens of *Times* journalists tweeted a screenshot of Cotton's piece with the comment: "Running this puts Black @NYTimes staff in danger."

The claim that words with which one disagrees are a form of violence is both an assault on the First Amendment and a common tool of censorship for the Left. On June 4, Sulzberger felt compelled to defend Cotton's piece in a staff memo. "I believe in the principle of openness to a range of opinions, even those we may disagree with, and this piece was published in that spirit," he wrote. "But it's essential that we listen and to reflect on the concerns we're hearing, as we would with any piece that is the subject of significant criticism."

When that failed to mollify the mob, editorial page editor James Bennet, whose department had commissioned the piece, issued an abject apology at a June 5 staff meeting. "I just want to begin by saying I'm very sorry, I'm sorry for the pain that this particular piece has caused," he said, adding, "I do think this is a moment for me and for us to interrogate everything we do in Opinion." Although Cotton described a rigorous back-and-forth process that included at least three drafts of the op-ed and line-by-line editing, the *Times* asserted that an internal review "made clear that a rushed editorial process led to the publication of an Op-Ed that did not meet our standards."

On June 7, Bennet, who had once been seen as a strong candidate to become the paper's executive editor, was forced to resign because of the internal uproar. Reflecting on the experience in a 2022 interview with the online media site *Semafor*, Bennet said: "My regret is that editor's note. My mistake there was trying to mollify people." The *Times* and its publisher, Bennet said, "want to have it both ways." Sulzberger is "old school" in his belief in a neutral, heterodox publication. But "they want to have the applause and the welcome of the left, and now there's the problem on top of that that they've signed up so many new subscribers in the last few years and the expectation of those subscribers is that the *Times* will be *Mother Jones* on steroids."

The *Times* steadfastly refuses to grapple with the critiques of former insiders such as Bennet and Weiss, who have pointed out how its stated commitment to traditional standards are at odds with the daily journalism it produces. Lewis Menand echoed these concerns in a 2023 essay in *The New Yorker*, "When Americans Lost Faith in the News":

> What people want is advocacy.... In the end, we don't
> care what the facts are, because there are always more
> facts. You can't unspin the facts; you can only put a
> different spin on them. What we want is to see our
> enemy—Steve Bannon, Hunter Biden, whomever—
> in an orange jumpsuit. We want winners and losers.
> That is why much of our politics now takes place in a
> courtroom.

During the past decade, the *Times* has transformed itself into a very different publication. It is not an honest broker, but an organ of advocacy. To its critics, this is a tragedy for journalism and the nation. But, as a free-standing business, that is also its right. Perhaps the *Times* could defend these changes. Its refusal to do so, to report on the world as it is, not as it would like it to be, does a grave disservice both to journalism and the nation.

THE DAVOS *TIMES*: BESPOKE PROPAGANDA

BY ASHLEY RINDSBERG

The debate over censorship has rarely been more prominent in American public life. But with all the focus on what cannot and must not be said, we have neglected its converse: the art of compelled belief we call propaganda.

In its optimal authoritarian state, propaganda is a black-and-white affair—a complete subjugation of public and individual beliefs and opinions to the dictates of state power. How, then, do we understand propaganda that lives in shades of gray, not in the glare of the authoritarian state but in the shadows of democracy where it remains ambiguous, difficult to grasp, and even more difficult to define?

The American media's embodiment of grayness, *The New York Times*, is difficult to pin down for precisely this reason. Despite mountains of criticism, investigation, and polemic directed at this one institution, we appear no closer to truly understanding the *Times*—and may actually be farther off. The great white whale of American influence is certainly adept at serving power. But it also defies many aspects of canonical propaganda. The *Times* frequently opposes the government's position on important issues. It is privately held (and publicly traded). It often successfully delivers news that meets some standard of accuracy and importance. It "listens" to its readers, going so far as to allow them to comment, directly on the digital page, on its coverage.

From this angle, the *Times* looks like a paragon of the free press, as its stakeholders very much believe it to be. But when we turn it on its side, we discover an institution that learned not to impose reality, as Stalin or Hitler's newsprint henchmen did, but *edit* it. This is not about mastering the brazen art of asserting falsehood as truth or vice versa (though no doubt the *Times* has at times veered into that cruder form of propaganda) but a deft, deceptively light-touch alteration of reality. This is propaganda of the bespoke variety. Raised to the level of craft, it draws on a rich tradition to produce a form of dark excellence.

In many ways, the *Times*'s ability to pull off the epistemological trick of editing reality is even more effective than the industrial propaganda it echoes. *Times* reporter Walter Duranty (1884–1957) is held up as the archetype of journalistic transgression not because he proclaimed that Ukraine of the early 1930s, then becoming subject to Stalin's brutal anti-peasant campaign of extermination-by-starvation, to be a Soviet wonderland. He didn't even assert that things were reasonably well. He simply reported that, yes, there were serious shortages, and, yes, there were hungry people on the streets; he referred to this as "malnutrition" and in 1933 called reports of famine "exaggeration or malignant propaganda."

This was a lie, but one that was shaved deliberately close to the truth. In his coverage of the U.S.S.R., Duranty rounded the edges enough to achieve the political end at hand, namely, smoothing of the path by which FDR's incoming administration would recognize the Soviet Union as the legitimate government of Russia—which it did in 1933. Stalin would later personally invite Duranty for an interview, where the dictator, admiring of the British-born American's skill as a propagandist, told him, "You have done a good job in your reporting the U.S.S.R., though you are not a Marxist, because you try to tell the truth about our country and to understand it and to explain it to your readers."

The reality is that Duranty's true reward was not bestowed in Moscow by the Georgian-born dictator but in New York City, at the hands of America's power elite. At a gala event at the Waldorf Astoria marking American recognition of the Soviet Union, the only man to receive a standing ovation from an audience that included both countries' ambassadors and the Who's Who of American society—including captains of American industry and titans of commerce eager to gain access to the rapidly industrializing Soviet economy—was Duranty. His service to the regime, to *both* regimes, had not gone unnoticed or unappreciated. Stalin was correct: Duranty was no Marxist. He was a Timesman, a main-chancer happy to serve himself as a means of serving power.

But the Duranty boogeyman eclipses the more damaging truth behind the affair, which is that the *Times* played an instrumental role in brokering U.S. recognition of the Soviet regime. This geopolitical watershed would not have been possible had the American public been aware that the Soviet leadership in question was bent on the murder of some 5 million of its own citizens, and for no particular reason. So, the famine was left out of America's Soviet story. According to *The New York Times*, it never happened. And that was all that was needed for the party to go on. Tellingly, the *Times* has refused all calls for it to return Duranty's 1932 Pulitzer Prize for foreign reporting published in 1931, pre-famine.

That six-word phrase—"according to *The New York Times*"— explains much about the role the paper plays in public life. For millions of people around the world, it is an unexamined heuristic of credibility. If *The New York Times* said it, then it's at least plausibly, if not probably, true. If the *Times* did not say it, then its status remains worrisomely uncertain. And if the *Times* denied it, its status lies somewhere between outright error and conspiracy theory. The question is, What gives the *Times* this power? Given all we know about the paper, why does it continue to function so successfully?

The answer lies, at least in part, in the fact that the *Times* sits at the very center of an ecosystem of acceptable thought and opinion. This ecosystem includes elite universities from which the paper's journalists hail; the Pulitzer Prize, which glazes even the paper's most precariously reported pieces (think the 1619 Project) with a resin of credibility; the network and cable news organizations that continually refer, and defer, to its journalism; and the policymakers who crave a glowing *New York Times* profile—and dread a takedown. As a result, in the always-buzzing social bureaucracy that governs American public life, *The New York Times* serves as a kind of Michelin Guide to RightThink, awarding its coveted stars (in the form of lavish coverage) to ideas like "white fragility," "gender fluidity," and "climate injustice" while deprecating American exceptionalism, traditional religion, nationalism, and any ideas that threaten the ideological objectives of the class it represents.

In the half-century stretching from Duranty's geopolitical sleight-of-hand through the 1990s, the paper's role in this ecosystem became ever more rooted. But that ecosystem had hitherto been constrained to the Acela power corridor between Washington, D.C., and New York as the broader ambitions of the *Times* were clipped by a diverse media market. Across the country, regional newspapers and local news channels dominated their respective markets. For most Americans, *The New York Times* was a far-flung notion—what espresso-sipping elites read when they wanted to know about the latest fusion restaurant, art installation, or book of experimental poetry.

But with the rise of the internet and the subsequent collapse of local news, the *Times*—as prescient and canny as it has frequently proved itself at adapting to new market conditions—began to evolve. It did this by precipitating a deliberate and painful transformation from the country's most prestigious regional news outlet into America's most powerful news media company. The centerpiece of this expansion was a series of acquisitions that would expand the company's reach, broadening its format and corporate synergies. This included its purchase of *The Boston Globe* in 1993 for $1.1 billion 0, its 1996 acquisition of two local TV stations in the Midwest, a 2003 decision to buy the *International Herald Tribune* and its purchase of web content company About.com in 2005. But in 1997, the company also revamped its core product, *The New York Times* newspaper itself, as part of what a *Times* article on the expansion described as "a series of major changes…to make the daily more widely available around the country." This included a four-section addition to the paper to cater to regions outside the Northeast, partnerships with nearly three dozen Northeast newspapers to deliver the *Times* with their own papers, and the expansion of its New York regional edition from four to six sections. Notably, the company would also re-orient its ad sales strategy from a regional to a national focus.

The *Times* did indeed emerge as one of America's few truly national newspapers, an effect powered by the very same force, the internet, which had created a vacuum in local news. With the web browser taking the place of printing presses and delivery fleets, the *Times* could become the "hometown paper" of a new, geographically abstracted elite that wasn't tied to the Northeast, but existed around the country. This was the "emerging global superclass" that Samuel Huntington had identified in 2004, which had emerged in response to worldwide populations that had grown not only in absolute size but, as a result of more interconnectivity (through the web, globalization, increased air travel and other factors), had expanded in *effective* size. This new, still-growing sprawl of public life demanded more and more centralized power to manage it.

What the *Times* had always understood is that the most effective form of influencing the behavior of millions of people is not determining what they think but shaping the contour of their very reality. Debating whether the Ukrainian famine constituted genocide was a losing bet for the American establishment pushing for American diplomatic recognition of the Soviets. But if that famine *never even happened*, the moral debate is emptied of value. Conversely, by asserting as a historical premise that America was a slaveocracy, as the paper did with its 1619 Project—an extensive editorial initiative that sought to "reframe" American history by putting slavery and what the *Times* considered to be its modern-day consequences, as its very center—it was able to position unceasing debate about America's original sin as a moral necessity.

With the 1619 Project, the paper added an important new weapon to its arsenal. Through the revisionist project, which was no doubt the *Times*'s greatest marketing, ideological, and editorial success of recent years, the paper has been able to not just reject American exceptionalism but shove it outside of the Overton window, turning the entire American project itself into a source of doubt. Patriotism once might have been excused so long as the nation in question fulfilled the deeply liberal promise of equal opportunity. But when the concept of equality itself is cast as a racist lie, the last ties to the idea of a nation separated from the rest of the world not just by geography but by a foundational story are dissolved. America becomes no longer a shining city on a hill but another island in the global archipelago. The nation's historical success—*according to The New York Times* built on a persisting foundation of slavery—suddenly becomes its most terrible liability.

This crowning achievement of "Woke," or subversive, Marxism-steeped ideological attack is essential to the *Times*'s most recent evolution. With what one might also call its great leap forward, the *Times* now seeks to use its base as the news outlet of the American establishment to molt itself into the news, opinion, and thought outlet of the global establishment. If Huntington had lambasted the rise of "Davos Man" in the 1990s, what we have in the 2020s is the emergence of something akin to the Davos *Times*. The policy démarches determined each year at the Swiss enclave of the World Economic Forum are spun into coverage by the world's most powerful global news organization located, appropriately, in the world's most powerful global city.

The *Times*, of course, is not alone in this. But key to the paper's unique role is its honed expertise—and perpetual willingness—to edit reality. The very existence of a global establishment depends on its ability to forge consensus out of an unimaginably huge, diverse, and diffuse landscape of countries, localities, cultures, and faiths. This divine task of corralling millions of minds requires a mental hierarchy in which sanctioned ideas take precedent over plain fact—and in which substantiated facts are deliberately labeled "misinformation" or its bigger badder brother, "disinformation," because they represent stumbling blocks to the prerogatives of that stateless establishment.

For the *Times*, the exemplar of centralized control in a globalized free market economic system is Chinese Communist Party (CCP)-led China. During the Covid pandemic—the recent event that, to the global establishment, constituted the most urgent and obvious imperative for total governmental control—the *Times* became openly exuberant, almost lyrical, on the question of Beijing's approach to information, expression, and personal freedom. "In the year since the coronavirus began its march around the world, China has done what many other countries would not or could not do," the *Times* gushed in a front-page news article in February 2021. "With equal measures of coercion and persuasion, it has mobilized its vast Communist Party apparatus to reach deep into the private sector and the broader population, in what the country's leader, Xi Jinping, has called a 'people's war' against the pandemic—and won." For the *Times*, this social and governmental success stood in stark contrast to the U.S., where a state-by-state response made for a disturbingly decentralized pandemic response. "While the United States and much of the world are still struggling to contain the coronavirus pandemic, life in many parts of China has in recent weeks become strikingly normal," the *Times* reported in August 2020, almost three years before the pandemic's end.

All this might very well have been true—if you were taking China's Covid mortality and morbidity numbers at face value. That was a difficult proposition for any thinking individual, who would have understood that China's reporting—in a country of 1.4 billion people with a bare-bones healthcare system through much of its vast rural expanse—no Covid-related deaths for many consecutive months during an eighteen-month period at the height of the pandemic, according to the website *Our World in Data*, was not just false but offensively absurd. Nevertheless, the *Times*, along with the rest of the mainstream media, not only took those numbers at face value but, in re-reporting them in its vaunted pages, legitimized them and made them quasi-official. After all, "*according to The New York Times…*"

At the same moment that the *Times* was trumpeting China's authoritarian excesses as effective public healthcare—all the while still tarring America as a slave nation—the paper was unnervingly silent about another moral event of global significance: the Uighur genocide. Echoing its cover-up of the Holocaust almost a century earlier, the *Times* has effectively covered the Uighurs in silence, prompting a scathing letter from Florida's Republican senator Marco Rubio in December 2021 when a trove of documents showed that the *Times* withheld critical information connecting Xi Jinping directly to the Uighur genocide. Instead, the *Times* has produced only the most tangential reporting—for example, on the geopolitical ripples of the genocide or its effect on fashion brands—while on-the-ground reporting has been all but absent. Much as the *Times* "buried" the Holocaust so as not to be seen as a "Jewish" newspaper, according to researcher Laurel Leff's book *Buried by the Times: The Holocaust and America's Most Important Newspaper*, and much as it denied the Ukrainian famine as a means of serving power, so, too, has the paper's Uighur coverage (or non-coverage) been rooted in both business and ideological aims.

The *Times* has long sought entry to the Chinese news market, from which it has been shut out after running an unfavorable story about corruption by a senior party official in 2012. The paper is well aware that deep reporting on the Uighur genocide would guarantee that it would never gain entrance to the world's biggest media market. But, even more important, covering up the genocide is about maintaining the illusion that CCP-style total centralization of power is an inevitability in a world in which the only truly meaningful problems— the pandemic, the "climate catastrophe," "structural racism," and gender injustice—are global problems of an inherently intractable nature. This matrix of universal, planet-sized issues demands an approach to policy and decision-making that flows from international bodies and non-governmental organizations such as the United Nations, the International Monetary Fund, and the World Bank.

In a panic-induced environment, when everything is at stake and disaster looms around every corner, virtually every attempt at exerting control, no matter how draconian or inept, becomes instantly rationalized. But chief among those attempts are policies concerning the control over information: who gets to know what, and why. For the *Times*, the flip from championing free speech (as the paper did loudly when its star reporter Judith Miller was imprisoned for not revealing her source on a story during the Valerie Plame affair) to an institution that openly *advocates* censorship appears to be its greatest act of reinvention yet. In the past five years alone, the *Times* has worked hand-in-glove with government agencies and officials to determine what constitutes misinformation and to control its flow; regularly casts as "disinformation" or "conspiracy theories" any claims, such as the Hunter Biden laptop story, that might damage its policy objectives; and spun a web of false narratives about Donald Trump's ties to the Kremlin and Russian intelligence, none of which was corroborated and all of which have been debunked.

When the *Times* reported in 2021 on Clubhouse, an app that allowed people to join audio chat groups, the paper unselfconsciously described the exchanges going on in these rooms: "In thousands of chatrooms every day, Clubhouse's users have conducted unfettered conversations on subjects as varied as astrophysics, geopolitics, queer representation in Bollywood and even cosmic poetry." What stuck out in this sentence was the word "unfettered." Though it was mocked, the paper was deadly serious: The conversations were unfettered from the oversight of the trust-and-safety committee of the public consciousness that the *Times* embodies. Unfettered conversations are a threat not just to the power structure that the *Times* serves, but to the paper itself. Alternative channels for truth—or, to use a more prosaic term, naked facts—are a direct threat to the paper's mission, which is to be the sole arbiter of what is considered true and false.

On aggregate, this might appear to be a paradigm shift for the paper. In reality, these features are central to the *Times*'s very nature. Seen from the outside, the paper is an implement of American power.

Seen from the inside, it's more than a powerful institution—it's America's last real dynasty of influence. For all its talk about glass ceilings and "dead white males," power at the paper has been handed down from male heir to male heir (most of whom were named Sulzberger) for the past 120 years. As with any dynasty, the primary incentive has become the maintenance and expansion of the wealth, power, and prestige of the family's ownership dynasty and the socio-economic class it inhabits.

The *Times* is once again riding a surging wave of power, this time toward what is envisioned as a centralized future where citizenship is defined as fealty toward a set of global policies, and morality is a procedure for obeying the regulations consequent of those policies. The *Times* is editing reality to ensure that reality matches its ideology. While the set of circumstances giving rise to the ascendant political system are new, the role that *The New York Times* plays as the self-appointed midwife to the emerging elite stretches back more than a century. For millions of people caught in this scream of change, it's a brave new world. For *The New York Times*, it's business as usual.

PART THREE: THE PAST AS PROLOGUE

THE FOUNDERS' NOTIONS OF THE FREEDOM OF THE PRESS

BY ARTHUR MILIKH

Freedom of the press didn't always exist. At only four hundred years old, it's relatively new. Before then, official limits always determined what could and couldn't be published. Sometimes there was harsh and exacting censorship, as in sixteenth-century Europe, which famously prosecuted and destroyed Galileo for challenging church authority. Sometimes the censorship was looser, as in ancient Athens, where philosophical writings circulated quietly though somewhat freely. Nonetheless, Athens put Socrates to death for speaking against the city's gods. Censorship always was the default position.

It was not a historical accident or some evolutionary process that brought the freedom of the press into existence. To the contrary, it was created by a handful of European men, then transformed into a bedrock political principle, and implemented in the Constitution by America's Founders. As originally understood, the liberty of the press would cover all publications: books, essays, journals, and magazines—not just newspapers, as we like to believe today. Its creators were thinkers of high rank, who had deep and far-reaching reasons for establishing it. First among them is the freedom of the intellect, an end in itself. But best known to us is the political justification: that a free people can neither rule itself nor defend itself adequately and peacefully without a free press. Indeed, without it, the Founders thought the opposite would reign—tyranny, mediocrity, and corruption. They were right then and are still right today. Moreover, many of its founders also believed that a nation cannot have scientific progress and enlightenment without the freedom for scientists to publish and disseminate their findings. Freedom of the press, we forget, is essential to the scientific enterprise.

For most of American history, we took for granted the freedom of the press, including its intellectual origins and its enormous benefits. But today many Western elites are demanding a return to the era of censorship. There is less and less support for free speech in America, and the call for government to censor speech and publications—either directly (like the Biden administration's Disinformation Governance Board) or indirectly through the federal government's Big Tech proxies—is growing louder. These censors boast that justice, equality, and peace will blossom from censorship, but what they'll create is suffocating tyranny, filled with corruption, nauseating mediocrity, governed by resentments, political instability, and the end of science.

Almost 150 years before America's Founding, John Milton, author of *Paradise Lost*, published the classic elaboration of the freedom of the press, *Areopagitica* (1644). Milton assailed the British Licensing Order of 1643, which required authors to submit their works for pre-publication approval to government officials. These censors also had the power to seize and destroy disapproved books. Milton saw that such laws turn citizens into flatterers and courtiers, rather than public-spirited men concerned for the common weal. Censorship would destroy, he also contended, the possibility of sound policy by silencing thoughtful and critical voices. And it would smother the flourishing of genius:

> We should be wary therefore what persecution we
> raise against the living labours of publick men, how we
> spill that season'd life of man preserv'd and stor'd up in
> Books; since we see a kinde of homicide may be thus
> committed, sometimes a martyrdome, and if it extend

to the whole impression, a kinde of massacre, whereof the execution ends not in the slaying of an elementall life, but strikes at that ethereall and fift essence, the breath of reason it selfe, slaies an immortality rather then a life.

Knowledge cannot defile, nor consequently the books, if the will and conscience be not defil'd. For books are as meats and viands are; some of good, some of evill substance...wholesome meats to a vitiated stomack differ little or nothing from unwholesome; and best books to a naughty mind are not unappliable to occasions of evill. Bad meats will scarce breed good nourishment in the healthiest concoction; but herein the difference is of bad books, that they to a discreet and judicious Reader serve in many respects to dis-cover, to confute, to forewarn, and to illustrate.

Milton's *cri de coeur* succeeded in liberalizing England's harsh censorship regime, and greatly influenced America's Founders. In fact, Milton's definition of the liberty of the press was summarily used by James Wilson during the ratification debates: A free press means that—absolutely—there be no government censorship prior to publication.

About eighty years later, John Trenchard and Thomas Gordon, using the pen name "Cato," wrote a series of letters published in the *London Journal* and the *British Journal* in defense of freedom of speech and the freedom of the press. They had an immediate effect on public opinion in Britain and in the American colonies, and especially on the sixteen-year-old Benjamin Franklin, who republished excerpts under the name of "Silence Dogood" in 1722. A sample:

Without freedom of thought, there can be no such thing as wisdom; and no such thing as publick liberty, without freedom of speech: Which is the right of every man, as far as by it he does not hurt and control the right of another; and this is the only check which it ought to suffer, the only bounds which it ought to know. This sacred privilege is so essential to free government, that the security of property; and the freedom of speech, always go together; and in those wretched countries where a man cannot call his tongue his own, he can scarce call any thing else his own. Whoever would overthrow the liberty of the nation, must begin by subduing the freedom of speech; a thing terrible to publick traitors.

The Founders built upon these principles, elevating them to the status of a right. Madison explained the logic in his essay *On Property*: As free and equal individuals, our minds belong to us, for no one has the right to control them. Similarly, our speech, an extension of our mind, also belongs to us, as no one has a right to control our speech. And by extension, our writings and publications are the products of our minds, just as is our speech. This is half-way to explaining the unity of the First Amendment: Our conscience, speech, publications, are all products of our mind, and are thus inviolable.

Freedom of the press is a radical departure from all the past, with enormous political and moral stakes. It was never only about newspapers and journalists. It's about the very possibility of enlightenment, and its two core components: the flourishing of political liberty and the flourishing of science. Thomas Jefferson thought most deeply and clearly about this double goal, as he nicely summarized in an 1804 letter:

> No experiment can be more interesting than that we are now trying, and which we trust will end in establishing the fact, that man may be governed by reason and truth. Our first object should therefore be, to leave open to him all the avenues to truth. The most effectual hitherto found, is the freedom of the press.

The Founders had five major arguments justifying this core institution's *political* effects: (1) the freedom of the press allows a free people to check its elected and appointed government officials through publications, (2) it allows a free people to organize itself in opposition to a government which violates rights, (3) it creates common sentiments and ideas among the people, (4) it encourages the blossoming of the intellect, and (5) it cultivates rational habits of mind in the public. The Founders believed that these benefits cannot be established and safeguarded otherwise. Which is precisely why so many powerful forces want to limit what can be said or written today.

Regarding the modern theory of government, a free press has the power and duty to compel the responsibility of its government by vigilantly guarding against corruption and abuses of power. This is a novel understanding of the word "responsibility," which was never used in quite this way until the Founding era. Our broader system of government, with its famous checks and balances, employs ambition to counteract ambition, and antagonistic institutions to square off against one another. Responsibility is produced by this kind of antagonism or compulsion. Contrast this with the old view—prevailing in monarchies and aristocracies—where traditions, or honor, or oaths were heavily relied upon to ensure good behavior. The press, in following this logic, has an institutional role in preserving republicanism.

The British philosopher David Hume, who also greatly influenced America's Founding generation, states most clearly this role of the press in his 1741 essay, *Of the Liberty of the Press*:

> The spirit of the people must frequently be rouzed, in
> order to curb the ambition of the court; and the dread
> of rouzing this spirit must be employed to prevent that
> ambition. Nothing so effectual to this purpose as the
> liberty of the press, by which all the learning, wit, and
> genius of the nation may be employed on the side of
> freedom, and every one be animated to its defence.

Preventing government's usurpations through fear of public anger is difficult to achieve without a free press. Moreover, in nations where private avarice is encouraged and serves as the engine of prosperity and innovation, those who govern are especially open to corruption, foreign influences, and forgetting of their national or constitutional loyalties. Under the First Amendment, the press is supposed to maintain this check on their appetites. While in theory rational politics originates in compelled responsibility, Hume also foresaw that where the press is free, it will often mindlessly oppose *any* governmental action, regardless of the harm this may cause to a nation.

It is also meant to expose and attack dogmas hostile to political liberty. No doubt a free press creates great rancor in the public square, as it did at the time of the Founding. But in theory, the truth (of natural rights teaching, or of science) would be defended and would eventually win out. A free press would thus defend republicanism against all forms of anti-republicanism—against tyranny, monarchy, slavery. In this sense, the press is a form of proto-warfare which prevents genuine domestic warfare by weakening and eventually dissipating the passions the Founders so feared by filtering them through the gauntlet of reason. In idealized form, it is this warfare of reasoned argument that compels the public to make and grasp arguments rather than default to the use of force.

Republican government requires a free people to be able to communicate among themselves. This is especially true of a large, diverse republic of vast territory. As the anti-Federalist author or authors known as the "Federal Farmer" wrote in the *Poughkeepsie Journal* in 1788, "a free press is the channel of communication as to mercantile and public affairs [by which citizens] are enabled to unite, and become formidable to those rulers who adopt improper measures." The press, in mobilizing public sentiment, prevents the usurpation of rights by government powers, just as the right to bear arms has many times almost invisibly restrained tyrannical governmental impulses. Moreover, since the public often cannot organize in person (in part, the justification for so large a republic), it must share common sentiments

and ideas. A free press encourages the development of common sentiments, and thus establishes a common bond.

Publications would train citizens' toward intellectual independence, habituating them to a rational bent of mind. Citizens are cul-
tivated to develop the intellectual and emotional means to resist rule
by mob, and to resist falling in love with impossible moral and political fantasies. For a people to be free it must be tutored in reasoning
about the public good, public affairs, and small-scale political pru-
dence. Benjamin Franklin pointed out that the freedom of the press
especially concerns the "Liberty of discussing the Propriety of Public
Measures and political opinions."

Not only do ordinary citizens benefit from this civic and practical education, but opportunity is offered to the ablest among them
to cultivate their intellects and their political virtues, especially public-spirited courage. The freedom of the speech and the press "is the
great bulwark of liberty; they prosper and die together: And it is the
terror of traitors and oppressors, and a barrier against them. It produces excellent writers, and encourages men of fine genius," Cato
observes in Letter 15. It is difficult if not impossible to cultivate the
mind without books and other publications. More broadly, for a number of reasons modern democracy is often hostile to the excellence of
the mind. But freedom of the press would preserve the greatest books,
suited for the rarest natures, which require space to blossom. This is
another element of what Jefferson meant by the pursuit of the truth, in
philosophy and religion.

But the preservation of political liberty is only half of the story.
The other half, as noted, is the promotion of science, which is nearly
impossible without the freedom of the press. Again, the stakes are
much greater and deeper than newspapers and journalists; the possibility of enlightenment itself is at stake. As strange as it is for us to
hear, because today we all live in the atmosphere of science, modern
natural science is an innovation with enormous moral and political
consequences. No one elaborated these consequences better than
the French philosopher René Descartes (1596–1650), a founder of

modern science, and a great influence on Jefferson, along with Locke, Francis Bacon, and Isaac Newton.

In *Rules for the Direction of the Mind* (written in 1628 but not published until 1700) Descartes says that the past was defined by two types of scientists and inventors. The first were those who wanted to impress the crowd with fake science to gain power over it, by which he means alchemists, and less obviously, also priests. The second type were those who really did possess scientific knowledge or made real discoveries, but who wanted to keep them secret. It is very hard to distinguish one from the other—but the freedom of the press will solve this millennia-old problem. Both types will be required to publish their secrets. In exchange for revealing their secrets, but only after genuine discoveries have been verified via the scientific method, will the discoverers gain the glory, influence, and the wealth that they hoped for all along.

The freedom of the press is political in the highest sense as it spreads the scientific view of all things in the battle for modernity and enlightenment. In doing so, it gets rid of false sciences (alchemists and divine conjurors); it makes the ignorant (as Descartes calls them) see the distinction between the true and the false; and it universalizes a new uniformity of thinking where material and efficient causality become the only forms of causality upon which minds turn, rather than teleological and miraculous thinking. In this new world, scientists are the keepers of the truth.

Despite this new era of press freedom, from Milton to today, it has been broadly understood that laws could legitimately punish certain kinds of publications. The Founders were greatly informed by William Blackstone's *Commentaries on the Laws of England* on this point:

> The liberty of the press is indeed essential to the nature of a free state; but this consists in laying no previous restraints upon publications, and not in freedom from censure for criminal matter when published. Every freeman has an undoubted right to lay what sentiments he pleases before the public; to forbid this, is to destroy the freedom of the press; but if he

publishes what is improper, mischievous or illegal, he must take the consequence of his own temerity.

These limits served as guardrails to preserve, rather than limit, political liberty. These guardrails are still on the books in many American states, though they have been considerably weakened by Supreme Court jurisprudence over the past century.

There are three basic common-law categories, as the scholar David Lowenthal lays out in *No Liberty for License* (1997): obscenity, libel, and seditious libel. Obscene publications covered pornography and erotica, and gratuitous violence. The former were banned because exacerbating prurient sexual desires was universally viewed as bad for individuals and society, encouraging young people to become sexual beings before maturity, and undermining families by drawing fathers and husbands out of their homes; the latter, because gratuitous violence shocked and harmed decent morality, and made citizens insensitive to crime.

Moreover, libelous writings that destroy the reputations of individuals—including public officials—were also punishable. In fact, Jefferson believed that restraining the press against false and defamatory publications, "renders a service to public morals and public tranquility." Until the 1964 Supreme Court case *New York Times Co. v. Sullivan*, there was a broad belief in states and in federal courts that no honorable society would allow politicians, let alone private citizens, to have their reputations destroyed on false pretense. Newspapers were held to a standard of "reasonable care and diligence to ascertain the truth." If a careless publisher harmed someone's reputation (which it is difficult, if not impossible, to restore), he should be punished. It was a fair deal between the press and citizens that lasted for more than a century. This standard required the press to carefully consider, and prove, what it published. But "actual malice," the standard created by *New York Times Co. v. Sullivan* has in practice given the press a free pass to libel and slander anyone—never to suffer consequences, and never to think twice before ruining reputations.

The last major limitation emerging from the Founding is seditious libel, which includes speech or publications that make legitimate government so vilified that it cannot function, and can lead to it being overthrown. In a different era, this category was viewed as common sense: Every nation has a right to protect itself or prevent its self-destruction by publishers and writers. Even Socrates did not object to the city's right to put him to death for questioning its gods.

There were other minor categories of restrictions, in which state and federal statutes restrained journalists from snooping on private citizens, and court gag orders which protected the judicial process from being illegitimately influenced by newspapers inflaming public passions. But, again, all these limits were viewed as facilitating the ultimate goals of the freedom of the press—political liberty and liberty of the mind.

For all the promised utility of a free press, many involved in its intellectual creation showed trepidation about what it would unleash. Jefferson was famously angered by how quickly it descended into calumny, malice, and falsehood. But among the Founders, the critic most clear-minded on the harm done by the press is Benjamin Franklin. Franklin was himself the founder and editor of many newspapers and made a fortune doing it. In a short masterpiece published toward the end of his life, *An Account of the Supremest Court of Judicature in Pennsylvania, viz., The Court of the Press* (1789), as I have previously argued in *National Affairs*, Franklin explained that unlike any other republican institution, the press does not fall under any explicit constitutional check. By its very design it is motivated to act viciously—attacking bad dogma, false knowledge, and political corruption—but it is neither limited nor moderated by either its own idealism or by any institution. It pretends to act like a court, conducting hearings and inquiries against public and private citizens, and all other institutions. But unlike a real court, it is not subject to the same limiting procedures, precedents, checks, evidentiary standards, and appeals which moderate the power of courts.

Nor does a sense of justice restrain it. Franklin half-joked that the press is like the Spanish Inquisition in its moral authority to force and shape belief through fear and intimidation, reaching into individual minds and compelling belief through its power to destroy reputations, or turns mobs on its enemies. It can transform decent citizens into villains overnight. The press reminds citizens of their vulnerability, and it enjoys this power, sometimes sadistically. Franklin feared this behavior would undermine rational habits of thought among citizens by using driving passions to manufacture judgments, rather than by paying respect to their rational faculties by persuading through the careful elaboration of evidence.

In effect, the freedom of the press has created a new human type, now entrusted with guiding the public intellect, deciding citizens' fates, and even determining the future of the nation. Since there are no appointments by an executive authority on the basis of tradition, honor, or intelligence, any man, no matter how untutored, can suddenly have great power—neither "Ability, Integrity, [nor] Knowledge" are needed. And what often unifies this class, for Franklin, is the motive to possess the "privilege of accusing and abusing [other citizens] at their pleasure." Though the press began with the mission of preventing despotism, it may itself have a despotic soul. Further, its continued power over the public depends on a "natural Support" in the soul—resentment. Resentment is desiring that harm befall others in order to protect one's good opinion of oneself. In amplifying and dignifying resentment of citizens, the press extends its own popularity and reach.

Franklin's solution? "[L]eave the liberty of the press untouched, to be exercised in its full extent, force, and vigor; but to permit the *liberty of the cudgel.*" Franklin—a media man himself—thought the only check on the press would be the public consequences that restrain it; he wanted the public to keep in mind its power to humiliate, and for the press to fear it. The public can unite against the press if it is sufficiently affronted by its abuses. One solution would be stronger libel laws in the wake of the overturning of the Court's infamous *Sullivan* decision.

Many Western elites today do not understand the stakes of maintaining a free press, though they sometimes pay lip service to it. In siding with the government or the ruling faction in their hopes of crushing their political opposition once and for all, they are creating something far worse than we have today. The absence of a responsible and free press means the coming of a new era—not of establishing social justice once and for all, but of political corruption, governmental mismanagement, usurpations of rights, and national decline, all of which at some point become irremediable.

More to the point, today's journalists who use their powers to side with an increasingly tyrannical state do not see that the position they currently occupy is temporary. The transition from democracy to tyranny is facilitated by a seemingly free press, which obtains for itself the petty benefits from assisting the government (the career boosts, the access, the doggie treats). But the next phase of the tyranny they help to usher in will make of the press an unwilling house pet. Not only will this mean a clearly subordinate role rather than a partnership, but worse: It means suffering real threats, manipulations, and a forced drive toward unchosen, illegitimate goals, by a power far stronger than it, now unfettered and unrestrained.

Nor do they yet see the effects on the country and the Constitution that currently protects them: the end of any objections to the state's direction, but only flattery and compliance; and the ensuing corruption, theft, the death of innovation and originality, the selling-out of the country; the criminality (national and local); the loss of prosperity, and the unchecked losses in foreign policy abroad, will be beyond the press's control to stop.

CHECK YOUR OPINIONS WITH YOUR PARKA

BY PETER PRICHARD

It's a weekend morning in January 1976, and a gust of lake-effect snow sweeps across the picture window of the *Times-Union* newsroom, obscuring our view of downtown Rochester, New York. The fifteen reporters and editors on the weekend shift look up in unison as our leader, managing editor John L. Dougherty, enters the newsroom, shaking the snow from his coat. He pulls up a chair, props his feet on the City Desk, lights a Marlboro, and begins scanning the proofs of our copy.

The Rochester *Times-Union* is an afternoon newspaper, one of two highly profitable Gannett papers that serve this thriving mid-sized city and its surrounding towns. Dougherty is around sixty, a trim, wiry scribe whose weathered face reflects all the miles he's logged and all the editions he's put to bed. This morning, the sixth day of his work week, he's slogged through mounds of salty slush to sign off on Saturday's final edition.

Like most good editors of that era, John read virtually everything in the newspaper before it went to press. As "J.D." speed-read our news stories, work came to a standstill as we awaited his verdict. He was judicious in his judgments, usually not changing much, because over the years he had drummed into every one of us, again and again, the need for accuracy, fairness, balance, and objectivity. He was a stickler for getting things right. He liked the old city room saying, "If your mother says she loves you, check it out."

Occasionally he'd say something like, "You need a quote from Steve May [Rochester's mayor] in that item about the unplowed streets in Irondequoit." Or "Can't we get Walter Fallon [Eastman Kodak's CEO] to say something about Kodak's fight with Fuji? Their PR people are useless."

Every reporter and editor knew that when you entered J.D.'s newsroom, you checked your personal opinions with your parka. We were reporters, not editorial writers or columnists, and we tried hard to approach every story with an open mind. We strove to be blank slates; our role was to discover what happened, to try hard to determine what was true and what was false, and to always include two or more perspectives in our stories.

There was very little discussion of anonymous sources because we almost never used them. In many if not most cases, the reliability of what anonymous sources told us was questionable. We had learned over decades of experience that any source who asked to be anonymous often had an axe to grind and was seeking to use us, and the *Times-Union*, to discredit a rival or boost an ally. So, we only granted people anonymity as an absolute last resort, for very important news we believed to be true.

That powerful focus on the mission—to find and report the facts—was rewarded during the 1971 riot at Attica prison. After a lot of digging, the pathologist told a *T-U* reporter, on the record, that "gunshots, not knives" had killed nine prison guards whom the inmates had taken hostage.

The State Police had claimed that the inmates cut the hostages' throats when officers stormed the prison. Dougherty had edited that story himself, insisting that reporters triple-check it and corroborate it from two sources before printing it, and the *T-U* won a Pulitzer Prize for general local reporting.

All that said, the *T-U* newsroom was certainly not perfect. Our staff was not as diverse as it should have been. We did not employ many people of color or many women, and as a result, we short-changed some perspectives in our community, most notably those of black Americans. Al Neuharth, soon to be Gannett CEO, would later insist that the diversity of newsroom staffs should reflect our readership, and our hiring of women and blacks increased, improving our coverage.

Despite that shortcoming, most of us surely believed that our job was to illuminate the objective truth of the given situation, and refrain from injecting our own opinions into the story. Objectivity, as it had been defined by the dominant news agency of that day, the Associated Press, was our byword. We believed that our role was to report the facts, without fear or favor. By reporting the news in a fair and balanced way, we felt that we were providing a vital service to America's experiment with democracy. As Abraham Lincoln said, "Let the people know the facts, and the country will be safe."

Sometimes we were the public's guardians against corruption and government overreach. Sometimes, we dared to think that our work had made the world a little bit better.

The Demise of the Daily Newspaper

The *T-U* was a medium-sized newspaper. When I was a reporter there in the mid-1970s its circulation was nearly 142,000, close to its peak. We had a staff of about eighty journalists covering the Rochester metro area. Reporters were assigned to regularly cover city and town halls, school districts, police departments, the courts, business and lifestyle beats, and long-form projects. We had a popular local news columnist, and we had strong features and sports departments. Six days a week, our readers could expect to receive a reasonably complete report of what was happening in Rochester. Opinion was quarantined on the editorial page, along with letters to the editor and guest opinion pieces.

And when we missed something, the morning newspaper on which I started in Rochester, the *Democrat and Chronicle*, circulation 139,000, would almost surely cover it. Even though both newspapers were owned by Gannett, then a very profitable public company, the reporters of each newspaper competed fiercely with one another. Taken together, there were about 170 reporters and editors on the two newspapers.

Fast forward to today. The *Times-Union* published its last edition in 1997 and merged operations with the *D&C*. The *D&C* still exists, but is a shell of its former self, with a circulation of less than 28,000. The two newspapers had a combined annual pre-tax profit north of $30 million in the mid-1970s; today the *D&C* probably struggles to break even. The hedge fund that is the company's largest shareholder doesn't disclose the profits of individual newspapers.

Readers of the Gannett Rochester newspapers had a resource that kept them well-informed about every big issue in the region. We covered their elected representatives thoroughly, reported what they stood for and how they voted. And we covered the thriving companies who called Rochester home then—Kodak, Xerox, and Bausch & Lomb.

In cities and towns across the country today, newspapers have been decimated. Total U.S. weekday newspaper circulation in 1974 was about 62 million copies. By 2020, that number, including digital subscriptions, was had shrunk to about 24 million—a 61 percent decline. The Pew Research Center estimated that the average time spent by visitors to the nation's fifty largest newspapers had declined to two minutes per day.

By comparison, the average amount of time spent by visitors to five social media networks that same year—Facebook, Instagram, Twitter, TikTok, and Snapchat—was between twenty-eight and thirty-five minutes per day. And the total amount of time people spent in front of their screens on an average day had ballooned to seven hours.

So today readers spend two minutes a day on newspapers but seven hours a day on internet content, some of it news but much of it useless gossip, memes, pranks, and salacious posts by "influencers" seeking to turn clicks into cash. And some still wonder why millions of Americans are ill-informed about serious issues.

First the digital revolution took away newspapers' readers, and then it took most of their advertising revenue. Newspaper advertising revenue peaked in 2005 at about $49 billion a year. By 2021 it had collapsed to $8.8 billion, an 82 percent decline. Social media took in $58 billion in 2021, seven times as much as newspapers. The trend continues today.

Faced with the digital revolution that looted their revenue bases and sent almost all the advertising money to Google, Facebook, Instagram, and Craig's List, the remaining news outlets still standing have drastically cut costs. Across the country, these newspapers—or more accurately, websites that used to be newspapers—have become empty shells with skeleton staffs that provide threadbare coverage.

In 2006, the newspaper industry had 74,000 employees. By 2020, it had only about 31,000, about the same number that just one company, Gannett, had in the 1990s.

The Rise of News Deserts

According to a *U.S. News & World Report* article, over the past fifteen years the United States has lost 2,100 newspapers, leaving at least 1,800 communities that had a local news outlet in 2004 without a single one in 2020. One small example: One million people live in Montgomery County, Maryland, and it has no local newspaper. Newspapers that once covered an entire state have retreated to serve just a few counties.

News coverage has been drastically reduced as well. In 1991, *The Baltimore Sun* published nearly 87,000 stories; by 2009, that number was under 24,000. And, in many cases, the articles that were printed were not as meaty or thorough as they were in the 1990s.

Newspaper owners tried to save their way to prosperity, but that was impossible. As staffs collapsed, so did the quality of the news pages. There are fewer newspapers, fewer reporters, fewer stories. "There's nothing in the paper," longtime readers used to frequently complain. Now, they're right.

When the digital revolution started in the early 2000s, newspapers were slow to adapt, similar to the way some buggy-whip manufacturers ignored the first horseless carriages on their streets. Most did establish websites and put content online. But they didn't charge for it. As a result, consumers became accustomed to getting news for free.

As the downward spiral worsened, some mainstream legacy news sites spent increasing amounts of energy chasing eyeballs with click-bait. Some newsrooms installed monitors that recorded how many "hits" each story got, often supplanting traditional news judgment by experienced editors with the whims of the crowd. Some news sites later converted these whims into algorithms that determined content.

Long gone are the days when you could discover in your morning news report some interesting, well-written story about a subject that you never dreamed you would be interested in. An editor at your local newspaper had spotted it and a writer had written it.

Most consumers today get their news from social media. The algorithms of those sites spew out stories that the machine has decided, based on something we users clicked on or a random comment we made that was harvested by the software that resides in an electronic device—a wireless speaker, a phone, or a TV—that knows more about us than we realize. The well-balanced structure of a good newspaper, curated every day by talented and dedicated human beings, has been largely replaced by machines spewing sales pitches and trivia.

National Journalists Became Propagandists

As the 21st century unfolded, a more pernicious trend emerged, especially among journalists working for the national media. The rise of the "woke" culture and the near-complete domination of liberal reporters and editors of a few national news sources led to agenda-driven journalism. *The New York Times*, for decades arguably the best newspaper in the world, began giving more space and attention to causes that fit its staff's woke leanings.

Here's a partial list of the pet causes the *Times* embraced: hatred of Donald Trump, enthusiasm for Democrats and dislike or outright contempt for Republicans, distrust of Big Business and capitalism, demonization of the rich, fear of global warming, condemnation of

Israel, hostility toward religion and support for death to infants in the womb, advocacy for gay rights and "gender transition," and a default preference to trust activist government to solve most problems. This was the agenda the newspaper's staff had established for the news columns, not the opinion pages.

Except for a tiny number of moderate voices, the *Times*'s opinion pages rarely printed any opinion columns by conservatives. You would never read Rush Limbaugh, Mollie Hemingway, or Thomas Sowell in its pages. The liberal tilt became so severe that a deputy editorial page editor was forced out because, in the wake of George Floyd's death, he dared to publish an op-ed by a U.S. senator that advocated using the military to quell riots, looting, and attacks on police in American cities. The *Times* was not the only newspaper to promote this partisan agenda. Other large newspapers and television networks, with the partial exception of Fox, joined the march, too.

Sadly, *USA Today*, where I was the top editor for more than six years, was one of them. When Al Neuharth started the newspaper, he established a no-endorsement policy in elections. The paper abandoned that policy in 2020 and endorsed Joe Biden, thus ending a thirty-eight-year tradition and, in effect, attaching a political bumper sticker to its nameplate.

The Death of Objectivity

The news media is still the only private business that enjoys constitutional protection, but more and more voices are asking if the media deserves it. Neuharth often said: "The First Amendment guarantees a free press, but we in the media must make sure it is a fair press."

That emphasis on fairness is certainly out of fashion in the national media now. As newspapers declined, journalists tried to shore up audiences by turning to blatant opinion and sensationalism. Those stories were easy to write—or worse, Tweet—and resulted in more internet clicks by readers. So, reporters spent less time reporting and more time tweeting, often abandoning moderation, thorough report-ing, and respect for opinions different from theirs.

The rise and election of Donald Trump provided some national reporters with an unprecedented opportunity to amplify the lies of his most vociferous opponents. Mainstream reporters joined the progres-sive crowd that was trying to bring down an elected president. They cheered Trump's enemies and advanced their agendas, while largely ignoring the opinions of the 74 million Americans who'd voted for him.

Faced with this tsunami of opinion and reliance by woke reporters on what "feels right," long-time editors threw in the towel and just went with the staff's flow. Leonard Downie, Jr., former top editor of *The Washington Post*, wrote in an op-ed in which he said that

> today, newsrooms are debating whether traditional objectivity should still be the standard for news reporting. "Objectivity" is defined by most dictionaries as expressing or using facts without distortion by personal beliefs, bias, feelings or prejudice...
>
> But increasingly, reporters, editors and media crit-ics argue that the concept of journalistic objectivity is a distortion of reality. They point out that the standard was dictated over decades by male editors in predomi-nantly White newsrooms and reinforced by their own view of the world. They believe that pursuing objec-tivity can lead to false balance or misleading "both-sidesism" in covering stories about race, the treatment of women, LGBTQ+ rights, income inequality, climate change and many other subjects. And, in today's diver-sifying newsrooms, they feel it negates many of their own identities, life experiences and cultural contexts, keeping them from pursuing truth in their work.

Abandoning objectivity is a profoundly misguided approach. The original idea behind having a diverse newsroom is that you would have a much better chance to reflect the diversity of your audience if your staff is representative of all your readers. The intent was to reflect many perspectives, not elevate any one perspective over all the others.

The media-bias problem has been compounded because nearly all the journalists on the staffs of America's largest newspapers consider themselves "progressives" who uniformly vote for Democrats, and they aren't shy about advertising it. Journalists working for national news organizations today frequently parrot the daily talking points distributed by the Democratic National Committee—and are proud of it. The triumph of opinion over objectivity has resulted in networks that regularly promote political points of view. For example, the cable network MSNBC is pro-Democrat, while the Fox networks are largely pro-conservative (although Fox offers several balanced news programs).

We've reached the point in recent years where the top editor of *The New York Times* declared that the election of Donald Trump had ended the debate over whether practicing "objectivity" was a valid approach to news coverage.

"Trump has changed journalism," the *Times*'s then-managing editor Dean Baquet said. "We didn't know how to write the paragraph that said, 'This is just false...' We struggle with that. I think Trump has ended that struggle. I think now we say stuff. We write it more powerfully that it's false." (Although half the country may not think it's false.)

It is certainly true that Donald Trump's relationship to "truth" is often tenuous. But instead of simply being skeptical about what Trump said, reporters at the *Times* and other leading media outlets decided that almost everything he said was a lie. They abandoned any pretense of fairness and allowed their coverage to descend into malignancy and hatred. Apparently, Trump was so bad that it was fine for reporters to trash standards that had served journalism well for more than century.

It turned out that the forty-fifth president of the United States was so objectionable that most of the media thought it was fine to cover him unfairly and adopt the lies about the president's "collusion" with the Russian government that his enemies told, day after day, in the run-up to the 2016 election. Powerful television networks and other large newspapers and news sites piled on, broadcasting outlandish claims, such as that the future president took part in "golden showers" when he was in Moscow. Exhaustive and very expensive government investigations found no evidence of any Russian collusion. It turned out that the collusion claims were lies funded, orchestrated, and leaked by Trump's opponents, including Hillary Clinton. "We couldn't collude with ourselves," one Trump staffer said.

As those charges unraveled, instead of correcting their mistakes or investigating how they happened, these prominent news sources doubled down and continued their vendetta against a president who just didn't fit their taste. They hated him, so it was okay to defame him. They hated him, so it was okay to print almost anything his political enemies said, with minimal investigation or context. *The New York Times* and *The Washington Post* won Pulitzers for their "Russian collusion" stories, prizes the Pulitzer board should have rescinded. Neither the journalists nor their employers who got it wrong ever apologized. In some cases, they kept producing the same agenda-driven stories, even after it was obvious that they were false.

After their chosen candidate Joe Biden won the presidential election, today's national reporters miraculously morphed from attack dogs to lap dogs. Their persistent refusal to find out the facts about Hunter Biden—where he got all that money, where it went, what the donors received for it, and whether his father received any of it—is another egregious example of where reporters' biases won out over the truth. In the old world of journalism, reporters would be keen to find out why various governmental entities were so eager to indict Trump while slow-walking any allegation about the Bidens into oblivion. Equal justice under the law? Not likely.

In this environment, public figures have figured out that it's very easy to manipulate today's reporters. It's especially easy if you are a "progressive" politician, because the reporter you're leaking the story to is already playing for your team.

Or you can just ignore the media and say very little about what you're doing because there are no consequences for being wrong or even corrupt. Many of today's national reporters won't follow up, they just move on to the next shiny object. And in many instances, the bent politicians, police officers, or executives don't have to worry that the press will find them out, because there usually aren't enough reporters on the beat to discover their malfeasance.

Instead of digging for the news, many of the journalists who are on duty spend hours tweeting and "building their brands." As David Simon, the former *Baltimore Sun* reporter who produced the TV crime series *The Wire* told Congress: "it's a great time to be a crook in America."

To sum up:

* Newspapers knew that the digital age was coming, and they failed to adapt fast enough and were too slow to charge for content. Digital competitors took away newspapers' revenues and never paid a fair price for the news that they created.
* Silicon Valley produced portable personal computers—cell phones that are really mighty computers—and destroyed legacy media. The resulting loss of ad revenue led to drastic budget cuts that crippled the media's ability to cover the news and be democracy's watchdog.
* The rise of social media demolished the base of shared knowledge that legacy media had built, exacerbating our political divide, and contributing to the rise of "low information voters" who were easy targets for demagogues on both sides.
* Academia compounded the problem by turning out "woke" reporters who were often more interested in promoting their personal politics than serving the public. Many shaped their coverage in their heads before conducting a single interview. Perhaps our media landscape would be improved if the remaining newsrooms hired more people who earned their reporting chops covering night meetings in small towns rather than attending glitzy colleges.

* The government's hands-off approach to regulation of Big Tech hasn't always served us well. Arguably, government should have paid more attention to the downside of the digital revolution and its resulting effects on children, community, and democracy. In recent elections, tech companies have acted like totalitarian governments by frequently censoring speakers, especially conservatives. Regulators may make the same mistake if they ignore the unintended consequences of machine learning and artificial intelligence for journalism and news coverage.

* The members of the media have amplified they country's political divide by their constant emphasis on conflict and extreme positions. In politics today there is no middle, and very little, common ground. Politicians are largely to blame, but journalists play into their hands every day. Peter Vanderwicken once put it this way in an article in the *Harvard Business Review*: "The U.S. press, like the U.S. government, is a corrupt and troubled institution. Corrupt not so much in the sense that it accepts bribes but in a systemic sense. It fails to do what it claims to do, what it should do and what society expects it to do."

What Can Be Done?

I'm a lifelong optimist, but the loss of the Fourth Estate is a defeat from which democracy may not recover.

For years, people referred to the press as the Fourth Estate—almost a fourth branch of government. Journalists used to believe that they had a near-sacred responsibility to keep citizens well-informed, through a commitment to accurate, fair, and objective news coverage. The Founders of our country believed that a free and unfettered press was necessary to a functioning democracy, and that is why they included freedom of the press in the five freedoms of the First Amendment—the bedrock of our liberty.

The public has certainly noticed the decline of fairness in news sources. A 2022 Freedom Forum survey found that only 14 percent of Americans trust journalists. Only Congress has lower ratings. And political divisions exacerbated by partisans on both sides and the media have caused millions to censor themselves—45 percent say they've done this.

The Newseum, the interactive museum of news and history in Washington, D.C., which closed in 2019, defined the mission of the media this way:

* The free press is a cornerstone of democracy.
* People have a right to know. Journalists have a right to tell.
* Finding the facts can be difficult. Reporting the story can be dangerous.
* Freedom includes the right to be outrageous. Responsibility includes the duty to be fair.
* News is history in the making. Journalists provide the first draft of history.
* A free press, at its best, reveals the truth.

Thanks to the First Amendment, the journalists who serve us enjoy nearly limitless freedom to practice their craft. They would be wise to reflect on and follow those worthy principles.

The digital revolution has wrought many miracles: seamless communication, the opportunity for billions of new voices to express themselves, the means to readily research anything, and a simple way for people around the world to easily collaborate to solve problems. But its consequences for a free and fair press have been disastrous, and as a result, democracy has been damaged.

I hope that I will live long enough to see journalists begin to revive an honest commitment to facts, fairness, and the truth.

MEDIA OBJECTIVITY, 1920–2024, RIP

BY JOHN FUND

Objectivity in the media—the idea that news stories should be fair, undistorted, accurate, impartial, and offer an open-minded look at the evidence—is a concept that's just over one hundred years old.

It was born out of a famous 1920 essay by two-time Pulitzer Prize winner Walter Lippmann called "Liberty and the News." Lippmann believed that opinion pieces had their place and acknowledged that they excited readers far more than dry accounts of events. But he called on news reporters not to serve any cause "no matter how worthy" and to strive to truthfully report what they learned. His arguments won the day and were adopted by the vast majority of newsrooms all over the country, from small dailies to major networks.

But times and trends change, and it's fair to say that the formal burial of media objectivity occurred on January 30, 2023. On that day, former *Washington Post* executive editor Leonard Downie, Jr., wrote a lengthy piece in Downie's old paper headlined "Newsrooms That Move Beyond 'Objectivity' Can Build Trust."

After surveying seventy-five key sources in the media elite, he found a "generational shift" among them had concluded that objectivity "is a distortion of reality." Downie wrote that male editors in predominantly white newsrooms had created "false balance or misleading 'bothsidesism'" in covering stories about race, the treatment of women, LGBTQ+ rights, income inequality, climate change"—and the list goes on. He and former CBS News president Andrew Hayward both said that their survey of media elites "convinced us that truth-seeking media must move beyond whatever 'objectivity' once meant to produce more trustworthy news."

The quotations they collected from their media sources in their search for truth are indeed revealing. Kathleen Carroll, the former executive editor of the Associated Press, asked of Lippman's rules, "Objective by whose standard? That standard seems to be white, educated, fairly wealthy."

Emilio Garcia-Ruiz, editor-in-chief of the *San Francisco Chronicle*, said that a new generation was demanding a revolution: "The consensus among younger journalists is that we got it all wrong. Objectivity has got to go." *Los Angeles Times* editor Kevin Merida sounded like a teacher who now wanted his students to run the classroom: "We're trying to create an environment in which we don't police our journalists too much. Our young people want to be participants in the world."

What Merida must have actually meant was that he wanted his writers to be "activists." Nothing else can explain his paper's bizarre series of drive-by character attacks on Larry Elder, the attorney and radio talk show host who was the Republican candidate for governor of California in the 2021 recall election against incumbent Gavin Newsom.

On July 14, *Times* columnist Jean Guerrero said that Elder, a native of majority-black Compton, and black himself, was effectively a race traitor through building a niche career "enabling white victimhood" and "white grievance politics," which "were once the purview of neo-Nazis and the Ku Klux Klan." The next month, *Times* columnist Erika Smith wrote a piece titled "Larry Elder Is the Black Face of White Supremacy. You've Been Warned." She called him the racist "troll that no one was supposed to feed."

Like the conquest of Constantinople in 1453, the siege and eventual fall of the Church of Objectivity didn't occur without some brave resistance.

On Bill Maher's HBO show—increasingly a refuge for those who believe in free speech along the lines of the old ACLU—*New York Times* columnist Bret Stephens expressed his alarm at Downie's stab at the heart of objectivity: "If he were to get his way that would be not just the end of any serious journalism in the United States, I think it would be the end of the United States."

Marty Baron, editor of *The Washington Post* from 2012 to 2021, then responded in a speech titled "We Want Objective Judges and Doctors. Why Not Journalists, Too?" He admitted his stance is "terribly unpopular" among today's journalists. "Objectivity is not always achieved," he acknowledged, but "failure to achieve standards does not obviate the need for them. It does not render them outmoded. It makes them more necessary. And it requires that we apply them more consistently and enforce them more firmly."

Baron had an ally in David Greenberg, a professor of media studies at Rutgers University, who defended objectivity as "the relentless attempt to correct subjectivity and, therefore, approach what people of diverse viewpoints can agree to be the truth." He championed the value of having "places where anyone can go to get roughly the same reliable, accurate account of news events, before moving into a political debate about the implications of those events. And it seems to me, if you were to survey people in newsrooms, they would largely agree that that is worth preserving."

Greenberg's observation may have been true up until 2016, but in that year, Donald Trump broke the brain synapses of most elite American journalists. As Trump accepted the Republican nomination, *The New York Times* ran a front-page article by its media columnist Jim Rutenberg titled "The Challenge Trump Poses to Objectivity."

Rutenberg asserted that so many reporters viewed Trump as "potentially dangerous" that their reporting would inevitably move "to being oppositional." Because Trump was "conducting his campaign in ways we've not normally seen," reporters could be excused for not using objective standards in covering him. Peter Boyer, a former reporter for both *The New York Times* and *The New Yorker*, said that the Rutenberg column proved that Trump "had baited the elite news media into abandoning the norms of traditional journalism—a central tenet of which was the posture of neutrality."

The *Times* itself used to vigorously police its objectivity standards. Abe Rosenthal, its executive editor from 1977 to 1986, was such a believer that he had his tombstone inscribed with "He Kept the Paper Straight." As late as 2015, the year that Donald Trump rode the Trump Tower escalator down to the press conference at which he announced his presidential candidacy, the *Times* Style Book was a model of clarity.

"Writers and editors should guard against word choices that undermine neutrality," the 2015 Style Book directed. "If one politician is firm or resolute, an opponent should not be rigid or dogmatic. If one country in a conflict has a leadership while the other has a regime, impartiality suffers." By the next year, the *Times* was routinely referring to Trump "lies" and "fabrications."

The shift attracted criticism from Liz Spayd, a former managing editor of *The Washington Post* and editor of the *Columbia Journalism Review*. In 2016, she was the *Times*'s public editor and she responded to Rutenberg's farewell to objectivity with a piece titled "Why Readers See the Times as Liberal." She concluded her piece with what some called an obituary for the old *Times*:

> Imagine what would be missed by journalists who felt no pressing need to see the world through others' eyes. Imagine the stories they might miss, like the groundswell of isolation that propelled a candidate like Donald Trump to his party's nomination. Imagine a country where the greatest, most powerful newsroom in the free world was viewed not as a voice that speaks to all but as one that has taken sides. Or has that already happened?

Spayd paid a price for her candor. In May 2017—four months into Trump's presidency—the *Times* announced her firing and the elimination of her position as an in-house ombudsman. In her final column,

Spayd lamented that the *Times*'s ombudsman role was part of "having an institution that is willing to seriously listen to [the] criticism, willing to doubt its impulses and challenge the wisdom of the inner sanctum." She wasn't optimistic that the *Times* would "keep the paper straight" in Abe Rosenthal's famous phrase, and her fears were proven right.

A few months after Spayd's departure, the *Times* dismantled the one-hundred-plus-member copy editor desk, eliminating what it called an archaic assembly-line model of news production. Abe Rosenthal considered the copy desk not only to be a guardrail against errors, but also fundamental to his mission of maintaining objectivity.

In January 2019, every major media outlet in Washington seized on a *BuzzFeed* story alleging that Trump had ordered his former attorney Michael Cohen to lie to Congress. The next day the story was firmly shot down by the prosecutors investigating Trump. Jeffrey Toobin, CNN's fiercely anti-Trump legal analyst, had to concede: "the larger message that a lot of people are going to take from this story is that the news media are a bunch of leftist liars who are dying to get the president, and they're willing to lie to do it."

Later, it was revealed that pretty much the entire basis of the "Russiagate" probe of allegations that Donald Trump had colluded with Russia to sway the 2016 election had collapsed. Its central pillar—a dossier by a compromised former British spy Christopher Steele—had been covertly paid for by Hillary Clinton's campaign and relied on easily discredited sources.

Not only did the collapse of the Russiagate conspiracy theory not lead major media outlets to rethink their stance toward Trump and the truth, many reaped benefits from the story. In 2019, the Pulitzer Prize committee awarded its National Reporting prize to *The Washington Post* and *The New York Times* for their "deeply sourced, relentlessly reported coverage in the public interest" of the imaginary Russiagate non-scandal.

Coverage of Trump—both accurate and flawed—was also a bonanza of a business model for elite media outlets. Both executive editor Jill Abramson and her successor Dean Baquet boasted that

Trump had been big box office for the *Times*. "Given its mostly liberal audience," Abramson wrote in her memoir, "there was an implicit financial reward for the *Times* in running lots of Trump stories, almost all of them negative: they drove big traffic numbers."

Indeed, the company's stock price had hit a three-year low of $10.80 on November 3, 2016, five days before Trump's election victory; when Trump left office in January 2021, the shares had reached $49.86, just shy of their all-time high. Former *Times* investigative reporter Jeff Gerth, who wrote a definitive, four-part, 24,000-word take-down of the *Times*'s sloppy coverage of Russiagate for the *Columbia Journalism Review* that appeared in early 2023, referred to the paper and Trump as "sparring partners with benefits."

But like the addict who experiences a short-term high after taking narcotics and then crashes but can't change his habits, the media is paying a long-term price for its farewell to objectivity. In 2018, *Washington Post* executive editor Martin Baron told a journalism conference at Oxford University that the news media seemed to be losing the power to influence events. "Journalism may not work as it did in the past," Baron said. "Our work's anticipated impact may not materialize."

One factor is the loss of public trust and confidence. An October 2022 survey by Gallup and the Knight Foundation found that only 34 percent of Americans trusted the mainstream media to report the news "fully, accurately and fairly," and that was only because 70 percent of Democrats took that stance.

Only two weeks after Leonard Downie published his obituary of objectivity in *The Washington Post*, a February 2023 Gallup/Knight survey found an even grimmer picture. Asked whether they agreed with the statement that national news organizations do not intend to mislead, fully half the respondents said they disagreed; only 25 percent agreed. Only 23 percent of those surveyed believed that journalists were acting in the public's best interests. The Associated Press said the results "showed a depth of distrust and bad feeling that go beyond the foundations and processes of journalism."

Can anything be done? Objectivity is unlikely to have a Lazarus-like resurrection from its grave anytime soon. But there is a country that seems to have struck a better balance.

The British public is not keen on the quality of its wide array of national newspapers—a recent survey found that only 37 percent of people trusted the British media. But the U.K. certainly has a wide diversity of newspapers that do not hide that they have a distinct point of view, while they also work to produce an accurate, comprehensive product. From *The Guardian* and the *Independent* on the Left to the *Daily Telegraph* and the *Times* on the Right, British newspapers offer readers an ideologically much more varied product line than exists in the U.S.

"There is a smorgasbord of papers and websites for every taste, and people are free to sample several," says John O'Sullivan, a former editor of *National Review* magazine who was once a speechwriter for Margaret Thatcher. "If you have a dissident or minority viewpoint it isn't automatically trashed as 'misinformation' and the roughly equal power of competing publications means that journalists often actually debate the conclusions of competitors."

Given the parlous post-objective state of journalism in America today the British media environment is a promised land by comparison.

Clive Crook, a British journalist who has been deputy editor of *The Economist* and a former senior editor at *The Atlantic*, is no stranger to journalism on both sides of the Atlantic. He unequivocally comes down on the side of those who say that objectivity in journalism should not be abandoned as a goal.

First, he says, striving for objectivity "would make the truth more accessible, because the discipline of suspending feelings, opinions and personal bias opens the mind." Second, "it would give readers greater confidence in the news that's set before them."

If the search for objectivity and the pursuit of truth is to be abandoned, journalists of the future should have little confidence that their words will have influence beyond partisan sects, the ideologically rabid, and the purely credulous. Who wants to write or report merely for those audiences?

PARTISAN MEDIA?
'TWAS EVER THUS

BY JOHN J. MILLER

"Good evening," said Dan Rather on the *CBS Evening News* on
September 8, 2004. He had greeted viewers this way countless times
before, but today everything was different. His show that night would
mark the sunset of what was once called the "mainstream media."
The anchorman continued: "There are new questions tonight about
President [George W.] Bush's service in the Texas Air National Guard
in the late 1960s and early '70s and about his insistence that he met his
military service obligations. CBS News has exclusive information..."

Many readers will remember the rest of the story. In the notorious segment that followed, Rather and his crew accused a president of
having exploited political connections to avoid military service in the
Vietnam War. The allegation had surfaced previously, but now CBS
claimed to have explosive new documents that proved Bush's dereliction of duty.

Presented as objective journalism, Rather's report aired during the
heat of a close presidential contest. Bush, an incumbent Republican,
faced Democratic candidate John Kerry, a senator from Massachusetts
whose own service in Vietnam had become controversial. The provocative claims of CBS News had the potential to turn the election against
Bush—and in an earlier era, without the feedback channels of the
internet, they might have succeeded.

Within hours of the broadcast, however, several writers took to the blogosphere, which at the time was a new and untested medium. They questioned the authenticity of what came to be called the "Killian documents," focusing on problems of typography and arguing that typewriters from the early 1970s could not have produced them. In other words: CBS News was fake news. The documents were forgeries, meant to unseat a president, and plugged uncritically by a major news organization and its star correspondent.

A fierce debate erupted as little-known bloggers took on a media titan. In less than two weeks, they convincingly exposed the sloppiness and dishonesty of CBS News. On September 20, Rather apologized for his bogus broadcast. The sorry episode came to be called "Rathergate," and it essentially ended Rather's career. Journalists make mistakes all the time, but the blunder of Rathergate heralded so much more: the demise of an old media that falsely claimed to represent the "mainstream" and the rise of a new media that was more open to heterodox ideas.

Most notably, Rathergate marked the onset of radical changes that paradoxically have returned American journalism to its deepest roots. Today, in the 2020s, the media is closer in spirit to the media of the Founding Fathers than it is to the media of just a generation ago. To be sure, the technologies are vastly different. The Founders had printing presses and we have screens. What our two ages share, however, is a boisterousness that can produce the worst kinds of journalism but also some of the best—and, perhaps not coincidentally, some of the most nakedly partisan.

Rathergate ended journalism's century-long charade of "objectivity," which supposedly rejected partisanship but instead merely disguised it. For decades, the media establishment and its celebrities had masked their political biases behind claims of impartiality. Postwar conservatives came to see the ruse: They knew that the so-called mainstream media was in league with liberalism and often a mouthpiece for the Democratic Party. Insiders occasionally admitted as much. Just a few weeks before Rathergate, the public editor of *The New*

York Times asked a striking question in a headline: "Is The New York Times a Liberal Newspaper?" Daniel Okrent answered it in the first line of his column: "Of course it is." He went on to list a series of "social issues," such as "gay rights, gun control, abortion and environmental regulation, among others." Then he confessed: "And if you think The Times plays it down the middle on any of them, you've been reading the paper with your eyes closed."

In today's confusing and confounding media environment, it's easy to yearn for a time when honest reporters and editors played it down the middle and aspired "to give the news impartiality, without fear or favor, regardless of party, sect, or interests involved." That's how Adolph S. Ochs put it in 1896, shortly after he bought *The New York Times* and began to turn it into what is often regarded as America's newspaper of record. For decades, a version of his quote was etched into the wall of the newspaper's lobby. Rendered as an airy abstraction, however, the quotation lost its vital context. As Susan E. Tifft and Alex S. Jones explained in *The Trust: The Private and Powerful Family Behind The New York Times*, their comprehensive history of the publishing family behind the *Times*, Ochs had a political purpose in mind. "His aim was to reassure Republicans of the paper's political objectivity," wrote Tifft and Jones, because his paper was widely regarded as loyal to the Democratic Party.

Opinions may vary on how well the *Times* has lived up to its supposed standard of objectivity—or people simply may agree with the words of another prominent newsman from an earlier era, when newspapers were loudly and proudly partisan. "Protestations of impartiality I shall make none," wrote William Cobbett in 1797. "They are always useless and are besides perfect nonsense, when used by a news-monger."

During the days of the American Founding and the early republic, Cobbett and other news-mongers were commonly aligned with political parties—not just on their editorial pages, which did not yet exist in their modern form, but in everything from their accounts of events to their business models. Publishers received patronage payments from political actors and printing presses earned government contracts based on their partisan loyalties. The link between party and press was so strong, the period is sometimes called the "Party Press Era."

Hack writers flourished, praising their paymasters and hurling insults at their foes. The results could be maddening. Thomas Jefferson, who hired writers to advance his political interests in print, held conflicting views. In 1787, he wrote that given a choice between "a government without newspapers or newspapers without government, I should not hesitate a moment to prefer the latter." Twenty years later—and, it must be said, after a newspaper's attack artist accused him of fathering children with his slave Sally Hemings, in a charge that has echoed through history—he expressed his frustration with the press: "[T]he man who never looks into a newspaper is better informed than he who reads them; inasmuch as he knows nothing is nearer to the truth than he whose mind is filled with falsehoods & errors."

This roiling media environment produced some of the most scurrilous journalism that Americans ever have read as well as some of the most remarkable prose ever published. *The Federalist Papers*, after all, were a series of newspaper essays written by Alexander Hamilton, James Madison, and John Jay in 1787 and 1788. Today, we would call them "op-eds," though this specific term had not yet been invented. These masterworks of political theory—and products of journalism—argued successfully for the ratification of the Constitution, whose First Amendment and its commitment to press freedom is another bounty of a partisan age.

Well into the 19th century, Americans expected blatant partisanship in their media, and newspapers often advertised their loyalties in their very names. Many of these have survived into the current era. The largest are probably the *Arkansas Democrat-Gazette* of Little Rock, and *The Republican* of Springfield, Massachusetts, followed by the *Tallahassee Democrat* in Florida and the *Democrat and Chronicle* in Rochester, New York. Each day, tens of thousands of people still read these newspapers. The most remarkable relics of the party-press era may be the *Herald-Whig* of Illinois and the *Cecil Whig* of Maryland, both of which remain in print, long after the demise of their partisan namesake.

More familiar partisan names live on in small-town publications: *The Appeal-Democrat* of Marysville, California, *The Bloomfield Democrat* of Iowa, *The Corydon Democrat* of Indiana, the *Delta Dunklin Democrat* of Missouri, the *Durant Democrat* of Oklahoma, *Foster's Daily Democrat* of Portsmouth, New Hampshire, *The Marshall Democrat-News* of Missouri, *The McDonough Democrat* of Illinois, the *Mountain Democrat* of Placerville, California, *The Press Democrat* of Santa Rosa, California, and the *Weatherford Democrat* of Texas. Additional newspapers continue to bear the name of the other major party: the *Bethany Republican-Clipper* of Missouri, the *Bureau County Republican* of Illinois, the *Cazenovia Republican* of New York, the *Daily Republican* of Marion, Illinois, *The Garrett County Republican* of West Virginia, *The Kane Republican* of Pennsylvania, *The News Republican* of Boone, California, the *Press-Republican* of Plattsburgh, New York, the *Republican-American* of Waterbury, Connecticut, the *Republican Herald* of Pottsville, Pennsylvania, the *Times-Republican* of Marshalltown, Iowa, and *The Woodville Republican* of Mississippi.

The economic system of partisanship began to change in the 1830s, as new technologies allowed printers to publish newspapers at lower cost, liberating them from the need for party patronage. As publishers realized that they could generate revenue from readers by selling cheap editions at high volume, the era of the party press moved into the era of the penny press. The first edition of the New York *Sun*, which sold for a penny in 1833, came with a populist slogan: "It shines for all." *The Sun* and its ilk were not just for Democrats, Whigs, or Republicans, but for everyone. Plenty of newspapers maintained their partisan ties, but many editors announced their political independence. Horace Greeley is best known for an apocryphal line that became a slogan of manifest destiny: "Go West, young man." He also founded the *New-York Tribune* in 1841, proclaiming his freedom from "servile partisanship." Separating his paper from partisanship did not mean separating himself from politics, though, and Greeley remained a colorful political actor who served briefly in Congress as a Whig, supported the creation of the Republican Party, and even ran for president in 1872 on a doomed ticket that had the support of many Democrats.

The advent of the telegraph also pushed newspapers away from partisanship. Wire services such as the Associated Press, founded in 1846, sought to sell their content not to factions but to the masses. Moreover, the costs of telegraphic transmissions encouraged short bursts of information, rather than long and winding narratives that veered into idiosyncrasy and opinion. Concision was both cheaper and more general in its appeal. It encouraged writers to stick to facts. So did the arrival of photography, especially as new printing technologies allowed these images increasingly to appear in newspapers. Could the best journalistic prose mirror the realism of a photo? Many editors and writers wanted to rise to the challenge.

Around the turn of the century, the emerging progressive movement and its commitment to social reform through expert knowledge began to reshape the industry. Newspapers and magazines often descended into to the corrupt sensationalism of yellow journalism and embraced the earnestness of muckraking crusades, but journalists increasingly saw themselves as professionals with ethical obligations to empiricism and impartiality. They developed codes of conduct whose highest principle was "objectivity."

Objectivity is the opposite of subjectivity, and in philosophy it refers to truth that exists apart from the perceptions and emotions of observers, or subjects. In science, objectivity recognizes the ability to uncover truth through disinterested investigation. In journalism, it tends to mean telling stories without personal bias—and from the start, both journalists and readers have argued whether this is possible or even desirable. Editorial decisions about what constitutes news, after all, is a subjective choice. War is news. So is famine. But what about the divorce of a politician? Or the arrival of a new consumer product? Or a sports score? The "inverted pyramid" approach of hard-news storytelling is supposed to be journalism's rough equivalent of the scientific method, with writers conveying accurate information in the order of its importance—and this, too, requires subjective judgment. Reporters who summarize a president's State of the Union address, for example, must decide what to highlight and what to leave out. If they truly aspired to objectivity, they would become stenographers. Author bylines, which were rare in the 1920s but common in the 1930s, are tools of journalistic accountability, but also concessions to the fact that behind every supposedly objective news article is a subjective observer.

This is not to deny the reality of truth or to say that good reporters can't achieve something like fairness, but to show that the ideal of journalistic objectivity is a contested concept that always has drawn challenges and complaints. In the second half of the 20th century, its strongest critics argued that "objectivity" in the media disguised liberal bias. In the first half of the 20th century, however, the reverse was true: Liberals were the dominant skeptics of objectivity, believing that conservative capitalists controlled the media.

An early critic was the muckraking writer Upton Sinclair, best known for his 1906 novel *The Jungle*, which sought to expose the restrictive employment practices and filthy conditions of the meat-packing industry and proposed socialism as a solution. In 1919, he published a nonfiction attack on the media. In *The Brass Check*, whose title referred to tokens that served as currency in whorehouses, Sinclair claimed that "American newspapers as a whole represent private interests and not public interests." He argued that publishers and editors protected their businesses by refusing to examine corporate corruption and failing to cover or promote the views and activities of socialists. In the 1930s, as media historians Sam Lebovic and Michael Schudson have shown, the New Dealers believed that the media was aligned against them. In 1936, when President Franklin Delano Roosevelt won re-election with 60 percent of the popular vote and carried forty-six of forty-eight states, only 37 percent of daily newspapers had endorsed him. Following Roosevelt's victory, mobs of the president's supporters egged the building of the *Chicago Tribune* and set fire to one of its delivery trucks. Democrats complained about conservative media bias into the 1950s, when they argued that the press was hostile to Adlai Stevenson, a Democratic presidential candidate who lost a pair of elections to Republican Dwight Eisenhower.

Around this time, however, conservatives flipped the script. The radical Left never has quit accusing the media of capitalist bias, in critiques that are mostly updated and refined versions of what Upton Sinclair had alleged soon after World War I. Yet by the middle of the 20th century, liberalism was in ascendance. "In the United States at this time liberalism is not only the dominant but even the sole intellectual tradition," wrote Lionel Trilling in 1950. "For it is the plain fact that nowadays there are no conservative or reactionary ideas in general circulation." This included the media, according to William F. Buckley, Jr., who founded *National Review* in 1955 as "a responsible dissent from Liberal orthodoxy"—an orthodoxy that he and other conservatives increasingly observed in a media that equated liberalism and objectivity. (Trilling's use of the term "circulation," from the world of media, is telling.) By the 1960s, liberal media bias had become a major concern of conservatives who felt that their favored politicians, such as the Republican Barry Goldwater, suffered from prejudicial treatment in the press.

New technologies had the inadvertent effect of merging liberal political ideas with journalistic objectivity. As radios became a major source of news in the 1920s, and televisions in the 1950s, print journalism faced existential threats: For the first time, people could receive authoritative news accounts from other sources. Now, when they looked at newspapers at the breakfast table in the morning or in the living room after dinner, they were reading about news they first had heard from different forms of media. Many newspapers responded by doing what magazines had known to do for a long time: They still wanted to break news, but they also turned more and more to providing context for the news and offering interpretations of it, which print journalism is much better able to do than radio and television. At the same time, they still regarded themselves as objective, even though their work was riddled with the subjective judgments of liberalism.

Although *The New York Times* continued to pay lip service to what was supposedly its greatest principle—"impartiality, without fear or favor"—its own leaders knew that they had a problem. In 1968, as media historian Matthew Pressman has revealed, A.M. "Abe" Rosenthal described it in a letter to fellow editor James Reston: "There are more reporters at the paper who seem to question or challenge the duty of the reporter, once taken for granted, to be above the battle," he wrote. "Inevitably, more young reporters reflect the philosophy of their age group and times—personal engagement, militancy, and radicalism." Rosenthal amplified the point the following year in a memo to editors: "I get the impression, reading *The Times*, that the image we give of America is largely of demonstrations, discrimination, antiwar movements, rallies, protests, etc.... I think that because of our own liberal interest and because of our reporters' inclinations, we overdo this."

Critiques of media bias are heavily subjective and anecdotal, but data also has confirmed the liberal dominance of the media, such as surveys that have shown that the White House press corps votes overwhelmingly for Democrats. In 2011, political scientist Tim Groseclose published *Left Turn*, based on his quantitative analysis of media content. He demonstrated that despite claims of objectivity, top media outlets were replete with liberal bias, that right-of-center companies, such as Fox News, were less conservative than so-called mainstream companies were liberal, and that the media's overwhelming liberalism had in fact pushed the political views of Americans to the left.

Journalists sometimes respond to this evidence by claiming that their political preferences do not affect their objectivity. "I don't think there's one reporter now—I'm not talking about columnists—who acts out of an ideological bias that can be detected," said George Stephanopoulos in 1994, when he was a top advisor in the Democratic administration of President Bill Clinton, and shortly before he became a host and correspondent for ABC News. Conservatives scoff at such claims, concluding that journalists are either in denial or lying. Whatever the causes or excuses, the results are clear: Journalism in the age of so-called objectivity was partisan, even though its practitioners refused to admit it.

Dan Rather's predecessor at CBS News was Walter Cronkite, who signed off his broadcasts in the 1960s and 1970s with an authoritative claim that was also an appeal to his own alleged objectivity: "And that's the way it is." He was widely described as "the most trusted man in America," though the empirical basis for this claim never was strong. He was also indisputably a liberal. When Democratic presidential nominee George McGovern needed to select a running mate in the summer of 1972, he briefly considered Cronkite but decided not to ask the newsman. McGovern feared that Cronkite would turn him down and wanted to avoid the embarrassment of a rejection. At the time, McGovern was probably the most leftwing candidate in U.S. political history—and years later, Cronkite said he would have jumped at the chance to join the ticket. "I'd have accepted in a minute," he said. Yet he refused to acknowledge his liberalism. "If people knew how I felt on an issue, or thought they could discern from me some ideological position of [CBS], I had failed in my mission," wrote the secret Democrat in his memoir, *A Reporter's Life.*

The age of the internet has made it harder to hide bias from an audience, as Rather discovered to his humiliation. It also has upended the media's economic models. Just as the penny press loosened the connection between newspapers and political parties in the nineteenth century, social media has made it more difficult for networks and publications to generate revenue. The result is a proliferation of websites and media companies whose political perspectives are obvious to everyone. They may not be sponsored by parties, which are weaker today than they were during the era of the party press, but they draw support from politically minded investors and subscribers. In the 2020s, journalism is awful, full of misinformation and propaganda, just as it was during the time of the Founding Fathers. Journalism also is wonderful, as Americans never have enjoyed news and commentary that is so accessible and diverse—and, perhaps, objectively better than it used to be.

CHECKING THE "FACT CHECKERS"

BY MARK HEMINGWAY

Among the myriad of ways that America turned into a dystopian nightmare in 2020, the hysteria over Covid and Donald Trump's possible re-election created an information landscape that Americans thought was unthinkable a decade ago: Powerful institutions have normalized widespread, Soviet-style political censorship. What's more, the American media have been the biggest cheerleaders for singling out and punishing people for no other reason than they have departed from the enforced ideological consensus by being willing to state demonstrably true facts.

There's much to be said about how we got to this place, but it's worth zeroing in on two particular mechanisms responsible for this state of affairs. The first is the rise of politicized media "fact-checkers," and the second is Facebook, the social media site. The fact that these two entities have now joined forces means that speaking freely online without an algorithm slapping a warning label on innocuous opinions is now impossible. The Facebook-owned site Instagram has actually run a "fact check" on a meme that criticized lawmakers who "spend trillions on bills they haven't read, but want details on how you spend $600." They also have algorithms psychoanalyzing the potential for extremism. People in Facebook groups dedicated to canning food have been receiving warnings that say, "Are you concerned that someone you know is becoming too prepared?"

While I confess that I didn't see this censorship algorithms regime gaining power so quickly, as a reporter in D.C. for more than twenty years, I did see plenty of warning signs. One in particular was hard to ignore: In the summer of 2018, I was sitting in a staff meeting at the now-defunct magazine *The Weekly Standard* when an editor at the publication started yelling at me.

At the time of the argument, *The Weekly Standard* was four months away from being shuttered, and though no one in the meeting knew we were facing the axe, a profound sense of unease had descended on the place. A hardline opposition to Trump wasn't universally shared by the magazine's staff, but for the two years following his election, top editors at the magazine regularly lambasted Trump and indulged in some regrettably erroneous Russia-collusion reporting. This approach was not appreciated by our regular subscribers who had overwhelmingly voted for the president.

And the argument that led to me getting yelled at was another exhibit in prosecuting the case for how things at *The Weekly Standard* had gone wrong: We had gone from being an outlet that regularly published hard-hitting media criticism to enabling the worst media innovation in decades—so-called fact checking.

In 2017, editors above my paygrade decided that we were going to be one of a handful of media outlets that agreed to collaborate with Facebook for the social media giant's "fact checking" program. In exchange for a few crumbs from a company with $700 billion, we would write "fact checks" taking politicians and pundits to task for spreading "disinformation" that Facebook would then use to make content-moderation decisions. In addition to writing fact check columns for our website, we would be hiring and employing an in-house fact checker whose salary was paid by Facebook. This fact checker would also be serving as a traditional in-house fact checker, going over magazine articles pre-publication to root out "errors." The editors saw this as a win-win.

I was never consulted by the editors about this decision to work with Facebook for several obvious reasons. In 2016, I wrote a piece for the magazine's website bluntly calling Facebook's plan to collaborate with outside media organizations to fact check content on the plat-form "a terrible idea." And years before that, in 2011, I had written a cover story for the magazine headlined "Lies, Damned Lies, and 'Fact-Checking.'" It was the first major—and deeply critical—examination of media "fact checking" organizations, such as PolitiFact and *The Washington Post* Fact Checker. The article made a splash and I spent years afterwards writing tens of thousands of words inveighing against the dishonest tactics of corporate media "fact checkers" that were now working for Facebook.

The actual track record of media fact-checker malpractice and dishonesty isn't up for debate. Long before Trump, there were criti-cal university studies showing that fact checkers accused Republicans of lying three times as often as Democrats. Further, fact checkers' reticence to fact check Democrats was pretty clearly tied to helping Democrats win elections. PolitiFact rated Obama's famously dishon-est 2012 campaign promise about the Obamacare law—"if you like your health insurance, you can keep your health insurance"—as "true" six different times. When the law phased in after Obama had lied to secure his re-election, millions of Americans were suddenly kicked off their health insurance plans. PolitiFact then disingenuously made it "lie of the year" in 2013, one year after telling the truth about the law might have made a difference in the election.

Once upon a time, editors at the *Standard* would have agreed with me about how corrupt it was that Facebook was now paying PolitiFact to produce these partisan hatchet jobs, but now we had taken Facebook's money and hired our own "fact checker." The editors pre-sumably thought that, as a conservative publication, we would bring some balance to the endeavor. I felt like they should have known better.

As it happens, the guy they hired as our fact checker was a diligent, if inexperienced, journalist in a relatively thankless job. Somewhat to his credit, he seemed to know his limits, and one day spoke up in our staff meeting. He said he was concerned about doing his job because of the growing power of Facebook. He explained that whenever he did one of his fact-checking columns, part of his gig involved going into a special portal in Facebook's backend created for its fact-checking mercenaries, where he entered details about his fact check. When he entered a claim of "false," he was asked to enter the URL of the story where he found the claim—at which point Facebook, according to its own press releases, would then kill 80 percent of the global internet traffic to that story. Our fact checker explained that this was making him uncomfortable. Some of these fact checks were complicated, and he felt that his judgment wasn't absolute.

It was a record-scratch moment in the staff meeting. After a beat, I spoke up and said something to the effect of "you mean to tell me, that a single journalist has the power to render judgment to nearly wipe a news story off of the internet?" Where our publication had once taken pride in challenging the dishonesty and bias of the corporate media, it dawned on me and more than a few others in the room that whatever influence our failing publication had, was being leveraged to act as part of terrifyingly effective censorship regime controlled by a hated social media company run by one of the world's richest men.

And that's when one of *The Weekly Standard*'s editors began to yell at me. It was a stressful time, and we were all on the verge of losing our jobs. I don't recall much of what he said in the moment, except that to my astonishment and just about everyone else's in the room, he said that Facebook needed to ban even more people. That editor is now running a publication whose sole reason for being is airing grievances about the post-Trump Republican Party.

The origins of Facebook's fact-checking program are not a mystery: Trump won.

And following his victory, it was the uproar over Facebook's alleged role in the 2016 election that really sowed the seeds of the media's complete implosion. It was quite the fall from grace—in 2012 the Obama campaign maximally exploited Facebook's data to reach out to voters, and this was greeted with a chorus of hosannas from the press, eager to praise this technologically savvy electioneering. Carol Davidsen, the analytics director on Obama's campaign, later admitted that the campaign had access to all of Facebook's data and that

Facebook "allowed us to do things they wouldn't have allowed some-one else to do because they were on our side."

But where Facebook was eager to be credited for Obama's vic-tory, almost immediately after Trump's election the knives were out internally. "Facebook employees have formed an unofficial task force to question the role their company played in promoting fake news in the lead-up to Donald Trump's victory in the US election last week," reported *BuzzFeed* in November 2016. The employees were operating in defiance of CEO Mark Zuckerberg, who said the idea that Facebook had unfairly tilted the election in Trump's favor was "crazy." And by all accounts the suggestion that Facebook as a company wasn't in the tank for Democrats was, in fact, crazy. Earlier in 2016, former Facebook workers told *Gizmodo* that employees at the social network were actively suppressing conservative news so that it didn't trend on the site. Trump had run a savvy digital campaign, for sure, but there was no way his campaign received the access to the platform that the Obama campaign had.

The media and Democratic politicians continued to pounce on post-election reports about trivial amounts of Russian propaganda appearing on Facebook and other social networks. It didn't matter these claims were almost universally overstated and fueled irrespon-sible speculation that Trump's election in 2016 was illegitimate. (For obvious reasons, the media was far less interested in how the Russian-sourced Steele Dossier, bought and paid for by the Democratic National Committee and the Hillary Clinton campaign, was a far more likely and impactful source of misinformation and election interference.) Zuckerberg was facing mounting public pressure to do something, anything, to convince liberal America that he was taking the problem of disinformation at Facebook seriously.

Still, addressing growing complaints about "fake news" on Facebook went well beyond kicking off a few foreign troll farms. How could Facebook institute the kind of sweeping censorship that would be necessary to placate its angry critics and dissenting employees?

Thanks to the infamous Section 230 of the Communications Decency Act, Facebook was spared legal liability for any harmful content that appeared on its site, premised on the understanding that it was neutral platform for third-party content. The belief that Facebook and other social media sites weren't exercising the same kind of sweeping editorial judgments that made traditional publishers subject to libel laws was always a farce, but Facebook didn't want the additional legal exposure or scrutiny that would come with telling political organizations and media outlets what they could and could not say on a website that, fairly or not, presented itself as a public forum. Facebook needed to bring outside media organizations in to help it in its quest to censor the news.

Once upon a time, the media would have seen Facebook's decision to ask media outlets to act as outside censors as an indecent proposal—but by 2016, media organizations were thoroughly compromised. The internet had largely killed off direct subscription business models, so they were all dependent on social media platforms, such as Facebook, for revenue. And if the American media once had a classically liberal reverence for the First Amendment that enabled their business, America's newsrooms were now so politicized they were happy to choose the form of their destructor if it meant keeping Republicans out of power. It took no time at all to get the media on board with Facebook's grand censorship plans.

In December 2016, Facebook announced that it was partnering with media fact checkers "to combat and bury 'fake news,'" according to *Business Insider*. That this program was launched just two months after Trump won should make the motivation behind the program abundantly clear. Try as they did, the media and Big Tech oligarchs had been unable to play a decisive role in the 2016 election. Now they were teaming up to exert even more control over which information voters would be allowed to see and hear. And sure enough, under Trump the normalization of censorship occurred much the same way that Ernest Hemingway described how bankruptcy happens—slowly, then all at once.

Five years ago when I was in *The Weekly Standard* staff meeting getting yelled at for questioning Facebook's ability to fairly adjudicate

PART THREE: THE PAST AS PROLOGUE

political disputes, I don't think anyone in the room anticipated that the next few years would see the media and Big Tech doing anything as threatening as censoring the sitting president of the United States as Twitter—now X—did in 2020, or the broad suppression of legitimate reporting on political scandals, such as Hunter Biden's laptop, which even *The Washington Post* and *The New York Times* have now begrudgingly admitted was real. And yet, I have seen very little in the way of regret, much less any self-awareness from journalists, which would indicate a recognition of this dramatic erosion of free speech.

Suffice it to say, I have since parted ways politically and professionally with the editor that yelled at me that day in defense of Facebook. Since then, he's very publicly and unironically argued "We Need More Social Media Bans." And, after we all lost our jobs, *The Weekly Standard*'s former fact checker, the one who dared to express concern about Facebook becoming an engine of global censorship, got a job doing "fact checks" for CNN, and has since been promoted to reporter.

The editor-in-chief of *The Weekly Standard* who signed off on our Facebook partnership has since gone on to start a new publication called *The Dispatch* that still participates in Facebook's fact-checking program. In 2020, just before the election, a fact check from *The Dispatch* got the ads from one of the largest pro-life groups in the country banned from Facebook. Its fact check said it was unfair to claim that Joe Biden supports late-term abortion. *The Dispatch* would later admit that its fact check was "published in error."

Facebook's third-party "fact checking" program has also grown extensively since then. Facebook now funds more than eighty different fact checkers and has spent more than $100 million on the program to date. "We know this program is working and people find value in the warning screens we apply to content after a fact-checking partner has rated it," says Facebook's website. "We surveyed people who had seen these warning screens on-platform and found that 74% of people thought they saw the right amount or were open to seeing more false information labels, with 63% of people thinking they were applied fairly."

In sum, the evidence that people are happy with Facebook's censorship program is that Facebook says they are. Even if Facebook's touting of its own internal surveys was credible, it's still that admitting 37 percent of Facebook users don't think that the misinformation warnings are applied fairly. That's a huge number, and Facebook's own surveys should be telling it that its misinformation policies are creating distrust among a very large segment of the population. But bizarrely, Facebook is hyping this number as if it's reassuring. To quote one of the more incisive critiques of modern journalism, the 2004 comedy, *Anchorman: The Legend of Ron Burgundy*: "They've done studies, you know. Sixty percent of the time, it works every time."

Facebook's indefensible justifications can't just bulldoze past the reality of the situation that Americans now face. In just a few years, the country went from concerns about disinformation that were vague and hysterical in equal measure, to allowing one of the world's largest corporations wide latitude to capriciously censor the news with the goal of influencing elections on behalf of Democrats. The press, the one group that is supposed to warn the public about the dangers of this kind of fascist arrangement, is completely fine with submitting to and enabling this unprecedented exercise of power. And no, that's not hyperbole—the textbook definition of fascism is the merging of corporate and state power, typically achieved by an alliance with a political party. That seems to accurately describe the situation.

Given the lines that have already been crossed, history doesn't suggest many examples of people restoring a culture of free speech once it's been taken from them. The good news is that the Big Tech-Corporate Media censorship regime is still relatively new. Recent, more authoritative, surveys show that voters are increasingly distrustful of both Big Tech and the media, even if they don't fully understand exactly how this corrupt alliance is controlling the news they see and hear.

But for those of us who do understand what's happening, the censorship that's been forced on us is dire—and it's time we started yelling about it.

THAT
SULLIVAN DECISION

BY CLARICE FELDMAN

From the Founding of this country, states were empowered to define what constituted defamation, that is, publication of false statements injurious to one's reputation. In 1964, sympathetic to the nascent civil rights movement, the Supreme Court upended that principle in the landmark case of *New York Times Co. v. Sullivan*. In cases that followed in its wake, the Court dramatically relaxed the definition of publishers' duty of care and thus stripped virtually all Americans of the traditional, customary, and recognized right to redress for defamation.

There is increasing pressure to scale back these decisions, which have given publishers a free ride to engage in character assassination of those with whom they disagree. Justice Abe Fortas first expressed dissent from the path the Court was taking. More recently, Justices Neil Gorsuch and Clarence Thomas have, as well. Will the court someday overrule *Sullivan* or will it find it sufficient to pare back the progeny of that case?

In a 2023 case involving a criminal prosecution for online stalking, and thus not a defamation case, *Counterman v. Colorado*, six judges reaffirmed *Sullivan*'s central holding that the test of permissible speech lies in the recklessness or "actual malice" of the speaker. Nevertheless, the possibility remains that future cases may limit the knock-on effects of *Sullivan* that have tipped the balance in favor of "public figures," including politicians, thus allowing the press a free hand to libel those with whom it disagrees.

The Sullivan Case

Though neither man was named in a March 1960 advertisement run by *The New York Times* under the heading "Heed Their Rising Voices," Alabama's governor, John Patterson, and one of the commissioners of the city of Montgomery, sued the paper and four of the Alabama ministers whose names appeared below the advertisement: Ralph Abernathy, Solomon S. Seay, Fred L. Shuttlesworth, and Joseph Lowery. In May, the paper retracted the claims affecting the governor, but not the commissioner, L.B. Sullivan. It turned out that those four "signatories" had been added to the list of endorsements by civil rights leader A. Phillip Randolph without their knowledge or consent, which left only the *Times* as a defendant. As the court acknowledged, "the advertisement included statements, some of which were false, about police action allegedly directed against students who participated in a civil rights demonstration and against a leader of the civil rights movement." As it turned out, the *Times* had done no independent checking of the facts asserted in the ad, some of which it might have detected had someone in the newsroom merely run to the paper's own archives.

Regardless of the long history of state court prosecutions for defamation under state law, the clearly false and libelous nature of some of the charges in the advertisement, and the paper's failure to check its own reporting before running the ad, the justices held that the First and Fourteenth Amendments prohibited a state court from awarding damages to a public official "for defamatory falsehood relating to his official conduct unless he proves 'actual malice'—that the statement was made with knowledge of its falsity or with reckless disregard of whether it was true or false." A more detailed history of the case is found in Anthony Lewis's book *Make No Law: The Sullivan Case and the First Amendment*, noting that even such conservatives as former Chief Justice Rehnquist fully accepted the First Amendment rationale of *Sullivan* "as assuring the tight to criticize government...in robust, uninhibited terms."

Sullivan's Progeny

In subsequent cases, the definition of defamation became looser, and the persons entitled to protection, as well. *Sullivan* dealt with defamation of public officials; later cases covered the publisher's defamation of "public figures," which allowed mudslinging on anyone who might be considered a "celebrity." As Glenn Reynolds wrote in *The Wall Street Journal* on March 24, 2021:

> In *Gertz v. Robert Welch Inc.* and *Time Inc. v. Firestone*, the category of public figures was further expanded to include ordinary citizens who "thrust" themselves into the debate. Anyone, however obscure, who spoke out would lose traditional protection against libel and slander. The term "thrust" suggests it is vaguely inappropriate for ordinary citizens to take part in public affairs; at any rate, the price for doing so was to make your reputation fair game, a tax of sorts on speech.

Subsequent cases, in particular, *St. Amant v. Thompson*, *Curtis Publishing Co. v. Butts*, *Bell Atlantic Corp. v. Twombly*, and *Ashcroft v. Iqbal*, have further expanded the free range of publishers to disseminate what once might be deemed libel without recourse.

In *McKee v. Cosby*, where the Court declined a petition for *certiorari*—the means by which litigants seek judicial review by the Supreme Court—Justice Thomas, echoing a commonly held view by many Supreme Court watchers, describes the *Sullivan* case as "policy-driven decisions, masquerading as constitutional law." He called for overruling *Sullivan*. "If the Constitution does not require public figures to satisfy an actual-malice standard in state-law defamation suits, then neither should we." Thomas concluded: "The States are perfectly capable of striking an acceptable balance between encouraging robust public discourse and providing a meaningful remedy for reputational harm. We should reconsider our jurisprudence in this area." Others, such as Glenn Reynolds, a professor of law at the University of Tennessee in Knoxville, have asserted that it would be sufficient to protect libeled persons if the cases subsequent to *Sullivan*, such as those noted above which expanded its reach, were reversed.

How far has the law been expanded since *Sullivan*, which, as Justice Thomas summarized, was intended to encourage public discourse on matters of civil importance? Much too far.

In *Amant*, a 1968 case involving the publication in a political speech of a false charge by another person that claimed a public official had engaged in criminal conduct, the Court expanded upon its *Sullivan* holding that the "reckless disregard" test in *Sullivan* would not be met unless the person defamed could demonstrate by sufficient evidence that the defendant had serious doubts about the truth of the publication. While in tort law (civil actions to redress wrongdoing) the normal test is whether the one charged behaved as a reasonable and prudent person would, the *Amant* test was much lower—whether there was "sufficient evidence to permit the conclusion that the defendant, in fact, entertained serious doubts as to the truth of the publication."

Think about this for a moment. Under this test, if a publisher receives information from someone, even someone without a history of credibility, and runs with it without checking, unless the person defamed can show somehow that the publisher had serious doubts about its probity, or simply didn't care, he's still free from liability (the "reckless disregard" test). Justice Byron White, who authored the majority opinion in *Amant*, offered up an unpersuasive rationale:

> It may be said that such a test puts a premium on
> ignorance, encourages the irresponsible publisher not
> to inquire, and permits the issue to be determined
> by the defendant's testimony that he published the

statement in good faith and unaware of its probable falsity. Concededly the reckless disregard standard may permit recovery in fewer situations than would a rule that publishers must satisfy the standard of the reasonable man or the prudent publisher. But *New York Times* and succeeding cases have emphasized that the stake of the people in public business and the conduct of public officials is so great that neither the defense of truth nor the standard of ordinary care would protect against self-censorship, and thus adequately implement First Amendment policies. Neither lies nor false communications serve the ends of the First Amendment, and no one suggests their desirability or further proliferation. But to insure the ascertainment and publication of the truth about public affairs, it is essential that the First Amendment protect some erroneous publications, as well as true ones.

Justice Fortas dissented, finding it unpersuasive. He found that statement broadcast by Amant had been made with "actual malice." His reasoning was sound. He contended that Amant had a duty to check the reliability of libelous statement he broadcast:

> The First Amendment is not so fragile that it requires us to immunize this kind of reckless, destructive invasion of the life, even of public officials, heedless of their interests and sensitivities. The First Amendment is not a shelter for the character assassinator, whether his action is heedless and reckless or deliberate. The First Amendment does not require that we license shotgun attacks on public officials in virtually unlimited open season. The occupation of public officeholder does not forfeit one's membership in the human race. The public official should be subject to severe scrutiny and to free and open criticism. But if he is needlessly,

heedlessly, falsely accused of crime, he should have a remedy in law. *New York Times* does not preclude this minimal standard of civilized living.

(This ignores the fact that in *Sullivan*, the *Times* had only to check its own archives to see that some of the allegations in the ad were false.)

As noted in the *McKee* case, Justice Thomas indicated a desire to reverse *Sullivan*. In 2021, in *Berisha v. Lawson*, he was joined by Justice Gorsuch in asserting that *Sullivan* went too far and has evolved into allowing publishers to "cast false aspersions on public figures with near impunity." Said Gorsuch: "Not only has the doctrine evolved into a subsidy for published falsehoods on a scale no one could have foreseen, it has come to leave far more people without redress than anyone could have predicted."

He added that previous tests that courts have used "seem increasingly malleable and even archaic when almost anyone can attract some degree of public notoriety in some media segment." In 2022, Thomas again dissented from a denial of *certiorari* in *Coral Ridge Ministries Media, Inc. v. Southern Poverty Law Center*, saying it was time to re-examine the "actual malice" standard and its application to public officials. "A person may now be denied ordinary rights under defamation law if you "voluntarily inject" yourself or are "drawn into" a "public controversy." Unless you lock yourself in your home and never engage in any public activity—that's you!

You need only a cursory examination of media coverage since *Sullivan* to see how partisan the press has become and how likely any conservative—any private citizen who takes a stand that the press considers unpopular, or any public official—will be subject to defamatory coverage on, little, if any, factual basis. Will three other justices join Thomas and Gorsuch in overruling the post-*Sullivan* defamation cases? Your First Amendment rights are substantially diminished if things remain as they are.

In October 2023, the Court refused to hear an appeal in *Blankenship v. NBC Universal, LLC* by then-candidate for Senate Don Blankenship who was falsely accused of being a felon when his conviction had been for a misdemeanor. Once again Justice Thomas called for a reconsideration of *Sullivan*. Neither Justice Gorsuch, who'd earlier been critical of the holding in *Sullivan*, nor Justice Kagan who had done so in 1993 before becoming a justice, joined him. Does this mean that neither *Sullivan* nor the cases which expanded its reach will never be overturned or limited? As was the case with *Sullivan*, the particular facts of the case and sentiment concerning the parties always plays a role, in the Court's deliberations, and it remains conceivable that a case with claimants more sympathetic to the jurors may yet become the vehicle for paring back the overly broad protections against defamation.

SPIES AND JOURNALISTS: A VERY SPECIAL RELATIONSHIP

BY KYLE SHIDELER

A public uproar broke out on receiving the news that America's spy agencies have penetrated the media, using the power of mass communication for their own ends. Congress demanded an investigation into the coziness between the intelligence apparatus and its media lackeys. In response to the outrage, the CIA promised it won't happen again—while avoiding any real responsibility.

The year was 1977.

Carl Bernstein of Watergate fame authored an article for *Rolling Stone* magazine in which he detailed the CIA's program for recruiting media figures as assets and sources, alleging that more than four hundred journalists participated in the program, which had been ongoing since 1953. Intelligence insiders claimed that the number was closer to one hundred but did not dispute that the CIA had recruited journalists and given them operational responsibilities, such as delivering messages, seeking out information, and sharing what they learned with Langley. The piece was titled, "The CIA and the media: How America's Most Powerful News Media Worked Hand in Glove with the Central Intelligence Agency and Why the Church Committee Covered It Up."

Today, we may find ourselves wondering if anything ever really changes, as we learn that social media organizations have been thoroughly penetrated by CIA and FBI people, and that current and former spooks routinely appear on nightly newscasts to help to shape a narrative for the mainstream media. Now it is conservatives, not progressives, who demand a new Church Committee to rein in the "rogue elephants" in the intelligence community.

Bernstein's revelations in 1977 are most interesting, not in comparison with today's illicit coupling of journalists and spies, but by contrast. Done correctly, intelligence work and journalism are similar occupations. Both professions seek to acquire information, sift it for value, and package it with other information before providing it to customers. For American intelligence agencies, those customers are supposed to be the elected policymakers who need to make hard decisions about our national security. For the reporter, the customers are the audience whose subscription fees and ad revenues pay his salary.

Most of the work of such CIA journalist-assets was described as mere reporting, as Bernstein admitted, noting that often the CIA wanted to establish ground truth about basic facts, like whether the streets in some Eastern bloc backwater were fully paved. Much of the cooperation happened at the highest levels, with the consent and support of the publishers. Journalists were valued for such observations because they often did long tours abroad as foreign correspondents while CIA officers under official State Department cover were frequently rotated. Additionally, America's human intelligence (HUMINT) collection capability was always woefully inadequate compared to its Soviet opponents, which also explained the need to leverage American reporters.

"The notion that a newspaperman doesn't have a duty to his country is perfect balls," columnist and CIA asset Joseph Alsop declared in response to revelations that during his time as a foreign correspondent for *The New York Herald Tribune* he also did work for American intelligence. This view was not uncommon in the 1950s and 1960s. Many journalists had close ties to the CIA's forerunner, the Office of Strategic Services, and had done honorable service during World War II. The notion that one might share observations with representatives of the

U.S. government was not viewed as a hardship or a compromise of journalistic objectivity, provided that one strictly reported facts. *The New York Times* claims that not one of the journalists involved in the CIA program ever alleged that the Agency asked them to slant or water down their reporting in any way, a claim that could be true given what we know about how the program worked. News organizations are also known to skew their reporting in order to ingratiate themselves with sources and others, so the CIA would not need to apply overt pressure for a news slant.

The exposure would result in the termination of the program, no doubt helped along by changing attitudes among the journalists of the 1970s, who no longer saw loyalty to country and objectivity as compatible, and who viewed the CIA and FBI as adversaries, not allies. These revelations ended cooperation between journalists and spies, at least for the good of the country.

Such alliances continue now from baser motives.

It's hard to understate the irony of Bernstein's complaining about journalists collaborating with intelligence officials when he had served as the unquestioning recipient of leaks by Mark Felt, the one-time head of FBI counterintelligence, motivated by Felt's bureaucratic beef against the elected president of the United States. Bernstein's relationship with Felt can be thought of as the alternative model of intelligence-journalist cooperation, where the eyes of the intelligence services are not on foreign foes, but domestic political and bureaucratic opponents.

Even in exposing the CIA's relationship with journalists, Bernstein was likely little more than a patsy. As the late Angelo Codevilla observed from his time as a staffer on the Senate Select Committee on Intelligence, a leftwing faction of the intelligence services used the Church Committee and other revelations of bad behavior, not to clean up shop but to target internal opponents—and to establish a dominance over the security organs which has never since been challenged. Instead of journalists being the eyes and ears of American spies, it's now the spies who observe and report to their journalist assets, not to relay facts, but to spread narratives that serve the opaque purposes of the government mandarins.

Journalists seeking to remain in the good graces of the intelligence community have returned the favor by pre-emptively tailoring their reporting to the needs of the spies. *The Intercept* has reported how CIA favorite Ken Dilanian, first of the *Los Angeles Times* and later of the Associated Press, was one of several journalists who routinely gave the Agency preclearance of stories to ensure that the coverage portrayed the CIA in a positive light.

Coziness between spies and journalists has grown exponentially worse as society has progressed further into the digital era. Media outlets have closed foreign news bureaus and sent veteran foreign correspondents into retirement. In their place have settled swarms of young, eager J-school grads, some responsible for writing as many as a half dozen articles a day, with no requirement for multiple sources and no fact checking, posted to news websites where the ability to stealth-edit an error has replaced pro-active high-quality and knowledgeable editors. Eventually even writing articles became too time consuming, and journalists now rush to scoop each other on social media, hammering out 140-character pieces for the benefit of their Twitter (now X) followers, who sometimes outnumber the total official subscribers of the outlets where they are employed.

These are the twenty-seven-year-olds who "literally know nothing" as former Deputy National Security Advisor Ben Rhodes once pointed out. Rhodes was describing the method by which, as an official in the Obama administration, he built a foreign policy "echo chamber" that would successfully spin a narrative to justify a nuclear deal with Iran. Rhodes's partner in the scheme was a CIA officer seconded to the National Security Council, Ned Price. Price and Rhodes realized that reporters who lacked worldly experience or access to foreign correspondents of their own were completely reliant on intelligence officials in Washington to tell them what's really going on.

What little HUMINT capability the intelligence agencies had was decimated in the 1970s, thanks in part to Bernstein and company.

So today the intelligence doyens of D.C. don't really have any better understanding of the ways of the wider world than do the know-nothing journalists to whom they leak. But what the intelligence services do have is extensive electronic surveillance. And this tool also has been turned inward, in attempts to produce more goodies to leak to their aligned journalists.

Accompanying Rhodes's narrative-shaping was the tactic of unmasking identities of Americans caught in electronic surveillance, which began with congressional opponents of the Iran nuclear deal who were surveilled while they spoke with Israeli officials also opposed to the deal. As Lee Smith, author of *The Plot Against the President* has pointed out, the Iran deal surveillance was a dry run for the "Russian collusion" hoax launched against Donald Trump. The plot contained all the same elements: eavesdropping on political opponents engaged in conversations with foreigners—whether those conversations were legitimate, or the result of foreign assets being introduced by the services to justify surveillance—and using targeted leaks to favored reporters to create a false but prevalent narrative which in turn justified more extensive surveillance.

Ironically, central to the scheme was the use of the Foreign Intelligence Surveillance Act (FISA) court, which had been instituted as a post-Church Committee reform, sold as an effort to rein in the intelligence community. Instead, provided they can sell their story to the court, the spies have carte blanche to indulge in bad behavior with a judicially clear conscience. Exactly as Codevilla had repeatedly warned would happen. Like Bernstein with Felt, journalists are perfectly comfortable being the patsies of deep-throated spies if the target is a Republican, and not some foreign foe.

But perhaps more revealing of the true dynamic between intelligence and media is when the target is not a conservative, but a Democrat. For example, following the disastrous withdrawal from Afghanistan, anonymous intelligence officials rapidly threw the Biden administration under the bus, blaming their supposed political masters for everything that went wrong, and insisting to their preferred reporters that they'd predicted the situation accurately, only to be foiled by the troublesome reality of civilian-elected government.

During a Q&A with Biden after the Afghan collapse, one could see an almost physical change overtake a previously sleepy White House press corps which had allowed the Biden press secretary to run circles around them on a regular basis. This same group were furiously swarming, peppering the Democratic president with questions that were noticeably detailed and exceedingly specific, certainly fed to them by their intelligence sources.

So, while the intelligence services have outraged conservatives with their partisan interference, perhaps the largest motivation for the spies is to maintain the appearance of omniscience. What passes for intelligence analysis now is often little more than a self-licking ice cream cone; leaks from intelligence officials to journalists become news articles, which are in turn cited as open-source evidence in intelligence analysts' reports, the publication of which is breathlessly reported on by the spies' favored journalists. This trick can routinely be spotted for Department of Homeland Security terrorism bulletins and other intelligence products which appear in the public discourse, if one knows where to look.

With the rise of social media, the intelligence services have found something that they believe is more than mere ground truth—virtual reality. Having embarrassed themselves for decades for failing to understand what's going on in the streets of Damascus, Cairo, or Kyiv, American spies have realized that it's easier to manufacture public opinion about what's going on instead of doing the hard work of reporting. If journalism is the "first draft of history," social media is the first draft of journalism. Indeed, social media accounts for a major part of how news articles are distributed and read. If you cannot use social media, or if your reach is squashed, you are dead in the water as a journalistic outfit.

For social media, all questions of fact are subject to spin and interpretation. Whatever claim gets the greatest number of likes and shares becomes the truth. Are the rebels of the Arab Spring budding democrats or literally Al Qaeda? Is the Ukrainian counteroffensive succeeding or failing? Are school board protestors the most dangerous terrorists? Controlling social media narratives means that spooks never have to be embarrassed about getting the facts wrong, ever again. To paraphrase Orwell's Winston Smith in 1984, whatever happens on social media, really happens. And what appears on social media is decided by The Algorithm. Or rather he who controls The Algorithm. Social media has become the effective top editor and final arbiter of what constitutes news.

Understood from this perspective, the obsession of the intelligence services with information hygiene on social media becomes clearer. The Department of Homeland Security's Cybersecurity and Infrastructure Security Agency (CISA) has adopted the role of determining what qualifies as "Misinformation, Disinformation, and Malinformation" online. Misinformation is defined by CISA as incorrect information not intended to cause harm. Disinformation is deliberately false information intended by an enemy to manipulate public opinion. Malinformation is true information perceived as out of context or harmful, as determined by the security organs. While Mis-, Dis-, and Mal-information may be within the right of any American to post, the intelligence services don't believe that you have a right to puncture their carefully constructed social media reality bubble. Indeed, posting information that the intelligence community disagrees with has become increasingly compared to literal terrorism.

Fifty-one former intelligence and national security officials, organized by former CIA director and Biden campaign advisor Mike Morell at the request of then-Biden campaign official Tony Blinken, authored a letter which claimed that a laptop abandoned by Hunter Biden, containing evidence of the Biden family's criminal conduct and corruption, was mere "Russian disinformation." According to evidence gathered by the House Judiciary Committee, the CIA itself may have played a role in helping to gather signatures for the letter. America's mainstream journalists then aggressively reported on the letter as evidence that the laptop's falsehood was an established fact. In turn, the censorship departments of social media organizations Facebook and Twitter took action to squash such "false" claims. The *New York Post* was for a time banned from social media for attempting to share its thoroughly researched article on the Hunter Biden laptop.

Not only was it subsequently shown that the article was entirely accurate, but it was revealed that the FBI itself had a copy of the laptop's hard drive and had already verified many of the claims made in the *Post* piece. The very FBI agents who convinced social media companies that the Biden laptop was part of a "hack and dump" Russian disinformation strategy *knew* that was a lie. The intelligence community's favorite puppet journalists unapologetically cheered on the *Post*'s social media ostracism.

Following Elon Musk's purchase of Twitter, we came to learn that the social media giant had hired so many ex-FBI agents that the former Feds had their own internal company Slack channel where they translated Twitter corporate culture into Bureau-ese. The FBI possessed an open portal into Twitter, with which it and other government agencies, such as CISA, relayed demands to silence "misinformation" opponents, and even paid millions to Twitter for the privilege. Twitter executives were granted clearances so that they could be the recipients of classified information from the FBI supposedly justifying bans on whatever accounts were inconvenient.

When Musk tried to reveal evidence of the Bureau's misbehavior, the very man charged with reviewing the files to be released to journalist Matt Taibbi was former FBI General Counsel James Baker, who had left the FBI after being outed for his key role in perpetrating the Russian-collusion hoax against Trump. It turns out that the Twitterverse is balanced precariously upon the backs of FBI agents.

Censorship is seldom effective at squashing misinformation. It breeds more misinformation. This lesson is easily learned from observing the public discourse in any Arab or former Eastern bloc country in which the security services maintain a symbiotic relationship with the official press. In such a system Joe Public quickly learns not to trust official media organs which put out only that information that has been approved for them by the intelligence services.

In the absence of good information, private (or social media anonymous) discourse devolves into an endless fractal of increasingly implausible, but not entirely disprovable, theories. Such chaos is an advantage for the type of regime that former Defense Intelligence Agency intelligence officer John Dziak calls the "counterintelligence state." The counterintelligence state relishes the spread of misinformation, disinformation, and deception: the creation of virtual reality. Not as a means of defeating foreign opponents, but in order to keep the domestic populace confused and intellectually disarmed.

Increasingly, America's remaining sober minds pour through preferred, politically charged media organs like *Politico*, *The New York Times*, and especially *The Washington Post*, the way the old Sovietologists used to read *Pravda*, trying to make some sense of stories consisting of "a senior intelligence official said…" and "according to sources close to the operation…" Meanwhile the less sober-minded are busy reading the stories about UFOs which seem to flood social media every time a major hearing into the bad behavior of the intelligence community comes up on the congressional schedule.

Could a new Church Committee fix these problems? Doubtful. The previous committee was helped along by intelligence insiders who knew where the bodies were buried, and who were motivated to throw their colleagues to media wolves who, at least in public, portrayed themselves as opponents of the intelligence services acting on behalf of the public's right to know.

By contrast, the present intelligence community is in ideological lockstep, reinforced by its dominance over the social media environment and surrounded by a media cohort as docile as kittens. In Congress, Republicans traditionally have shown an ability to ask questions and generate headlines, but seldom to hold people accountable and drive real reforms, particularly when the Democratic Party has benefited from the intelligence services' misbehavior. Since most congressmen remain addicted to media attention, their focus is easily swayed by any number of shiny objects that appear in the press as part of a "limited hang-out," an espionage term used to describe the deliberate release of information to lessen the damage caused by the uncovering of a real secret. Their questions in oversight hearings are usually limited to three- or five-minute soundbites suitable for TV and social media, but not for getting to the bottom of things.

What, then, can be done? Ultimately only ground truth can defeat deception, only reality can trump virtual reality. What is needed is not a new Church Committee, but to rebuild what the Church Committee destroyed. Not as a bureaucracy, but as a private network of analysts and reporters who can provide genuine information to the public, and to those elected officials who wish to hear it, like our official intelligence services and media companies are supposed to offer, but no longer do. A deliberate campaign to rebuild the wisdom exhibited by those early foreign correspondents, whose insights were so prized by the CIA before the purge, would go a long way toward piercing the veil of the counterintelligence state.

Such a thing has been attempted before. As detailed in his autobiography *Free Agent: The Unseen War, 1941–1991*, former *Economist* and Reuters reporter Brian Crozier helped to forge a network of think tanks, together with a newswire, that offered accurate reporting and analysis after the decimation of Western services' human intelligence capabilities in the 1970s. His team would play a quiet but important role in the successes of Margaret Thatcher and Ronald Reagan, two elected leaders often at odds with their own official intelligence services. It is a model which can work, provided it avoids falling into the social media trap of emphasizing clicks and shares over ground truth, and instead focuses on building long-term capability and awareness.

Faced with genuine publicly available competitive analysis, the intelligence services will not be able to hide behind anonymous leaks to enforce the illusion of omniscience. Their incompetence and inability to do their job will be exposed. They will either be forced to reform themselves and offer a product which their customers genuinely need, or they will find themselves replaced.

PART FOUR: THE MEDIA VS. AMERICA

NIXON AND THE WEAPONIZATION OF MEDIA HATE

BY MONICA CROWLEY

One day in the 1990s, my first real-world boss, former President Richard Nixon, summoned me to his office. I knocked, and upon entering, found him in his usual corner chair, feet propped up on an ottoman, glasses on the tip of his nose. In a fit of frustration, he was angrily balling up the entire front section of *The New York Times*. "Mr. President?" I said as I approached him. "Everything okay?" He glanced up and playfully tossed the newspaper ball at me. "Given this biased bullshit coming at us all day long, it's a miracle any Republicans get elected to anything at all. Ever."

I had become the former president's foreign policy assistant after having read one of his brilliant policy books and written him a substantive letter while still in college. During the four years I worked for him, until his death in 1994, I became the professional confidante of a man who had transformed American politics, changed global balances of power—and who had become the first significant modern casualty of a newly aggressive, partisan, and activist American media.

His decades-long war with the press has become legendary, and in many ways, has set the framework for all successive Republican politicians and presidents, including most dramatically, Donald Trump. Relentlessly adversarial and often outright hostile, Nixon's relationship with the press began a destructive era of dishonest, nakedly partisan reportage in the name of defeating political actors the media didn't like; halting the conservative agenda while advancing the progressive one; and becoming the enforcement arm of the Democratic Party and leftist radicalism.

The modern American press has always been biased toward the Left. The difference in the Nixon era was its level of intensity and transformation of its bias into overt action. Rather than hold fast to their supposed ideal of objectivity, members of the press embraced shameless advocacy. And instead of holding all powerful leaders accountable, they investigated and lied about some while giving passes to others. They became ever more intoxicated with their power to destroy their political opponents, to set the national agenda, and to determine the direction of the country.

And, in their corrupt judgment, Nixon was too odious to be allowed to succeed. Once they perceived his intellectual brilliance, political acumen, and transformational agenda as existential threats, they bit into him like a junkyard dog and never let go.

The origins of the press's Nixon hatred go back to his earliest political days. From the moment he first ran for Congress in 1946, he was a staunch anti-communist, committed to fighting Marxists both abroad—and at home. And rather than cast his lot safely with the Establishment, he stood for and with the American people—whom he later famously called the Great Silent Majority—and championed them and their interests ahead of those of permanent Washington. He was America First long before Donald Trump came down the escalator in Trump Tower.

This forever earned him the deep, abiding enmity of anti-American agitators, communist sympathizers, and garden-variety leftists everywhere, including in the press, among the Democrats, and in what we now know as the Deep State.

That enmity was evident right from the start of his political career. In 1948, freshman Congressman Nixon was a member of the House Un-American Activities Committee, investigating communist infiltration in the U.S. government. The Committee became aware of Whittaker Chambers, a former communist functionary who left the party completely disillusioned and later went on to be a senior editor at *Time* magazine. In his blockbuster testimony to the committee, Chambers identified the depth of communist infiltration, pointing directly to senior members of the government, including Alger Hiss, a former State Department official and prominent Democratic functionary involved in the creation of the United Nations.

Hiss was a darling of the press with the perfect establishment pedigree: A graduate of Harvard Law School, he served as secretary to Supreme Court Justice Oliver Holmes, was a top adviser to President Roosevelt at the Yalta Conference, and was a major force behind the creation of the United Nations. Tall and handsome, Hiss glided through the corridors of power with ease. The only problem was that he was a communist who had passed secrets to the Kremlin, and Nixon proved it. Hiss was eventually convicted of perjury, and Nixon was catapulted into the national political limelight. That sensational event set Nixon on a collision course with the press, many of whom had communist sympathies and hated that he had exposed one of their own. Nixon himself identified the Hiss case as the origin story of his war with the press.

Nixon ran for and won a seat in the U.S. Senate from California in 1950, in part by insinuating that his opponent, Helen Gahagan Douglas, was a communist sympathizer. One of his campaign's leaflets, comparing her record to that of a notorious communist party-line congressman from New York, was printed on pink paper, and later in the campaign, Nixon suggested that she was a "pink right down to her underwear."

These tactics were condemned as below-the-belt and set many in the press off on career-long jihads against Nixon, including Herblock, *The Washington Post*'s star political cartoonist, who first drew Nixon as a sewer rat after the Senate race—and never stopped vilifying him. But the tactics worked: Nixon won that race and further cemented his anti-communist credentials.

In addition to the Hiss case, another event accelerated his sour relationship with the press. In late 1952, as he headed into the general election as Dwight Eisenhower's choice for vice president, he was hit with allegations that he had misappropriated campaign funds. Reporters smelled blood. Sensing that his place on the ticket might be in jeopardy, Nixon delivered a national primetime address—known as the Checkers speech—in which he laid out the facts, attacked the smear merchants behind the story, and asked the audience to let the Republican National Committee know if he should stay on the ticket. The public response was overwhelmingly in support, Nixon became vice president, and the press once again was proven wrong. Prior to the speech, Nixon and some in the press still courted each other, but following the address, they turned on each other. When some reporters were late for a campaign bus, Nixon reportedly snapped, "F-ck 'em, we don't need 'em." His press secretary, Jim Bassett, summed it up: "By the end of the '52 campaign, he had utterly no use for the press."

After the Hiss case and the Checkers speech, Nixon never expected fair or honest coverage in the media. Reporters continued to have no use for him; they ceaselessly targeted him with smears, unfair criticisms, and outright lies, and of course never apologized or corrected the record when their lines of attack were disproven. During the 1960 election, journalists drooled over the handsome scion of the incipient Kennedy dynasty while spitting vitriol at Nixon. *Washington Post* columnist Mary McGrory wrote, "He was just so icky, so yucky—humorless, self-righteous and smarmy," while *The New York Times*'s Harrison Salisbury said he had "a terrible sleazy quality that crept into many of his appearances."

Nixon's frustration with the press boiled over after he lost his next race—for California governor in 1962—when he declared in his "last press conference" that the reporters wouldn't "have Nixon to kick around anymore."

His absence lasted all of six years, when he ran again for president and won, driving a fresh cycle of hate from the press. The 1968 election coincided with a change in newsroom culture toward more investigative and openly adversarial reporting. The Vietnam War had lit the flame: Much of the media's coverage went from straight report-age to ardent opposition against official Washington under President Lyndon B. Johnson. When America's most respected news anchor, Walter Cronkite, turned against the war, it was game over: "If you've lost Cronkite," the saying went, "you've lost America."

Once reporters began to regard the presidency as an institution that could not be trusted, it came under withering journalistic fire, led primarily by *The Washington Post*. The newspaper's hard-bitten editor, Ben Bradlee, recalled, "As far as the Presidency was concerned, there was an awe for the office under Wiggins, my predecessor. I guess I changed all that. By the time Nixon got in, we were already anti-White House, and we sure stayed that way."

That they certainly did, leading the Watergate charge with report-ers Bob Woodward and Carl Bernstein. They hated Nixon and thought the presidency was too powerful. It was a perfect storm into which Nixon unknowingly stumbled. In a conversation with me, he expressed a belated awareness of that brutal truth: "There are stan-dards for Democrats, standards for Republicans; then there were stan-dards for me," he said.

> I was in a totally different category. The press didn't trust me after Hiss, and they were just out there, circling and waiting...they weren't interested in Watergate as much as they were interested in getting me on Hiss and on Vietnam. I gave them what they needed, but believe me, Watergate was just the excuse.

For Nixon, Watergate made obvious the hidden consequence of the Hiss case: that as a force immune to the intellectual pathogens of the Left, he had to be brought down.

If that sounds familiar, it's because once Nixon's enemies—includ-ing the press—claimed his scalp, they grew increasingly emboldened to hunt other high-profile Republicans, including and most notably President Trump. During Nixon's long political career, the press tested the limits of weaponized hatred and ultimately succeeded in taking him out. Armed with that kind of trophy, they kept going, ramping up their efforts to destroy whoever threatened their agenda and that of those they protected.

Realizing this, Nixon hated the fact that he needed the media to get his message out. When he wrote books and op-eds and gave television interviews and speeches, he needed the amplification that the press afforded those efforts. And before the age of cable news and social media, he had no choice but to cooperate with the Corporate Media. His valid complaints about his press coverage were often derided as paranoid or lacking in self-awareness. But he was, in fact, routinely and unfairly targeted by reporters, editors, and publishers who only cared about "getting Nixon." The number of media outlets have expanded greatly since then, but in most cases their leftwing mania has only gotten more extreme.

Watching the glowing coverage that then-President Bill Clinton received during a 1993 trip to Asia, Nixon blasted the media:

> No wonder no one watches the damn networks anymore. God, the news is bad. It's all entertainment, not really news. And the news they do give you is so slanted to the left that it's just outright biased. Anyway, [NBC's Tom] Brokaw really built up Clinton and Hillary in Tokyo, saying Hillary was a real heroine to the young women. Now, what the hell. When we were there in 1953, women were nothing, and Mrs. Nixon went out among them and talked to them, and the damn media never gave her any credit. Why?

"You were in the wrong party," I said.

"That's it," he replied.

Of course, the answer went far beyond his Republican affiliation to his strategic genius, ideological principles, political effectiveness, and strong personality. The press hated him for all of that and more—and their rage culminated in the ultimate battle known as Watergate.

The scandal that began with a "third-rate burglary" of the Democratic National Headquarters in Washington in June 1972 led to the first presidential resignation. Fresh research from historians such as Len Colodny and Robert Gettlin (*Silent Coup: The Removal of a President*) and Geoff Shepard (*The Nixon Conspiracy: Watergate and the Plot to Remove the President*) indicate that shadowy malign forces in the security state conspired to destroy Nixon's presidency and remove him from office. In retrospect, Nixon was fed tainted information about a break-in he did not order and knew nothing about, made decisions based on that bad information, and ended up driving his own political demise.

At the time, of course, he had no concept of the dark machinations swirling around him. Even in his later years, he still had a tenuous grasp on what had actually happened and his role in it. But he never doubted that the press eagerly helped to bring him down. The fact that Nixon saw himself as surrounded by enemies caused many of them to deride his "paranoia." But his adversaries were real and actively bent on his destruction; most, including those in the press, wore their fierce opposition to him with pride.

In addition to Hiss and Watergate, Nixon ascribed their relentless hostility to the other defining issue of his political career: the Vietnam War, which divided the nation over the need to stop communism in Southeast Asia. Despite having been correct about Hiss and having ended the war, Nixon had earned the permanent animosity of those on the Left. They sought his removal from the political scene as the only way to stop his powerful anti-communist mission. After all, how could they keep advancing Marxism in America if the American president were exposing and halting it at every turn?

Confounding his enemies became less about revenge and more about his own unwillingness to accept the ruin they had tried to impose on him. He was committed to remaining visible and controversial, which of course drove his enemies in the press even crazier. They never stopped trying to destroy him, and he kept coming back, his voice ever-more important.

AGAINST THE CORPORATE MEDIA

In the modern era, Nixon was truly "patient zero" in the battle against a weaponized media. Once they claimed his scalp, no other conservatives were safe from their dirty game. That contentious relationship set the precedent. We haven't had a healthy republic with an honest press corps in a very long time. Maybe we never truly had one. But the advent of Richard Nixon turned journalists into hunters, and leaders with whom they disagreed into the hunted.

This corrupt dynamic has had an increasingly corrosive effect on our republic. And if Nixon were still with us today, he would be appalled by how much worse the media's hostility, dishonesty, and activism have gotten. He would be standing shoulder to shoulder with the rest of us in fighting the war for truth.

THE MEDIA VS. DONALD J. TRUMP: THE RUSSIA HOAX

BY STEVEN F. HAYWARD

When a large number of organs of the press come to advance
along the same track, their influence becomes almost irresistible
in the long term, and public opinion, struck always from
the same side, ends by yielding under their blows.
—Alexis de Tocqueville, *Democracy in America*

A free press has long been considered a bulwark of a thriving democracy, not primarily because of the theoretical perspectives of Milton or Mill, but from the practical view that the news media would shine a light on government perfidy, "hold the powerful to account," and so forth. Even if the legend of the media's role in driving the course of the Watergate scandal is a gross exaggeration, the fear of media exposure likely provides some deterrent to bad behavior and tyrannical acts from our government and large private institutions.

But what happens when the members of the news media take a side in partisan conflicts? And what if that side is the side of corrupt or authoritarian government itself? The tale of the Trump Russia hoax from 2016 to the present represents more than just an isolated failure on the part of the media, but the culmination of decades of catastrophic decay. This was more than an instance of media bias or

malpractice, however, as it ultimately involved the active participation of key institutions and leaders of our national security apparatus, which is as scandalous as it is ominous. Yet it seems unlikely that
there will ever be any serious accountability or reform as a result of
its exposure.

Once upon a time, from the nation's Founding and until the early
decades of the 20th century, most American newspapers were openly
partisan (also true in Great Britain and France), with papers widely
understood to be Republican Party—or Democratic Party—affiliated
papers. The honesty of this, along with competition for readers and
advertisers, meant that the public could be fully informed on different
sides of a story if it wished to. Reporting in those days—it wasn't called
"journalism" yet—was a working-class occupation, on par with police
officers and other tradesmen who came to their craft armed with a
good high school education in English usage, and ample opportunities
for apprenticeships similar to carpenters and pipefitters. There was
true "diversity" in the social rank and opinions of reporters.

Gradually, over the course of the 20th century, reporting became
a high-prestige profession, in which "journalists" were regarded (or
self-regarded) on par with lawyers, accountants, and doctors, that is,
people with a specialized body of expert knowledge, though what constitutes the necessary specialized expertise to report on events is seldom specified with any coherence. Nowadays most elite media journalists are graduates of Ivy League universities, and many have advanced
degrees in journalism from the likes of Columbia or Northwestern
that are as leftwing in ideology as the rest of universities today. The
parallel pretense is that contemporary journalism is non-partisan and
"objective," unlike during those grubby days of partisan newspapers.
In addition to the ideological and demographic homogeneity of newsrooms, this exalted professional cadre has come to have a class interest parallel to the government officials they cover. Members of the
American media still pretend to be adversarial, but this is a pose, and
in any case the intensity of their adversarial attitudes palpably differs
between the two major political parties.

This bias has significant consequences, affecting both public opinion and government policy. The political scientist Tim Groseclose, employing multiple and widely accepted advanced statistical techniques of social science, has concluded that the leftward bias of the major news media skews public opinion at least five points to the left of where it would be if the general public were exposed to a more balanced spectrum of news and opinions. A five-point difference may not sound like much, but Groseclose and several other scholars working independently have found that this skew has made a difference in a significant number of recent elections—all of them favoring the Democratic Party.

These findings can hardly be dismissed as a special grievance or excuse of the right. Let's not forget that in 2008 Barack Obama said, "I am convinced that if there were no Fox News, I might be two or three points higher in the polls." And in 2004, *Newsweek*'s Evan Thomas remarked on PBS that media favorability toward the Kerry-Edwards ticket "was going to be worth maybe fifteen points." (Thomas later revised his estimate down to five points—coincidentally the same estimate as Groseclose and his colleagues.)

Sometimes it's not ideological bias but a simple herd mentality at work, which reinforces ideological bias. Few reporters (or their editors) have enough independence of mind to present a story line or angle that departs from what the herd is reporting, or that defies the narrative template set forth in the prestige press such as *The New York Times* or on major TV network news. The social pressures backstopping groupthink inside the demographically uniform bubbles of New York or Washington, D.C., newsrooms are overpowering.

The media herd mentality is most pernicious when it is congruent with a narrative that a government entity or powerful politically preferred interest has formulated to serve its own political interests. The media amplify every claim of an environmental "crisis" from the Environmental Protection Agency or Consumer Product Safety Commission with complete credulity. The coverage of the George Floyd's death while in police custody and the coverage of the riots in

AGAINST THE CORPORATE MEDIA

its aftermath were derelict distortions of reality because no one in the media had the courage to express any doubt about the claims of Black Lives Matter. Perhaps the most grotesque media sycophancy of the past fifty years was the McMartin Preschool scandal in Los Angeles in the early 1980s, when a wholly fabricated "child molestation" epidemic was week after week breathlessly reported without a scintilla of skepticism or diligence by the media, all of which buttressed the ambitions of headline-seeking prosecutors and "recovered memory" quacks who were treated as though they had the credibility of Nobel Prize winners in physics. (This episode was repeated in several other cities around the country until it was belatedly recognized as a fabrication in every instance.)

This kind of media malpractice can have serious political consequences beyond elections or criminal prosecutions. Perhaps the most significant example is the media coverage of the January 1968 "Tet" Offensive during the Vietnam War. By 1968, the media was already hostile to the war and was reporting the Johnson administration's prosecution of it with deep skepticism and cynicism. When the attack of the Viet Cong and North Vietnamese army caught U.S. and South Vietnamese forces by surprise, the media ran with the story line that the attack was a major defeat for the U.S. and South Vietnam, arguably the greatest military disaster America had ever suffered, including Pearl Harbor. The decisive media blow came from CBS News anchorman Walter Cronkite, then called "the most trusted man in America," who closed a gloomy news special in late February with what he labeled as his *subjective* opinion (though this qualification was lost on the public): "[I]t seems now more certain than ever that the bloody experience of Vietnam is to end in a stalemate... [I]t is increasingly clear to this reporter that the only rational way out then will be to negotiate, not as victors, but as an honorable people who lived up to their pledge to defend democracy, and did the best they could."

President Johnson is reported to have said, "If I've lost Cronkite, I've lost middle America." As measured in opinion polls, the American public, growing weary of the war, turned decisively against it. What

North Vietnam could not win on the battlefield was won on the campuses and in the newsrooms—and finally in the living rooms—of America. Two weeks later, Johnson was nearly defeated in the New Hampshire primary by anti-war candidate Eugene McCarthy, and two weeks after that Johnson startled the nation by dropping out of the 1968 presidential contest.

Yet a closer look, which all subsequent military analyses confirmed, shows that the Tet Offensive was a decisive *defeat* for the Viet Cong and North Vietnam. You would have looked in vain for any media coverage of the event that reflected this reality, a "malfunction" told in extensive detail in Peter Braestrup's magisterial account published a decade later, *Big Story: How the American Press and Television Reported and Interpreted the Crisis of Tet, 1968 in Vietnam and Washington.* Braestrup's book on this mis-reporting ought to be assigned in every journalism course in America, but likely it is not read anywhere.

The Russia hoax—the baseless, indeed preposterous, claim that Donald Trump colluded with Russia to steal the 2016 election—dwarfs the media malpractice in the Tet Offensive by at least an order of magnitude. Media hoaxes involving Russia are not new. *New York Times* reporter Walter Duranty won a Pulitzer Prize in the 1930s for his protective, favorable coverage of Stalin's Soviet Union. The *Times* has never admitted this misprision of journalistic duty, nor returned the Pulitzer.

In the early 1980s, the media bent over backwards to create a favorable Western image for the first new Soviet leader in twenty years, the former head of the KGB, Yuri Andropov. *The Washington Post* reported that Andropov "collects abstract art, likes jazz and Gypsy music," and wears Western-tailored suits. *The Wall Street Journal* said that Andropov "likes Glenn Miller records, good scotch whisky, Oriental rugs, and American books," such as, improbably, those by Judith Krantz, and Jacqueline Susann's *Valley of the Dolls.* *Time* magazine reported that he listened to Chubby Checker albums. *The Christian Science Monitor* gushed that Andropov was a poet "of a comic variety." *The New York Times* declared that Andropov "is said by his associates to be more cosmopolitan than his predecessors," and that he was fluent in English, though strangely no American diplomat or reporter could recall having ever spoken with Andropov in English. There was no evidence for any of this. Edward Jay Epstein called it "a portrait worthy of 'Saturday Night Live': the head of the KGB as one wild and crazy guy." Sometimes credulous media treatment of Russia was simply partisan churlishness. In 1990, *Time* magazine selected Mikhail Gorbachev as its "Man of the Decade," in a 5,000-word article that mentioned Ronald Reagan only once, and just to dismiss as "smug" the central features of his Soviet strategy.

But the Trump Russia hoax is the granddaddy of them all. We now know that the "Russian collusion" narrative was cooked up as an opposition research project against Trump initially by the conservative *Washington Free Beacon*, but soon acquired and propelled by the Hillary Clinton campaign in the middle of 2016, after it became apparent that Trump had a slim but realistic chance of winning the election. The irony of Hillary Clinton and the Democrats mounting accusations of collusion with Russia is that there is scarcely anyone in American history with a deeper record of corrupt collusion with Russian interests than the Clintons.

As President Obama's first secretary of state, Hillary Clinton famously attempted to "reset" U.S.-Russia relations that had soured during the George W. Bush administration. Behind the scenes, Bill Clinton was assisting Rosatom, a Russian energy company, to acquire complete ownership of Uranium One, a Canadian mining company, that would make Russia a dominant supplier of the world's uranium supply. (The acquisition required U.S. government approval because some of the company's mines are in the United States.) Bill Clinton collected $500,000 for a single speech in Russia in 2010, his fee paid by an investment bank that was financing the Rosatom acquisition, and during which visit he met privately with Vladimir Putin.

During these years the Clinton Foundation was scooping up huge overseas contributions (the largest country of origin was Ukraine), all the while denying that Secretary of State Clinton exerted any influence over Russian transactions involving her husband and his foundation. Hillary said she had adopted strict conflict-of-interest rules, but everyone over the age of six understood the value to foreign donors of sending cash to the former president and possible next president. The simple proof of this is the complete collapse of foreign contributions to the Clinton Foundation immediately upon the defeat of Hillary in November 2016. The foundation still has more than $300 million in assets.

Following the Rosatom acquisition of Uranium One, the chairman of the Canadian-no-longer subsidiary sent a contribution of $2 million and $350,000 to the Clinton Foundation that the Clintons "forgot" to disclose. Other investors in Uranium One contributed a further $8.5 million to the Clinton Foundation between 2008 and 2010. To their credit, *The New York Times* and *The Washington Post* reported these dodgy dealings, though the reporting behind these stories was not done by *Times* or *Post* staff, but by independent investigative journalist Peter Schweizer, who gladly supplied the *Times* and the *Post*.

Naturally there was blowback in the newsrooms over these stories, and there was little to no follow up by the mainstream media. It is little wonder that Hillary Clinton thought she could easily get away with having an insecure private email server, and with a preposterous slander of her 2016 rival, Donald Trump. In any case, given that the Clintons had serious problems with their own Russia connections, it was perhaps a simple matter of what psychologists call "projection" to gin up an attack on Trump based on nothing more than Trump's campaign statements expressing criticism of NATO and optimism about achieving the better relationship with Russia that Hillary Clinton and the Obama administration had promised and failed to deliver. In fact, the Clinton campaign's own internal polling showed that her dubious ties to Russia were one of her largest vulnerabilities with voters.

Is it merely a coincidence that the principal agents in the Trump collusion hoax were former corporate media journalists? If there is a "patient zero" of the Trump collusion hoax (aside from Hillary), it is

Glenn Simpson, a former reporter for *The Wall Street Journal*, who founded Fusion GPS in 2011. Fusion GPS is described as a "strategic intelligence" consultancy based in Washington, D.C., and is the kind of enterprise that can only exist in Washington. Like many other such firms, its "assets" are the personal contacts of its principals (mostly other former reporters like Simpson), engaged in the political version of private investigative work (most frequently known as "opposition research"). Fusion GPS's first target in 2012 was Mitt Romney, but other targets the company was hired to damage included anti-abortion activists and foreign business figures implicated in Russian money-laundering schemes.

Having done initial opposition research on Trump for the *Free Beacon* in 2015, Fusion GPS shopped its portfolio to the Clinton campaign and the Democratic National Committee in the spring of 2016, reaching a deal to continue the work in April. Payment for the work was routed through Democratic super lawyer Marc Elias and his firm Perkins Coie. In June, Simpson linked up with a foreign source, Christopher Steele, a former British spy with a mixed reputation, who was engaged to conduct further intelligence-gathering about Trump's attempted business ventures in Russia. Steele began compiling every rumor and speculation about Trump in Russia from whatever source came to hand.

Hillary Clinton's campaign got its money's worth, though peddling a preposterous claim of Russian collusion with Trump was pushing on an open door in most newsrooms. A theme quickly took hold in the media: Donald Trump's statements of respect for Putin on the stump, along with his criticisms of NATO, were manifestations of a more sinister corrupt bargain between Trump and Putin. Typical of the first stories was a mid-June 2016 *Washington Post* feature discussing Trump's financial ties to Russia, which mostly reported Trump's repeated *failures* to close any substantial business deals in Russia. Unlike Bill Clinton, Trump never met Putin despite personal requests from Trump. Putin called off a tentative meeting in 2013 at the last minute, and the two never met in person until after Trump became president in 2017. Despite the premise of Trump's "30-year history" of business with Russia, the only concrete Trump-Russia business ties the *Post* could find was a $14 million Russian investment in the 2013 Miss Universe contest (owned by Trump at the time) held in Moscow that year, and Trump's sale of a Florida mega-mansion to a Russian oligarch in 2008. That's it. The rest of the feature was a classic of "ventriloquist journalism," in which a series of foreign policy grandees were quoted about how Trump's statements about Russia were "troubling." This is the kind of reporting the prestige press calls "news":

> Michael McFaul, who stepped down in 2014 as the U.S. ambassador to Russia, said Trump's stance toward Russia "makes everyone I talk to around the world nervous—and it makes me nervous." David J. Kramer, who served as deputy assistant secretary of state dealing with Russia during the George W. Bush administration, said he was "appalled" by Trump's approach.

In hindsight, these early stories featuring the deep thoughts of potentates such as Michael McFaul should have been seen as a warning of what was to come. Serving as a megaphone for the establishment view of Trump became the template for countless identical news stories that followed right through the election and beyond, which, if stacked up, could probably build a Trump tower in Moscow with enough left over for a second one in St. Petersburg. *The New York Times* and *The Washington Post* were subsequently awarded a Pulitzer Prize for their "deeply sourced, relentlessly reported" coverage of the Trump-Russia fable.

Not that there wasn't a legitimate news story about Russian interference in the American election; it was just not the one the media chose to report in depth or frame accurately. In the spring of 2016, Russia-based computer hackers successfully penetrated the Democratic National Committee (DNC). The hack revealed not simply embarrassing and confidential material from DNC computers that damaged Hillary Clinton, but above all how poor the DNC's cyber-security was. The fruits of the hack were soon released publicly on WikiLeaks and other internet outlets.

Beyond the email hack, Russia mounted an online campaign that spoofed social media accounts in support of Trump and critical of Hillary in the runup to the November election. Multiple subsequent investigations found that there was no collusion between the Trump campaign and the Russian mischief on the internet. Beyond the collusion angle are several odd angles and absurdities to the scene. First, can anyone take seriously the proposition that Russian interference on social media changed the outcome of the election? To do so would require believing that the $1 billion spent by the Hillary Clinton campaign was overcome by $100,000 in paid Facebook ads and phony social media posts. No one has produced evidence that Russian efforts reached a target audience of swing voters in the Midwest states that turned the election to Trump. Political scientists, employing their most advanced voodoo regression models, have been unable to come up with a finding that the Russian intrigues affected the result. The explanation is simple and straightforward: The overwhelming majority of the Russian messaging appeared on or was targeted at Trump-supporting individuals and groups.

There is a second glaring anomaly of the collusion hypothesis that the media never considers. Objectively, Trump's policies were more adverse to Russian interests that the policies of Democratic administrations. In particular, Trump's domestic pro–fossil fuel energy policies exerted downward pressure on global oil and gas prices, substantially reducing Russian export earnings. Trump's withdrawal from the Iran nuclear deal, his skepticism toward further arms control agreements with Russia, and his Middle East policies all ran contrary to Russian policies and interests, not to mention the military attacks on Russian mercenaries in Syria that Trump ordered. Even Trump's skepticism of and pressure on NATO, which panicky foreign policy elites thought threatened the existence of the alliance, was not unambiguously a boon for Russia, since stepped-up defense spending by NATO

European member states (albeit sluggish and recalcitrant) would present Russia with a more potent foe. And it might well have been Trump's bluster that led to Russia pausing its aggression on Ukrainian territory until a Democrat was back in the White House. From the standpoint of which candidate or party is more congenial to Russian interests, clearly a Hillary Clinton presidency would have been preferable.

Why, then, would Russia do it? A Senate investigation concluded that the most likely motive was to undermine trust in American institutions and elections. One wonders why Russia would bother when we have the media and academia performing that task already, but a little accelerant on a fire never hurts. One also wonders whether Russia had the media in mind as its primary target all along, as such tactics had a long history during the Cold War when the Soviet Union was highly effective in injecting disinformation into the Western media. Disinformation campaigns of this kind put our administrations on the defense, and cause difficulties in relations with our allies.

Badly slanted partisan media coverage of Republican presidential candidates is nothing new. The prestige press insinuated in 1964 that Barry Goldwater was a barely closeted Nazi who secretly consulted ex-Nazis in Europe, so it was not a leap for the media to settle on the preposterous idea that Trump was a Russian agent. Any possibility that the Trump Russia collusion hoax might start to settle down after the election was scotched with the release of one of Fusion GPS's most sensational opposition research products, Christopher Steele's whole-cloth dossier of unverified gossip and rumors about Trump.

The pure salaciousness of the dossier guaranteed a long half-life in the media. The most attention-grabbing detail was a supposed bacchanal in a luxury suite of a Moscow hotel, in which Russian prostitutes performed "golden showers" on Trump, for which videotape was alleged to exist. Anyone who knows the famously germophobic Trump would have immediately doubted the story and much else in the dossier of unverified (or "raw" as is said in the intelligence trade) information. Needless to say, no tape of any Trump presence in Moscow has emerged. The publication of the Steele dossier by the anything-goes

Buzzfeed allowed the prestige press to engage in a cynical ventrilo-quist two-step, by which the veracity of the dossier was doubted while nonetheless passing along its sensational contents. Bob Woodward called it "garbage," and NBC's Chuck Todd called it "fake news." But the idea that Russia might have *kompromat* material on Trump took wing for a fresh flight as Trump prepared to take office.

Beyond the alleged tape that had the media practically peeing itself was a superficially more believable charge that Trump was com-promised on account of deep debts to Russian financiers—but who could tell since Trump's financial architecture was so opaque and he refused to release his tax returns? This led to countless more "news" stories consisting of little more than speculation by "experts" about how Trump's Russian creditors might hold the key to understanding why Trump was a Putin lackey. Once again, the media overlooked an obvious fact, which is that Trump's track record of stiffing creditors and sticking banks with huge losses meant that if any Russian bank or financier did hold Trump paper, it was *the bank* that had the problem.

Neither the facts—or more to the point the lack of facts—nor com-mon sense could restrain the media for the simplest of reasons: Trump was good for business. He was very good for business. Subscriptions to *The New York Times* and *The Washington Post* soared, at a time when newspapers had been shedding subscribers at a rapid clip. Ratings for rabidly Trumpophobic CNN and MSNBC soared. Their leftist audi-ences couldn't get enough confirming dirt on Trump. The untalented, obnoxious, and egomaniacal Jim Acosta became a cable TV celeb-rity on CNN.

The Trump Russia hoax would stand as a massive case of media bias and malpractice were it not for a second major factor that pro-pels it into what ought to be regarded as the largest political scandal in American history, certainly far greater than Watergate. This is the role that the intelligence and law enforcement apparatus of the federal government played in targeting Trump and amplifying the collusion hoax. The FBI denies that the Steele dossier or any of the other Clinton campaign opposition research on Trump prompted its "Crossfire

Hurricane" investigation into Trump, but it is clear that individuals at the highest level of the FBI decided to use the Bureau's investigatory powers to damage Trump, and maybe even prevent him from taking office if he won the election.

The smoking gun of partisan political motives and actions on the part of senior leadership of the FBI was discovered early in the Trump presidency, though deliberately obfuscated by congressional Democrats who persisted in claiming they would reveal concrete evidence back the Trump collusion hypothesis. (No such evidence was ever produced.) That the entire matter was a perpetrated falsehood concocted by the FBI was confirmed officially in the report of Justice Department special counsel John Durham in May 2023. This part of Durham's summary only begins to describe the full dimensions of the corruption involved:

> At the direction of Deputy Director Andrew McCabe, Deputy Assistant Director for Counterintelligence Peter Strzok opened Crossfire Hurricane immediately. Strzok, at a minimum, had pronounced hostile feelings toward Trump. The matter was opened as a full investigation without ever having spoken to the persons who provided the information. Further, the FBI did so without (i) any significant review of its own intelligence databases, (ii) collection and examination of any relevant intelligence from other U.S. intelligence entities, (iii) interviews of witnesses essential to understand the raw information it had received or (iv) using any of the standard analytical tools typically employed by the FBI in evaluating raw intelligence. Had it done so, the FBI would have learned that their own experienced Russia analysts had no information about Trump being involved with Russian leadership officials, nor were others in sensitive positions at the CIA, the NSA, and the Department of State aware of such evidence concerning the subject.

Durham's report goes on to offer details on the FBI's abuse of the secretive Foreign Intelligence Surveillance Act (FISA) to obtain warrants to wiretap several figures who were close to Trump. Durham brought three criminal indictments against an FBI agent and two sources who provided false information to the FBI. The FBI agent pled guilty (receiving probation) to altering evidence, while the other two were acquitted by Washington, D.C., juries despite solid evidence of their guilt. Getting a D.C. jury to reach convictions implicating federal government lawbreaking is an uphill climb. Durham was undoubtedly hoping to emulate the time-honored playbook of Justice Department mob and drug-ring prosecutions, building a case from the bottom up by getting low-level actors to roll over on the higher-ups. It didn't work against the FBI. Durham's investigation closed, and there will be no further accountability from anyone in the FBI—or among the news media that dutifully reported what can truly be called "fake news."

Durham went on to note a partisan double-standard at work at the FBI:

> The FBI elected to end an investigation [of Hillary Clinton] after one of its longtime and valuable CHSs [confidential human sources] went beyond what was authorized and made an improper and possibly illegal financial contribution to the Clinton campaign on behalf of a foreign entity as a precursor to a much larger donation being contemplated. And in a third, the Clinton Foundation matter, both senior FBI and Department officials placed restrictions on how those matters were to be handled such that essentially no investigative activities occurred for months leading up to the election. These examples are also markedly different from the FBI's actions with respect to other highly significant intelligence it received from a trusted foreign source pointing to a Clinton campaign plan to vilify Trump by tying him to Vladimir Putin so

as to divert attention from her own concerns relating
to her use of a private email server.

Aside from the problem of Hillary's illegal (but excused) use of
an insecure private email server that was surely penetrated by foreign
intelligence, it is well established that Bill Clinton's 1996 campaign
for re-election involved laundering illegal foreign campaign contributions, so there was ample reason for the FBI to have been vigilant
about a rerun by the Hillary 2016 campaign.

The determination of the FBI to prevent a Trump presidency was
made explicit in text messages between FBI counterintelligence chief
Peter Strzok and FBI agent Lisa Page, who turned out to double as
Strzok's mistress:

> July 21, 2016: Strzok: "Trump is a disaster. I have no
> idea how destabilizing his Presidency would be."
>
> July 27, 2016: Page: "Have we opened on him yet?"
>
> Strzok: "Opened on Trump? If Hillary did, you know
> 5 field offices would…"
>
> August 8, 2016: Page: "[Trump's] not going to become
> president, right? Right?!"
>
> Strzok: "No. No, he's not. We'll stop it."

This should not be regarded as a novel breach by the FBI, given
that it was a senior FBI agent, Mark Felt (lionized as "Deep Throat"),
who took it upon himself to use FBI resources to bring down President
Nixon. Democratic Senate Leader Chuck Schumer—no ally of
Trump—put his finger on the problem of the American "Deep State"
when he commented to MSNBC shortly after the 2016 election, "You
take on the intelligence community? They have six ways from Sunday
of getting back at you."

The Trump Russia hoax did not wholly cripple the Trump presidency, but it was a major distraction and made an impeachment of Trump an inevitability, though it required contriving a case through a peripheral issue once the Mueller investigation failed to substantiate any of the wild claims about Trump and Russia. And it likely contributed to Trump's defeat for re-election in 2020, though this can never be known for certain.

Just to be sure, however, the wider intelligence community rallied in 2020 to undermine Trump's chances when Hunter Biden's abandoned laptop computer was discovered to contain highly compromising information about the extensive corruption of the Biden family. The Biden campaign denied the authenticity of the laptop, and although the FBI knew that the laptop and its content were genuine, fifty-one former senior intelligence officials, luminaries of both parties trading on their bipartisan reputations including five former CIA directors, signed a public statement declaring the laptop to have "all the classic earmarks" of a Russian fabrication. (It emerged later that the letter was instigated by the Biden campaign.) No lie was too big to support in service of the interests of the Deep State. The equivocal statement was good enough for the media to declare a new Russia hoax and to downplay the Hunter Biden story, and for social media platforms to cancel the accounts of the *New York Post*, the only major media outlet to report accurately on the laptop, and anyone else who promoted the *Post*'s independent work.

The point is that the major media organizations today are not merely slanted to the left, but wholly compliant with carrying out the wishes and protecting the interests of authoritarian government. When proud members of the prestige press adopt slogans such as "democracy dies in darkness," or wring their hands about supposed "threats to democracy," they ought to look in the mirror. This outcome is surely a delight to the Russians and other enemies of the republic.

HOW THE MEDIA MISSED WHAT I SAW ON JANUARY 6

BY NICK SEARCY

In 1976, the film *All the President's Men* made journalism sexy and noble in my young mind. Because of it, I was thinking of majoring in journalism at the University of North Carolina. I wanted to "speak truth to power," and "question authority." I dreamt, just for a moment, of becoming a bold, brave truth-seeker, of holding the feet of the powerful to the fire, keeping those in government honest, and standing up for the "little guy" against the almighty state, just like Dustin Hoffman and Robert Redford did.

Thank God I came to my senses and majored in drama and English instead. As I have learned in the decades since, those lofty ideas are utterly unwelcome in today's media. Now journalists strive to *obey* authority, to *silence* the powerless, to *support* the powerful, to *cover up* lies—and if the "little guy" dares to stand up to his government masters, he must be crushed, vilified, demonized, and destroyed, and, whenever possible, imprisoned.

Today, journalists are more like unscrupulous prosecuting attorneys uninterested in truth and only interested in winning their case at any cost. If the truth hurts the narrative advanced by the powerful, it must be suppressed. In the words of the late great Rush Limbaugh, today's journalists are nothing more than "stenographers for the regime." And rather than holding the state accountable, they are actively persecuting and vilifying private citizens whom the state targets, and they are giving the neighbors, friends, and customers of these people permission to hate, despise, and persecute them as well.

I learned this by going to Washington, D.C., on January 6, 2021. I went there along with somewhere between 1.5 million and 2 million other people, who had come, at their own expense, to protest an election they honestly believed had been stolen. I saw people praying, people singing the national anthem, reciting the Pledge of Allegiance with their hands over their hearts—happy, patriotic people who loved this country. I saw people of all ages, all races, all religions. I saw "Chinese-Americans for Trump," "Blacks for Trump," "Hindus for Trump," "Sikhs for Trump." I even saw a man wearing a T-shirt that read "Fags for Trump." I saw people waving flags, a lady with a portable stereo playing Twisted Sister's "We're Not Gonna Take It" on a loop that everyone sang along with. From where I stood, it looked more like a tailgate party than a riot.

But when I turned on the television that night, I didn't see any of that. All that the media showed was violence—which involved a tiny percentage of the people who were there. The narrative was set, long before the day even happened, that everyone who went there that day was a violent white supremacist terrorist racist subhuman redneck who was trying to kill everyone in Congress and "destroy democracy"—and that this was not a protest, but an *insurrection*. The media had launched their mission, which continues to this day, to destroy, utterly, as many of the January 6 attendees as possible. And make no mistake—the media has relentlessly backed the demagoguery coming from Joe Biden, Kamala Harris, and the rest of the Democrat party machine, intentionally and relentless planting the idea that *everyone* who went to Washington that day was a criminal, an "enemy of democracy," and must be destroyed.

These lies by the national media, the major networks, and the newspapers have been chronicled quite well by truth-tellers like Julie Kelly, Tucker Carlson, Glenn Greenwald, and others; and their lies about the coronavirus, "Russian collusion," the Hunter Biden laptop, Joe Biden's laughably obvious corruption, and the "mostly peaceful" Black Lives Matter riots have been revealed so often by now that it seems repetitive to bring it up. They are proven liars, and proven propagandists for the federal government, and everyone knows it.

But what struck me as being different this time was how even local reporters had turned into slavish mouthpieces for the state, as they set about utterly destroying the lives of anyone that went to Washington that day. In case after case, these people were vilified in their home papers and on their local news reports, resulting in the loss of their jobs, their homes, their businesses, and the respect of their neighbors, and even their liberty—all before any trials had taken place. For the media, these "insurrectionists" were guilty until proven innocent.

To be clear, this did not come about because of some vast, coordinated conspiracy, with higher-ups in the media giving orders to local reporters and news anchors. They are not patsies, but willing, avid participants. It is difficult to advance in the news business without being in agreement with the leftists above you and beside you in the newsroom. Heck, it's hard to graduate from a college with a degree in journalism if you aren't "one of them." They do it instinctively, because that is how they have been trained throughout their personal, academic, and professional lives. Their concept of "justice" is not the one that most Americans grew up with, the blindfolded Lady Justice holding the scales. These reporters think their bias *is* justice, that justice is whatever serves the "progressive" narrative.

The result of the media breathlessly regurgitating whatever the government accused these people of doing, while never committing any acts of real journalism by exploring the facts—that most of these people were law-abiding citizens who had never been arrested for any crime before in their lives—was that their communities, their neighbors, their customers, all turned against them. The media gave permission to hate these people—after all, every single one of them was called a violent, racist, white supremacist insurrectionist who deserved the scorn and hatred of anyone who believed in "democracy." America, however, is a representative republic, designed as such to protect us all from mob rule.

For example, Lewis Easton Cantwell, an Army veteran living in Sylva, North Carolina, owned three tea shops in the western part of the state, specializing in teas for those struggling with drug and alcohol addictions. He was in D.C. on January 6, but never entered the Capitol building, committed no violent acts, caused no property damage. Nevertheless, he was arrested outside his tea shop early one morning, with a show of force worthy of a serial killer or a drug dealer—twenty or thirty vehicles, SWAT teams, long rifles. They marched him out in leg irons, as if he were a dangerous, violent criminal. After the local papers reported his arrest, he was subjected to hate mail, Yelp reviews calling him a traitor and a racist, and eventually eviction from his business. Not one reporter ever tried to get his side of the story. He was vilified, bankrupted, and left practically unemployable because his reputation in the community had been destroyed.

Like so many other January 6 defendants, Cantwell eventually decided to plead guilty to one count, because of the exorbitant legal costs, and the cruel fact that there is absolutely no possibility of winning a jury trial in the 93 percent rabidly Democrat jury pool that is Washington. Almost all defendants have asked for a change of venue so that they can be tried in their home states by a jury of their actual peers, and every single change of venue request has been denied by the venal, partisan D.C. judges who preside over these kangaroo courts.

So now Cantwell has served five months in a federal prison, is back at home, and is considering changing his name as soon as he legally can, as any search of his name brings up a characterization of him as a criminal.

Countless others have faced the same character assassination, and the same destruction of their businesses, reputations, and lives. By now, the government has charged more than a thousand over January 6. Many of them have trouble finding employment, even in the most menial jobs, because of what pops up about them when their potential employers Google them. Consumers of the propaganda from the news media have believed the lies, and openly cheer on social media when they hear how these individual lives have been ruined, not only by the corrupt D.C. legal system, but also by their communities having turned against them so that they have no way to make a living.

George Tanios, a successful restauranteur in West Virginia, another "J6er" who never entered the building and participated in no violence or vandalism, had to close his restaurant after headlines about his arrest caused his neighbors and customers to tape hateful messages to the door of his restaurant, calling him a terrorist and a racist, a white supremacist. He was falsely accused of ten felonies, including attacking police officers. All ten felonies initially were dropped, but then, a year later, two other felonies were added to his case, and this forced him to make the painful decision to plead guilty to two misdemeanors, to stop the financial devastation caused by mounting his legal defense, thinking he could restart his life after more than two years of being prosecuted. In his plea deal, he was forced to say that he entered the Capitol, which he never did—but these are Soviet-style confessions, in which the truth is irrelevant. You must sign what the government tells you to sign, or you will be destroyed. To this day, he has trouble finding any employment because of the media's constant characterization of him as making "terroristic threats," even though all those charges were dropped. He has received hundreds of pieces of hate mail from people poisoned by the lies in the news.

J.D. Rivera, a Marine veteran, father of six, and once an aspiring journalist in Pensacola, Florida, did enter the Capitol on January 6, and filmed every second of the twenty-two minutes he was inside. He had the promise of a job from a local TV station, and he thought that this footage would be valuable in securing a position. The video shows that he committed no violent acts, simply chronicling what was happening inside the building. He went to trial and was sentenced to seven months in federal prison for misdemeanor trespassing—yes, *trespassing*—all felony charges having been dropped before trial. Leading up to his trial, the TV station never allowed him to start working because of the charges against him, and it was the only news outlet camped in front of his house filming him the day he was arrested. He was unable to find any kind of employment. Even when he applied at Burger King, just to get some money coming in to feed his family, he was rejected because of what came up online under his name search.

Eric Christie from Los Angeles, a person whom I had met briefly earlier at a Trump rally in Los Angeles, and whom I saw and waved to on January 6, also never entered the building. He was arrested on December 22, 2022—almost two years after January 6. The article written about him carried the headline: "Jan. 6 Insurrectionist Arrested After Standoff in Van Nuys." The media apparently does not believe in that annoying "innocent until proven guilty" Fifth Amendment nonsense. He's an "insurrectionist." The government said so.

While I have never been targeted or persecuted by the FBI or the Department of Justice—and many times I have wondered why I have not—they most assuredly have had a negative impact on my career. I certainly am not equating my experience with those who were jailed without bond for over two years, but I have felt a little bit of their wrath.

It happened because I made the mistake, early on the morning of January 6, of speaking to a reporter from *Politico*, who approached me as I walked by myself toward the Ellipse, where President Trump was going to speak. He identified himself and asked if he could ask me why I was there. I was quoted in his article, published on January 7, 2021: "'It's a historic day. And I wanted to be here for it,' said Searcy, best known for a recurring role in the FX show *Justified*. 'I want to witness what happens, and if this is the last day of the republic, I want to be here to see it.'"

The tone of the article made my statement seem much more ominous than I had intended it to be. I was referring to the installation of the illegitimate, addled moron Joe Biden as the "end of the republic," not the protests surrounding it. But this article, unbeknownst to me, lit a small fire in the Hollywood community.

On the Saturday evening after January 6, I was in bed when I got a call from my theatrical agent at the time. This shocked me, because my agent almost never called me anyway—we communicated primarily through email at that time—and never on a weekend after business hours. I answered, with a surprised "Hey Dan, what's up?"

"I just have to ask you one question. Did you go into the building?"

"What building? What are you talking about?"

"You went to Washington on January 6, right? Did you enter the Capitol building?" he asked.

"No, I didn't go into any buildings. I didn't even see anybody go into the building. I had no idea anyone went into the building until I saw the news. Why?"

"Well, there is a casting director out here passing a picture around to all the agents and casting directors of someone there that day that she claims is you, and she is telling them you should never work again." Dan was quite breathless and excited. I got the feeling that Dan had called me fully prepared to drop me as a client.

"Send me the picture," I said.

It was a picture of a man wearing a cap and with a mask covering his face, waving a flag, standing on the Capitol steps, in front of a mural. Even though his head and face were covered, it was obvious that it wasn't me.

"Dan, come on," I said. "That guy outweighs me by about fifty pounds. You know that isn't me."

"Well, I didn't think so, but I had to make sure."

"Well, who is spreading this rumor?"

Shockingly, the casting director was someone I had known for thirty years, since my days starting out in New York City. She had cast me in some of the most important projects in my career. I had once done, as a friend, a public reading of her husband's play. We were friends, or so I thought. It was hard to believe.

Since I had her personal email address (and she had mine as well—she could have just asked me herself, instead of spreading this rumor and contacting my agent, but I suppose she was afraid I might be a dangerous anti-democracy racist insurrectionist terrorist), I dropped her a line, saying in part:

215

We've known each other a long time. I remember doing a reading of your husband's play about how awful Republicans are. I believe that people have the right to express themselves, and tell the stories they want to tell. As a professional actor, I am willing to participate in that, even if sometimes I don't agree with the POV.

You write my reps and tell them that you're "disturbed" by my perspective? Sounds like an attempt at intimidation to me. You could have reached out to me for verification. Why didn't you? That is disturbing to me...

I find it very sad, after knowing you for 30 years or so, that you would treat me this way. But having worked in Hollywood for the same amount of time, I can't say that it surprises me.

See you around,
Nick

Her response was:

I reached out your reps after another casting director sent me a photo of you on the Capitol steps waving a flag with a big mural behind you and it turns out it wasn't you. I only did it out of concern for you and for your career. We have known each other for forever and I want you to know that I would never prevent you from getting work. I can separate politics from acting. I'm still a fan. And when it comes to politics we can agree to disagree.

I never heard from this person again, nor have I since been offered a role by the major network for which she is head of casting. And she is not the only one. There are at least three casting directors with whom

I had worked so many times over the years that I knew their families, their children's names, and they knew my family as well. After January 6, I never heard from any of them again.

Furthermore, Fox News—you know, the "conservative" news network—never had me on again, after years of doing guest appearances on Greg Gutfeld's show and others. The network also refused to allow me even to buy advertising for my documentary about January 6, *Capitol Punishment.*

I am fortunate that I have reached a point in my life where I won't suffer much if I never work again. The people in my business who have been given permission to despise me by the media can't really hurt me. But for the other Americans who went to D.C. that day along with me, whose lives, businesses, marriages, relationships with their children, and friendships have been permanently damaged by a government that wants to crush the powerless and a media that slavishly supports the powerful, it is a tragedy and a shameful chapter in American history. Where are the Woodwards and Bernsteins of today when we need them? (And, of course, I'm talking about the Redford/Hoffman movie versions of Woodward and Bernstein. The real Woodward and Bernstein were never anything more than part of the leftwing machine.)

A republic cannot function properly without a free and honest press, one that looks for truth and holds the government accountable. The vast majority of American journalists today have abdicated their responsibilities and become simply a mouthpiece for the regime in power—as long as it is a Democrat regime, of course. Any individual who opposes that regime must be targeted, intimidated, and crushed.

This must change, or America will not survive.

HOW "WOKE" CONQUERED THE MEDIA

BY SEBASTIAN GORKA

Sometimes one just has to pause and take stock, as we now live in a world that daily beggars belief. A sizable portion of the adult population believes that there are hundreds of genders, that the freest nation in the world is endemically oppressive, that men can become women, that math is racist, and that a child can chose its gender.

Just a few years ago this would have all been deemed clinically insane. Or at least been perfect fodder for a Monty Python or *Saturday Night Live* skit when SNL was still funny. Now these "facts" are articles of faith for those who worship at the altar of Wokism. How did we get here, and what was the role and the culpability of the corporate media? What follows is a sketch map of the perverse route taken by our society.

First, let us deal with the word "Woke." I for one don't like the term, since in general usage the word means something good, the state of being conscious, awake to the world around us. Instead, I prefer to see "Wokism" as just another form of political correctness, whereby ideas are segregated into the permissible and the déclassé, the approved and the prohibited. Nevertheless, in order to understand the Left's journey from "normal" politics to reality-denying cultism, we need to understand the etymology of the term and the context of the ideology of which it is a part.

Whilst there is a 20th-century pre-history of the term's limited use, by the likes of Marcus Garvey and the singer Huddie Ledbetter, the broader political application of the term "Woke" came with the rise of the so-called Social Justice movement, and specifically a 2012 tweet from the black American singer Erykah Badu exhorting her followers to support Pussy Riot, the anti-Putin punk group. Soon #StayWoke would become shorthand for those who subscribe to a whole panoply of twenty-first-century progressive tropes, a collective term applying to all aspects of the New Left's ideology, from Critical Race Theory to transgenderism. Soon "Woke" would become the moniker to describe those who were on the ideological cutting edge of the Left. Not only that, it would become the yardstick by which Americans would be judged on social media, in popular culture, and corporate media, a metric that, if not met, would lead to one's "cancellation," as happened in the case of actress Gina Carano, whom Disney fired from *The Mandalorian* after a non-Woke post on Instagram.

How did this repackaged ideology of the New Left attain such dominance in American culture? Before we look at the role of the mainstream media in mainlining radical, counter-factual views, it is essential to understand not just the origins of the term "Woke," but the modern metamorphosis of leftwing politics.

It all began in an Italian prison cell after World War I. There, a crippled communist, imprisoned by Mussolini's regime, had an epiphany. Antonio Francesco Gramsci realizes that the leftwing "worker's paradise" of Karl Marx could not be effected by violent revolution, except in semi-feudal, backward societies, such as turn-of-the-century Tsarist Russia (and later in predominantly peasant China). In developed countries, such as Italy, or America, with a vibrant middle class, strong Judeo-Christian values, and an emphasis on the rights of the individual over some abstract vaunted "collective," revolution can never be a mass phenomenon.

Instead of violence in the streets and bloody revolutions, the resilient "bourgeois" societies of the West must be dismantled, undermined from within. This crucial observation of Gramsci's would lay the basis for what the Left has become today and for the transmogrification of political correctness into "Wokism."

The road would not be obvious and straight, rather complex and circuitous instead, but the milestones and key actors are readily identifiable if one takes the time to dig for the origins of how an adult today can believe in the utterly absurd, such as that America should have no border and that a man can become a woman just by incanting that it be so.

Gramsci's ideas were reflected by the attempts of Hungarian writer and politician Gyorgy Lukács, who implemented them in the short-lived Hungarian Soviet government in Budapest after World War I. From there they were picked up by a philosophical playboy in Germany called Felix Weil, who used his inherited wealth to build a home for the radical ideas of the New Left, the Institute for Social Research or, latterly, the Frankfurt School. Weil gave a political home to Lukács, and one Max Horkheimer, a man whose name most Americans have never heard, but whose anti-Western ideas would become the bedrock of all so-called "Critical Theory."

Critical Theory, the documented existence of which in our schools the Corporate Media has labeled a conservative conspiracy, states that the current political, economic, and social power dynamics in the West must all be ruthlessly and relentlessly challenged since power is in the hands of those who do not deserve it, especially the members of the white heterosexual "cisgender" patriarchy, aka the oppressors, and must be given to the colored, LGBTQ, non-gender-conforming minorities, aka the oppressed. But how to do that? How can the powerful be brought down and the "downtrodden" liberated in the freest nations of the world? In steps.

Thus, Herbert Marcuse and his "repressive tolerance." (That is not a parody; he and his New Left colleagues used that phrase on purpose.) Since America is uniquely unburdened by a class structure—at least by comparison to the nations of Europe—Marcuse realized that a class war in which the "workers" rise up against the "capitalists" is a fantasy. So, he needed a new victim group, or groups. Women victimized by men, homosexual Americans oppressed by straight Americans, "people of color" exploited by white oppressors. These are the constituents of wokism who were to be made "class conscious" and empowered by a new "just" form of totalitarianism.

In his 1965 essay "Repressive Tolerance," Marcuse explains that in order to effect a just society, tolerance must be made partisan. In this Orwellian redefinition of the word, tolerance would not permit the expression of views deemed "oppressive." Only that which undermines the repressive, established order will be tolerated.

I know this all sounds insane, but these weren't just the musings of ridiculous navel-gazing academics stuck in Germany. Fleeing Hitler, these radicals who hated Western civilization would escape, first to Geneva and then, in 1935, to America, ensconce themselves in the ivory towers of our most prestigious colleges, influencing the likes of "community organizer" Saul Alinksy and radical civil-rights activist Eric Mann, who would in their turn indoctrinate and train the likes of Hillary Clinton, Barack Obama, and the founders of the Black Lives Matter movement. Today's insanity makes sense if you understand the connective tissue from that Italian prison cell to the infernos of violence and looting of the Summer of George Floyd 2020.

My brief with this chapter was ostensibly to explain how the corporate media adopted "Wokism, and how it spread the ideology so rapidly across all sectors of society. My first thought was, well the Corporate Media has always been "Woke." Did *The New York Times*'s Walter Duranty not receive the Pulitzer Prize for lying about "Uncle Joe," simply because it served the "greater good"? That was back in the 1930s! Are *The Washington Post*'s Bob Woodward and Carl Bernstein not still bloviating on cable news as the brave Watergate "journalists," despite the fact that the source, "Deep Throat," who made them famous, was a disgruntled deputy director of the FBI, and to this day there is no proof that President Nixon knew anything about the bungled burglary or committed any subsequent crime? I put it to you that media has never been "unbiased."

But something has indeed changed—from the depth of the media's ideological corruption to its seeming irreversibility. Here I proffer two possible reasons: social media and my former boss, President Donald Trump.

First, social media's impact. I remember when journalism was a profession. A proper trade. One would apprentice and work for years or even decades. Excellence in writing and research would lead to investment in the individual. In the days of real investigative journalism, an established name would be trusted, given a lavish expense account, and told to come back in six months with a real story, or not at all, whether the subject was "Who is bin Laden?" or "What is the truth about Thalidomide?" Today that breed is gone or has left for Substack. Now there is no money from full-page ads or the classifieds. Gone are the professional journalists, replaced by twenty-somethings with a Gmail account, a laptop, and a goal to get as many "clicks" as possible to drive internet ad revenue—accuracy be damned.

Second, one cannot underestimate the effect that the former president had on the state of the Corporate Media and its bitter commitment to political lies. A billionaire businessman who had never run for office, but who had captained one of the most popular reality TV shows for fourteen years, Donald Trump knew just how vacuous and morally corrupt the members of the "news media" had become. And he called them out. They've never recovered.

It is rather ironic that the phrase "fake news" was first coined by a future *BuzzFeed* editor, Craig Silverman, to attack and undermine conservative outlets like Fox News or Breitbart. Then the archbrander who is Donald Trump, flipped the derogatory term back onto the mainstream media like a deft aikido champion to show its members up for their rank corruption so effectively that it is now a moniker they are unlikely to shake for the foreseeable future.

There is a deeper aspect to my brief that I feel unable to answer. And that is the moral aspect of what we have witnessed. Not only has Corporate Media wholeheartedly internalized the New Left's political correctness in the form of "Wokeness, it has lost all sense of moral decency, or even just a moral compass.

How else does one explain what we witness today about the "Russian Collusion" hoax, or the coverage of the Covid pandemic? For six years, the likes of *The Washington Post, The New York Times,* CNN, and MSNBC have peddled the smear that President Trump and his campaign covertly collaborated with the Kremlin to subvert the 2016 elections. Despite the $20 million spent on the Mueller probe and two impeachments that failed to bring a conviction, despite no evidence of collusion ever presented, the purveyors of this lie—originally propagated by a former MI-6 agent funded by the Clinton campaign—have yet to retract one word of their "coverage," let alone apologize.

As a minor figure in all these, as a former deputy to the president, this is also personal. I understood the attacks on my boss, and the attacks on me by way of proxy when I worked in the White House. But when journalist after journalist baselessly attacked me as a literal Nazi—despite my father's having protected his Jewish friends from the Germans as a child in occupied Hungary—or even attacked my teenage son in an article with a headline calling him a "traitor" simply because his father worked for the duly elected president, then I fail to comprehend the utter loss of any decency or even humanity that the mainstream demonstrates on a daily basis. And this isn't just about MAGA conservatives like me or my former employer.

All during the Covid pandemic, the Corporate Media was prepared to lie. Whether it was about the danger that the disease from Wuhan represented to children—it didn't—or how being vaccinated would make it impossible to spread the virus—it doesn't—its members repeated Woke lies because the collectivist in them told them too. And now we know the truth—about children needlessly kept out of school, or masked; about grandparents who died alone, and otherwise healthy young Americans harmed by experimental vaccines. About how healthy children were not truly in danger but have been psychologically scarred, perhaps for life, thanks to masks and isolation and absence from school, nary a confession, let alone an apology.

So, I can explain where "Wokism came from, and how it infected the media and was propagated by it. But I can't explain how all those so-called journalists have lost their souls.

Perhaps when then say, "sorry," they'll tell us.

WE SHALL
NEVER OVERCOME
BY ROGER L. SIMON

Did the Corporate Media ever do anything worse than to put the final kibosh on the civil rights movement? It was tantamount to taking a wrecking ball to the American dream and letting it fly until nothing was left, not a thing, really. Everything else was meaningless. White people were terminally evil, and black and white could never live together.

Remember "We Shall Overcome"? How, back in the '50s and '60s, we would sing, tears in our eyes, "Oh, deep in my heart, I do believe, we shall overcome someday." Or "Black and white together we shall not be moved"? It's hard today to wrap your mind around how that spirit could ever have existed.

I only dimly remember it myself although I was very much there, in South Carolina in 1966 just three years after Martin Luther King had delivered his "I Have a Dream Speech" in Washington, D.C., and just one year after my grammar school best friend Andy Goodman had been shot to death by the Klan in Mississippi. A movie was made based on that.

When I saw my first black power salute, I told myself, and others told me, it was just a phase. We were trying to do good in our small ways and, for a while, it looked as if we had—were it not for the Corporate Media. Well, not by themselves, of course, and not for a while.

The Corporate Media was preceded in its racial recidivism by white radicals and black separatists as superbly detailed by Shelby Steele in his book *White Guilt: How Blacks and Whites Together Destroyed the Promise of the Civil Rights Era.* But bad as that was, progress had been made. By the beginning of this century the American people, it seemed, were starting to put what has been called "our long racial nightmare" behind us.

Nowhere was this more evident than in a *60 Minutes* interview that Mike Wallace conducted in 2005 with Morgan Freeman, among the more famous black men in the country at that point. Wallace had asked the Oscar-winning actor if he was planning on celebrating Black History Month. Freeman pooh-poohed the idea, replying that it was "ridiculous," continuing to Wallace: "You're going to relegate my history to a month? What do you do with yours? Which month is White History Month?"

Wallace said he was Jewish, so Freeman asked if he wanted a Jewish History Month. Wallace didn't. "Oh, why not? Why not? You don't want one? I don't either," Freeman continued. "I don't want a Black History Month. Black history is American history." And then Wallace asked, "How're we going to get rid of racism?" At that point, Freeman dropped what is these days called on the internet a truth bomb: "Stop talking about it."

Stop talking about it? What an original thought for a racially obsessed nation. It might even work. In fact, it was the only thing that could work. But tell that to the likes of the Reverends Al Sharpton and Jesse Jackson. They would have been out of a job.

Freeman amplified his suggestion. "I'm going to stop calling you a white man, and I'm going to ask you to stop calling me a black man. Call me Morgan and I'll call you Mike." That was 2005.

I recall this interview being discussed—hashed and rehashed—in myriad venues. A few were sympathetic to Freeman at first, understood that he just might be making sense, but gradually their voices were drowned out. Great actor that he was acknowledged to be, Freeman was being cornered, possibly even cancelled in an early version of what would become a common occurrence. The media played a role in this, praising Freeman for his artistic skills, but implying that he should "clarify" what he "meant."

Needless to say, Black History Month and the rest of the noxious identity politics parade prevailed. It was a necessity for the poor and downtrodden, according to sources in and out of the media. Never could there be equality without it. This was a few years before we were introduced to the concept of "equity," which was still the province of arcane academics. Whatever else, this idea of "stop talking about it" had to be squelched at all costs. Talking about race and then talking about it again was to be of paramount importance, the only solution, as we would learn later from Attorney General Eric Holder, Barack Obama's self-described "wing man."

The Corporate Media never met a better partner than Obama. They were made for each other. Looking back now on those massive crowds that celebrated his accomplishment immediately after the election, how even those of us who didn't vote for him were moved that finally a black man—still spelled with a lower case "b" in the press in those halcyon days before the Corporate Media and its allies took that same wrecking ball to the English language—would be elevated to the presidency. It made us all look and feel good about ourselves. This was the man who, after all, had inspired us a few years before with a speech at the 2004 Democratic Party convention, assuring us that we were not politically oppositional red and blue states, on the brink of separation or, worse, civil war, but all joined at the hip in common cause as the *United States of America.*

We were snookered, of course. Beneath it all, the Obama administration, even though it pretended otherwise, was among the most racially divisive in American history and the direct antecedent of the yet more divisive Biden administration.

This is when the corporate media began to come to the fore. The Democratic politicians and pundits plus their extensive cadre of media allies had realized for some time their absolute dependence on the votes of black Americans for power—but now a black man had been elected president. What if racism became in the public mind a thing of the past, even relatively? Without it, what did the Left have? Nothing much really but a collection of academics who wanted to recycle Marx for the umpteenth time despite the mass murders, and maybe some soccer moms. Later they would have more.

Actually, this lust for the black vote goes back well before 1964 when Lyndon Johnson signed the Civil Rights Act. But that's when LBJ is reputed to have used the n-word to register his pleasure in having secured the black vote for generations with that legislation.

Where would the Left be without the black vote? Racism simply had to survive. It was up to the media to remind us, even to bring it back, to fan it. And they were more than willing with their ally Barack Obama. Racism, after all, was under every tree. Just watch MSNBC or CNN and you would know it.

One of those trees, of all places, was Cambridge, Massachusetts, where a local cop arrested Henry Louis Gates after a 911 caller reported the Harvard professor and public television star for breaking and entering his own house. The call was understandable since Gates, having just returned from China to find his front door stuck, was trying to force it open with the help of his driver. This arrest might have been a normal matter of urban confusion, easily written off and forgotten by all concerned, but Gates was a famous black man, and Obama was president. What resulted was a "beer summit" for all parties on the White House grounds—in other words, a media show. That the cop was anything but a racist—he had given mouth-to-mouth resuscitation to Boston Celtics star Reggie Lewis when Lewis collapsed during practice—was beside the point. Publicity for even the whiff of racism was all. The media beat the drums.

But this was little compared to the 2012 killing of black teenager Trayvon Martin by George Zimmerman in Sanford, Florida. The neighborhood volunteer watchman Zimmerman had caught the suspiciously hooded Martin skulking about a housing development at night. A tussle ensued during which—accidentally or on purpose, it was never clear—Zimmermann shot Martin. Immediately the shooting was reported as "white man kills black kid." Around the world it went—we were back to the Klan. We soon learned that Zimmerman was Hispanic, another minority. How embarrassing. Almost as immediately a new term was invented, or possibly resurrected, "white Hispanic." The media gobbled it up.

But not nearly to the extent that its members relished Obama saying, "If I had a son, he'd look like Trayvon." Well, maybe. Others might look askance at a mixed-race child of privilege like Barack—who attended Punahou, the fanciest, whitest, private preparatory school in Hawaii, followed by stints at Occidental College, Columbia University, and Harvard Law—identifying himself with a kid from the streets, but no matter. The media had its red meat.

All this prepared the ground for the media fiestas that lay ahead—the shooting, and riots surrounding them, of Michael Brown in Ferguson, Missouri, on August 9, 2014, and the May 25, 2020, death of George Floyd in Minneapolis with its ensuing turmoil during the Trump administration.

The Michael Brown affair was a particularly egregious case of Corporate Media manipulation. It took nearly a year—in the case of *The Washington Post* until March 16, 2015—for much of the media to admit that Brown had never said "Hands up, don't shoot!" before being shot, supposedly execution-style, by Officer Darren Wilson. The media allowed, actually encouraged and publicized, "Hands up, don't shoot" to become the mantra of a new civil rights movement that had nothing to do with real civil rights, only rage and vengeance. By lying, the media fanned racial flames that brought attorney general Holder to Ferguson to fan the flames some more, all based on something that never happened.

Some conservative media told the truth. *What Killed Michael Brown?*—a documentary by Shelby Steele and his son Eli did so, extensively. But by then the damage was done. It was Churchill's "a lie goes around the world before the truth can put its pants on" on steroids.

The George Floyd affair was, if anything, worse. The once great city of Minneapolis has effectively been destroyed by the turmoil that flowed from it. Yes, it is bad, even tragic that Floyd died. But this was a behemoth of a man, six feet four inches tall and weighing 223 pounds, a locally known felon convicted of eight crimes who had served four years in prison for a case of aggravated robbery in which he aimed a gun at a woman's abdomen and demanded drugs and money. He was a heavy user, as he obviously was that day when police were warned of his floating a possible counterfeit twenty-dollar bill and pursued him.

Did he deserve to die? Of course not. Did police use excessive force? Probably. Did they do this because Floyd was black? Who knows? One of the officers was black himself. Whatever the case, who among us of whatever ethnicity could know how we would have behaved in such a situation faced with such a man? And yet he has been lionized as if he were St. Francis of Assisi, his face emblazoned on city walls, not just in Minneapolis.

Who started this? Partly the Corporate Media, of course. Its members publicized it everywhere. Something that was sad, they helped to turn into a cause. If you think about it, excessively praising a person like Floyd, making him out to be some kind of secular saint to be venerated, is sadistic toward black people while pretending to be on their side. It is the real racism of which they accuse others.

Enter critical race theory and "anti-racism," the extreme duplicity that had been cooking in the academic oven for decades. As its purveyors tell it, America didn't begin in 1776. It began with a "slave ship"—in reality, an English privateer that wasn't even a slave ship that put to shore in Virginia in 1619. The Corporate Media didn't care. Its members applauded straight from the front pages of *The New York Times* in something called the 1619 Project. Race was now everything, our national character nothing. Dr. King? Who's he?

Racism is something that the Corporate Media lies and lies and lie about, ignoring the most heartbreaking subject of all, that the overwhelming majority of the murders in our country are black on black, often of children, and therefore helping to preserve their tragic status quo. Understanding why the Corporate Media does this is not all that difficult. It's a question of power. If racism were to go away, the media would lose it.

Meanwhile, the American people are the big loser in all of it. If Corporate Media is not defeated, indeed, we Americans—black and white—will never overcome.

THE MEDIA VS. THE NATION'S BORDERS

BY MARK KRIKORIAN

> We just follow the story wherever it goes. We don't have an
> agenda, we don't have professional opinions on immigration.
> We try very hard to keep those out of the stories.
> —Kevin Rothstein of WCVB-TV Boston, co-recipient of the 2017
> Eugene Katz Award for Excellence in the Coverage of Immigration

For two decades, the Center for Immigration Studies (CIS), which I
head, presented the Eugene Katz Award for Excellence in the Coverage
of Immigration. The goal was to counter the tide of bad reporting on
the subject by highlighting informed and fair coverage of such a complicated and contentious issue.

CIS strove to recognize mainstream media outlets, and usually
succeeded. Over the years, we bestowed the award on reporters from
The Washington Post, the *San Francisco Chronicle*, *The Dallas Morning
News*, Copley and Newhouse, local television news stations (as in the
epigraph above), and others. Even when the award went to writers at
ideological outlets, such as *City Journal* or *National Review*, it was for
real reporting.

The award is no more.

This isn't because immigration coverage was great before Donald
Trump and now, post-Trump, there isn't a single reporter in conventional media covering the issue knowledgeably and fairly. But the

chattering-class freak-out over Trump's success at tapping into discontent over immigration to win the 2016 presidential election seems to have swept away journalistic standards and dialed up to eleven the pre-existing flaws in immigration coverage.

Take *BuzzFeed News*. Before Trump announced his candidacy, its investigative team—yes, *BuzzFeed* had one—took the nearly unprecedented step of launching a deep dive into the abuses caused by guest-worker programs, reporting on the abuses suffered by both the foreign workers and the Americans they displaced. The stories had titles like "The New American Slavery: Invited to The U.S., Foreign Workers Find a Nightmare," "All You Americans Are Fired," "The Jobs No Americans Can Get," and "Employers Abuse Foreign Workers. U.S. Says, By All Means, Hire More." In December 2015, *BuzzFeed* also ran "Trump Resort in Florida Relies on Foreign Guest Workers." Fair enough—he was a presidential candidate and had made use of the very foreign-worker visas the team of reporters had spent so much time investigating. (I offered the investigative team the Katz Award, but they declined it.)

Once Trump started to gain traction and potentially became a real threat, *BuzzFeed* swung into action. Its original journalistic instinct to dig into dark corners gave way to Trump Derangement Syndrome. Concerns about work-visa programs and other aspects of immigration were pushed aside, and the foreign-worker coverage was all Trump, all the time: "Trump's New York Golf Course Seeks Foreign Workers," "Trump Seeks More Foreign Guest Workers for His Companies," "Trump's Florida Clubs Absent from Job Fairs to Hire U.S. Workers," "Trump Beach Resort in Florida Seeks More Foreign Workers," and so on and on and on. And on.

Punching Up, Punching Down: The Narrative of Immigrant Victimhood

The underlying flaw in media coverage of immigration is that it is shoehorned into a narrative of victimhood, with the foreign-born in general, and illegal aliens in particular, treated as a protected class. This narrative dovetails with the broader narrative of whites oppressing non-whites, because most immigrants have been, and will likely continue to be, what our current race laws classify as "non-white." Of the approximately 22 million legal immigrants since the year 2000, about 87 percent have been from countries outside Europe and Canada. (Of course, a large share of those from Latin America likely considered themselves to be white until being told in the U.S. that they're oppressed minorities: "Hispanics.") Race aside, immigrants are, by definition, outsiders—the "other" in a xenophilic media culture that values the fringe over the mainstream.

Thus, reporting fairly on the realities of immigration—covering both the tech entrepreneurs *and* the criminals, both those Americans who benefit from immigration and those who are harmed by it—is seen as "punching down," heaping abuse on those lower on the status hierarchy. Immigration must always be good, and illegal immigration is undesirable only in that it causes difficulties for the illegal aliens themselves. This solicitude for immigrants—and by extension, for the whole project of *de facto* unlimited immigration—expresses itself in a variety of ways. Let's start with the very words that the Corporate Media uses to discuss the phenomenon.

Whatever You Do, Don't Call Them Illegal!

In *1984*, Orwell has one of Winston Smith's colleagues say, "In the end we shall make thought-crime literally impossible, because there will be no words in which to express it." It was shortly before Orwell's titular year that the media began its effort to make thought-crime on immigration impossible. It started with the euphemism "undocumented" for illegal aliens.

The explicit purpose of replacing "illegal" with "undocumented" is to remove the moral culpability of foreigners who have entered our country illegally, or overstayed their permission to be here. Illegality requires some kind of punishment or accountability, whereas being undocumented can simply be remedied by getting documents. If you can't say "illegal," the thought-crime of supporting immigration enforcement becomes, if not impossible, then more difficult, and easier to dismiss as bigotry.

Civil rights activist Leonel Castillo was appointed by Jimmy Carter in 1977 as the first Hispanic commissioner of what was then known as the Immigration and Naturalization Service (INS). Among his other innovations to undermine the agency's culture of enforcement was the mainstreaming of the term "undocumented" into the immigration lexicon. Castillo didn't invent the term, but a Google Ngram search, which charts the frequencies of any set of search strings, shows that "undocumented alien" and "undocumented immigrant" were all but unknown in published sources before the mid-1970s. *The New York Times* used the adjective "undocumented" as early as 1859, but for a century, almost all uses of it related to vessels—*ships* that didn't have the requisite paperwork to dock. The *Times*'s first use related to immigrants came in a 1935 subhed mentioning "undocumented aliens." This wasn't a precursor to the later euphemistic use of the adjective, though, because the story also referred to "undesirable aliens" and "illegal immigrants." It seems likely that the use of "undocumented" for illegal aliens began by analogy to the adjective's application to ships, many of which also carried aliens.

The *Times*'s first use of "undocumented" in the current politically correct context, to avoid drawing attention to the illegality of the aliens' presence, came in late 1976, in an unbylined story on page 56 referring to Haitian illegal aliens suing to receive political asylum. But it was an April 18, 1977, frontpage story that introduced the euphemism to the public. A report on an amnesty proposal by the Carter administration said that the policy "would stress humane treatment of the illegal, or 'undocumented,' workers," the quotation marks clearly signaling that this was a new and unusual term.

The displacement of "illegal alien" did not happen immediately; the phrase was still used well into the 2000s, though increasingly only in quoted comments, while "illegal immigrant" remained acceptable.

Even the phrase "undocumented alien" was increasingly replaced with "undocumented immigrant." It was during the Obama administration, however, when activists ramped up the pressure on media organizations to use the new phrase exclusively, and new reporters arrived in newsrooms having emerged from the woke madrassahs of higher education to oblige. The National Association of Hispanic Journalists took up the cause, writing in 2009 that "undocumented" should be used instead of "illegal." The loudest single voice for policing the terms used by the media to describe illegal aliens was Jose Antonio Vargas. Vargas was an illegal alien himself, who worked—illegally—as a reporter at *The Washington Post* and the *Huffington Post*. In 2011, he founded an advocacy group called Define American (his definition of "American" included himself, naturally), and in 2012, he began specifically targeting the *Times* and the Associated Press to get them to stop using "illegal" to describe illegal aliens.

In April 2013—not coincidentally the same month the Gang of Eight amnesty bill was introduced in the Senate—both the AP and the *Times* submitted. The Associated Press in 2011 had actually pushed back and defended "illegal immigrant" as an acceptable, neutral term, rejecting both "illegal alien" and "undocumented worker." But two years later it capitulated, barring any use of "illegal" to describe a person, saying that only actions should be described as illegal. The *Times* responded to the pressure from Vargas and others by further discouraging the use of "illegal immigrant" but not prohibiting it, though "undocumented" has clearly become the preferred usage. And it ends the style-book section on immigration this way: "Do not use *illegal* as a noun, and avoid the sinister-sounding *alien*."

The language of broadcast news has also been successfully scrubbed. The Media Research Center examined the newscasts of the three major broadcast networks over a nearly ten-month period in 2022 and 2023. It found that "throughout all 254 minutes of border coverage, they never once used the terms 'illegal immigration,' 'illegal immigrant,' or 'illegal alien.'"

Think of the Dreamers!

One area in which the media narrative of the noble immigrant who is never wrong but can only be wronged is most evident is the coverage of the so-called Dreamers. Even using that advocacy label skews the perception and coverage of the issue of illegal aliens who came here at a young age.

The original DREAM (Development, Relief, and Education for Alien Minors) Act was introduced in 2001. There have been many iterations of the proposal over the intervening two decades, but they all would have given a green card (that is, permanent residence with a path to citizenship) to illegal aliens who came here as minors, had lived here for a certain number of years, had completed school or were in some educational program, and who had not been convicted of certain crimes. The rationale was that since they were minors when they came to the U.S. illegally, they should not be held liable for the actions of their parents. The bill came closest to passing in the lame duck session of Congress at the end of 2010, when it passed the House but failed in the Senate.

Barack Obama's 2012 campaign, fearing that anemic Hispanic registration numbers would threaten his re-election, decided to implement something like the DREAM Act administratively to generate enthusiasm among Hispanic voters (even though the president had earlier said he lacked the authority to do that). The result was Deferred Action for Childhood Arrivals (DACA), which gave two-year renewable work permits (but not green cards, which only Congress can do) to more than 800,000 illegal-alien "Dreamers" (though some have dropped out in the interim).

The original DREAM Act and its DACA simulacrum targeted the most sympathetic group of illegal aliens in order to make the case for a broader amnesty for all the rest of the illegal population. While insufficient numbers of voters and lawmakers were persuaded, the media ate it up. Who better to represent the immigrant oppressed by the white supremacist phallocentric patriarchy than children!

This led to some exceptionally bad reporting. The most notable flaw in reporting on DACA wasn't so much that sympathetic reporters feasted on sob stories—we would expect nothing less. Rather, the press corps, almost as one, misrepresented the program's requirements in order not to cast doubt on its beneficiaries. It's not that they lied, but that they either uncritically parroted the rhetoric of activists and their allies in Democratic administrations, or they ironed out important wrinkles that they judged inconsequential.

*   **Brought here as children.**

This is the starting point of media falsehoods about DACA. There is no requirement that children be "brought" here by parents "through no fault of their own" to be eligible for the program The use of the verb "brought" is intended to paint a picture of babes in arms exercising no agency. Even a decade after DACA was decreed by Obama, the *Times*, for instance, still referred to "some undocumented immigrants brought to the United States as children."

But to be eligible for DACA, one only had to have come here illegally before age sixteen, with or without parents. While many, probably most, of the beneficiaries were, in fact, "brought" here by parents, one of eight were teenagers when they arrived, some of them almost certainly coming on their own, since a fifteen-year-old is considered to be of working age in much of the world. To give a sense of how common it is for teenagers to travel illegally on their own: During the first two years of the Biden administration, about a third of a million unaccompanied minors crossed the border illegally, most of them teenagers.

*   **Americans in all but paperwork.**

This is a lobbyist phrase that journalists thankfully avoided, but they accepted the premise unquestioningly. Contrary to the old "if your mother says she loves you, check it out" reportorial ethos, reporters expressed little skepticism about this assertion that was so central to the case for DACA—just *how* American were these illegal aliens?

A useful proxy for that would be proficiency in the English language. The DACA recipients served up by advocacy groups to be interviewed by reporters all spoke English, of course— mostly with standard American accents—but were they typical? Inquiring media minds should have wanted to know, but not in this case. As it turns out, the DACA application form has a box to check if an interpreter filled it out for the applicant. If any reporters had asked how many applicants used interpreters, they would have learned that Obama's Department of Homeland Security didn't tabulate that information, so there is now literally no way to know without going back through 800,000 pieces of paper by hand. You can see why the Obama administration would not want that known, but there was no excuse for the crusaders of the Fourth Estate to ignore the question altogether and let the White House get away with it.

A CIS estimate using results from a test of English proficiency for people with the characteristics of DACA beneficiaries concluded that perhaps one-fourth of DACA recipients are functionally illiterate in English. But this knowledge might have undermined the public sympathy for the DACA beneficiaries and thus undermined support for future amnesties, so only rightwing media noticed.

* **No criminals need apply.**

Another way the Corporate Media misrepresented DACA was how its members described DACA as only for those who "have a clean criminal record," in the words of a *Times* reporter who should have known better. Anything else might have undermined the image of "Dreamers" as paragons of virtue and fully deserving of amnesty.

But there is no such requirement. While there is, indeed, a level of criminality beyond which one is ineligible, that's different from a "clean record." To be considered for DACA, an applicant must merely not have been convicted of a felony, a significant misdemeanor, or "multiple misdemeanor offences," in the words of the Department of Homeland Security memo that created it. "Multiple" was taken to mean three or more, and in implementing the program, multiple misdemeanors committed on the same date counted as only one offense.

Further, only convictions were considered. More than 50,000 successful DACA recipients had arrest records, including for serious crimes. In the words of L. Francis Cissna, director of U.S. Citizenship and Immigration Services under Trump, America "let those with criminal arrests for sexually assaulting a minor, kidnapping, human trafficking, child pornography, or even murder be provided protection from removal."

It was the same with gang membership, which was the subject of a question on the DACA application. But like the question discussed above about use of an interpreter, the government didn't want anyone to know the share of DACA beneficiaries who were in gangs so it didn't record the information on its own forms. And no one in the press expressed the slightest interest in the subject.

The point of all this is not to make a case for or against DACA. It is merely that the press had no interest in relaying, or even gathering, facts that would have cast the program in a negative light. To do so would have been seen in newsrooms as punching down, even racist. "The public has a right to know" morphed into "the public can't be trusted with such knowledge."

What border crisis?

These patterns reached their culmination in the legacy media's reaction to the border crisis sparked by President Biden. Starting on Inauguration Day in 2021, the new administration rolled back almost every immigration policy put in place by the Trump administration.

The result was predictable and predicted: In the first three years of the Biden administration there more than 7 million illegal-alien apprehensions at the border with Mexico, exceeding anything the United States, or any country, has ever experienced.

Some of those people were arrested multiple times, and many were expelled, but more than 3 million illegal border-crossers were taken into custody and then released into the United States on Biden's watch and at his appointees' behest, supposedly to apply for asylum. In addition, there were nearly 2 million known "got aways," aliens whose illegal entry was detected (by remote cameras, ground sensors, and other means) but who were not apprehended because the Border Patrol was overwhelmed. Those number have only worsened since.

And yet the legacy media expressed less interest in this historic crisis than in the much smaller surge in illegal border crossings in 2019 under Trump. From March through June 2019, the Border Patrol arrested 419,864 illegal border-jumpers at the Southern border, the highest number during the Trump presidency, in a surge sparked by the cancellation of the zero-tolerance policy at the border (and quickly ended by the institution of the Remain in Mexico policy, which required illegal aliens claiming asylum to wait for their hearing dates on the other side of the border). From March through June 2022, during some of the heaviest flows of illegal border-crossers under Biden, there were 831,854 Border Patrol arrests—nearly double the same period three years earlier under Trump.

So, did news coverage reflect this dramatically greater threat to the nation's sovereignty? Search *The New York Times* for "border" and "Mexico" for the four-month period in 2019 and you find that 583 stories were published. The same four-month period in 2022 under Biden shows only 302 stories.

Twice the news, half the coverage. The reason is clear—in intensely covering the short-lived surge under Trump, the media could champion the cause of the downtrodden immigrant while attacking Trump. But under Biden, during a much worse illegal-immigration surge caused by his policies, to draw attention to the greatest mass-migration crisis in history would potentially stir the hoi polloi against immigrants, undermining reporters' preferred party and administration.

The reluctance of the legacy media to cover immigration once Biden took office was clear from a 2021 Pew Research Center report. It looked at coverage of the first two months of the Biden administration and found that media outlets with a rightwing audience were twice as likely to cover immigration as outlets with leftwing or mixed audiences. You might think this is merely a question of dueling partisan websites, but the imbalance between those media outlets that covered immigration intensely and those that did not was stark. The outlets that Pew defined as having leftwing audiences included *The New York Times*, *The Washington Post*, CNN, *Politico*, NPR, and PBS—much of the leading media in the country. Even among the outlets deemed to have "mixed" audiences, only the *New York Post* did not have a primarily leftwing audience; the others so listed were the three broadcast networks, *The Wall Street Journal*, and *USA Today*.

Among the outlets with rightwing audiences that Pew found covered immigration more heavily were Fox News, of course, plus the *Washington Examiner*, Breitbart News, Newsmax, and the radio shows of Mark Levin and Sean Hannity. While Pew implied that its findings suggested that rightwingers were obsessed with immigration, a more accurate headline for the report would have been "Corporate Media Trying to Ignore Biden's Border Disaster."

And even as the border crisis gathered steam, the legacy media *reduced* its coverage of immigration. NewsBusters found that compared to March 2021, the three broadcast networks' coverage of the border dropped 94 percent in August 2021, with a grand total of six and a half minutes of stories. This, despite the fact that border arrests had jumped 20 percent since March, which was already double the level of January, Trump's last month in office. And of the three networks, ABC World News Tonight had not a single story on the border during the entire month.

The legacy media seemed as reluctant to go to the border as Vice President Kamala Harris. That's why Bill Melugin of Fox News was able to scoop all other media outlets on the first really big, un-ignorable story of Biden's border crisis. On September 15, 2021, Fox aired shocking drone-camera footage of a rapidly growing shanty town of Haitian and other illegal aliens under the International Bridge in the Texas border town of Del Rio. Word had spread that the cartel that controlled the Mexican side of the border there, unlike elsewhere, didn't force border-jumpers to pay a fee, so thousands came running.

Only after Fox's broadcast of the alarming images did the rest of the large media outlets feel compelled to end what amounted to an embargo on border news. And even then, the legacy media and its Democratic allies leapt at the opportunity to change the narrative by confecting a fake story about Border Patrol agents on horseback "whipping" Haitian illegal aliens. The *Times* initially reported "images of agents on horseback chasing, and in some cases using the reins of their horses to strike at running migrants." When the news photographer himself said that no one had been whipped, the paper had to publish a correction. But the damage was done.

When they weren't ignoring the border, the members of the mainstream media parroted their administration's talking point. In March 2021, as illegal-alien apprehensions at the border reached double the level before he took over, Biden was asked about it. His response: "The truth of the matter is, nothing has changed…. It happens every single solitary year. There is a significant increase in the number of people coming to the border in the winter months of January, February, March—it happens every year."

And what did *The Washington Post* publish on that very date? "The migrant 'surge' at the U.S. southern border is actually a predictable pattern. Evidence reveals the usual seasonal bump—plus some of the people who waited during the pandemic." Biden's comment was a "if you like your doctor, you can keep your doctor" level of brazen falsehood, but instead of calling him out, the prestige media tried to cover for him.

Something similar happened in spring 2023. In May, the Biden administration finally lifted Title 42, the pandemic-era public health measure that enabled Border Patrol agents to expel border-jumpers back into Mexico without entertaining their (often phony) asylum claims. It was feared that a huge wave of illegal crossings would follow, so the Department of Homeland Security came up with what it presented as a carrot-and-stick approach to reduce illegal immigration. It would bar border-jumpers from applying for asylum if they hadn't first applied for asylum in any of the countries they passed through before reaching the U.S. border, but said that those who used a Department of Homeland Security cell phone app to, in effect, schedule their illegal immigration at a port of entry would be let in. This was described as "expanding legal pathways," even though there was nothing at all legal about letting in inadmissible aliens and then releasing them into the U.S.

The goal of the policy was to reduce the number of illegals caught by the Border Patrol (by increasing the number waved in "legally" by immigration inspectors, who are part of a different component within Customs and Border Protection). The goal of the policy was to get a compliant media to report that illegal immigration was down, and it succeeded. The coverage of the June 2023 border arrest numbers (the first month after the new policy was in place) was a White House press flack's dream.

For example: "Unlawful Southern Border Entries Down 70 percent from Record Highs Since End of Title 42" (ABC News), "Border Encounters Remain Low Nearly a Month After Title 42 Lifted, DHS Says" (CNN), and "Southern Border 'Eerily Quiet' After Policy Shift on Asylum Seekers" (*The Washington Post*). None reported that the number of aliens employing the alternate means of illegal immigration by making appointments to come through ports of entry reached a record high in the very same month, triple the number in the prior June, and quadruple the level of June 2021. But no amount of media water-carrying could obscure the fact that Border Patrol arrests jumped right back up in July 2023.

There may be other policy areas where reporting by the legacy media is broadly reliable (or maybe not). And even in immigration, there are still individual reporters who cover the topic fairly. But the partisan culture of the established media outlets is such that immigration is unlikely to ever be covered broadly and fairly and thoroughly, with all perspectives fully aired. Immigration is a polarized issue, and the members of the legacy media have chosen their pole.

THE MEDIA VS. THE MILITARY

BY KURT SCHLICHTER

My sergeant was one of those lean, hard guys from out in some Western state where it would never occur to his betters to visit, wielding a moustache worthy of a '70s porn protagonist and a binary perspective fitting for a terrain where there was sky and dirt, and nothing else. "Sir, if a reporter comes around," he asked me, "can I shoot him?"

If it was 2023 instead of 1991, I would have had to chastise him for assuming that a journalist would be a man instead of a woman, or someone with no gender at all. But during the Gulf War, lieutenants like me had been trained by the same guys who rebuilt the Army after the Vietnam debacle, and we were focused on serious things, like winning, rather than on carefully regurgitating the clichés and tropes of a ruling elite that we were barely aware existed.

The soldier, even in a civil war, tends to physically separate himself from the people when choosing where to do his business. Little Big Horn and Iwo Jima were distant and remote, and even Gettysburg was fought in the fields outside of the town. There are exceptions, of course—crazy-brave Red Army Russian peasants fought it out knife-to-knife with the Wehrmacht in Stalingrad as civilians trapped in the hellscape huddled nearby in the cellars. But usually a battlefield somewhere is far off, away from the people, and the people want to know just what their boys are doing.

Enter the war correspondent, though until recent years the reporter was part of the team rather than posing as some neutral outsider. Sometimes he was a soldier, too. The Athenian Pheidippides was a *hemerodrome*, a courier, who ran all the way home from the Battle of Marathon to report the Greek victory over the Persians, then promptly dropped dead. But he filed his story first.

Sometimes he was even the commander. Julius Caesar's remarkable *The Gallic Wars* was not originally a memoir but pure reportage. He wrote his missives during his campaign and sent the dispatches home to the Eternal City to be devoured by the Senate and curious citizens eager to know what their men faced at the edge of the world. "All Gaul is divided into three parts, one of which the Belgae inhabit, the Aquitani another, those who in their own language are called Celts, in our Gauls, the third," it famously began. Caesar's purpose—he rarely had just one purpose in anything he did—was not only to feed the Roman people's appetite for news but to burnish his own *gravitas*. Another young noble seeking adventure and fame was Winston Churchill, who would head out to war as a soldier, resign his commission in theater to then report for the London tabloids, then re-up again with some local regiment to get in on the next battle.

But the dilettante model gave way to the ink-stained-wretch model as newspapers were able to fund their own correspondents instead of having to rely on rich kids' letters home. World War II saw an explosion of war correspondents sent overseas to satisfy the hunger of the people back home for news about their 12 million menfolk deployed to all corners of the globe in the Great Crusade against the Axis. These young civilian men with notepads were not that different from the young military men with M1 Garands—they even wore the same uniforms (albeit without rank). But more important, they came from the same kind of places and the same kind of families and the same social class.

Ernie Pyle was the quintessential war reporter of the era, the man who told the story of the dog-faced infantrymen and their harrowing, often-short, lives at the front. Pyle was no Yalie slumming it with the proles. Born to a tenant farmer in Indiana, he dropped out of college and did a short stateside hitch as a swabbie in the Navy Reserve during World War I, then took up the pen. He followed the troops through the European theater, sharing their misery, reporting their suffering. His poignant columns were printed in hundreds of newspapers. Then he went to the Pacific theater, and during the fight for Okinawa on April 18, 1945, while accompanying U.S. Army soldiers, he caught a Japanese machine gun bullet below the lip of his helmet. He died at age forty-four, looking seventy-four.

His legacy was demonstrated by the honors bestowed upon this civilian at the behest of the grateful troops whose story he told. Pyle was awarded the Purple Heart, and he was buried among the heroes in the Punchbowl, the National Memorial Cemetery of the Pacific at Honolulu. And Ernie Pyle was never unclear about whose side he was on.

The World War II model of the correspondent serving alongside the soldiers limped on even into Vietnam, where it finally expired during the Tet Offensive when Walter Cronkite treacherously pronounced the war lost to millions of American TV viewers even as U.S. troops were annihilating the Viet Cong troops foolish enough to rise to face them. Joe Galloway of UPI was the exemplar. General H. Norman Schwarzkopf knew him in Vietnam and called him "the finest combat correspondent of our generation—a soldier's reporter and a soldier's friend." During the first Battle of the Ia Drang Valley in 1965, immortalized in Galloway's book written with General Hal Moore, *We Were Soldiers Once...and Young*, he was rumored to have picked up an M16—there were plenty of them lying around—and fought off the North Vietnamese forces attempting to overrun the American 1st Battalion, 7th Cavalry Regiment. What is not in dispute is that Galloway was the only civilian to receive a Bronze Star medal for bravery in Vietnam—he carried a wounded soldier back to cover under fire. Like Associated Press stringer Marcus Henry (Mark) Kellogg, who was scalped by the Sioux alongside Custer's men, Joe Galloway knew what side he was on.

By contrast, during a famous 1987 seminar on war reporting in which the moderator posited a scenario where the reporters had learned that an American unit was walking into an ambush, both Mike Wallace and Peter Jennings stated that they would *not* warn the GIs. In other words, the model from Pheidippides to Galloway of the reporter on the side of the soldier has been replaced by a model embracing some arbitrary, manufactured "higher principle" that privileged a false neutrality over keeping a fellow American from catching an AK-47 round in the belly. Don't imagine that the soldiers do not know it.

The advantage of professional distance is objectivity, as a reporter too deep in the military hierarchy risks becoming a mere font of propaganda. But the objective reporter model began to create problems as soon as it arose. The Civil War gave rise to technology—the telegraph—that gave reporters the ability to pass on tactically relevant information about future operations rather than just to provide an account of the aftermath. General William Tecumseh Sherman, whose understanding of the essential truth of war ("war is hell") and utter ruthlessness in achieving his objectives was second to none, thought reporters were little more than "spies" whose dispatches were "false, false as hell," and banned them from his formations.

But then, reporters would never be banned today because the senior military leadership is perfectly comfortable with the media. The professional distancing is from the grunts, not the brass. Today, reporters are informally embedded within the military hierarchy, mostly in the Pentagon press room, and the result is just what the distance model was proposed to prevent—today, the senior military establishment and the media are working together to jointly push their shared agenda. It's the grunts who are left out, their stories untold, the incompetence of their leaders covered up by professional courtesy and the cultural affinity those senior military leaders and media figures share.

The reporters and the generals are all of a kind—they went to similar colleges (no one becomes a general without at least one advanced degree), they share similar cultural mores and, especially in Washington, D.C., they physically live among each other. A general has gone to the Army War College in Carlisle, Pennsylvania, where any residual rough, Cro-Magnon edges are sanded off. It is not a combined-arms school but a charm school. The seminar participants do not ruminate on how Napoleon might have won at Waterloo or on the secrets of Alexander's leadership; they talk about the strategic threat of the weather and assure each other that diversity is our strength, not the number of howitzers that you can dial in on a target. The military saw a civilian-military gap widening several decades ago and made the decision to bridge it by making the military more like the civilian world. Not coincidentally, the U.S. has not won a war in those several decades.

But while the reporters and the generals share the same social class—and, not coincidentally, the same politics—the troops are left out of the lovefest. The media's military coverage today consists of passing on leaks that advantage the brass and ignoring the scandals created by the brass. The fact that much of war today is special-ops fighting in the shadows instead of mass armies of conscripts on a battlefield means that there will necessarily be much less of the kind of coverage an Ernie Pyle or Joe Galloway might provide. Still, where are the stories of individual soldiers? Absent without leave, but on the networks' news shows, there are plenty of clips of impeccably uniformed O6s conducting briefings on the latest successes, such as the Afghanistan withdrawal. And the members of the press nod as their military pals explain how the Kabul retreat was actually a triumph while the names of the thirteen troops killed by the senior leaders' gross incompetence are left unspoken and their stories go uncovered.

But does some lowly E4 from Rancho Cucamonga even register with the modern media? Does he even exist? He doesn't, if the reporter never goes and looks for him and his story, but why would it occur to the reporter to do that? The reporter went to NYU; the soldier graduated from high school, found that community college was not for him, and enlisted. The reporter has a BLM sticker on his MacBook; the soldier will blow his re-up bonus on a new F-150. The reporter considers it essential that the military integrate trans awareness into everything it does, and the flag officers agree; the soldier just wants to kill people, break things, then go fishing back home on leave.

The media and the soldiers are utterly alien to one another. How many reporters have a brother in the Marines? Probably a lot fewer than have a brother in Antifa. Their paths rarely cross in real life and certainly never will unless the reporter goes to seek the grunts out. But why would he? He is not sympathetic to the soldier or to the soldier's class—he finds them bigoted and ignorant and probably extremist, inferiors who believe in Jesus and the Constitution. The reporter hates the soldiers, and the readership of the *Times* or the *Post* or whatever has no interest in reading about the challenges and sacrifices of a bunch of knuckle-draggers in camo. They are proles, heavily armed janitors or gardeners doing the dirty work of society so those of the reporter's social class can live their soft, comfortable lives. The soldier does not matter. The men whom Pyle and Galloway held up as icons are now merely a cautionary example—"Kaden, you need to make sure your Pride Month essay is perfect so you get an 'A' and then get admitted to Harvard, or else you might have to join the Army!"

The truth is that today the military and the media, as institutions, are not adversarial but aligned. Instead of marching through a conquered enemy capital, the military leadership has allowed a Gramscian march through its institution, at least at the top levels. Down below, where the rubber meets the road and the bayonet meets the guts, the fighting men are still the same. They want to do what warriors do. But it is unclear whether elite America is willing to tolerate warriors today, other than those in FBI SWAT teams busting down the doors of families who illegally pray outside abortion mills.

I do not remember exactly what I told my sergeant in response to his question about busting a cap into any reporter who ventured into our platoon's area of operation. None ever did, so it remains unclear whether this was a rare joke from the taciturn NCO or a serious query. I tend to think it was a bit of both. Out in the Old West, strangers were presumptively dangerous. An unknown trio on horseback approaching your homestead might well be coming for your horses; if they were

Comanche, they might take not just your horses but your sister and your scalp. Prudent suspicion was in his blood.

It has gotten worse since, with the generals and the journalists expressing their class solidarity while forgetting the soldiers. They share their class's aversion to the idea of victory, in no small part because demanding victory provides a clear metric—you win or you lose, and losing demands accountability. So, in the aftermath of the Afghanistan debacle, the media kept quiet about the ugly truth, and the generals kept their jobs and future gigs on the Boeing board. As always, the guys who pay the price were guys like my sergeant. The reporters and the brass may think the troops are just rural rubes, but my sergeant was wise enough to recognize his enemy.

WHAT THE MEDIA DOESN'T KNOW ABOUT GUNS

BY ELIZABETH SHELD

Americans get their information about firearms both actively and passively from Corporate Media outlets. Across the country, people tune in to daily news programming on television or read the news on websites and newspapers to find out what is happening in their communities. Families gather around the television to watch the latest episode of their favorite television series or plan a weekend to catch the new Hollywood blockbuster. America's worldview is informed by the firearm narratives presented in the media.

That media presents itself as an authority on firearms. Whether in a news article, on television or video, the agents of the Corporate Media deliver the facts about the rising crime rates, the latest gangland shootout, or updates on a school or workplace shootings. But do they present the facts? The media message is uniformly predictable: We need "sensible gun control" or "we need to ban assault weapons" or "we need universal background checks" or "we need more gun laws," but the members of the media dismiss instances of existing gun laws being broken to commit crimes. They are not familiar with thousands of firearms restrictions, and they don't know how guns function.

It is easy to say that the media folk don't know about guns and firearm policy because firearms are not part of their lifestyle. The

Corporate Media conglomerates are headquartered in big cities, their million-dollar talent live in fancy urban buildings with doormen and cutting-edge security systems. They take private vehicles to and from work and do not walk among the filthy casuals in New York City or Washington, D.C. The Hollywood faction lives in mansions situated in gated communities under the watchful eye of security patrols and away from the hoi polloi. Firearm laws do not apply to this rarefied breed because they have outsourced their security. "Why would anyone need an AR-15 to protect their home?" they wonder while dialing the access code to enter their fortified neighborhood of estates.

One of the most frequent propaganda tools the media deploys to manipulate the public is that of the *activist-expert*. The guests appearing on television or referenced in newspaper articles have titles and associations with the illusion of gravitas. "Surely a fellow at the Highfalutin Institute knows what he is talking about," the audience might think to themselves as they listen to an anti-gun lecture presented as social science. The cloak of authority is persuasive and effective at shaping opinions, which is precisely why the media refuses to feature any authority figure who does not push anti-gun policies. When pro-gun representatives do appear in the media, they are almost always outnumbered or shouted down to undermine their viewpoints.

On television, a frequent favorite activist-expert is an anti-gun character from the fake grassroots group known as Moms Demand Action. In the case of print and digital media, news stories reference the latest "research" published by a website called *The Trace*. But both Moms Demand Action and the pseudo-research institute The Trace are bankrolled by notorious anti-gun nut Michael Bloomberg. Bloomberg has spent tens of millions of dollars of his personal fortune on his anti-gun crusade, funding numerous fake grassroots entities and research outlets. The media is aware of exactly who it is featuring in its reports but never tells the audience that the experts are paid political operators. The members of the media don't announce that the "Moms" are paid to spew leftwing talking points or that "The Trace" exists to conceal a gun-control agenda behind a patina of social science research. But they certainly do let their audience know about the rightwing, pro-gun National Rifle Association if a representative is lucky enough to get an invitation to appear on a show.

There are plenty of knowledgeable people and organizations the media can hire as consultants for news stories or feature on television news shows to discuss firearm issues. The media outlets have failed to do so, regardless of how many times their ignorance has been exposed or corrections have been published to their reporting. In fact, though, they are not ignorant, they are intentionally misleading their audiences. In 2015, the Associated Press was forced to issue an embarrassing correction to its news story about a biker-gang shootout in Waco, Texas. The AP initially reported that "a semi-automatic weapon can shoot more bullets in less time than a small-caliber weapon"—which makes no sense whatsoever—and was forced to correct the description and explain that "an automatic weapon can fire multiple rounds more quickly than a semi-automatic weapon."

There are semi-automatic small-caliber firearms—those two attributes of a firearm are not mutually exclusive. Ammunition size has nothing to do with the mechanism that feeds a cartridge into a gun chamber. The AP also seems to confuse large-caliber weapons (the size of the bullet) with semi-automatic weapons (which automatically chamber a new round, but still require a pull of the trigger for each shot fired). The author and editor responsible for this news story could not be bothered to check with any number of groups that could have provided facts and accurate information on firearm engineering, such as the National Shooting Sports Foundation or Gun Owners of America.

The media's bias against guns is not limited to factual inaccuracies or the stable of fake experts; it also applies to the media's prestige talent. News anchor Jake Tapper has an extensive media resumé, including stints at CNN and ABC in various capacities. Many viewers, however, aren't aware that Tapper has a political history: He was the press secretary for a Democratic member of Congress, Marjorie Margolies (now Chelsea Clinton's mother-in-law) before working in the Corporate Media arena. The cherry on top of Tapper's credentials is his work for gun-control activist group Handgun Control, Inc., now known as the Brady Center to Prevent Gun Violence.

When reporting stories about gun violence for CNN, Tapper does not let his audience know that he used to work for a gun-control advocacy group. In 2018, following the school shooting at Marjory Stoneman Douglas High in Parkland, Florida, Tapper moderated a debate on gun policy for CNN. He did not inform the audience that he was aligned with one of the sides participating in the debate. Rather, he presented himself as a moderator between two sides on the topic.

The media's bias against guns is evident not only in the narrative it promulgates to the public, but also in the content omitted in its news stories and broadcasts. An excellent example can be found in reporting of the defensive gun use by Kyle Rittenhouse. Rittenhouse defended himself against violent aggressors and rioters in Kenosha, Wisconsin, during the George Floyd riots in the summer of 2020. He fought off and deterred three malefactors who intended to kill him, but a story of successful defensive gun use is not one the media wants to tell. As the media was demonizing and lying about Rittenhouse, claiming he was a white supremacist and a kid who "crossed state lines" looking for trouble, it paid little attention to Gaige Grosskreutz, who now goes by the name of Paul Prediger. Grosskreutz was Rittenhouse's third assailant. He is a career criminal and felon who illegally possessed the gun he pointed at Rittenhouse just before Rittenhouse shot him in self-defense. Grosskreutz received a fraction of the media scrutiny Rittenhouse did, and a fraction of the headlines and think pieces devoted to Rittenhouse, because the media did not like the moral of Rittenhouse's story: Americans need firearms to protect themselves from people like Grosskreutz.

Similarly, the media was entirely disinterested in Hunter Biden's gun-related crimes. President Biden's son admitted to illegally possessing a handgun despite being a drug user and lied on his federal 4473 form. The 4473 form is used to conduct a background check prior to making a gun purchase. The form reads:

> The information you provide will be used to determine whether you are prohibited by Federal or State law from receiving a firearm. Certain violations of the Gun Control Act, 18 U.S.C. 921 et. seq., are punishable by up to 10 years imprisonment and/or up to a $250,000 fine.

While members of the media are loud proponents of placing more restrictions on law-abiding citizens, they pay little attention to inconvenient individuals who break existing gun laws. In fact, the media never blames gun violence on the lack of current gun law enforcement but only on a perceived lack of even *more* gun laws. In Hunter Biden's case, the gun laws were designed to keep a firearm out of the hands of a drug addict, which seems to be a good idea in the service of public safety. When the Department of Justice made a sweetheart deal to give Hunter a slap on the wrist for his gun-related crime, the media showed no outrage. There were no representatives from Moms Demand Action or Everytown USA and no research studies from *The Trace* to talk about Hunter's gun crimes.

Another tactic of the anti-gun media is to direct the audience toward its preferred narrative with an obsessive focus on the presence of a firearm during a crime and away from the individual responsible for the violence. Media coverage of the Parkland school shooting paid little attention to the intentional breakdown of the existing system to keep guns out of the hands of violent maniacs. The Parkland shooter had multiple, serious disciplinary problems at school, yet had never been referred to law enforcement. Previous behavior included repeated animal cruelty, statements of a desire to shoot or kill people, and an announced intent to shoot up a school. The police had visited the shooter's home thirty-nine times on account of domestic turmoil involving a gun, and his disturbing social media posts had been sent to the FBI by an alarmed citizen.

Instead, the media crafted a narrative of a troubled eighteen-year-old who was able to purchase a firearm because there weren't enough restrictions on gun purchases. The real story is that the shooter was able to buy a gun because every guardrail to prevent it was intentionally disregarded by various institutions: The school system was de-incentivized from referring him to the police. The police never arrested the shooter despite numerous visits to his house, and the FBI never got around to checking into reports of his threat to shoot up a school. There was no official documentation that would prevent him from purchasing a gun, despite multiple laws to make sure that he was prohibited from doing so.

There is no better example of the media's ignorance of existing firearm policy than the example of the documentary *Under the Gun*. In 2016, "America's sweetheart" Katie Couric along with Stephanie Soechtig narrated and produced the anti-gun documentary. Couric calls herself a journalist and has an extensive pedigree that includes ABC News, CNN, and NBC News. Most people remember her as a host of the *Today* show. Couric went on to become the first female anchor on a Big Three network when she landed the job as solo anchor for the *CBS Evening News*. By all representations, Katie Couric was in the news business not the activism business.

Couric's *Under the Gun* documentary was marketed as an investigation into America's gun violence epidemic, but it was more like a gun-control commercial than an investigation. A common story line used to promote anti-gun sentiment by the media is to document an experience buying a firearm and follow up with a "gotcha" story telling the public how easy it is to buy a gun. Couric's documentary includes such a scene, or rather a *crime scene*. In the documentary, producer Soechtig had one of her employees, a Colorado resident, make private firearms purchases in Arizona in a Wendy's parking lot. But what really happened is that the team committed four separate felonies by purchasing four separate firearms across state lines without a background check. In an effort to show how easy it is to buy a gun in Arizona, all they did was to show how ignorant they are of federal firearms law:

> SOECHTIG: We sent a producer out and he was from
> Colorado. He went to Arizona, and he was able to buy

a Bushmaster and then three other pistols without a background check in a matter of four hours. And that's perfectly legal. He wasn't doing some sort of underground market.

But it's *not* perfectly legal. All interstate gun purchases must go through an entity with a Federal Firearms License (18 U.S.C. 922(a)(3) and 922(b)(3); 27 CFR 478.29). The unsuspecting viewer of Couric's documentary might be shocked at the fake "gotcha" moment and have no idea that he or she just witnessed numerous firearm felonies. Astute members of the firearms community recognized and pointed out the documentary's gun crimes, but Soechtig simply insisted that what she had directed her employee to do was legal. She asserted that Arizona law allows out-of-state residents to purchase long guns without a background check. However, individual states do not regulate interstate firearm purchases, which is the territory of the federal government. None of the crew of *Under the Gun* was pursued by the relevant agencies for breaking the law.

The Corporate Media's malign influence on the American public continues unabated. There is seemingly no amount of correction or shaming that deters its members from their gun-control crusade. They know what they are doing. So, you can bet that the next time there's a media story about firearms, the media's agents will be working in concert with a stable of fake experts to manipulate the public with tired calls for yet more gun restrictions.

GREEN MEDIA, GREEN MONOLITH

BY TOM FINNERTY

Few articles are as embarrassing to read as *Newsweek*'s notorious cover story of April 28, 1975, titled "The Cooling World." Embarrassing, because it combines specific and portentous predictions of doom—which were never realized—with confident scientific assertions that run counter to what we know today to be true. Here is the opening of the piece, written by science editor Peter Gwynne:

> There are ominous signs that the Earth's weather patterns have begun to change dramatically and that these changes may portend a drastic decline in food production.... The drop in food output could begin quite soon, perhaps only ten years from now... The evidence in support of these predictions has now begun to accumulate so massively that meteorologists are hard-pressed to keep up with it.

After listing a variety of costly extreme weather events in various countries, Gwynne continues:

> To scientists, these seemingly disparate incidents represent the advance signs of fundamental changes in the world's weather. The central fact is that after three quarters of a century of extraordinarily mild

conditions, the earth's climate seems to be *cooling down*. Meteorologists…are *almost unanimous* in the view that the trend will reduce agricultural productivity for the rest of the century. If the climatic change is as profound as some of the pessimists fear, the resulting famines could be catastrophic…. [Some scientists] regard the cooling as a reversion to the "little ice age" conditions that brought bitter winters to much of Europe and northern America between 1600 and 1900. (Emphases added.)

Needless to say, there was no global famine due to a new Ice Age in the 1980s. Quite the reverse, in fact. Since "The Cooling World" was published, American agricultural output has doubled, and the global story is much the same, with crop yields having significantly outpaced population growth. Both have likely been aided by global temperatures, which have generally trended upwards—the opposite of what was predicted—in the years since the article was published.

There's no other way to put it—*Newsweek* was spectacularly wrong. But it wasn't alone, not by a longshot. Two years prior to the *Newsweek* story, *Science Digest* published "Brace Yourself for Another Ice Age," which predicted that the Earth might soon be faced with year-round winter, and that American cities would be "buried in snow and an immense sheet of ice [which would] cover North America as far south as Cincinnati." The following year, *Time* magazine published an article titled "Another Ice Age?" It claimed that "a growing number of scientists are beginning to suspect that many seemingly contradictory meteorological fluctuations are actually part of a global climatic upheaval" brought about by the fact that "the atmosphere has been growing gradually cooler for the past three decades." And shortly after the *Newsweek* piece, former *New Scientist* editor Nigel Calder wrote in *International Wildlife* magazine that "the threat of a new ice age must now stand alongside nuclear war as a likely source of wholesale death and misery for mankind."

One might think that being so wide of the mark on such a major topic—in the media's telling, the most important topic there is—would inspire a certain amount of humility in the journalistic community. But a brief perusal of any mainstream media publication today, including those which were taken in by the "global cooling" scare of the 1970s, would indicate that the opposite is the case. In fact, journalists have continued to use the same apocalyptic language, while appealing to a supposed "expert consensus" pointing to a quite different diagnosis.

Here's a representative sample of stories from the past few years: *The Washington Post*: "Extreme Climate Change Has Arrived in America"; NBC News: "Heat Waves, Wildfires & Drought: How This Summer Is a 'Preview' of Earth's Coming Climate Crisis"; *The Guardian*: "'The Era of Global Boiling Has Arrived,' says UN Chief"; *The Toronto Star*: "It's So Hot that Canada's Sea Creatures Are Cooking to Death in Their Shells"; *Buzzfeed*: "Climate Change Is Driving an Increase in a Deadly Flesh-Eating Bacteria"; *The Guardian* again: "The Gulf Stream Could Collapse as Early as 2025, Study Suggests"; *The New York Times*: "Damage to Great Barrier Reef from Global Warming Is Irreversible." And on and on.

The contention is that a new "climate crisis"—originally designated as "global warming," now generally referred to as "climate change"—has arrived. In the telling of most major news outlets, it is having devastating effects on our environment and our way of life, it is increasing the frequency of extreme weather events, and it can only be addressed by spending trillions—that's trillions with a "T"—to change course.

None of these claims is true. At best they are misleading, lacking key contextualizing information. So, for instance, after years of the *Times* publishing articles about the impending death of the Great Barrier Reef—"Large Sections of Australia's Great Reef Are Now Dead"; "Great Barrier Reef Imperiled as Heat Worsens Die-Offs"; "The Great Barrier Reef Has Lost Half Its Corals"—the Australian Institute of Marine Science released a study in 2022 showing record amounts of coral cover in two-thirds of the reef, and high levels in the last third as well. Specialists have referred to the past several years as part of the "boom and bust" cycle of the Great Barrier Reef. But the "paper of record" contained no big headline stories about the study. Indeed, it seems not to have mentioned the study at all.

The media's transition from one doomsday scenario to another began in earnest in the late 1980s, after the previously mentioned decades of cooling had given way to ten years of warming. A watershed moment occurred in 1988, which saw a blistering heat wave and drought spread over large swaths of the country. That summer, Chicago, Philadelphia, and Kansas City each had more hundred-degree days than they'd had in the previous thirty years combined, and on June 21, nearly every state in the union registered temperatures north of 90 degrees.

In the midst of the heat wave, Senator Timothy Wirth, convened a hearing of the Senate Energy and Natural Resources Committee with the object of pinpointing the problem. (Senator Wirth would later claim that he'd made it a point to open the committee room windows the night before, so that it would be extremely hot inside, and the cameras would capture all of the experts sweating.) The testimony of Dr. James Hansen of NASA caught the particular attention of journalists. According to a front-page story in the next day's *New York Times* titled "Global Warming Has Begun, Expert Tells Senate" (subhead: "Sharp Cut in Burning of Fossil Fuels Is Urged to Battle Shift in Climate"), Hansen testified that it was "99 percent certain that the warming trend was not a natural variation but was caused by the build-up of carbon dioxide and other artificial gasses in the atmosphere."

Thus a "consensus" was born. Not, it must be noted, a *scientific* consensus. Many scientists pointed out that the months after that summer heatwave saw a notable decline in temperatures, such that Hansen's prediction that 1988 would be "the warmest year on record" was ultimately not borne out. Even at Senator Gore's committee hearing there was countervailing expert testimony. Dr. Lester Lave of Carnegie Mellon University, until then something of an environmentalist hero for his work linking urban air pollution to declining health outcomes, testified that the theory of anthropogenic global warming remained "controversial" in the scientific community. He was ignored.

The consensus was one of narrative. In short order, major publications began treating claims like those of James Hansen as gospel, while turning a blind eye to, or actively suppressing, differing opinions. Dr. Richard Lindzen of MIT has written about how, almost overnight, "climate change" became a topic about which one could not dissent. According to Lindzen, less than a year after Hansen's testimony he authored a paper critiquing the theory of global warming, only to struggle mightily to find anyone who would publish it. *Science* magazine claimed in its rejection that the paper held "no interest to [its] readership." Once Lindzen found a publication willing to print his paper, however, *Science* began ferociously attacking it before it was even released.

This trend has only gotten worse in the intervening decades. Nowadays, major publications regularly devote uncritical coverage to "climate doom" stories. Every extreme weather event—heatwaves, tornadoes, hurricanes, even cold snaps and blizzards—is cited as evidence of "anthropogenic climate change." Seemingly unrelated stories often include an obligatory climate angle—surges in illegal immigration become reports on "climate migration," for instance. And every aspect of our lives is considered fair game for climate critique, as is evidenced by the frequent think pieces about the necessity of making bugs central to our diet. A few headlines just from *The Atlantic*: "Why Insects Are the Most Eco-Friendly Meat," "Why You May Soon Be Eating More Insects," and "To Save the World, Eat Bugs."

Skeptical engagement with these perspectives, whether from scientists like Lindzen, Judith Curry, or Freeman Dyson, or data and policy analysts, such as Steven Koonin, Ross McKitrick, Michael Shellenberger, or Bjørn Lomborg, is either ignored outright or mentioned perfunctorily and then dismissed. And discussions of the cost or wisdom of going all in on "green" policies—replacing cheap, dependable fossil fuels and nuclear energy with unreliable and inefficient wind and solar power, or banning gas-and-diesel powered automobiles altogether within the next decade—meet the same fate.

The question is, Why? Why has the mainstream media sold its soul to the environmentalist movement, its narrative, and desired outcomes?

Well, clicks for one. Which is to say, disaster sells, and journalists who write, and editors who approve the umpteenth story about how the world is going to end in twelve or seven or five years due to "global warming" are at least in part responding to the same market pressures that inspired the short-lived "global cooling" freak out of the '70s. It's cynical and short-sighted, but their job as they see it consists in attracting eyeballs, selling papers, garnering clicks, and thus making money.

That's not the only role that avarice plays in this story, however. Often the profit motive is more direct. For example, the Media Research Center has documented the "explosion" of climate-centric stories published by the Associated Press in the wake of a multimillion-dollar grant from a group of leftwing environmentalist-tinged foundations, including the Hewlett Foundation and the Rockefeller Foundation. In return, the AP pledged to assemble a "climate swat team" to "enhance the global understanding of climate change and its impact across the world."

For a news organization to allow its reporting to be dictated by wealthy donors is shocking. But it is an increasingly common practice, and as advertising and subscription revenues have declined precipitously in recent years and newspapers across the country have folded, it's difficult to turn down that kind of money. Still, it remains a dereliction of duty and an especially egregious one in this case since many publications simply pick up and rerun AP reports directly. Even when the Associated Press notes the environmentalist funding of particular reports, as it often does (at least in the fine print at the bottom of the page), the publications rerunning those reports may not.

That said, it isn't just money that inspires the Fourth Estate to carry water for Big Climate Change. Modern journalists are often true believers, who've been educated and socialized into the narrative. Ideologically, they are much further left than the average American, with only about 3 percent of them identifying as Republicans. They come disproportionately from upper-class backgrounds. They've followed the religious trajectory of their WASP ancestors, away from Judeo-Christianity and toward a kind of spiritual-but-not-religious pantheism, which makes them particularly predisposed toward environmentalist millenarianism. American journalists are also much more likely to be college graduates than the average person. More than 95 percent of journalists hold at least a four-year degree, while less than 40 percent of the general adult population does so.

No doubt many of them would say that this last fact makes them smarter than the average American, better able to assess the relevant evidence. In reality, it often serves to insulate them from how regular people think and live their lives. And, since the modern university is latterly ordered less toward the pursuit of wisdom and truth than indoctrination, journalists' academic credentials have a tendency to distort their perception.

That isn't hyperbole. The "long march through the institutions"—the stated goal of the Marxist intellectuals who began at places like Frankfurt's Institute of Social Research and moved westward during World War II—has been wildly successful. Their influence is felt from the Ivy League to state universities, Catholic colleges, and even our military service academies. (America's future commissioned officers can minor in Diversity and Inclusion Studies at West Point these days.) And an underappreciated aspect of "critical theory," the distinctive strain of mid-century Marxism which set American academia on fire after the war, was its environmentalism.

This was a deviation from traditional Marxism. Indeed, it was originally the National Socialists, not the communists, who were known for being romantic about the natural world. Meanwhile, as the Frankfurt School's Herbert Marcuse would grouse about his intellectual forebear, Karl Marx "had wanted to turn the whole world into a workhouse." The factory assembly line was a classic Marxist image of a utopian workers' paradise, where individuality was subsumed into a mechanistic societal project.

But the working classes on whose behalf Marx and his followers claimed to speak had, for the most part, failed to sign up for their imagined workers' revolution. Consequently, the disciples of the Frankfurt School turned on the working classes, whom they believed to be corrupted by capitalism to such an extent that they had enabled the rise of fascism in Europe; never mind that fascism itself was conceived of first and foremost as a rejection of Anglo-American capitalism. From there, the critical theorists came to turn on all of industrial society, which they held to be a capitalist plot to generate wealth by despoiling the natural world.

This was an important point of departure, which laid a foundation for what would become the New Left. No longer did it emphasize a workers' revolt. In fact, it could be called a class war in the other direction, with the privileged raging against their economic and cultural inferiors, that is, regular people who aspired to earn an honest wage, live reasonably comfortable lives, and raise a family. For the Cultural Marxist New Left, these were all markers of the bourgeois "consumer culture," which they disdained partly because, they claimed, it necessarily harms the environment.

Modern journalists are, by and large, the spokesmen of this elite and over-credentialed class, which helps to explain their credulous reporting on approved climate-related topics and their extreme indifference toward stories that undercut or complicate the accepted account. That includes angles that would catch the eye of even old-fashioned leftists—the effect of elevated energy prices on the poor, for instance, or the actual environmental harm done in third-world countries by mining for minerals to make electric-vehicle batteries.

The influence of critical theory and the New Left on modern journalism can be seen even in the method of argumentation. Or lack thereof. Because rather than calmly and logically laying out facts with the intention of building a convincing case, New Left disputation came to be characterized by angry, urgent assertion, and a rejection of all discourse that didn't serve the revolution. In his book *Green Tyranny*:

Exposing the Totalitarian Roots of the Climate Industrial Complex, Rupert Darwall observes:

> The aim of critical theory was not genuine understanding of social phenomena, derided as the "fetishism of facts," but bringing about social change. Truth was not immutable.... Disinterested scientific research was impossible in a society in which men were themselves not autonomous and empiricism a capitulation before the authority of the status quo.

Hence the notable incuriosity about the actual, and extremely complex, science surrounding climatic variations. Because, despite their panegyrics about how we must "follow the science," most journalists, like their comrades in the activist world, have accepted the belief that truth itself is merely an assertion of power.

Of course, the idea that truth is malleable undermines the media itself. The role of the journalist is to lay the pertinent facts before the public in a coherent form. If he rejects the "fetishism of facts," if he continually molds the truth toward his own ideological priors, eventually people will start to notice that what they're reading in the papers doesn't match what they're experiencing in reality. They'll start to suspect that something is up.

And they have. As journalists have invested a great deal of their profession's reputational capital, built up over a century or so of generally impartial reporting, in ideologically inflected narratives, with "climate" rivaling race as the most significant, that capital has become exhausted. This is evidenced by the fact that public trust in the media has plummeted to record lows.

That doesn't mean the members of the media haven't done serious damage to our body politic. From the 2021 cancelation of the Keystone XL pipeline, which cost tens of thousands of jobs on both sides of the Canadian border, to the "renewable energy" mandates that ensure our subservience to the People's Republic of China (a country that powers its dominant solar panel industry by means of coal-fired power plants), and passing the deceptively named Inflation Reduction Act—called by *New York Times* columnist Paul Krugman "a climate change bill with a side helping of health reform"—which exacerbates inflation by shoveling billions of dollars of recently printed money into the gaping maw of the Green Industrial Complex, they have aided an assault on our nation's economy, energy independence, and way of life.

Worse still is the personal cost. Americans—especially young Americans—report extremely high levels of "eco-anxiety," constant terror that the world is going to end within their lifetimes, along with a reluctance to have children, because they've been convinced that humanity is destroying the natural world. This phenomenon has gotten so bad that even the Left has started to grow concerned about it—*The New Yorker* published an article titled "What to Do with Climate Emotions?" about Americans who can't function because they're overwhelmed by anxiety and depression about "climate change."

That, however, is to be expected since, for their entire lives, young people have been subjected to the constant drumbeat—in their education, their entertainment, and the news—of a malicious narrative irresponsibly embraced and propagated by the media for its own cynical ends.

THE MEDIA VS.
THE POLICE
BY JACK DUNPHY

From 1955 to 2009, the headquarters building of the Los Angeles Police Department was Parker Center, at 150 North Los Angeles Street. Named for former LAPD chief William Parker and made famous in the *Dragnet* television series, the eight-story building came to be, like Parker himself, an emblem for the transformations that occurred in society in general and police work in particular over that period. Hailed in the beginning as innovative and modern, both the building and the man for whom it was named came to be condemned as retrograde or even evil.

Perhaps no single room in Parker Center symbolized those changes more than a small office on the ground floor, near the building's rear entrance facing San Pedro Street. In the early 1980s, as a young street cop with the LAPD, I would sometimes pass by the room when my duties took me to Parker Center, and I had done so several times before my curiosity compelled me to step inside and speak with the men working there.

A sign in the hallway identified it as the Norman "Jake" Jacoby Press Room. Like most offices in the building, it was spare, small, and cramped, as though designed to accommodate three desks but containing four. On those desks were typewriters, telephones, notepads, and, perhaps shockingly to today's sensibilities, ashtrays full of stubbed-out cigarettes. I would not have been surprised to find a bottle or two of strong spirits in some of the desk drawers.

Sitting at two of those desks were men in late middle age, one of whom was Jacoby himself, who in his fifty-six years as a police reporter occupied the office for most of its existence. He started with the City News Service in 1935, then served in the Army and wrote for the *Stars and Stripes* during World War II. After stints at the now-defunct *Herald Express* and *Herald Examiner*, he returned to the City News Service and served as the unofficial dean of L.A. crime reporters until his retirement in 1991 at age seventy-five.

"So," I said, stepping into the room and addressing Jacoby and his colleague, "what goes on in here?"

The two men received me graciously and explained how they worked the phones and walked the hallways of Parker Center, talking with cops in search of stories that would run in the *Los Angeles Times* and on local radio and television stations. I wasn't aware of Jacoby's iconic status at the time, but I would come to learn that he had been given the run of the building and had contacts at every LAPD and L.A. County Sheriff station, as well as those in every suburban city in Southern California. Though he did not ignore police scandals, of which there were a few, Jacoby was regarded among LAPD detectives as something just short of a trusted colleague. He wasn't a cop, but he understood the job and those who performed it as few outsiders ever did.

The LAPD moved from Parker Center to a modern headquarters building at First and Main Streets in 1999. While Parker Center had come to be recognized as a symbol for the LAPD and, through its depiction on television, for cops everywhere, to the uninformed passerby the current Police Administration Building might be just another ten-story building housing a bank or an insurance company. Proposals to retrofit and repurpose Parker Center were entertained but found to be impractical and costly, and the building was demolished in 2019.

That demolition might be viewed as a punctuation mark on the end of an era. Before I retired from the LAPD ten years ago, I had few occasions to visit the current headquarters building, so I'm unaware if it contains a press room. I doubt it does, as the very idea of someone like Jacoby, or any reporter, having unfettered access to the place is unthinkable today. The truth is that there *are* no more reporters like Jacoby, whose current heirs in the trade would, in the current fashion of chrono-chauvinism, surely regard him and his contemporaries as unsophisticated embarrassments.

Jacoby attended a two-year college before embarking on his reporting career, and I would be surprised if any of the men (they were all men) with whom he shared the Parker Center press room all those years had received any more education than he had. Like many of the cops among whom he circulated, Jacoby was a military veteran and proudly working-class, harboring not a trace of ambition to insert himself among the elites in the city's government and entertainment classes.

How things do change. The addition of women's names to the masthead of today's newspapers is of course a welcome development, but accompanying it has been the transformation of the news business from a trade in which a man like Jake Jacoby was viewed as an ideal to one whose practitioners would spurn anyone so uneducated and rough around the edges as he. The term "reporter" has given way to "journalist," the path to which title leads not through the military or years spent on the police beat, but through elite universities and graduate schools.

As "reporters" became "journalists," they grew detached from and even dismissive of the people they covered. Whereas on any given night during his long career Jake Jacoby might have been found knocking back a few highballs at one of the downtown L.A. saloons frequented by LAPD and sheriff detectives, few of today's journalists would deign to so lower themselves.

And today, truth be told, few cops would welcome them if they did. Buffeted by years of hostile and at times dishonest coverage in the media, most cops have come to view the press as a dangerous adversary. In Los Angeles, this adversarial relationship was cemented with the March 1991 arrest of Rodney King, who was roughly subdued by LAPD officers at the end of a car chase in the San Fernando Valley. The fashionable narrative adopted in the media and repeated ad nauseam was that King was the victim of rough treatment that blacks typically received at the hands of the LAPD, treatment that was at last exposed when the incident was captured on tape by a nearby resident with a handheld video camera, at the time still a rarity.

There was no room in the narrative to disclose the fact that a local television news station had selectively and provocatively edited the tape, omitting those portions leading up to the moment when officers began striking King with batons. Nor was there room in the narrative for a discussion of changes to LAPD use-of-force policy that had abandoned the use of carotid neck restraints in favor of metal batons, with which officers were literally trained to break the bones of resisting suspects.

Absent this crucial information, public expectation grew that the four officers charged with beating King would be convicted when they stood trial in 1992. When the jurors viewed the unedited tape of King's arrest, and when they heard evidence that had been suppressed in the media for a year, they acquitted three of the officers and failed to reach a unanimous verdict on the fourth. With the expectations of convictions so thoroughly dashed, it came as no surprise that days of rioting in Los Angeles promptly followed, resulting in dozens of deaths, thousands of injuries, and more than $1 billion in property damage from fires and looting.

Even after the verdicts and rioting, even after two of the accused officers were convicted of civil rights violations in a federal trial (the two others were acquitted), the media narrative remained largely unchallenged. Only with the 1997 publication of *Official Negligence*, by former *Washington Post* reporter Lou Cannon, was the narrative exposed as the incomplete version of events it was. In nearly seven hundred pages of his meticulously researched book, Cannon, a biographer of Ronald Reagan and a newspaperman of the old school, explored every element of the Rodney King affair—his arrest, the relevant local politics, the officers' state and federal trials, and the riots—bringing to light facts ignored, negligently or willingly, by the local and national media.

But "progressive" narratives die hard, and the LAPD's reputation as a racist institution persists today, owing largely to the coverage it receives from Southern California's dominant news outlet, the *Los Angeles Times*. The *Times*'s antipathy for law enforcement in general and the LAPD in particular has been openly displayed on its pages for years, even long before the Rodney King affair, and its writers and editors seem to exult in the reporting of stories damaging to the department's reputation. Recognizing this is not to say that the LAPD, or any police agency, should be immune from examination and criticism when warranted, and over the years it has indeed been beset by a number of scandals great and small. But when the *Los Angeles Times* turns a blind eye to the realities of crime in Los Angeles, one cannot help but suspect that facts inconsonant with the narrative, as in the Rodney King affair, are deliberately being concealed from readers.

The *Los Angeles Times* is fond of reporting on the demographic disparities between those stopped, questioned, and arrested by the LAPD and the city's overall population. "LAPD Searches Blacks and Latinos More," reads the *Times*'s headline from a typical story of the genre, this one from October 2019, "But They're Less Likely to Have Contraband than Whites." In the story, as in so many others like it, little or passing attention is paid to the actual demographics of crime in the city, which are heavily skewed toward black and Latino offenders. Blacks make up 8 percent of L.A.'s population, yet they commit 41 percent of the city's violent crimes, 39 percent of its homicides, and 50 percent of its robberies. These numbers offend the sensibilities of the writers and editors at the *Times*, just as similar numbers from any city one can name offend those of its media elites. On those rare occasions when these statistics are mentioned at all, in the L.A. *Times* or any major daily, they are buried deep within the story.

Not only are the racial realities of crime largely ignored in the *Los Angeles Times*, but in 2020 the paper engaged in a sackcloth-and-ashes campaign for the expiation of its sins in having reported on those very realities nearly forty years earlier. In a September 2020 editorial, the *Times* issued a groveling apology for a story that ran in July 1981 under the headline, "Marauders from Inner City Prey on L.A.'s Suburbs." The story described the trend, which continues to this day, of gang members ranging afield from inner-city Los Angeles to commit crimes in middle- and upper-class suburbs, "sometimes with senseless savagery."

According to the editorial, the story

> reinforced pernicious stereotypes that Black and Latino Angelenos were thieves, rapists and killers. It sensationalized and pathologized the struggles of poor families and painted residents of South L.A. with a broad brush. It quoted police and prosecutors unskeptically and implied that more aggressive policing and harsher judicial sentencing were the only effective responses to crime.

Nowhere in the editorial did the *Times* say that anything in the earlier story was untrue, only that it "lacked nuance and context." If the realities of crime are to be obfuscated in such a manner, how much more difficult will it be to address crime when and where it occurs? In Los Angeles and elsewhere, violent crime is most often committed by and against those very minorities whom today's elite journalists would cocoon in ignorance within layers of "nuance and context."

Oddly, the crisis in today's journalism may have been best described by *New York Times* columnist David Brooks, who as a graduate of the University of Chicago is at once a chronicler of the problem and an example of it. In an August 2023 column, he wrote of American society's stratification into layers divided between the elites and everyone else, with the former having little to do with the latter save for lecturing people on how better to behave. "When I began my journalism career in Chicago in the 1980s," he wrote, "there were still some old crusty working-class guys around the newsroom. Now we're not only a college-dominated profession; we're an elite-college-dominated profession."

Those elites, sheltered from the effects of the policies they advocate, have contempt for those who neither share their strata of society nor aspire to, none more so than police officers. Jake Jacoby was one of those "old crusty working-class guys" whose absence from the newsroom Brooks today laments but will not, lest he alienate himself from his fellow elites, bestir himself to attract to the profession.

I very much doubt that Jake Jacoby, in his long career covering murder and mayhem in Southern California, lost even a minute's sleep fretting over a lack of "nuance and context" in anything he wrote. The journalism trade would do well to see his kind return but, alas, the elites occupying today's newsrooms would never allow it.

PART FIVE: FOREIGN AFFAIRS

INSIDE THE WOKE BBC

BY IAN GREGORY

Let me start with a mistake. In early 2023, I was due to speak at a university debating society about the British Broadcasting Corporation (BBC). Given my fierce disdain for the wayward broadcaster, I relished the prospect. But then, shortly before the debate, I was startled to find that I was down to speak *in favor* of the BBC. I mulled it over. And then decided to go ahead, persuaded by John Stuart Mill's dictum that "he who knows only his own side of the case knows little of that."

Despite the debating society not being well disposed to the BBC, I won handsomely. Perhaps I spoke well. But more important is that I knew that there are many good arguments for the BBC. This is crucial because the BBC's critics condemn themselves to being ignored, if they appear blind to these strengths.

What are they? Having spent a decade working inside the BBC, I know it has talented staff. I can speak of their efforts toward fairness, such as using stopwatches on political programmes to ensure equal time for each participant. There are also moments when its journalism is brilliant: The winning argument at the debate concerned a BBC investigation into China's persecution of its Uighur population, reporting that caused exquisite discomfort to the country's dictators. There is also the BBC's exceptional natural history programming anchored by David Attenborough.

I also know that broadcasters can never please everyone. Not all perspectives can be heard. Not all issues covered. So why, despite all that, do I feel that the BBC is becoming ever more biased?

First, its blindness. For, just as its critics are prone to confirmation bias, so are its staff. This human weakness is made harder to avoid because the BBC recruits in its own image. Those from outside the progressive orthodoxy keep their heads down. In editorial meetings, this leftwing mindset is sitting all around you. The staff's lives revolve around like-minded souls. Try as they might, they do not naturally come across alternative stories or more varied interviewees.

Increasingly, this mindset leaks into the coverage. In 2022, moments after Boris Johnson had decided against seeking to become prime minister again, a BBC News presenter declared on air: "Am I allowed to be this gleeful? Well I am." That was artless.

A demonstration of arrogance came a few months later when the BBC's highest-paid presenter—Gary Lineker—took to Twitter to denounce the government's key proposal for reducing immigration. Lineker said that the policy—flying illegal migrants to Africa while their claims were processed—was "immeasurably cruel." He accused the government of using Nazi-style language. The BBC's top manager, its director-general Tim Davie, knew that Lineker's remarks were so politically charged that he had to act. He suspended Lineker.

But then the BBC's staff unwittingly confirmed their commitment to Lineker's point of view. They went on strike. There followed a stand-off when management could have reshaped the BBC toward impartiality. But management blinked. The presenter was more important than the corporation's reputation. So QED: The BBC remains biased.

After losing against Lineker, the BBC's management gave up policing its presenters. Their main countryside presenter, Chris Packham, was so emboldened by this weakness that he told the media that climate protestors were "too timid," and could consider "blowing up an oil refinery." Impervious to the irony, Packham also threatened legal action against the government over its net zero plans.

Let us take another perspective. The BBC can tell you the ethnic breakdown of its staff, their sexualities, disabilities, and social class—even down to whether they had free school meals as children. But the one metric which would expose the BBC's partiality—its political affiliations—is not counted. Why? Because the answer would be embarrassing.

Why does this matter? The BBC is the overwhelmingly dominant media voice in Britain. Its broadcast and online news services are used by 76 percent of the British population. Its nearest competitor is ITV with 38 percent. This means that the BBC controls the contours of acceptable policy. Its editorial decisions starve issues it dislikes of publicity. For those it favors, it acts as a launch pad.

Where would the name recognition of Greta Thunberg, the Swedish environmental activist, be without the BBC's avalanche of coverage? A teenage idealist evokes sympathy, so helps to push the cause. The BBC's cause.

By contrast, it vilifies those it disagrees with—not least rightwing politicians with strong working-class support. For instance, the BBC has characterised the Italian prime minister, Giorgia Meloni, as "Italy's first far-right prime minister since Benito Mussolini." Why this bracketing with the fascism of a century ago? Meloni's skillful leadership has made her the most popular leader in the European Union—but not at the BBC.

And what about Donald Trump? The BBC's contempt has oozed from its programs just as from MSNBC's. Every accusation made against him breathlessly reported. Journalistic scepticism about anonymous sources disregarded. No thought given to the vested interests behind the allegations. This was not an exhibition of the BBC's mission of holding power to account—although Trump had much to be held account for. No, this was propaganda—campaigning designed to create derision.

Those watching the BBC would have assumed that, in terms of mental capacity, Trump was so impaired as to warrant his removal from office. But not Joe Biden. As for corruption allegations? The BBC gave Biden a virtually free pass. The corporation rarely strays from Democratic talking points. No surprise when its journalists portray *The New York Times* as an impartial source.

Just as Trump's success blind-sided the left-leaning BBC, so did the Brexit vote. Over the following years, the BBC enthusiastically reported every establishment attempt to dilute the referendum outcome. It also displayed its bias through proxies: Its producers chose endless interviewees whom they knew would deride Brexit supporters as stupid bigots.

The BBC's editorial choices promote all the key tenets of progressive thinking. Take the Black Lives Matter movement. The death of George Floyd dominated BBC output not just in news but in sports for month after month. Yet he died in the U.S.A. One man in an often-brutal world. Hundreds die in other countries without the BBC even mentioning their fate. So why did the BBC latch onto this story, giving it a moral halo redolent of its coverage of Nelson Mandela? Why so much effort into fanning the moral outrage? Because it fit the BBC's narrative—that Britain is an inherently racist nation. The reality is that, compared with its European neighbors, Britain is a tolerant nation.

This tolerance includes attitudes toward sexual minorities. The success of the campaign to legalize gay marriage meant that some protest groups were in need of a new cause to fundraise on. They chose transgender rights and sold training programs to Big Business and government departments. They gave awards to the most "progressive" organisations. The BBC joined this competition for kudos—at one stage its staff training material declared the existence of 150 genders.

Yet the impact on the BBC was more than mere virtue signalling. The number of transgender story lines in BBC programs spiralled, despite the very small number of transgender adults. That had an impact on impressionable minds. There has since been a vast increase in the number of young women "transitioning," with life-changing consequences. The BBC has responsibility for this. Vulnerable teenagers, wrestling with who they are, need support, not indoctrination.

Then there is climate change. Here, the BBC has issued guidance to its staff warning them about the dangers of interviewing "deniers." Yet who are these bogeymen? The phrase denier could be used to describe someone who refuses to accept the physics that CO2 acts as a "greenhouse gas." Yet this is a vanishingly small number among Britain's intelligentsia.

What is going on here? The slur was needed by the BBC to justify excluding interviewees who would bring nuance to this critical debate. How capable is humanity at adapting? Should we focus on carbon reduction or removal? What are the costs and benefits of the various technologies? The BBC rarely moved into these details, preferring the superficial argument about whether we are doing "enough."

All these matters are of genuine importance. Yet instead of treating them as issues worthy of journalistic scrutiny, the BBC retreats into campaigning. Look at the protest movements it blatantly promotes. All the dominant campaigns in the U.K. over the past five years—Black Lives Matter, Extinction Rebellion, and Just Stop Oil—owe their existence to the BBC's launching them and sustaining them with blanket coverage. Their demonstrations do not just get reported but trailed beforehand. It helps with turnout.

The BBC has no problem with the shallowness of these protestors' arguments and stunts—one even glued his face to a road. High on narcissism, low on evidence, these are middle-class movements demanding vague "action" to deal with "existential crises." Government ministers working to solve these issues get denigrated by BBC interviewers as uncaring. Protestors get the kid gloves treatment.

That is, unless they are working-class protestors raising concerns about out-of-control immigration or the unique pressures they faced during the Covid lockdowns. They are treated with disdain, or simply ignored. The BBC did not treat the Covid waves as a chance to probe the evidence base or question the assault on liberties. It acted as cheerleader for the controlling elite's view.

Great journalism is perpetually curious. Yet today, the BBC preaches. Its one-sided coverage of intrinsically complex problems like race relations, sexual identity, and climate change demonises wrong-thinkers. Its emoting does not encourage nuanced adult-to-adult debate and the search for reasoned compromises. Instead, it skews and trivialises the discussion into playground politics. It catastrophises instead of offering context.

The hyping of these issues means that other worthy matters are squeezed out of its coverage. Will falling fertility rates harm Britain more than global warming? Does the country care more about pride in nation or pride in minority sexualities? Is it the media's progressive hectoring that is turning people toward conspiracy theorists?

The BBC gets away with its narrow progressive output because it can. It is effectively unaccountable, the judge and jury of its own complaints process. So why bother? Complaining about it is as much use as waving a placard denouncing Putin in Red Square.

The BBC has immense power through selecting interviewees, and then choosing what they are asked about. All of Britain's elite knows that the BBC has the capacity to bestow on them visibility and credibility. For scientists, business leaders, trade unionists, campaigners, and politicians, the BBC can make or break them. For a minister, alienating the BBC is career suicide. Governments know that the BBC will relentlessly attack whichever policies most offend progressive sensibilities.

This power is so great that Elon Musk had it wrong when he called the BBC state-controlled media. No, the BBC controls the state. It is state-*controlling* media. Even though the Conservative Party has been in power for more than a decade, levels of public spending and taxation have been pushed to record-breaking levels. On issues such as race, sexuality, and climate the BBC has been pushing the government around.

So, to quote Lenin, "What is to be done?" The scary reality is that nobody controls the BBC. It is a self-perpetuating organism run by people who enjoy being powerful. But the corporation does have an Achille's heel: its finances. Its billions come from an unpopular licence fee. Even those who do not watch the BBC's output have to buy one to in order to watch their TV. Enforcement officers visit homes to ensure that the fee has been paid and, because the door is usually opened by a busy mum, 76 percent of those convicted of non-payment are women.

Yet there is a solution to this abhorrent sex discrimination. Defiant pensioners. Until 2020 those over seventy-five did not have to pay the licence fee. Now they do. Or should. For, hundreds of thousands of the elderly have not paid. And yet the BBC has felt too scared to take a single one of them to court. There is a *de facto* amnesty. Which in turn is ripe for being turned into a signal to the elderly that they do not have to pay. This is a door that can be levered open until it turns into a floodgate.

Such a hemorrhaging of cash is the only way to wake up the woke at the BBC. Their jobs threatened, its managers might stop ridiculing concerns about bias. This bias is warping Britain's politics. Every day that the BBC drifts from institutional neutrality it becomes a greater threat to British democracy.

CANADA: THE MEDIA AS STATE COLLABORATOR

BY DAVID SOLWAY

Having spent several years in the early part of my writing career free-lancing for the Canadian Broadcasting Corporation (CBC) in music and public affairs, and maintaining ties thereafter with various CBC personalities, journalists, and interviewers, I eventually came to real-ize that the organization was not politically innocent, as I had assumed in my salad days. It became increasingly clear the extent to which the news was curated and shaped. Complicity with certain tenets and policies of government pervaded an institution that was, after all, the heavily subsidized state broadcaster.

In the words of the Honorable Brian Peckford, former premier of Newfoundland and Labrador and the last living signatory to the 1982 patriation of the Canadian Constitution,

> the CBC dominates the media landscape, thanks to an annual one billion two hundred million-dollar grant from the government. The public broadcaster is a leftist propaganda organization that never gives a fair hearing to conservative, small-government voices on their news and public affairs programs

—or in Twitter parlance, it is an organ of a "state-funded media," a fact routinely denied by the Canadian prime minister.

Upping the ante, dissident journalist Rodney Palmer testified before the National Citizens Inquiry held in April and May 2023 that "Canada's public broadcaster has morphed into...the type that is normally found in dictatorships." In any event, there can be no doubt that the corporate mission of the state broadcaster is to support the fortunes of the left-oriented Liberal Party ("the 'natural governing party') irrespective of which party is in ascendance at any given time. Liberal governments were in office in Ottawa for over two-thirds of the period between 1900 and 2000, and for approximately 60 percent of the current century.

With only a handful of exceptions, such as *Rebel News* and a clutch of smaller outriders, the communications infrastructure in this country has become almost entirely partisan. As Peckford notes, the CBC is not alone in serving as a bastion of political and ideological orthodoxy. The mainstream press is not far behind in its effort to influence the cognitive profile of the nation. Today, the two entities, national media and the Liberal government, are joined at the hip, much as National Public Radio and almost the entire media industry in the U.S. are extensions of the Democrat Party.

A hostile media ecosphere abets the forced sterilization of the classical principles of free speech, the rule of law, and representative government, helping to advance a series of repressive bills making their way through a clock-punching Parliament and Senate, such as C-4 (asserting gender fluidity), C-12 (forcing net-zero emissions), C-21 (gun control), and C-11 (limiting internet access), the latter passed into law on April 27, 2023.

Media also works to prepare the public for the deliberate destruction of the energy sector, dumping on the Alberta oil sands and petroleum industry, in line with the government's proposed "Just Transition" or Impact Assessment Act—colloquially known as the "No More Pipelines Act," a clear infringement on provincial jurisdiction. It attempts to soft-pedal the impending rollout of digital ID surveillance technology in complete lockstep with government. The effort to accelerate media censorship of dissenting voices is ongoing.

The conservative advocacy group CitizenGO reports that the Liberal government has devoted more than a billion dollars to research for finding new ways to censor content critical of the administration, such as "media moderation tools" that would combat "misinformation," "hate," and "racism"—ironically, the nameplate feature of the media itself.

The only patches of accurate information one can rely on are reports on traffic conditions, bridge closures, road accidents, and ephemeral items of merely local interest. Even the weather bulletins are surreptitiously crafted to promote the myth of "global warming" and the propagation of carbon levies, while the accounts of forest fires are slanted toward the "global warming" hoax. The strategy of massaging public naivety seems to have been largely effective. What Paul Rutherford in *The Making of the Canadian Media*, a welcome addition to the meagre literature on Canadian press history, called "the golden age of the Press" is no more.

Canada's first mass media outlets during the nineteenth century and up to the aftermath of the Great War were "the spokesmen of democracy," glorifying the common man. Rutherford cites, among several exemplars, *The Vancouver Sun* for November, 26, 1920, which praised "the composite public mind [as] keen, judicial, and in the long run always fair." The press at the time "popularized the mores of the urban middle class." All this has changed. Writing in 1978, Rutherford saw the print on the wall. "All in all, the multimedia have encouraged a climate of opinion hostile to the Old Dominion and Confederation." He worried that "an upsurge of authoritarianism could well undermine the democratic imperative and transform the multimedia into an elite institution."

Fifty years later his fears have come to pass. The "common man" is no longer respected, but exploited and misled. The urban middle class now veers consistently left. News has been supplanted by narrative. Reality is not so much justly mediated as deceptively media'd. The paper press often reads like a government document. The same is true of radio and TV broadcasting where discussion formats are distressingly often subtle forms of political advocacy, of persuading viewers to, as it were, ride the snake. To take a few resonant examples:

A CBC report for March 27, 2017, one of many, stated that the majority of First Nations tribes rejected oil pipelines crossing their territories. The truth was otherwise. A non-profit Canada Action study for November 25, 2020, showed that Native support for a Trans Mountain pipeline was, in fact, rather strong. In a June 12, 2023, summit, the National Coalition of Chiefs (NCC) met to form a pro-development partnership to "Defeat On-Reserve Poverty," to cooperate with Canada's National Resource Industry, and to support major project developments. For the indigenous community, a revenue windfall was at stake in pipeline construction, casinos, inns, fruit and vegetable markets, and golf courses, which the majority of Native bands were unwilling to let slip. To put it mildly, the media networks were not interested in drawing attention to an event which runs counter to the "renewables" mantra they have been tapped to promote.

The Osoyoos Indian Band in the Okanagan Valley of British Columbia is a case in point. Under the enlightened leadership of Chief Clarence Louis, it generates more revenue than it receives from the federal government, thanks to a vigorous spirit of entrepreneurship in eco-tourism, residential development, job creation, agriculture, vineyards, and a successful winery. "People think that economic development or being business people is new to native people. We were the first entrepreneurs here," Chief Louis has said. One would never have known this from the media.

Anyone who watched the news programs or read the dailies during the Trucker Freedom Convoy in the winter of 2022 was informed that the truckers' quite legitimate protest against the vaccine mandates was an illegal insurrection, resembling the January 6 canard in the U.S. The truckers were held responsible for what were obvious false flag operations—desecrating statues, waving Confederate and Nazi flags, attempting arson, and the like. Russian money was involved. The truckers' bouncy castles set up to entertain their children were treated like military pillboxes. This was not "news" but a blatant and reprehensible exercise in the dissemination of state propaganda justifying the acts of professional liars and paid provocateurs. The government's invoking of the Emergencies Act, specifically designed to meet a foreign invasion or deal with a natural cataclysm, was deemed appropriate and justified by the media. To make matters worse, names of donors to the trucker fund were leaked, some of whom found their bank accounts frozen in government reprisal.

The real story is told in Tamara Lich's *Hold the Line: My Story from the Heart of the Freedom Convoy,* a book written by the courageous Métis grandmother at the heart of the protest, including details about her atrocious treatment in jail and an abusive prosecutor with a vendetta. As she writes, "when it comes to a Métis grandmother, with no criminal record at all, peacefully protesting in the nation's capital to uphold Charter freedoms, there is no catch and release." According to publisher Ezra Levant, the book was smeared by Justin Trudeau's Liberals even before it was officially launched. The media accordingly painted Lich as a diehard insurgent or, when it became less acceptable to proclaim her *non grata,* sought to portray her as a weak apologist who, as the CBC put it, "downplay[ed] her involvement as one of the protest's leading voices."

Nothing could have been further from the truth. Lich was unapologetic. "We exposed the Liberal-friendly mainstream media for its agenda and lies," revealing how "the CBC, the *Toronto Star,* CTV, the *Globe and Mail* and many others were working to vilify peaceful protesters in service to a corrupt prime minister who writes their bailout cheques... We exposed the banking system [and] we finally broke the fever of the pandemic restrictions."

True to form, Canada's largest newspaper, the *Toronto Star,* with a circulation of 2.4 million copies per week, did its utmost to further the government's draconian vaccine mandate, suggesting that it might be time "for our political leaders to make vaccination against Covid the law." Its opinion writers denounced vaccine resisters as "lazy and irresponsible" and lobbied for vaccine passports, in accord with the government's false soteriological narrative, or doctrine of salvation. As a result of the collapse of journalism, the public is largely unaware of the fusion between state and media, incapable of seeing that the press has been willingly co-opted by the state.

The 2023 scam concerning the funneling of Chinese Communist Party (CCP) money to the Trudeau election campaign is another case in point. Mandarin-bloc influence inside the Liberal corridors has been a fixture for years. The yuans have been piling up. As *Rebel News* for March 6, 2023 reported, "According to a leak from Canada's intelligence agency CSIS, a trio of journalists from mainstream outlets like the *Toronto Star*, *Globe and Mail* and CBC"—which Canadian blogger Robert Orr cleverly dubs the Xi B Xi—"were all working as 'mentors' for the Trudeau Foundation when it received donations linked to the Chinese Communist Party." Without exposure by a CSIS whistleblower, none of this would have been known.

For the lackey media-at-large, aside from a few token hems and haws and some perfunctory posturing, there was nothing to see here; time to move on. The media had become a collaborator of the CCP in its attempt to influence Canadian affairs and choreograph electoral results. People's Party of Canada leader Maxime Bernier's political platform, unique among Canada's federal parties, affirms that "a free press that reports objectively on current events…is a fundamental pillar of a democratic society." How so basic a function can be doubted or scanted beggars the imagination.

These are only a modicum of instances showing how the media provides cover for government malfeasance, fostering its deliberate policies of managed decline, if not controlled demolition, and loyally pumping out the state narrative.

As Paul Rutherford writes in a follow-up volume, *A Victorian Authority: The Daily Press in Late Nineteenth-Century Canada*, there was always a connection with the political establishment, but the relationship allowed for considerable press freedom. Major papers like *The Globe* and *The Mail and Empire* (which later merged to form *The Globe and Mail*) and *The Evening Star* (renamed the *Toronto Star*) had been instrumental in forging a sense of national cohesion.

No longer. The media has now turned against its own founding principles. Its presumed objective of speaking truth to power, reporting faithfully, and holding government accountable has been ruthlessly expunged. This for two reasons: its having been bought by lavish government subsidies, including more than $600 million to the paper press and, as noted, double that sum to the CBC; and its voluntary adoption of a "social justice" or "woke" ideological crusade.

It is undeniable that a corrupt media predicated on, as a reliable servant of government doctrine and policy, is critical to the advancement of predatory control over society. The separation between State and Press (as majuscule collectives) is crucial to the evolution of representative government. It is a relatively recent historical development, dating back to legislation passed by the Swedish parliament on December 2, 1766, supporting the freedom of the press and freedom of information. Perhaps the strongest defense of press freedom from state censorship in the English-speaking world is to be found in John Milton's 1644 pamphlet *Areopagitica*, wherein he argued that "truth and understanding are not such wares as to be monopoliz'd and traded in by tickets and statutes."

The principle is rooted in the First Amendment of the American Constitution: "Congress shall make no law...abridging the freedom of speech, or the press." In Canada, the concept is entrenched—theoretically, as it turns out—in the Constitution's Charter of Rights and Freedoms, specifically Sections 2(a), 6(2)(a), and 7, which guarantee the "fundamental freedoms," namely, among others, freedom of conscience, freedom of thought, freedom of mobility, and freedom of speech and the press. But the Charter's force has grown weaker with time as whole sections have been rendered null and void by the Liberal hegemon and touted by its media handmaiden.

As Tucker Carlson observed in a 2023 interview with *Real Clear Politics*, the media is "the Praetorian Guard of a small group of powerful people" who should be treated "with maximum contempt." We need to remember that the media is not muzzled, as in some totalitarian countries; rather, the formula of operational mendacity is eagerly embraced by the contemporary media consortium, which is nothing short of a game changer. Of course, the media lie can be inwardly resisted by a savvy citizenry. Perhaps a considerable portion of the public in the U.S.S.R. understood that *Pravda* and *Izvestia* were merely arms of Party propaganda, a condition which the Russians called *vranyo*, discussed in David Shipler's bestselling *Russia: Broken Idols, Solemn Dreams* and Mikael Klintman's *Knowledge Resistance: How We Avoid Insight from Others.*

Vranyo refers to lying in such a way that everyone knows that everyone else knows a lie is being told and knows that the liar knows that he knows. Klintman calls it "lousy lying" and observes that this form of lying may be construed as a power move, "of not having to submit to truth and facts...one of the gambits in which the Left is adept." News was often regarded as nothing but a species of official lard and hokum, which led eventually to the emergence of *samizdat*, the clandestine distribution of literature banned by the state.

In many Western democracies, however, and especially in Canada, the propaganda effect is far more insidious. Although a well-known leftwing apologist, Michael Parenti's observation in *Inventing Reality: The Politics of News Media* is apt: "the structures of control" within the media are "less visible and more subtle, not monolithic yet hierarchical...essentially undemocratic," and as distorting as "the institutionalized formal censorship we might expect of a government-controlled press." He might have said: even more distorting, as a majority appears to assume that the press is free and impartial. *Vranyo* is inoperative. People are therefore easily deluded and rendered compliant, dupes of the managerial elite. Unlike their Russian counterparts, the majority of Canadians—and Americans—concede their will and belief to the indoctrinating power of the media. Canadians and Americans have been inching ever closer to becoming nations of credulous "news" consumers, stubbornly refusing to understand that the media is neither disinterested nor objective.

We recall how Justin Trudeau's mockery of those who opposed vaccine mandates as "women-haters, racists, and science deniers" was dutifully bull-horned by the media and uncritically swallowed, as polls indicated, by more than two-thirds of the Canadian electorate, a representative proportion of a media-submissive population. Polling by Maru Voice Canada, a leading online market research firm, for January 2022 showed that over half of these respondents agreed to short-term jail sentences for vaccine refuseniks, and that skeptics should be denied healthcare. Such numbers are deeply dispiriting. The media did its job, whipping the public into a frenzy. Like its political comrades, the media malingers in the belly of the whale, "bleached by gastric acids," as Patrick O'Neill writes in *The Only Certain Freedom*. No matter. Canadians continue to park their trust in media shills, largely oblivious to the sordid game being played at their prohibitive expense.

In *The Origins of Totalitarianism*, Hannah Arendt forcefully articulates the issue: "The ideal subject of totalitarian rule is not the convinced Nazi or the dedicated communist, but people for whom the distinction between fact and fiction, true and false, no longer exists." One might say that the Canadian electorate has been conditioned by the media to believe that *falsehood is truth*, without scrupling to ferret out the facts for themselves or exercise rudimentary discernment and good sense.

Writing in *The Cochrane Eagle*, one of the few, reputable, small-town newspapers remaining in the country, industrial technologist, army veteran, and political commentator Tex Leugner laments that the problem with Canada is the people in it. Major Russ Cooper, director of Canadian Citizens for Charter Rights and Freedom (C3RF), is of the same mind. "In essence, we are seeing a top-down imposition of radical, non-traditional narratives on the fat, dumb, and happy." Despite Tamara Lich's hopeful and endearing belief that Canada is not a divided country, that "we all want our freedoms," that "we are all the same nation," and that we will unite against tyranny, the media is having none of it. Neither is the preponderance of the electorate.

As Canada's unofficial ombudsman Brian Peckford warns, "We have not figured out that as democracies mature, more and more citizen involvement is necessary in order to keep that democracy, not less. Canadians refuse to see how precarious our situation really is." This is not surprising. The media, cloistered in its privileges, sees its readers and viewers as a rabble susceptible to its occlusions.

In Canada's system of parliamentary democracy, there are three branches of government: the executive, which prepares bills to submit to parliament; the legislative, which holds the executive accountable for its actions; and the judicial, which interprets laws and ensures legal and constitutional authority. All have been compromised. In addition, under Liberal suzerainty, a fourth branch has now been added *de facto* to the system: the media, which seeks like the other branches to regulate public life and consolidate the role of government.

As the fourth branch of a decadent parliamentary apparatus, it has been resoundingly successful. The media has now become a department of the state.

THE CBC: FROM CROWN JEWEL TO JACOBINS

BY ELIZABETH NICKSON

The Beast

Renegade governmental organizations are virtually impossible to rein in, especially if they have careened off the rails into destructive action. Take, for the sake of argument, the FBI or Environmental Protection Agency in the U.S., or the World Health Organization and the United Nations internationally, or the plethora of sovereign and sub-sovereign health ministries that went AWOL during Covid. If threatened, a throng of defenders rise, vocal to the point of shrill, defending the original idea, refusing to look at the slavering beast all that public money hath wrought.

"Reform or die," says prime minister after president after premier. Nodding subservience is followed by...nothing. Commissions are formed, recommendations are made. Cosmetic changes ensue. Like rogue elephants they continue to roam the heights of the culture, braying and stomping and breaking things. Power, once acquired, needs to be wrenched from bleeding hands.

In Canada, that raging elephant is the Canadian Broadcasting Corporation. Founded in 1936, at last count, the CBC sprawls across the country in twenty-seven over-the-air TV stations, eighty-eight radio stations, a flotilla of websites, podcasts, streaming TV, and multiple satellite radio stations. Its mandate is high-flown, to connect the multiple city-states of the country, its frozen north and isolated rural communities via dozens of offices big and small. It broadcasts in English, French, and eight indigenous languages.

The CBC's Toronto headquarters, finished in 1993, was a state-ment of extreme optimism at a time when the corporation was widely loved. Designed by Philip Johnson, its cost $381 million. It is de-con-structivist in form, a symbol of the CBC's purpose, which is to re-con-ceive Canada's founding as racist and the country in need of radical reform led by itself. Its orthogonal grid is "interrupted by skewed ele-ments," its interior dominated by a green elevator shaft set at an angle to the building grid. Outside, a forbidding Soviet box, windows are outlined in CBC red. Inside, it's confusing, echoing, and replete with empty studios. Despite effulgent funding, the aura of failure wears on those still employed. They don't understand why they are no longer astride the culture.

A behemoth, it demands $1.24 billion of direct subsidy from the government every year, and rakes in several hundred million more through licensing, advertising, and production subsidy. It eats up, say some analysts, half the media dollars spent in the country, yet is watched on its twenty-seven TV stations by fewer than 5 percent of Canadians. Its news outlets perform worse. Only 1.75 percent watch CBC news on broadcast channels or cable. *The National*, its star sup-pertime news show in Toronto, is watched by fewer than half a mil-lion people, while private-sector competitors in the same city crest at 1 million or even 2 million.

In June 2023, the editorial board of Canada's long-time national newspaper, *The Globe and Mail*, put its rather large bear paw down and suggested shuttering CBC TV entirely, and focusing on digital and radio, which are relatively successful. The editorial board (acting in its own institutional interest), pointed out that digital advertising for CBC should be halted because a subsidized CBC should not eat up ad dollars in a tight market. The editorial board also stated that more than 24 million CBC digital visitors a month is substantial. It is not. The media is undergoing explosive growth in every country; it is only legacy media that is not growing. Routinely in the U.S., popular digital sites host tens of millions of visitors a day, and more than a billion a year. Using that metric, the CBC reaches about 10 percent of the available digital audience.

Most Canadians agree with *The Globe and Mail*. In fact, in mid-2023, 62 percent of Canadians wanted it shut down, saying they would vote for conservatives if they promised to do so. Not reined in, not given less taxpayer money, not privatized, but shut down, its many buildings, its wealth of equipment sold, and its employees scattered to the winds. Among some 30 to 40 percent, the mother corporation (as it calls itself) is actively hated, loathed. When Pierre Poilievre, the popular conservative candidate leader, promised to shut down the CBC, his audience rose for a prolonged standing ovation.

How did this jewel of Canadian culture which, for sixty years was held in near reverence by every sentient Canadian, come to this?

The Original Purpose

Public broadcasters, in general, engage in state-building, in national and cultural integration. They "provide social cement," they build bridges, "witness" and connect. Or are supposed to. They are meant to be free, in order to serve those without the funds for cable or streaming subscriptions. In Ireland, Raidió Teilifís Éireann (RTE) provides an alternative to the deluge of British programming, those in Nordic countries promote "equality, solidarity and belonging," and in Australia, the Australian Broadcasting Corporation (ABC) sets itself against the dominance of wicked corporatist freebooter Rupert Murdoch.

In Canada, the CBC is meant to provide a Canadian voice in a country where, as the old saw goes, Canadian culture is in a distinct minority. This purpose has been served well in French Canada, where Radio Canada (best said with a French accent) is widely loved and has managed to act as a beacon for Quebecois culture, an impressive amount of it created to flout, humiliate, and laugh at the *maudit Anglais* to the south, east, and west.

The digital and streaming explosion of the early aughts left the CBC flailing to catch up, and this is typically given as the reason its audience numbers are so poor. However, this is not the case for the CBC's radio stations which are the only division of the corporation that truly service small-city and rural Canada and can compete in an admitted fever of ever-expanding competition. Their drive-time shows can reach as many as 20 percent of the audience, and are often in first place in the ratings.

There are other rather more convincing arguments for its decline. CBC hosts on radio and TV have historically been beloved figures. Today, few Canadians could name one of them; personalities seemingly are not wanted at the CBC anymore but Canadians still love them. Canadian YouTubers routinely attract hundreds of thousands of viewers and, in Jordan Peterson's case, tens of millions, trouncing the "mother corporation" by orders of magnitude. Podcasts are popular, but half of those listened to in Canada by rightwing Americans. Which indicates that, even given its radio successes, the corporation has lost touch with Canadians. It simply does not have news or entertainment product strong enough to compete in the new marketplace. And, as the proliferation of new media in Canada proves, its editorial policy is so backward, almost every single digital opportunity has been missed.

In contrast to received opinion—which is that the culprit is the explosion in digital and streaming outlets—the answer to the corporation's distress is far simpler, and far more reparable. A series of bad political decisions have been made by policy chiefs who craft the corporation's editorial policy every year. Reputedly that secretive department costs taxpayer $180 million annually, but it is as closeted as the Kremlin and few even admit it exists. But it does, and it is those policy setters who have created the wholesale repudiation of the CBC via a rough-shod political brinksmanship that was meant entirely to remake Canada in a fresh, socialist image. And to destroy the one political party standing in the way.

Political Headwinds and Terrible Decisions

The Canadian public's loss of affection for **the CBC** began with their twenty-seven-year-long attack on Prime Minister Brian Mulroney, which started in the late 1980s with his election and ended only in 2011 with his exoneration by the Oliphant decision, a commission forced by the media after repeated failed attempts to destroy Mulroney. The goal, it appears in retrospect, was not only to ruin Mulroney, who saw Canada as a potential capitalist titan using its vast natural resources, but to salt the earth so that no such animal could rise again. Like the later "Russian collusion" hoax employed against Donald Trump in the U.S., the Mulroney attacks were based on hate via creating a storm of noise and accusations, falsified evidence, and an egregious waste of taxpayer money. Like the Russia hoax, nothing was found. That was not the point. The point was to ruin Mulroney, deflect criticism, and silence conservative voices.

Mulroney, a brash-to-the-point-of-vulgar Irishman from Montreal, rode in on Ronald Reagan's coat tails with the North American Free Trade Agreement and the 1980s private-sector boom. Journalists in the Toronto-Ottawa-Montreal triangle hated him, and as an exhaustive study done at the time demonstrated, more than 90 percent of journalists in Canada were liberal or, more likely, socialist. In fact, as Barry Cooper and Lydia Miljan found in their 1993 book *Hidden Agendas: How Journalists Influence the News*, it was almost impossible to work in Canada's media as a conservative, unless you were tightly tied to the financial pages, and even then, if you had little to no profile as a columnist.

Immediately upon Mulroney's election, the CBC and the national newspaper, *The Globe and Mail*, went on the attack. One investigative reporter, Stevie Cameron, who worked for both, grabbed the beat and did not let go. What happened was a thorough-going illustration of a political hit job disguised as journalism.

Mulroney, possessed, it was thought, of an egregiously ambitious wife, was accused of taking a $300,000 cash bribe for awarding a 1988

Airbus contract. He had over his ten years in office acquired a "friend," Karlheinz Schreiber, a fixer/lobbyist who trolled capital cities for his clients. Schreiber, a native of Germany, was said to have promised Mulroney a job as a lobbyist when his ministership was over. In the end, this dubious choice in friends was the only charge that landed after twenty years of parallel investigations by the CBC and *The Globe and Mail*, a ten-year investigation by the Royal Canadian Mounted Police, several court cases, and finally a formal commission.

The CBC program *The Fifth Estate* produced nine documentaries trying to pin kickbacks on Mulroney, using as a principal source an accountant and friend of Schreiber who had spent time in Swiss, Italian, and American prisons. The newsmen were convinced by this man, Giorgio Pelossi, that Mulroney had a secret Swiss bank account in which he had allegedly stashed millions, and petitioned the Swiss government to release the evidence. Neither the millions nor the Swiss bank account were ever found.

Finally, Mulroney had had enough and sued the CBC for libel. He won and then won again on appeal. These two court cases and decades-long investigations cost the CBC $15 million. Publishers and editors—there were several books—allowed reporters to use dubious sources, contributing to the of one of the publishers, Key Porter Books. Schreiber, who was under deportation orders, told a *Fifth Estate* host *on air* that he would do anything not to be deported. The CBC ran with his "evidence" anyway.

Despite losing twice in court, the CBC continued its crusade and in 2010, twenty-two years after the Airbus contract was awarded, conservative Prime Minister Stephen Harper was forced to empanel a commission that cost the Canadian taxpayer another $14 million. Justice Oliphant found that "nothing inappropriate occurred during the meetings that Mr. Schreiber had with Mr. Mulroney."

The CBC even commissioned *Mulroney: The Opera*, a $3 million and $800,000 film supposed to be shown in theaters first and on the CBC second. According to columnist Brian Lilley, the film portrayed Mulroney as an "American wanna-be with no ethics and an unquenchable thirst for power." It was so terrible that not only did it not air on CBC, the CBC took its name off the disaster. Naturally, it was praised by *The Globe and Mail*.

During Steven Harper's prime ministership, the CBC led an attack on four nominally conservative senators who had claimed expenses in hometowns that they rarely visited. This was unfortunate, but a well-worn pattern. A few paid back those expenses—the largest bill was for $150,000—and three were criminally charged and acquitted, but not before their lives had been shredded. The "scandal" over relatively small sums was meant to counter the rising suspicion of Canadians that the CBC and the government had run amok with spending, and, in a masterful sleight of hand, proffered visible conservatives as punching bags. The "investigations" mirrored the attack on Mulroney and, as meant, affected the 2015 election, which was won by Justin Trudeau's Liberal Party.

By then, Canadians, particularly those right of center, were sharply aware that Liberal scandals, far more egregious in terms of money misallocated, were ignored or glossed over. By 2011, after the CBC again lost with the Oliphant Commission it had forced, the organization had lost 30 to 40 percent of the country along with it.

In 2010, Prime Minister Stephen Harper commissioned a report from the Senate Committee on Transport and Communications to come up with ways to rescue the CBC. More ads, the cessation of in-house cultural programs, playing recordings, and selling off all its studios and buildings were among the recommendations. In response, the CBC spent the next three election seasons—2015, 2019, and 2021—attacking conservatives with its every breath. In Justin Trudeau, the ideal leftwing pretty boy willing to be puppeted for power, the CBC had finally found a politician to love.

On the campaign trail, Trudeau and his team promised to increase the CBC's funding. The CBC in return mirrored Trudeau's campaign of conservative-hatred, oil-sands hatred, and full-throated promotion of the "climate change" narrative. Harper, a stolid man married to reason, was subjected to daily character assassination, his every move portrayed as evil. When the CBC ran out of attacks on Harper, evangelical Christians, George W. Bush, most Americans, and "the extreme Right," an almost psychotic hatred of Donald Trump and his "deplorables" poured from all 127 stations and their satellites all day, every day. There was simply no opposing view allowed, except those of nominal conservatives, tamed submissives brought on to bleat and cower.

Since Trudeau's victories in 2015, 2019, and 2021, the CBC has enjoyed bumps in its annual budget by hundreds of millions of dollars, despite its basement-level ratings. And most conservatives who are not politicians are intimidated into silence. Many will not answer the phone if the CBC calls and dodge on-air invitations, effectively cancelling themselves. It is simply too dangerous to counter the force and fury of the CBC. In this, the policy chiefs won their battle and very nearly destroyed conservatism in Canada. While also managing to destroy a beloved institution and arguably, their own futures.

Why Don't They Love Us Anymore?

It was the betrayal of the coronavirus pandemic that took the CBC from a rough 35 percent wanting reform to 62 percent wanting it shuttered in its entirety. During the spring of 2023, the citizen-funded National Citizens Inquiry travelled the country taking testimony from doctors, nurses, scientists, the vaccine-injured, morticians, and public health officials. Two former employees of the CBC, both veteran journalists with sterling careers, reported what had happened. One, Marianne Klowak, anguished by the betrayal of her profession, told the story from the inside. The other, Rodney Palmer, who had reported from Beijing during the SARS epidemic, closely tracked the breakdown of the journalism profession via its accommodation made with governments and NGOs, compromised Canada Research Chairs (a government-funded chain of research fellowships), and the vaccine industry.

Who were we to withhold information that the public
needed to know and had a right to know in order to make
an informed decision? It tore me apart. We failed our
audience, we let them down. It was a crushing burden.
—Marianne Klowak

"We betrayed our audience, we betrayed their trust." Klowak, an award-winning thirty-four-year veteran at CBC Manitoba was used to having her stories turned around in a day, aired on TV, radio, and the web without question.

> We depended on our reputation for excellence over the years and used that reputation to effectively shut down one side of the truth. How were we doing that? We branded the doctors and experts we used as competent and trustworthy and those who challenged the government narrative, despite their reputations, as dangerous and spreading disinformation. It changed so fast it left me spinning. The rules changed overnight. It was a collapse of journalism. We changed from newsgathering to pushing propaganda.

People called, emailed, and stopped her on the street, asking her what was going on, why wasn't the CBC reflecting their concerns? A province-wide study showed that over 60 percent were worried about the safety of the vaccine, but any story she proposed about safety concerns was shut down. Every story—about people who had lost jobs because of vaccine hesitancy, the vaccine injured, families broken, family members ostracized, depressed university students, suicides from lost businesses and incomes—that countered the government's narrative was refused.

By early 2021, she found that the language in story meetings had changed as well. Despite only 4 percent refusing the vaccine for religious reasons, anti-vaxxers were labeled as religious nuts, uneducated, rural. "We were laughing at them, ridiculing them, it was pejorative…

the opposite of journalistic practice." Klowak's breaking point came after Israel was starting to report evidence of inflamed heart muscles among vaccinated teenagers and people were calling her, worried about vaccinating their children. At the same time, the U.S. Centers for Disease Control and Prevention had noted on its website that there had been rare cases of myocarditis among young people.

Her story about these side effects was sent to Toronto where it languished for several months in the CBC's own freshly created "public health unit" before it was returned with the instruction to use instead a group of experts chosen by CBC management, who claimed there was no risk from the vaccine. She refused and the story was killed. In the meantime, many parents had been forced to vaccinate their children.

After another story was spiked, this one about a young woman runner with irreversible heart disease after vaccination, Klowak took early retirement, but not before requesting extensive exit interviews with local and national editorial types. Her concerns were dismissed. Brodie Fenlon, the corporation's editor-in-chief, stated that he thought the CBC had performed well.

> *The CBC is a public entity, we pay for it, it broadcasts on the public airwaves and we expect them to tell us the truth because they've done it for fifty years.*
> —Rodney Palmer

Rodney James Palmer had been a TV presenter, producer, reporter, and a ten-year veteran of the CBC, working in Israel and India as a bureau chief, and notably in Beijing during the SARS outbreak. Palmer had noticed a distinct difference in the response of the Chinese to Covid, especially by their quarantining Wuhan, and, his suspicion triggered, bent to studying the rollout of the pandemic.

He observed that a week into the pandemic, the CBC's star reporter, Adrienne Arsenault, had run a story speculating how to respond if "your father" thought that China had created the virus. She went on to lecture her audience on how to counter such "misinformation" and to use "trusted sources" from "legitimate organizations." Palmer pointed out that in the beginnings of any pandemic, all information is necessary for correct analysis. "What evidence did she have?"

He discovered that Arsenault had used as her source an organization called First Draft, which emerged in March 2020 to counter "vaccine misinformation" and recommend the use of only "trusted sources." First Draft supported a pro-vaccine narrative, but Arsenault didn't mention that. Further, Palmer pointed out that in the same month, both *The Washington Post* and *Vanity Fair* had published deeply researched pieces raising suspicions about the Wuhan lab, but the CBC was already telling Canadians not to trust their own family members.

A few weeks later, Brodie Fenlon announced on his blog that the CBC had joined four organizations—First Draft, Project Origin, the Journalism Trust Initiative, and the Global Task Force—whose focus was to counter "misinformation." One, the Trust Project, was joined by several dozen newspapers and broadcasters all over the world with the same mandate: to assert "trust" against "misinformation." Their purpose: "to develop a consensus and a single strong voice around the issues facing public media worldwide." In public media, The Trust Project was joined by the BBC, ABC (Australia) France-TV, KBS (Korea), ZDF (Germany), and SVT (Sweden). Palmer wondered what possible congruence the CBC would have with the Korean Broadcasting System (and why the word "truth" was no longer in use). He observed that developing "a single strong voice" was in direct opposition to actual journalism.

Palmer pointed out that the CBC's *Marketplace* program had reported eight hundred social media posts that it judged to be "misinformation" to the Center for Digital Hate, and complained when only 12 percent were taken down. "Who at the CBC was the arbiter of the truth, when Canadians prefer to determine truth for themselves?" asked Palmer. How dare "the CBC promote a new identifiable group of Canadians and foment hate against them?"

Many journalists, some former, some having resigned during the pandemic, have gone on record to protest the corporation's extreme bias. Others have left because the editorial policy has shifted from news gathering to promotion of the other-sexed and marginalized people of color and disability, whereby every story has to include some element reflecting the persecution of the less-abled by white supremacists. And while this is yet another reason for the CBC's audience shifting away, it does not explain the active dislike and distrust exhibited by the public at present. The betrayal of trust, ironically, was everything. Klowak, before she retired, called around to journalists in the CBC and at other newsrooms, asking if her experience was typical. It was, but many were, unlike her, in mid-career and afraid to lose their positions.

Then came the trucker protest.

During the trucker protest, Justin Trudeau's behavior mirrored his father's punitive actions against violent French-Canadian separatists in 1970. The FLQ (the Quebec Liberation Front) had kidnapped two public officials and killed one of them. Trudeau on the CBC and in other media, drew an equivalence. He was able to do this because on the second day of the massive protest in Ottawa, three photographs appeared of a Nazi flag, the American Tea Party flag, and the Confederate flag. These three photos were subsequently tracked down to timing, photographer, location, and lighting and are believed today to have come from the Prime Minister's Office. Two photos were by photographers who had taken official portraits of Trudeau. A CBC journalist was the first to tweet the photos, refusing to reveal his source. Trudeau used these photographs as a pretext to refuse to meet with the protestors. The CBC aired the photographs repeatedly, skewing public opinion against the truckers. During the protest, the CBC aired one blatantly critical piece after another and at no time interviewed a protestor, despite the protestors being right outside the broadcaster's Ottawa studios.

According to reporters on the ground and subsequent investigations, it took the government two weeks to bring in the numbers of police deemed necessary to shutter the protest. The morning the shut-down happened, the protesters were faced by a phalanx of black-clad, Kevlar-coated men in battle order. None of the uniforms carried insignia. What looked like a winter carnival of people who had been cruelly separated and isolated for two years, was swiftly shut down in a few brutal days, during which police rode a horse over an elderly woman, and organizers were jailed without charge for weeks. The CBC characterized protestors as rednecks, and as American-sympathizers, ignorant and anti-science, and claimed that money was coming in from American Republicans who wanted to take over Canada. The government confiscated $20 million dollars in donations to the truckers from Go Fund Me and Give Send Go, the money returned to the donors, on the order of Trudeau's deputy prime minister, Chrystia Freeland. Freeland then froze the bank accounts of ordinary people, waitresses and clerks, who had donated as little as $50 to the truckers. Despite the fact that the protestors were, by all accounts, 20 percent people of color, all were dubbed racist. So much for knitting the country together.

The CBC has flagrantly betrayed the public trust and that fact is now reflected in its rampant unpopularity. Founded to "reflect Canada and its regions to national and regional audiences," it has become a bully, a hysteric sowing division between every conceivable cohort, black against white, indigenous against settler, the other-sexed against "normals," and especially creating hatred against conservatives. By every conceivable metric the CBC has failed.

Moreover, it has almost destroyed the country's fiscal integrity by becoming a shrill advocate for destructive public policies such as aggressive "climate change" mitigation in the coldest, most treed country in the world, thereby gutting the one industry—oil and gas—upon which one-third of the nation's economy depends. Canadians now rank first among the G7 for debt-to-income ratio, and it is the public broadcaster's prejudice and ignorance, above any other cultural institution, that is responsible.

THE ONE-PARTY MEDIA STATE IN IRELAND

BY BEN SCALLAN

There was once a glorious time when politicians feared journalists, and the raw antagonism between the two groups was palpable. This was certainly the case in Ireland, where in 1982, the government was found to have authorized an illegal phone tapping of three particularly irksome journalists—Geraldine Kennedy, Bruce Arnold, and Vincent Browne—in an effort to figure out who was leaking damaging government secrets to the press. It was effectively the Irish equivalent of Watergate, and predictably caused all hell to break loose when the news reached the ears of the public.

The revelation that law-abiding journalists had been bugged by the authorities without justification led to a significant media firestorm at the time, and the government was ultimately forced to issue a full-throated, groveling apology. Not only that, but the embarrassing scandal ultimately led to the resignation of the *Taoiseach* (prime minister) at the time, Charles Haughey, who retired from politics in the aftermath of the incident. The event quickly went down in infamy in the annals of Irish political history and shook the nation to its core.

But while some might look at moments like this as a regrettable chapter of the past or a dark political low point, in a sense it was actually preferable to the present situation. After all, at least in the '80s there were journalists worthy of bugging, which is more than can be said today when, almost as one, the members of the state-run media and "independent" newspapers move in lockstep with the government.

In most Western countries today, journalists attack others for spreading alleged "misinformation"—accusations which ironically are often false themselves, and simply are used to shut down dissenting narratives or inconvenient facts. On the Emerald Isle, however, the press pool takes this conformity a step further: Irish media will attack you for spreading *accurate* information, which even the media members don't dispute the veracity of, all to protect the corporate government-sponsored message.

So ubiquitous is this message in Irish politics, in fact, that even the state's two oldest "rival" political parties, Fine Gael and Fianna Fáil, agree wholeheartedly on just about every major issue: from mass immigration, to the joys of being in the E.U., to the necessity of censoring "hate speech," to socially liberal policies like LGBTQI+ issues and abortion, to "climate" policies like a carbon tax, and more. While these parties trace their supposed mutual animosity back to the 1922 Irish Civil War—a conflict which is now more than a century old and has little bearing on modern politics—you'd be hard pressed to find a single contemporary issue that the two parties actually disagree on.

Indeed, recent polling has found that the demographic profile of a Fine Gael voter is virtually indistinguishable from that of a Fianna Fáil one, to the point that the two groups actually decided to go into government together after the 2020 general election—an unprecedented move, which, in a foreign context, would be as unthinkable as American Democrats and Republicans announcing a merger, or the U.K.'s Tories and Labour formally teaming up. It was a real "mask off" moment in Irish politics, and starkly revealed the faux-conflict of the Fine Gael-Fianna Fáil uniparty for the pantomime it was.

Similarly, other opposition parties like Sinn Féin are simply open and outright socialists who want exaggerated versions of the existing leftwing policies. Their only gripe with the government is that it's not implementing enough climate policies, or enough mass illegal immigration, or enough abortion. It's a funny kind of revolution whose sole demand is essentially "What do we want? More of the status quo! When do we want it? Now!"—but that is effectively the once-revolutionary, Ireland First, Sinn Féin's position.

As such, Irish politics may be the most lopsided and monolithic in the entire Western world. Bar a small group of independents—a group you could count on two hands—the Irish parliament is entirely bereft of right-of-center voices. There isn't a single mainstream Irish party that wouldn't fit comfortably into the U.S. Democratic Party.

The Irish media is no less monolithic. So, as disturbing as it was in years prior to have a government that illegally surveils members of the press, at least the public during that era could rest easy knowing that the members of the media were doing their jobs. There were no cozy love-ins between the Fourth Estate and the political classes back then—journalists were out for blood, and all the cabinet ministers knew it. Every politician's worst nightmare was a reporter's microphone flag, and that piece of equipment haunted them at night like the boogeyman. Each press conference felt like facing a firing squad, and if that fraught relationship led to dirty tricks by the politicians, well then that just demonstrated that the press was robust and operating as it should in a representative democracy.

So ironically, although the 1982 phone tapping was undoubtedly reprehensible, it arguably proved that the overall system was healthy, and that the media was effective enough to earn politicians' wary contempt. The same hostile relationship between legislators and newsmen was seen across much of the West during that time.

Today, of course, nothing could be further from the truth. The "journalist" of today is little more than a regime stenographer, whose job consists of slightly re-wording press releases and uncritically parroting the talking points of state officials, both in print and on the air. It's a job that could be done by an intern, and judging by the amount of typos and grammatical errors one routinely encounters in their work, you'd wonder in some cases if it actually is.

These days, rather than politicians sitting in backrooms colluding against the press, the press and politicians collude together against the public. Both groups team up as natural allies against the citizenry whenever the upstart plebs have the temerity to make "outlandish" requests. These requests include the public's complaints about being locked in their houses for months over what was generally, for most people, a mild illness (Covid), or protesting their town's population being doubled overnight by unvetted mass migration, as has happened routinely since the start of the Ukraine-Russia war.

In modern Ireland, if you are a normal person who wants things to remain the way they've always been, and don't want to radically "update" society with new definitions of nationhood, gender, the family unit, and everything else, then you will quickly fall afoul of the government and its henchmen in the press. That's the way these things go now: Both government and the media see themselves as activist agents of "progressive change" whose sole purpose is to remake and socially engineer society in the European Union's preferred image. Since Ireland signed the Lisbon Treaty in 2009—after initially rejecting it—this was inevitable.

Journalists today, either consciously or unconsciously, view their job as legitimizing government policy and delegitimizing any objection to state power. The job of the modern newshound, in his own mind at least, is essentially to regurgitate whatever the prevailing, politically correct state-sponsored message is on the issue of the day, and then to berate any members of the public who dare muster the gall to question it.

It's not that they've gone soft per se; the media has certainly maintained its pugilistic antagonism and aggressive attitude. Its members are just as ferocious as they were back in the 1980s. They've simply redirected their scorn and ire away from the government and toward a new target: the general public.

This may help to explain the plummeting sales and the overall financial woes of an industry bemoaning its own global decline while actively pursuing it. Media outlets are learning, much against their will, that launching daily attacks against their own customer base, and regularly denouncing readers and viewers as a pack of hateful racists and misogynistic scum, is not a winning business strategy. Modern news-papers are less broadsheets, and more broadsides against the reader.

The point is, it seems almost inconceivable that a modern Western government would bother to wiretap most journalists, because that would be akin to bugging themselves—it's entirely unnecessary. Today's media is simply an extension of the state, and almost serves as another government agency on its own. So why bug someone you already entirely control?

At the organizational level, many outlets rely on state funding to stay afloat financially, the most obvious examples being state broad-casters like Ireland's RTÉ, Britain's BBC, and America's NPR. It's hardly surprising, therefore, that these groups are also the most diligent when it comes to toeing the party line. But even many supposedly private outlets across the West are now in receipt of money from the public coffers, either from national governments, or supranational entities like the E.U., with predictably sycophantic results.

This is the worst kind of corporatism, and a threat to democ-racy. Whatever criticisms one wishes to level at capitalism, in which unchecked private business supposedly runs amok, that system is vastly superior to the malign despotism that is Big Business allied with state power. In the latter system, you get all of the ruthless greed of big corporations, married to the overwhelming authority of the govern-ment, amounting to a nigh-unstoppable match made in hell.

Ordinarily, if a private media company produced insipid headlines like "Why Getting a Tan Is Racist" or "How Roads Are Homophobic," readers would soon shrug and give up, allowing market forces to take over, causing the publisher to crash and burn financially. The system balances itself out. But when such outlets have an unlimited supply of the people's money courtesy of their friends in the Department of Finance, then the natural penalty for being bad at one's job vanishes, and the media can continue to churn out an endless supply of socially corrosive swill *ad nauseam*, whether the public wants it or not.

It's because of this artificial safety net that so many companies feel comfortable vilifying their own readers rather than trying to court the people's business. The government largely pays their wages using taxpayer funds, so they can safely risk alienating the ordinary person knowing that his money will end up with them one way or another.

As a result, the moment any significant challenge to the governing establishment is mustered, the political-media complex kicks into gear to suppress the people's outburst with wall-to-wall negative coverage. The press and the politicians are effectively interchangeable, and they close ranks like a Greek phalanx to attack any outsider candidate or unsanctioned political protest, the same way that white blood cells unite and swarm to attack a foreign entity invading the body.

Of course, this only applies to elite progressive politicians; as seen with Donald Trump, the press suddenly seems to find its voice again and revert to its earlier aggressive state when a non-liberal or right-leaning candidate assumes office. Anyone who has not been thoroughly catechized in the leftist madrassas of elite universities is encroaching on the establishment's turf, and naturally needs to be squashed.

On an individual level, an easy way to understand this relationship is to observe the sheer number of journalists who end up becoming handsomely paid "special advisors" to this or that minister. Far from being an isolated incident, this happens all the time. It's not even an unwritten rule, mind you—the press openly acknowledges it. As the *Irish Examiner* reported on July 15, 2020: "It has become a recent tradition that each new government poaches from Ireland's media pool." The revolving door is a well-established career path for those who go into the fields of both media and politics; for a washed-up politico, there's always a spot on telly as a "commentator" or "analyst."

While not every instance of this can be written off as "selling out," and there may be the occasional journalist-turned-advisor with integrity and a genuine love of politics, in most cases it's obvious that the arrangement is a recipe for a castrated press. After all, if in general journalists know that there is the potential of a lucrative six-figure salary waiting for them in a government department somewhere if they

play their cards right, does that make them more or less likely to criticize the government during their reporting?

Common sense would seem to dictate that it's the latter. No reporter
is going to bite the hand that may one day be feeding him. Naturally
enough, then, many choose to keep their mouths closed when it's time
to seriously critique something that the government is doing.

One might naively chalk this up to an unfortunate trend. More
cynically minded observers might speculate that governments are
aware of this effect, and that compromising the press is in fact the
whole point of the exercise. Armed with a very basic understanding
of human motivation, it would not be difficult to see how offering
well-paying cushy jobs funded by the taxpayer to any journalist with
the good sense to shut up would yield fruitful results for those in
power. It seems reasonable to conclude, therefore, that the whole thing
is by design.

This *cursus dishonorem*, therefore, is well established and widely
understood: Journalists know they might one day get rich by becoming politicians' lapdogs, and as such many of them simply start the
process early to ensure that they're sufficiently practiced for that fate-
ful day when opportunity knocks and a payday looms.

Even if a particular journalist is sincere in taking up an advisory
role—and I'm sure some are, no group is all bad or malicious—these
cases are undoubtedly noted by their colleagues in the same field, and
it makes an impression on them. The end result from the overall press
pool, then, is a daily barrage of pathetically soft articles and reports
that wouldn't look out of place if they came directly from the government press team—because that's effectively who's behind it. For many
people in the modern media industry, being a journalist is basically an
audition for a future career working for the political powers-that-be,
and that very much shows in their reporting.

This is why *Gript* receives not one cent of government funding
and maintains complete financial independence to hold the powerful
to account in the most meaningful sense possible. All journalists with

a shred of intellectual honesty should understand that he who pays the piper calls the tune.

Whether purchased at the individual or organizational level, in Ireland at least, the sector as a whole is firmly in the pocket of the state, and independent journalists are an endangered species. The modern media industry consists almost exclusively of bought-and-paid-for mercenaries and establishment activists, motivated solely by fringe ideology and personal ambition. And as such, the days of the tense or challenging political conferences are long gone.

The MO is, "if you can't beat 'em, buy 'em," and governments have certainly gotten their money's worth.

THE DUPLICITOUS MEDIA DOWN UNDER

BY PETER SMITH

In his autobiographical memoir, *Glances Back Through Seventy Years*, the British writer and publisher Henry Vizetelly (1820–1894) tells the tale of Henry Hetherington's penny periodical, *Poor Man's Guardian*, first published in London in 1831; and of other irreverent periodicals, such as the *Prompter*, which captured the *Zeitgeist* by proclaiming "down with kings, priests, and lords." Alas, those freebooting media days are long gone: Disdain for authority, a guiding precept of the press since its beginnings, has become a sick joke in Australia, and the Australian Broadcasting Corporation (ABC), the national broadcaster, is the punch line.

Seared into my marrow are those ghoulish daily Covid updates when premiers of states and their chief health officers spread confected alarm to justify lockdowns, masking, and, eventually, forced vaccinations with experimental substances. All to combat a relatively mild infection for all but the aged and infirm. Still, that wasn't the worst of it. The worst of it came in the form of the media howling for more. No restriction, no loss of freedom was ever enough for much of the press in Australia. A sad commentary on the state of the Fourth Estate and symptomatic of a broader malaise: disdain for authority replaced by support for authoritarianism.

Eminent Australian historian Geoffrey Blainey wrote that Australia suffered from a *tyranny of distance*. Distance from Europe and North

America and the distance internally between centres of population. Sixty-five percent of the total population of approximately 27 million live in the six state capital cities. Of the five mainland capitals, the shortest distance, at 452 road miles, is between Melbourne and Adelaide. The relatively small national population as a whole, diluted into distant population centers, has inhibited the development of national newspapers and also of a full spectrum of opinion. Pickings are thin on the right-hand side.

All but two printed newspapers are either state-based or regionally or locally based. On the national stage, the *Australian Financial Review* was born in 1951 but remains a specialized newspaper, focusing largely on business affairs. As to general news coverage, Rupert Murdoch filled the breach in 1964 by establishing *The Australian*. It remains the only printed national newspaper covering the gamut of domestic and international news. Supposedly center-right, it is far-right to greenies and leftists but a constant disappointment to genuine conservatives. To give an inkling of what I mean: While I buy *The Australian* each day, I cancelled my online subscription in 2016. The overwhelmingly negative and grossly unfair coverage of Donald Trump had become too much to bear.

The Daily Telegraph in Sydney offers a slightly more populist-cum-conservative slant than does *The Australian*, as for Melbournians does the *Herald Sun*. However, they are parochial; neither covers the wider news adequately. Both are also owned by Murdoch's News Corp, as are many regional and local newspapers. Sans News Corp, the media landscape is distinctly red- and green-hued with hardly a conservative commentator or reporter in sight.

Ergo, we conservatives in Australia, old enough to still read newspapers, have to make do. Put up with the wishy-washy editorial stance of *The Australian*. Accept that the paper is firmly on the "climate-change" bandwagon, was an early advocate of pricing carbon dioxide emissions, and pretty well bought into Covid hysteria, as did most of its journalists. Accept lies. "One officer who was beaten by Mr Trump's supporters died the next day," as Hugh Tomlinson wrote, apropos of January 6, in the *Weekend Australian* of May 6, 2023. The reward? It gives ample space to conservative commentary. For example, the paper allowed one of its senior writers, Steve Waterson, to periodically make the case, superlatively and powerfully, against the grotesque overreaction to the Wuhan flu. Almost alone, among Covid bedwetters, Waterson made buying the paper worthwhile.

The ABC is Australia's ubiquitous taxpayer-funded public broadcaster. It has a statutory obligation to be balanced. Yet, as media watcher Gerard Henderson, the founder of the Sydney Institute, a privately funded current-affairs forum, has pointed out, the ABC is "a conservative-free zone without one conservative presenter, or producer, or editor for any of its prominent television, radio or on-line outlets." A similar indictment applies to the government-funded multicultural-oriented broadcaster called the Special Broadcasting Service. Both stack panels on their current-affairs shows. Both choose interviewees to fit their agenda. And, for the most part, the three free-to-air commercial television channels are woke fellow travellers.

It is difficult to overstate the pernicious influence of the ABC. Its bias is unremitting and pervasive. Reflexively, for example, the ABC knew whose side it was on in January 2014 when Prime Minister Tony Abbott was turning back asylum-seeker boats. It falsely and fatuously accused the Australian Navy of forcing "asylum seekers" to clasp hot engine pipes. Commentary on the coronation of King Charles is mere pretext for airing tedious grievances about the Crown's complicity in Britain's colonial past. And, where it doesn't skew and cherry-pick information, it censors both news and people which sit at odds with its green-left agenda.

Listeners and watchers of the ABC often simply never hear about incidents which embarrass the narrative. For example, about an Aboriginal-activist federal senator, of the female sex, creating foul-mouthed mayhem outside of a strip club in the early morning hours. They do hear—at dramatic length, with accompanying mood music—about Trump's supposed collusion with Vladimir Putin, and about the scepticism surrounding the authenticity of Hunter Biden's laptop. But little or nothing about these confected narratives once they fall apart. And never do ABC listeners and viewers hear any apology, however much they've been misled. They would be excused for believing that the Great Barrier Reef is in perpetual peril of disappearing; that the North Pole is free of ice, and that Covid is a deadly pandemic of the un-vaxxed—all of which are staples of accepted belief. Only Sky News (Australia), a cable service, breaks the leftwing consensus by providing conservative commentary. Again, owned by News Corp. However, its viewership is small; not much more than 50,000 in prime time.

Was the left-centricity of media ever thus? I don't know about ever. But Bob Hawke, Labor prime minister from 1983 to 1991, use to say that "the ABC always attacks Labor governments from the left." So, the left-centricity of the media has certainly been evident for some considerable time. What has changed are the issues.

Go back to the 1980s in Australia when Hawke was governing. The domestic issues were about taxing and spending, balancing the budget, interest rates, inflation, and the like. Only later when John Howard became prime minister in the last half of the 1990s did dissonant issues come to the fore. "Climate change" of course. Followed by its unwholesome fellow traveller ESG (environmental, social and governance), a particular blight on the resource-dependent Australian economy. Then gay marriage. Spinning into transgender activism, among other facets of identity politics and Wokism. Seemingly, no degenerative leftward lurch is a bridge too far. Additionally, progressive leftism is ideally suited to the Aboriginal grievance industry. Blocking mining, perennially whining, creating national discord; a sinkhole for taxpayer dollars.

Throughout, the mainstream media hasn't missed a beat in moving from traditional leftism to the debauched leftism of the progressive kind. Whether it's undermining Christianity, traditional values and patriotism, or aiding and abetting the United Nations-orchestrated climate scam, it's all in a day's work for the progressive Left and its media mates. It remains to be seen whether a majority of Australians can retain their independence of mind in the face of a mainstream media which, on the evidence, is distinctly to the left of the population as a whole.

A university in Queensland (University of the Sunshine Coast) conducted a survey of Australian journalists between May 2012 and March 2013. Of the 605 respondents, it found that "more than half (51 percent) describe themselves as holding left-of-centre political views, compared with only 12.9 percent who consider themselves right-of-centre." And, right-of-center is probably left of where it used to be. But, cynicism aside, even at face value, the survey confirms a political schism between journalists and the population at large. Though what that means these days is not what it meant in past days.

Modern-day issues have changed the meaning of being politically left or right. What would hard-bitten journalists of yesteryear, of whatever political persuasion, make of it? They no longer exist, so we'll never know. As the issues have moved on, so have the journalists. A conversation with Roger Franklin, editor of the conservative site *Quadrant Online*, is illuminating. He started out straight from school in 1972 as a copy boy for the *Herald Sun* in Melbourne. From there he went to a number of regional newspapers. Was recruited by the Sydney Sunday paper, the *Sun-Herald*, before being despatched to New York. Where, before returning to Australia, he worked for twenty-six years. First as foreign correspondent for Australia's Fairfax Media, then for *Time* magazine, for the *New York Post*, and finally for *BusinessWeek*.

Three pertinent things to note: First, in common at the time with most of those entering journalism in Australia, he had no university degree. This meant that he knew that he knew very little. "While I subscribed to youthful leftism, I had neither the confidence nor the brazen cheek to insert my personal politics into the stories I was writing." There are now, he reflects, "in these lean years for legacy journalism, fewer journalists in newsrooms and less diversity." Many more women. And all have university degrees. Second, instructively, his early impression of newsrooms was of an abiding disdain for authority. Finally, he notes a telling switch from an emphasis on stories and facts to amorphous issues, which he attributes, at least in part, to the influence of both women and universities. "A news story means reporting your findings; an issues story means quoting academics and experts with particular perspectives."

Apropos women, the union representing journalists in Australia, the Media, Entertainment & Arts Alliance cited figures in April 2021 showing that "there are now more women than men journalists in Australia." It couldn't help adding: "gender inequity is worsening, with women journalists getting younger and worse-paid just as men journalists are, on average, getting older and better-paid." There it is. Older and more experienced journalists getting paid more than their younger less-experienced colleagues. Who would have thought it? Notice the way the equity agenda trumps any objective consideration of the facts; a dead giveaway. Issues trump facts. By the way, at the ABC, 60 percent of journalists and producers are women.

And the growing representation of women in newsrooms? It undoubtedly gives the profession a more feminine-leaning temperament. That's not a sexist comment; nor necessarily a pejorative one. It's an observation. Albeit a generalization, men and women tend to approach things differently. Among other differences, a feminine temperament is more expressive than goal driven. More prone to explore surrounding issues rather than simply focusing on what's happened. For those with long memories, think of the 1950s TV series *Dragnet* and Detective Sergeant Joe Friday's temperament: "Just the facts, ma'am." Masculinity personified.

And journalism degrees? Journalists now come out of university with views to share; and they're distinctly not conservative views. Disdain for authority? A highly selective disdain. Certainly disdain for the likes of Donald Trump and Marine Le Pen, Viktor Orbán and Benjamin Netanyahu; and the Catholic conservative Tony Abbott when he was prime minister of Australia.

Disdain, too, for Australia's most senior Catholic priest, the late Cardinal George Pell. Freed on the morning of April 7, 2020, by a seven-to-nothing decision of the High Court, Pell had served 405 days in prison for a crime of child molestation that, logistically, he could not possibly have committed. Pell's real crime was being both a staunch conservative and traditional Catholic. The media perverted the course of justice by poisoning public perceptions. In his 2021 book on the deplorable events, author Gerard Henderson noted that more than "a hundred Australian journalists, commentators and the like took part in the Pell media pile-on. There were a few who spoke up for George Pell...but not many."

The campaign against Pell was symptomatic of an Australian media lacking a sense of balance and fair play. Having little regard for the rule of law and the presumption of innocence. Replacing fact-based news and stories with tendentious opinions; and, in the Pell case, with rabid activism.

Indeed, finding and presenting facts has given way to exploring issues and pushing agendas. "Climate change" is the quintessence of an agenda masquerading as news. Hot and stormy weather, floods, droughts, and bushfires, despite being ho-hum historically, are inevitably portrayed by the Australian media as being a product of catastrophic man-made "climate change." The then-prime minister Scott Morrison was pilloried by parts of the media for his perceived inaction on this mythical phenomenon - about which, even if it were real, Australia could do nothing - during the widespread bushfires of 2019 and 2020.

As things stand, the mainstream media, save a rare few maverick commentators, is fully committed to the received ignorance on "climate change." There are no thundering headlines chastising national, state, and territory governments for destroying Australia's abundant, cheap, and reliable hydrocarbon energy. Factoids lurk, free from the risk of being exposed. The phony climate crisis is prominent among them.

Another, equally destructive of the fabric of national life and particular symptomatic of media malfeasance, is the concocted tale of the "Stolen Generations." A report titled "Bringing Them Home," hatched by Australia's Human Rights and Equal Opportunity Commission in 1977, purports to show that Australian governments systematically "stole" tens of thousands of part-Aboriginal children from their families between 1910 and 1970. In fact, it maligns those who took neglected and abused Aboriginal children into care. Not one case, in this litigious age, has ever passed muster in a court of law. Author, editor and historian Keith Windschuttle in *The Fabrication of Aboriginal History* comprehensively demolished the myth with peerless scholarship. Yet it lives on, as robustly as does the climate myth.

Why? The media in Australia kowtows to authority; including, as need be, by being dutifully duplicitous. And, rest assured, no apologies will be forthcoming however much the confected narratives fall apart.

PART SIX: CRITICISM AND ITS DISCONTENTS

WHO NEEDS CRITICISM, ANYWAY?

BY ARMOND WHITE

Film critics' desperate embrace of *Top Gun: Maverick* in 2022 was another sign of media failure. Reviewer-shills cheered the film's box-office success based on the predictable repetition of the inane 1986 *Top Gun*, while conservatives celebrated its air-show spectacle, calling it "patriotic." However, the action flick's facile military procedural was unclear as to which adversarial nation had sparked the climactic armed U.S. response. The movie ultimately proved irrelevant to the contemporary reality of America's fighting potential and defense readiness.

Producer-star Tom Cruise had cannily sussed the moment of American weakness (after the embarrassment of the 2020 Afghanistan withdrawal) and resolved it by replaying his own familiar hotshot career themes. Cruise's rebooted Captain Pete Mitchell and his relationships with some remaindered or revamped characters and a new generation of eager recruits proved popular enough that elite media could not deny the film's impact in that insidious way mainstream reviewers have of ignoring movies that go against liberal partisanship. In this case, the film was critic-proof. It did not illustrate a film industry shift to the middle but was just the latest, lucky example of Hollywood formula. Yet any critic who could not see that *Top Gun: Maverick* was silly was just being silly.

The decline of criticism is consistent with contemporary main-stream journalism's undeniable failure at reliable, honest reporting. One witnesses the same lack of inquiry, the same refusal of qualitative standards, the same uninformed arrogance whether reading literary, music, or movie reviews. None of this is exactly new, despite whichever bylines strike you as credible, and it can be traced back to the 1980s when mainstream journalism hit a peak of power-driven celebrity worship in the guise of reportage. At that same time—the "high concept" era—culture writing took on a craven approach to the arts, specifically highlighting the film industry's financial interests by emphasizing box office results or reviews that rubber-stamped the narratives sold in marketing campaigns, misconstruing advertising hyperbole for the essence of a film's content. These perspectives gained hold because they enabled professional opportunism—journalists were rewarded for being shills.

Since then, this confusion has become the expectation of both critics and readers. Even some editors feel comfortable should a positive review be consistent with powerhouse advertising. When journalists presume that they are entitled to the flattery and status that comes from bowing down to Hollywood, it corrupts the entire exchange of communication. Criticism, and all of journalism, becomes ineffective and untrustworthy. No longer a means for understanding culture and the world, its purpose is lost.

Readers who think they can do without criticism devalue it as much as the critics who don't realize the importance of being objective or adversarial. Each side forgets that the truth-telling profession is crucial to the stability of the culture at large. Now that we've entered an age when reporting contains open and overt ideological bias, the opinion trade is no longer distinct. (The term "critic" is now a lazy reporter's euphemism for an unnamed oppositional source.) A situation this dire is part of the corrupted professionalism occurring in our culture. People who don't appreciate the necessity of criticism as part of journalism don't understand what either strict criticism or strict reporting are for. Both have become forms of hype.

Bad artists who are highly esteemed—those who habitually practice the coarsening of the world, the desensitizing of human relations, the barbarity of unskilled or dishonest expression—gain status and *carte blanche* reassurance from equally vulgar media touts.
Filmmakers Christopher Nolan, Damien Chazelle, Todd Field, Spike
Lee, Park Chan-wook, Alfonso Cuarón, Alejandro González Iñárritu,
Guillermo del Toro, Jordan Peele, Martin McDonagh, Barry Jenkins,
Yorgos Lanthimos, and Noah Baumbach represent the degradation
that now defines critically acclaimed movie culture. Like their films or
not, these are the advocates of millennial nihilism.

Worse than the comic-book-based time-killers from the Marvel
and DC cinematic universes and "multiverses," the art-house trash
that vendors have exhibited, first in theaters and then in streaming
services, cannot be taken seriously, yet are given prestige for their
depraved audacity. Because they insist on mistrust and viciousness
via violence, anti-social narratives and ignoble characterizations,
their movies contribute to culture-wide cynicism. Films such as *The
Dark Knight, Babylon, Roma, Birdman, The Shape of Water, Get Out,
Three Billboards Outside Ebbing, Missouri, Moonlight, The Favourite,
BlacKkKlansman, Marriage Story*, and *Tar* exaggerate moral conflict,
extending it from adolescent sarcasm into jaded adult resignation.

By responding to even morally ugly movies simply as entertainment, camp-follower journalists and critics abnegate ethical and aesthetic judgment and fail the basic tenet of their vocation. This has gone
on for so long that it now has become habitual. A new generation of
aspiring critics and journalists dismisses cultural and political history;
it accepts promotional writing as part of the way one operates within
a cultural system that sees the latest releases as part of a "golden age,"
a term recently applied to television, although such ignorance can be
found in all forms of thumbs-up criticism. Contemporary reviewers
and journalists don't realize that criticism is not merely articulated
opinion. With education and expertise, criticism should always offer
an ethical response to new work, judging it as part of civilized living—
that is, politics.

It is the balance of politics and art that makes criticism essential to how we deal with real-life drama or the representation of social and psychological problems that Hollywood product exploits, then hypes as timely. Valuing art requires a concomitant regard for critical thinking—how else can one appreciate art's abstract conceptual presentation of ideas, the essence of storytelling? Just because the popular audience may prefer celebrity over honor and no longer hungers for moral expression at the cinema, having been swayed by sneering, sardonic television superficiality, doesn't nullify the fact that criticism exists for the same reason that art exists.

Daily rituals, conflicts, and puzzlements give us reason to pay attention to art, so we need criticism to help us through the existential thickets. This is crucial when we are inundated by the screwed-up philosophizing behind meretricious hits: the *Avengers* movies, the *Fast and the Furious* films, *Stars Wars* ad infinitum, *Jurassic World*, *Black Panther*, *Avatar: The Way of Water*. Contemporary cinema is dominated by banal, unoriginal recaps of genre movies made by undistinguished Hollywood hacks who specialize in gross kinetic sensation or boutique films made by indie hacks who specialize in political trends and social shock—the most egregious subset of millennial trash: *Get Out, Joker, Green Book, Parasite, Knives Out, The Batman, The Power of the Dog, The Banshees of Inisherin Barbie, Oppenheimer*.

We are long past what once was called "the heroic age of moviegoing." That was when both critics and filmgoers broke free of conventions that belonged to commercial (Hollywood) cinema and appreciated new, experimental, revolutionary innovations practiced by exciting mid-twentieth-century artists (Fellini, Bergman, Antonioni, Godard, Truffaut). The millennium's new auteurs who peddle false sophistication—making audiences aware of what's called "meta"—has cost most filmgoers and critics whatever sophistication ought to come from being alive at this presumed enlightened point in history.

Call it modernism or postmodernism, we're sidetracked by having to question the product put before us. Not exploring personal relations and social forces distances us further from the moral need that underpins our interest in art. We're bereft of critical insight to help us analyze the deficiencies and ambiguities of popular culture. Instead of satisfying us, millennial movies trick us by aiming to make us feel "smart."

The term "meta" intends to make us self-conscious, accustomed to the suspension of disbelief that was at the heart of Bertolt Brecht's influential theatrical distancing effects, yet entertained by Hollywood's various strategies of useless distraction. A critic should clarify the connection that occurs between the way one thinks and one's personal sensibility, linking aesthetics with emotions—the best artistic experience. A critic's primary responsibility is to free readers from naiveté and propaganda—whether the latter be advertisement or political fashion.

In today's film criticism, aesthetic scrutiny has been replaced by political style. As they have in political journalism, hive-mind and group-think trends have instituted conformity and consensus among critical elites. Reviewers are expected to go-along with majority opinion—received opinion—rather than trace new work back to traditional foundations and timeless standards of honesty or quality.

Here is where progressive social-engineering hijacks ethics and principles, rearranging attitudes and tenets and the way we learn and sustain our beliefs. In this sense the comic book movie should very simply and immediately connect to how we learn right and wrong, through demonstration of good vs. evil. Genre movies should be essential to contemporary society by acting out and distilling fundamental myths—as in Zack Snyder's mythic reconstructions *Man of Steel*, and his *Justice League* re-cut, both routinely dismissed by mainstream reviewers. The late French-Swiss filmmaker Jean-Luc Godard once advised that "genre is how we learn who we are." But the emphasis on action spectacle and special effects has taken away from our capacity for self-examination, thus self-discovery and social examination vanish from the screen. When a movie culture perpetuates adolescent indifference, its danger gets corroborated by criticism that, like political journalism, is written in a bubble.

The recent expansion of the aggregator website *Rotten Tomatoes* to include more bloggers within its round-up of critical opinion only stretches the proverbial bubble. The presence of professional journalist-critics is overwhelmed in favor of diverse representation according to gender and race quotas. The result merely increases the contagion of like-minded reviewing and amateurish language. Criticism becomes even more undistinguished than journalism, and less significant.

Great Britain's *Sight & Sound* magazine and its once-venerable decadal poll of international critics self-destructed after it made a politically correct expansion similar to *Rotten Tomatoes* but deliberately (stealthily) weighing it in favor of feminist academics so that the poll results upended years of critical tradition. *Sight & Sound* declared Chantal Akerman's 1975 feminist art movie *Jeanne Dielman, 23 quai du Commerce, 1080 Bruxelles* "the greatest film of all-time" over former long-standing poll winner *Citizen Kane*. This aggressive politicization of the critical circuit has weakened whatever stature that criticism once had, even among critics.

At the height of the early internet free-for-all that devastated traditional journalism, even *The New York Times* was kowtowing to the idea of "democratizing" criticism, but the profession has moved in the opposite totalitarian direction—prioritizing race and gender progressivism, worshipping the occurrence of 100 percent *Rotten Tomatoes* rating consensus.

Politically minded people who are alarmed by the current realization that mainstream media lies to us all the time have been unable to defend themselves by defending criticism. Some conservatives go along with Hollywood's output as though unheedful that its messages come from the headquarters of cultural depravity and therefore cannot be trusted. It's as if ethics do not translate to the arts where principles are dropped to favor a popular trend.

Passive film-watching should not automatically lead to passive journalistic habits; but the few critics sponsored by conservative media too frequently follow the fads of mainstream media. Tough-minded, principled, and informed criticism is often avoided by conservatives.

Even as society descends into chaos and pop culture descends into nonsense, we still need critics to help us to keep our bearings, to maintain aesthetic and ethical equilibrium. Like a compass giving a constant, reliable sense of direction, only critics can provide sanity and thoughtfulness in the face of unanimous enthusiasm for junk product, whether by Pixar or Marvel. The reflex to go along with the majority overpowers the risk of standing alone, knowing one's beliefs, defining and defending one's taste.

At this moment when our personal integrity is challenged all around, criticism is more necessary than ever because it helps consumers to develop the right way to use their minds. Criticism can function as a lifeline, especially as we struggle with distrust of the media, stemming from unacceptable political and class differences. Criticism that creates healthy skepticism could be the first step toward making critical analysis of the culture's prevailing, largely leftwing, shibboleths.

Criticism is one way of bringing our standards to bear on our tastes. If regime media perpetuates offenses to our principles, scrupulous, refined aesthetics are our best protection. Media that promotes the status quo has no defendable standard but has demonstrated a tendency to establish its own interest above others. Critics are needed to assess the moral test offered by popular culture.

Mark Wahlberg's *Father Stu* and Terence Davies's *Benediction* were spiritually centered films that mainstream critics unforgivably ignored. *Top Gun: Maverick* wasn't an artistic success, but it uncorked the nation's deep-seated nostalgia, and a perspicacious critic would have made that clear to his readers. Instead, most reviewers, whether America First or not, went along with the hollow Rah-Rah, Sis Boom Bah! The best recent movies—*Father Stu, Benediction, Marx Can Wait, Ambulance, Straight Up, Dragged Across Concrete*—were virtually suppressed by mainstream reviewers, and the motion picture Academy, in the same way that political journalists blackout events—news—that's inconvenient to a particular social narrative.

We've had enough of journalism that supports the authoritarian surge, either from Washington or Hollywood. The public may not actually distrust criticism as such, but readers are hard-pressed to find criticism that can tackle the influence of the corporate and the mainstream and inspire or renew their confidence in the media. As we await journalism that is informed, reliably honest and helpfully skeptical, we await real criticism.

HOW WE LOST IT
AT THE MOVIES

BY GEORGE MF WASHINGTON

For as long as there have been movies, there have been movie critics. The first movie reviews read more like police reports submitted by Sergeant Joe Friday. "Just the facts, Ma'am… is it any good, and should I pay to see it?" A little boring, maybe. But as in any competitive game, it's always better if the referees don't put a thumb on the scale.

That attitude began to change in the '60s and '70s as a new generation of critics changed the concept of a "review" from a simple recitation of the facts to something more like an academic "criticism." These newer critics jettisoned the concept of "movies" and exchanged them for a deeper artistic analysis of "film," and mostly sneered at the kind of mass popular entertainment that has always driven the Hollywood bottom line.

Here in the internet era though, modern film criticism is dominated by a different kind of animal altogether. The modern critic is often a person who started, not with an entry-level job at a newspaper overseen by an editor and an army of fact checkers, but with a simple WordPress account. These critics tend to substitute feelings and politics for any practical knowledge of the process of filmmaking, and often produce a work product that is fundamentally different from anything that has come before in both form and function.

These modern movie reviews are something more like cultural signifiers—no longer is the question "Should you see this movie?" but

"What does seeing this movie say about you as a person?" As more time goes by, it gets harder and harder to find someone, anyone, who actually knows something about filmmaking and whose only goal as a critic is to give you an honest assessment of whether a film is good enough to spend your time and money on.

The Internet of Things

There's a reason why The United States of America was conceived as a representative republic and not as a pure democracy, and that's because the moment that too many people get involved, you no longer have a government, you have a mob.

This is true of a lot of things beyond just government—culture and the arts, for example. The internet has democratized artistic pursuits, including the art and craft of criticism, and it has done so more quickly than Hollywood has been able to adapt to it. It has lowered the barriers to entry and now any fool with a social media account can become a film critic, with all the damage and mayhem that comes along with being awarded the title without first gaining any kind of expertise.

When Bruce Springsteen sang "57 Channels (And Nothin' On)," he verbalized, perhaps inadvertently, an axiom that applies to all American pop culture here in the Late Empire period of the twenty-first century: that the more of something you get, the lower the quality tends to be. Most of what you find on TV, cable, or streaming is, if not exactly good, at least professionally and competently made. But saunter over to YouTube or TikTok and you'll be forced to sift through thousands, perhaps even millions, of hours of terrible "content" to get to one single thing that's worth your time. Even the word "content" itself implies something disposable, something ephemeral, something lacking in any real substance or meaning.

And indeed, by lowering the barriers to entry we have spawned a vast wasteland of terrible "content," including in the business of film criticism: 57 million channels and nothing on.

Which is not to say that things were universally better before the internet. Just as too many participants transform government into a mob, too few transforms government into a dictatorship. Just because there were only a handful of dedicated broadcast and print outlets engaged in the business of reviewing movies before the internet doesn't mean that some of those gatekeepers weren't hopelessly corrupted by their own biases. Most of the "important" film critics of the past quarter of the twentieth century aimed their reviews at the high-brow movie goer, the "upper-class twit," for all you Monty Python fans. The old stereotype of the haughty critic who can't stomach the lowbrow fare that the masses enjoy, and so makes it his or her duty to scorn proletarian tastes at every opportunity has proven to be a durable one.

The New Yorker's Pauline Kael was the doyenne of serious film criticism from 1968 to 1991, defining the image of the Francophile film sophisticate, the kind of person who would use words like *auteur* and *mise en scene* unironically. But give critics like Pauline Kael, along with her West Coast mirror image, the *Los Angeles Times*'s Kenneth Turan, credit: They had at least a passing knowledge of the filmmaking process and, more important, they had access. I have no doubt that if or when Pauline Kael called, filmmakers like Warren Beatty, Sam Peckinpah, and James Toback ran to the phone to answer it.

But the problem was that Kael was reviewing movies for her pals on New York City's Upper West Side. Anything that a teenager from Fort Lauderdale or Peoria or Tucson might enjoy on a summer Friday date night would have been beneath Kael, outside her "ken," as it were. Part of Kael's mission in life was to let you know that your proletarian tastes were icky and embarrassing. Her famous, and also somewhat apocryphal, statement about Nixon—that she couldn't understand how he'd won because she didn't know anyone who voted for him—wasn't just an indictment of her elitism, it was also a kind of confession.

And then, the internet age changed everything. Much as cable news broke the stranglehold that the big three networks once had on the national news agenda, the internet absolutely shattered the tightly gate-kept universe of film criticism. Before the internet brought democracy, or anarchy, if you prefer, to the world of criticism, the average American probably couldn't name more than a handful of reviewers (Kael, Gene Siskel, Roger Ebert, Leonard Maltin, Gene Shalit, Rex Reed), most of them known from television, not print. We still lived in a world where a dozen or so people decided, more or less on their own, which movies would succeed and which would fail.

All that changed with three words: "Ain't It Cool." Certainly, there were online movie critics before Harry Knowles, but none had ever blown up as quickly or as loudly as Harry and his bizarre cast of online characters. Knowles wasn't like any reviewer that had come before him. He was "one of us" as his fans might've said. And that was both good and bad. Harry spoke to the kind of underserved moviegoer that would rather see a *Star Wars* or *Indiana Jones* sequel than *Five Easy Pieces*, and his reviewing style reflected that bias in the way it perfectly tracked the ongoing coarsening of the culture. Harry's multiple daily updates brought the same kind of barely contained adolescence that was already beginning to absorb popular entertainment to the previously ivory towered business of critiquing films.

On *Ain't It Cool News* you were just as likely to read about Harry's bodily functions, or whether the lead actress gave him an erection, as you were to hear about the quality of the direction or whether a script was well-written. Because when it came to the latter, Harry didn't know a whole hell of a lot. Harry also began to traffic in rumors, which the studios absolutely hated, and which led to the rise of other rumor-based "scoop" sites, such as Nikki Finke's *Deadline Hollywood*, although Finke had a solid journalistic background, including stints at the Associated Press, *Newsweek*, and the *New York Post*.

And while these developments might have been good for voracious audiences increasingly addicted to salacious insider Hollywood stories, it's hard to see how they helped to make movies better. Certainly, they did nothing to make movie criticism better. Harry Knowles, at least in the early days of his reign, didn't know very much about the nuts and bolts of movie making and his reviews reflected that lack of understanding back at an industry that must have found his arrogant pronouncements maddening.

In the end, Harry Knowles was proof that criticism does require guardrails, a certain sense of basic decorum. In other words, Pauline Kael wasn't necessarily wrong; she was just too committed to the bit.

Politics

What came next, on the other hand, has been arguably worse than the mass democratization of the criticism business. Not just for the movies, but for the culture, and ultimately for the nation as a whole. I'm talking about the relentless politicization of, well, everything. It's hard to say exactly when this started, but as with online movie reviews, it was the internet, and later social media, that broke everything wide open.

After the election of Donald Trump in 2016, movie reviews and indeed movies themselves became just another weapon in the culture wars. And here in the post-Trump era, a critic is almost never simply reviewing a movie on the merits, rather he or she is telling us which movies we must see and, more important, *enjoy*, if we are to remain Americans in good standing. It is not enough that we simply watch the lady *Ghostbusters* movie, we must also defend it out in the broader culture no matter what its faults, or else we are misogynists and probably also soldiers of the patriarchy.

And while these new critics must defend movies that are "woke" from the masses who are un-woke, they also must attack those films that are "bad," as "bad" is defined by the dominant culture—which is to say, by progressives. Which is why we've also seen movie reviews evolve into a political tool designed to subtly push audiences toward movies that are "good for them" rather than movies that they might simply enjoy on their merits. At the same time, critics now openly attack those movies, directors, and movie stars of whom the coastal elites disapprove.

To cite but one example from 2023: Take a moment to scan through the dozens of negative reviews of the wildly successful independently released *The Sound of Freedom*, and you'll see exactly what I mean. You'll read a lot about the conspiracy-mongering web presence called "QAnon" or the chemical compound adrenochrome, which is said by some to be a sexual elixir for elites, harvested from the blood of children, but not very much about the artistic merits of the film itself.

And here I'm going to risk contradicting everything I've said about the mass democratization of the review business to point out that this new system has indeed managed to create at least one reliable way to judge whether a movie is worth your time. The quickest and most accurate metric available to any filmgoer who wants an honest assessment of a film's worth is the ratio of "Critics Score" to "Audience Score" at the movie review website *Rotten Tomatoes*. If the critics score is significantly higher than the Audience Score, say, something like 85/35, then you can be fairly certain the movie is bad, or preachy, or unnecessarily political, and that the "legitimate" critics have decided that it is their duty to boost the film because they believe it is "good for you."

Similarly, if the ratio is reversed, if audiences rate the movie very positively but critics have savaged it, then you can be pretty sure that the movie is at least fun and entertaining. If there's anything we know about the modern, Corporate Media film critic, it's that there is almost nothing that he hates more than a movie that is both fun and entertaining. If a movie reliably exhibits these twin attributes, then it follows therefore, that no one in the theater is learning the necessary lesson.

This "Audience Score" ratio method is not, strictly speaking, criticism in any real sense of the word. But it is, at least, a reliable guide to current popular taste. And in a world where almost everyone is lying to you, including movie critics, it may be that "reliable" will have to do for now.

THE DEATH OF BOOK PUBLISHING

BY THOMAS LIPSCOMB

Unlike a newspaper, a magazine, or a broadcast network, book publishing is not targeted to a specific market. What the industry does, and its impact, is a mystery to most people and of little interest. Book buyers are a small minority of Americans. But the industry is still a deep, wide aquifer diffusing the influence of its books throughout all other media.

The U.S. book publishing market totals around $30 billion annually. It is a small industry compared to other, more specifically targeted, mass media such as the broadcasting and cable TV industry at more than $300 billion. But it is far more powerful. A newspaper may destroy a Nixon presidency; a TV broadcast may destroy a Senator Joseph McCarthy. But a book has destroyed an entire nation-state.

Johannes Gutenberg's creation of the printing press in 1454 had probably the most consequential impact on modern Western civilization of any development until the invention of the atomic bomb in 1945. Until Gutenberg's press, the only room for dissenters from either the church or the royal kingdoms, which completely controlled the culture, was in the prisons or execution yards.

Before Gutenberg's press there were only a few thousand books of all kinds in existence. But by the year 1500, in barely fifty years, more than 9 million books were in distribution. Only twenty-five years later, the works of a heretical Augustinian priest named Martin

Luther sparked a Protestant Reformation in which millions would die. The ensuing chaos redrew the map of Europe and the states within it. Luther's attacks on the authority of the clergy were designed to empower the individual to do his own thinking. And the arguments for and against various schemes, for and against different forms of government, have raged through the ensuing book publications ever since, right up to Francis Fukuyama's *The End of History and the Last Man* in 1992.

As the power of various states and religious and political organizations has waxed and waned over the centuries, so have the periods of a comparatively open publishing medium and then its suppression. The expansion of book publishing and the ever-changing powers of censorship have been locked in conflict since the very beginning of the new industry.

When book publishing was loosely regulated and populations were becoming more literate, the world endured history-changing revolutions in the United States, France, and Russia. When Abraham Lincoln was introduced to Harriet Beecher Stowe, he is said to have called her "the little woman who wrote the book that started this great war." That is a useful reminder of the impact of books such as *Uncle Tom's Cabin* and Thomas Paine's *Common Sense*.

Piracy of copyrighted material still rules much of the developing world as well as much of the digital marketplace. The underlying justification as articulated by the American writer and editor Stewart Brand is that while the manufactured product is market controlled, "information wants to be free." A dubious proposition at best ascribing volition to an abstraction, but for the past forty years Google and other digital media oligarchs have enriched themselves at the expense of publishers and authors and other copyright holders in a blizzard of litigation, foggy court decisions, and dubious copyright legislation. Xerox copies have a hard cost of their own in duplication, but the cost of digital pickup is miniscule. Not surprisingly, in those same forty years book publishing revenues have stagnated.

Book publishing is a core medium. Its basic product, the book, can appear in spinoffs as magazine and newspaper articles, broadcast and cable programming, film, video gaming, and other ways that permeate every level of society, passed on far beyond its original purchasers. But it is dependent on open access to a large and relatively well-educated market.

Its major problem is that it requires a lot of capital. Perhaps one in five books makes money. And as novelist and screenwriter William Goldman said of Hollywood, "Nobody knows anything... Not one person in the entire motion picture field knows for a certainty what's going to work. Every time out it's a guess and, if you're lucky, an educated one." Book publishing is at least as risky, and far less lucrative, when a book occasionally hits the jackpot.

By World War I, there were many small firms in the United States and many different notions as to what they wished to publish and which market options they had. There were many voices and many opinions, and the field was wide open. Some were the equivalent of playthings for rich heirs, others had a base business with an anchoring author, such as O. Henry or Jack London, and were bulked out with British imports.

Every now and then a real talent would pop up, like an accountant at a feisty publisher called Boni & Liveright named Bennett Cerf. He and his partner Donald S. Klopfer would buy out The Modern Library for pennies and end up the multimillionaire founders of Random House. Around the same time, Richard Simon decided that his aunt's fascination with crossword puzzles might be wide enough around the country to provide a market base for a publishing company. Simon was among the first to realize that instead of waiting to see what was submitted to his firm, he might do better using his market sense to assign what he thought were salable ideas and publishing those. The resulting Simon & Schuster proved to be the most market-responsive company in the industry.

Between Random House and Simon & Schuster there stretched the range of American book publishing for the next seventy-five years.

There were older houses like Lippincott; Little, Brown; Dodd, Mead; Scribner; and Doubleday, as well as newer firms like William Morrow and Putnam. And there were so many different editorial points of view, authors were able to challenge and even advance traditional thinking without censorship and without being denied access to publishing. It was a period of great and productive intellectual turmoil, creating a host of new paths and attitudes for Americans despite the emergencies of two world wars and the Depression. Book publishers saw their function as choosing the most marketable authors and helping them to reach their audiences. While avoiding legal problems was a priority, curtailing "wrong opinion" based on their own predilections did not occur to publishers of the day.

Academia has always been tied to book publishing by creating the latter's audience, many of its authors, and its intellectual climate. Postwar America reached its academic zenith in the late 1960s. The Scholastic Aptitude Test—the name has since been changed twice, to the Scholastic Assessment Test, and is now simply the SAT, standing for nothing—scores for college entrance exams reached their highest levels. Money flooded into education from panicked federal funding after the 1957 Sputnik scare when the Soviet Union lofted the first satellite into low Earth orbit.

However ironic his intention, David Halberstam was not wrong in terming Americans of this era as "the best and the brightest." And the future looked brighter. And at this peak, with its sunny view of the future, a combination of unrelated events brought it all crashing down. The Vietnam conflict, botched by both Democratic and Republican administrations, caused a patriotic postwar America to seriously consider for the first time whether its own government could be trusted. America's confusion was heightened by the release into intellectual bloodstream and academia of both home-grown Marxists long suppressed and a host of imported Marxist radicals, such as the members of Germany's Frankfurt School.

To this crowd, quasi-revolutionary liberalism was a waste of time and its baby steps only delayed creating a better America. The truth as they saw it was that American institutions were rotten to the core. America's Founders, its history, its aspirations, were contemptible as well. The radicals were brilliant, zealous, and tireless. They set about dismembering the curriculum of American education, department by department, school by school, for the next thirty years.

The much-needed Civil Rights Act of 1964, which sought to redress the moral wrongs of racial segregation, was corrupted into a compensatory "affirmative action" social-welfare campaign at every level of American society. And the triage system that had created the peak of American education by empowering a meritocracy was turned on its head. It was now devoted to finding any way it could to credential anyone, however weak and incompetent, who had been "discriminated against." It would lower its standards and fake its statistics to conceal the clear failure of its good intentions. American academia collapsed into the pathetic heap of incompetent faculty teaching the hollowed-out curriculum we see reflected in the intellectual sterility of its graduates.

I went into educational (college textbook) publishing just before this inflection. I saw the change take place as an insider on top campuses all over the U.S. When I arrived, I was selling superb textbooks by first-rate academics who were both challenging and a pleasure to work with, from Paul Samuelson's *Economics* to H.W. Janson's *History of Art*. Within a few years these texts were being replaced because they were "insensitive" and "insufficiently critical of the culture," and replaced by texts by radical nonentities with few scholarly credentials and much political baggage.

Almost simultaneously, American industry was undergoing its own evolution. A host of small companies was being acquired by emerging conglomerates. Presumably this would lead to efficiencies of scale and more available capital with less risk to the shareholders. At the very moment publishing-company owners and founders were worrying about what to do with their ownership problems that caused both estate and management grief, ITT, Gulf & Western, RCA, and others were making bids for them. One minute an aging Bennett Cerf was worried about having to sell out his interest in Random House at a loss and now he was looking at a huge profit in "undervalued" stock in some hot conglomerate that was going to the moon. What was not to like? They sold. And over a period of a little over a decade, the discordant, irascible opinions and practices of the highly competitive publishing leaders, from Nelson Doubleday to Charles Scribner were silenced by the corporate concerns of conglomerates.

My own job vanished in the whirlwind. My employer, who had plowed its profits from evergreen lucrative classics like *The Joy of Cooking* and *Raggedy Ann* into a text company taking advantage of the new federal funding, sold to ITT. I wasn't unhappy; I didn't like where academia and textbook publishing was going. I moved into "general book publishing," where best sellers come from. I now had a host of contacts among academic authors who were superb but not part of the incoming Red Tide, so they could no longer get their textbooks placed in educational publishing. It worked. I had bestsellers from academic authors, and they won Pulitzers and other awards as well.

I piloted my career through the still-independent publishers where I had much more ability to use and argue my judgement over what and how to publish. I became the youngest editor-in-chief at one of the oldest houses in publishing, Dodd, Mead & Co., that had grown rich on Agatha Christie and Winston Churchill. The industry went from the creative chaos that had been so intellectually constructive to more and more groupthink across the industry, just as it had in academia. A term began to be used more and more: "political correctness." At first, we thought it was funny.

But my publishing program was market-driven. I had no pretensions of knowing what the "truth" and "right conclusion" were about anything. In fact, I was intensely curious about the conclusions of my authors. I read their manuscripts like a mystery novel: always interested in the conclusions they proposed to the major questions of the day.

This led to a completely open approach to the politics and philosophy of our authors. One minute I would publish terrorist Che

Guevara; the next Diana Mitford, the charming Nazi sympathizer whom Churchill once had put in prison; then black radical Bobby Seale, a founder of the Black Panthers; or the Irish communist Claud Cockburn and his son, Alexander. I'd even arranged to publish New York's infamous "Son of Sam" murderer, David Berkowitz.

I found a Mormon newsletter writer named Howard Ruff, who thought his combination of food storage and hard-money investing in gold was just the thing for hard times. Millions of Americans agreed and made *How to Prosper During the Coming Bad Years* a number-one bestseller for over a year. I got food writer Craig Claiborne to turn the diet he invented for himself into a top bestseller. I nearly got fired for publishing *The Last Mafioso* by Ovid Demaris for offending Frank Sinatra, who went to my boss and demanded my head.

The increasing groupthink in the publishing industry decreed that no one would publish any of the books being proposed by the Watergate criminals. But I did. And Nixon aide H.R. Haldeman's Watergate story, *The Ends of Power*, was the number-one bestseller two weeks before it was published and made the front page of many newspapers and every television news broadcast. Across the book-publishing industry books like mine were coming out and enlivening the national policy dialogue. The point of these stories is to compare the politically incorrect nature of all these books, some from the Left, some from the Right, with the insipid books and authors coming out of the Big Five that dominate book publishing today.

To make matters worse, after these takeovers of so much of the publishing industry by conglomerates, pieces of it were then spun off to huge foreign companies. German giant Bertelsmann took over a large group under Penguin/Random House including Doubleday, Knopf, Crown and Viking; Holtzbrinck from Stuttgart took over the Macmillan group; France's Hachette grabbed Little, Brown; Rupert Murdoch's News Corporation bought HarperCollins; while investment bank KKR purchased Simon & Schuster. The Big Five now control 80 percent of American book publishing sales and 80 percent of them are international corporations with foreign ownership. What do they care about what might be vital issues to Americans? Domestic book publishing had enlivened the national discourse for two centuries. Until now.

Today the intellectual debate is stilled. Nonfiction today remains the largest seller, but it is largely irrelevant and tame. In the wake of the Covid scandal, the worst public health failure in a century, and the collapse of America's dream of "rule-based" globalist hegemony in the disastrous Ukrainian proxy war, as recently as late 2023 there hadn't been a single book from any of the Big Five on either subject.

Occasionally, attempts to challenge the reigning orthodoxy with a proposed book have led to internal staff revolts by recent credentialed products of academia. Woody Allen's important autobiography was cancelled by Hachette a month before release. Simon & Schuster cancelled a book on *The Tyranny of Big Tech* by Republican senator Josh Hawley of Missouri six months before its publication, although it was later picked up by another publisher. Even bestselling authors such as Canada's Jordan Peterson and Britain's J. K. Rowling have been affected by the woke brigades embedded in publishing.

The problem is always the same: These books threaten the ever-growing list of neo-orthodox verities that has strangled American culture and thought in every institution. Cancellation and censorship go only one way: against any challenge to the prevailing narrative. Meanwhile, a preposterous exercise in pseudo-scholarship, such as *The 1619 Project: A New Origin Story* by someone who calls herself Nikole Hannah-Jones, received wide distribution and won a Pulitzer.

A police state is perfectly ready to blind itself and its citizens from free inquiry if it believes that to be the price of its goals of imposed social justice, equity, and top-down direction at every level from sexual identity to washing machines. That's the main reason why the complete American Corporate Media is now government-controlled. The American federal government only need provide its citizens with an official explanation; that is the only "truth" the populace need. Anything else is a "conspiracy theory" or "disinformation." A free press just raises questions, and questions lead to problems.

Publishing under the Big Five is a puritanical paradise doing its best to deny publication to anything it might view as tainted by bad behavior or controversy, including, as Mike Pence found out, having been a former Republican vice president. According to Penguin Random House, it is "Committed to creating a positive impact on the world." The owner of the Macmillan group, Stefan von Holtzbrinck, wants his firm to support "worthy, essential causes." This sort of virtue-signaling takes up prominent space in the public statements of almost every publisher.

Since the big retailers like Amazon and Barnes & Noble are very much in accord with the Big Five, the ability of the few independent publishers left to get distribution is extremely limited. And with almost all publicity media outlets controlled by the federal government, print, broadcast, and digital alike, the ability to reach large numbers of potential book buyers is restricted as well. So, book publishing as it existed in the United States for four hundred years no longer exists. This wasn't the outcome of some long diabolical plot. Most of the damage was done between the '60s and the '90s with the acquisitions by the first conglomerates and then foreign ownership.

The overflow of sewage from American academia both in the collapse of standards and suppression of inquiry and in the miserable intellectual preparation of its graduates simultaneously eroded the publishing market and restricted the abilities of the personnel in publishing itself. There are now fewer book readers, and those who read, read less, as the average American now has the equivalent of a sixth-grade education. So, in the United States, which had perhaps reached the crest of the social and intellectual benefits of publishing a mere half-century ago, book publishing today is nothing more than a trivial ancillary to the entertainment business. In poet and publisher T.S. Eliot's words: The Gutenberg intellectual explosion six hundred years ago has ended in the United States, "not with a bang but a whimper."

THE TRIUMPH OF DEAF STOCKBROKERS

BY MICHAEL WALSH

"I could make deaf stockbrokers read my two pages on music," wrote a late-nineteenth-century London music critic who at first called himself Corno di Bassetto and later went by his initials, GBS. If a writer could reach such an audience, in the estimation of the man who later outed himself as George Bernard Shaw, then it was possible to interest anybody in the ongoing cultural dialogue of Europe and America. "Classical" music—the name is a misnomer—was not considered then as it is now: forbidding, elitist, exotic, esoteric, impenetrable to the layman. Rather, it was available to anybody who found it of interest, and had been for more than a century across both the European and American continents, and it was the critic's duty to arouse, inflame, and challenge his readers at every opportunity in his service to both journalism and art. Every newspaper of any size had one.

I wrote my first music review in late 1971 as a stringer for the Rochester *Democrat & Chronicle*, a mid-sized morning daily located in upstate New York, halfway between Syracuse and Buffalo. Despite its modest size (the population was then about 250,000), but thanks to the powerful falls of the Genesee River and its proximity to the Erie Canal, the city had been an important manufacturing center in the nineteenth century—the Flour City—and had made a transition to the new world of technology via Eastman Kodak, Bausch and Lomb, and Xerox in the twentieth. It was also the home of the Eastman School of

Music, my alma mater, which had become one of the top conservatories in the world under its longtime director, Howard Hanson.

Music criticism by then was undergoing a transition from commenting on new works and new trends in musical expression to reviews of works in the "standard repertoire" as performed by the leading artists of the day. The focus on the new was a legacy of the nineteenth century, during which critics had taken sides between the Music of the Future composers, chiefly Franz Liszt and his son-in-law, Richard Wagner, and traditionalists, such as Johannes Brahms, who could trace their lineage back to Beethoven and Mozart and Bach. Pitched battles were fought in the press—Shaw, who covered the very first performance of Wagner's complete *Ring of the Nibelung* cycle at Bayreuth in 1876, stood up for the Future; Eduard Hanslick, the dreaded critic of the *Neue Freie Presse* in Vienna, threw his lot in with the classicists. A great deal of ink was spilled, but no blood.

But with the closing of the musical frontier (as it were) with World War I—a war that ended Western European civilization and took the arts with it—the musical repertoire became frozen in time, with a handful of popular composers managing to squeeze in between the two world wars before the doors of the Standard Repertory prison clanged shut. The Great war was a significant blow to all the arts, but particularly to music, which suddenly lost its prized place at the forefront of European philosophical and even political thought, a position it had held since at least the time of Boethius (c. 480–524 AD)—senator under the barbarian emperor Theodoric, consul, scholar, translator, historian, music theoretician, and general fountain of knowledge in post-Western Rome until his execution on Theodoric's orders. Hardly anyone, it seemed, wanted to pay for the compositions of the twelve-tone school that gained sway in academe after World War II as music become gnomic, gnostic, and gnarly.

Music critics, therefore, became *performance* critics. Their job was to not to engage in the intellectual and musical life of the times—for, effectively, there was none any longer—but to assess, contrast, and compare performances of what had become the traditional "classical" repertoire from Bach (d. 1750) through Rachmaninoff (d. 1943), with some allowances made for men like Shostakovich, who wrote his music under the constant threat of censorship or, worse, death, from Josef Stalin and his "anti-formalist" and "anti-bourgeois" cultural apparat-chiks. Coverage of the standard operatic repertory of Monteverdi and Mozart through Puccini was similarly affected.

Shostakovich, by the way, was a grand but cautionary example of political engagement with musical thought—backed up by the full force of the state. Reviewing the now-memory-holed opera *The Great Friendship* by Vano Muradeli, the Central Committee of the All-Union Communist Party had this to say in 1948 (a year of great peril for all Soviet composers):

> The Central Committee of the All-Union Communist Party considers the opera GREAT FRIENDSHIP (Music by Vano Muradeli, Libretto by G. Mdivani) produced at the Bolshoi Theatre of the USSR on the Thirtieth Anniversary of the October Revolution to be vicious and inartistic in both its music and its subject matter... The music is feeble and inexpressive. It contains not a single melody or aria to be remembered. It is confused and disharmonious, built on complicated dissonances, on combinations of sound that grate upon the ear... The composer has not made use of the wealth of folk melodies, songs, tunes, and dance motifs in which the creative life of the people of the USSR is so rich, and especially the creative life of the peoples of the North Caucasus where the action of the opera is laid.
>
> The conference of Soviet musicians, conducted by the Central Committee of the Party, showed that the failure of Muradeli's opera is not an isolated case. It is closely linked with the unsatisfactory state of con-temporary Soviet music, with the spread of a formal-istic tendency among Soviet composers. As far back

as 1936, in connection with the appearance of Dmitrii Shostakovich's opera Lady Macbeth of Mtsensk, Pravda, the organ of the Central Committee of the Party, subjected to sharp criticism the anti-popular formalistic perversions in his music and exposed the harm and danger of this tendency to the future of Soviet music. Writing then on instructions from the Central Committee of the Party, Pravda formulated clearly the Soviet people's requirements of their composers.

The state of affairs is particularly bad in the field of symphonic and operatic music. The question at issue concerns composers who adhere to the formalistic anti-popular tendency. The very fullest expression of this tendency is found in the works of such composers as Dmitrii Shostakovich, Sergei Prokofiev, Aram Khachaturian, Vissarion Shebalin, G. Popov, N. Miaskovskii, and others whose compositions represent most strikingly the formalistic perversions and antidemocratic tendencies in music which are alien to the Soviet people and their artistic tastes.

Forty years later, when I was the guest of Tikhon Khrennikov at the Union of Soviet Composers in Moscow, portraits of several of those men hung in one of the building's principal rooms. Still, that was music criticism to be heeded, and not just by deaf stockbrokers. In the nineteenth century the function of the critic had been to seek out and encounter the new and then dive right into the argument, for which he needed a musical education and an aptitude for the art form. Whereas by the second half of the twentieth, he was more likely to be someone who had simply attended many performances of mostly very familiar music.

I was fortunate to have entered the profession when I did, fresh out of Eastman and at a time when "Darmstadtism"—the music of the twelve-tonalists (and by extension their mirror-images, the atonal-ists)—and its near-fascistic demands that henceforth all music should abide by the new "scientific" compositional rules was coming under a counter-reformatory attack. The first blow was struck by a former seri-alist, George Rochberg, with his String Quartet No. 3, written the year I graduated from Eastman and premiered the following year, 1972. At practically a single stroke, Rochberg had overthrown the prevailing aesthetic (or, more properly, anti-aesthetic) orthodoxy, and had "given permission" as the current phrase it has, to enjoy the sheer beauty of tonal music once again.

Rochberg's apostasy was heartily decried by the *bien-pensant* at the time, especially by avant-garde critics who, like the Soviet Union under Leonid Brezhnev and Stalin before him, had issued a standing order of Not One Step Back. Territory conquered by the dodecaphon-ists was under no circumstances ever to be relinquished to those who really would rather hear Haydn or Mahler. Although audiences con-tinued to be tortured by music they didn't like and didn't want to hear under any circumstances—especially not in the concert hall—within a decade, composers such as Steve Reich, Philip Glass, and John Adams had shouldered their way onto the performance stage and into the popular imagination.

One evening in late 1977 or early 1978, shortly after I had begun my tenure on the *San Francisco Examiner*, a young man of about my age approached me at a concert to welcome me to San Francisco. He was a composer, he said, handed me the score of a new work for piano and invited me to attend its premiere in my professional capac-ity the following week. I took the score home, played through it and liked it immediately. The work was *Phrygian Gates*—today regarded as his "opus one"—and the composer's name was John Adams, later to become one of the most successful of the "minimalist" composers who came to prominence in the late '70s and early '80s. By May 1981, I was already at *Time* magazine and happily took up the cudgel not only for these composers but for the cause of music's restoration in the forefront of contemporary thought. I believe I succeeded in the former but failed in the latter endeavor.

How signally I failed is proclaimed by the absence of serious musical coverage in today's media. Although I wrote cover stories on James Levine, Andrew Lloyd Webber, and Vladimir Horowitz, I was never quite able to get my major piece on Phil Glass on the cover, although we came close on several occasions before the assassination of Indira Gandhi in 1984 killed our last chance and the story eventually ran inside. After leaving *Time* (which today exists only as a shell of its former self, a zombie version of Harry Luce's once-proud and influential magazine), I was not meaningfully replaced and such stories as appeared were concerned with the new forms of rap and hip-hop. In a sense, the magazine and other journalistic outlets were once again covering music as news—throwback stories to the 1920s when the newspapers joyously chronicled the glamourous doings of Gangland, with its snazzy thugs, opulent nightclubs, fast cars, loose women, and sudden demises by gunfire. It just wasn't something I cared to write about.

As for contemporary "classical" music, it has latterly become beset by all the modish ills of contemporary life, including the transient sex rumpuses of the #MeToo movement, both gay and straight; the "underrepresentation" of racial—but not sexual!—minorities, unsurprising regarding a European art form in which they have almost zero interest; and mostly because time and tide have passed it by. Performers today—nth-generation Xeroxes of Xeroxes that perhaps can trace their pedagogical lineage back to the late nineteenth century—have lost emotional touch with their sources, playing the notes but not the music. What then is left for the critic to do? No wonder the craft has essentially disappeared.

Few critics, it's true, can or ever could match Shaw at his most perceptively barbed. But because art music was vital to the pre-Great War civilization, because an informed citizen or subject in any Western country was expected to have knowledge of high culture (nineteenth-century Americans were positive whizzes at Shakespeare and quoted him right along with the King James Bible), and because Shaw was a great writer, his editors published him and his readers read—nay, were compelled to read—him.

As music itself ran out of gas, however, so did the critics. By failing to engage with the development of the art form, and being content to "fact check" performances, they put themselves out of business. Editors and publishers, who were trying desperately to hold on to their readership, eventually cut them loose in a fit of democratizing that was, however, too late to save their publications. Music has, therefore, been forced to return to its roots as a plaything of princes, a minority pursuit—now, however, subject to the cultural ill winds that can come for it at any time and bring it up on charges of insufficient diversity, cultural appropriation, unauthorized syncretism, and elitism.

In other words, the censors of the Central Committee of the All-Union Communist Party are back, this time flying the banner of "social justice" and "progressivism." And, just as in the old U.S.S.R., the state-adjacent media is marching right along in lockstep with them. To hell with the past, to the things which were once of value. Times have changed, comrade: In an era of declining readership and limitless gullibility, the media simply gives the people what it decides they want to hear, and lots of it.

In the end, it was not the deaf stockbrokers, those former avatars of middle-class Colonel Blimpism, who turned out to be the threat after all, but the commissars who monitor every movement to make sure that the orthodoxy of cultural and political conformity—they are now once again the same—is enforced. We have met the enemy, and he really is us.

PART SEVEN:
WOMEN
AND SEXUALITY

HOW WOMEN CHANGED JOURNALISM

BY PRISCILLA TURNER

The legendary Gilded Age journalist Ida Tarbell, whose investigation of Standard Oil brought J.D. Rockefeller's infamous monopoly to its knees, is a problem for feminists. Scan any list of the best female journalists of all time and you'll find Martha Gellhorn, maybe Barbara Walters, even Jane Mayer or Christiane Amanpour. (If you're looking for a trailblazing Ida, there's always Ms. Wells, the early civil rights activist.) Tarbell, if she's there at all, is down near the bottom. The legendary pioneer of investigative journalism has been ruthlessly relegated to the cheap seats.

Why? A born iconoclast, Tarbell was skeptical of women's suffrage.

Give feminists credit—they are committed! To the Agenda, if not the facts. And that is especially true for the women journalists who today hold sway over the profession, never mind that, at least theoretically, journalism is supposed to be *about* the facts.

Writer and literary critic Carol Iannone might have been thinking of journalism's sisterhood back in 1989 when she wrote:

> Feminism is a series of self-indulgent contradictions and anyone following it for a while is going to find her thought coarsened… Women are the same as men, women are different from men, according to the ideological need. Women are strong and capable. And yet have been the slaves and victims of men

359

throughout history. Women are angry, even rebellious in patriarchy, but also superior to men because loving and tender.

Now that those "self-indulgent contradictions" are inscribed as inerrant scripture, it's useful to revisit pagan times when women journalists were expected to cover the news more or less objectively—that is, like their male counterparts. Remember the great 1940 comedy *His Girl Friday*? An adaptation of a stage play, the film swapped out Hildy Johnson's sex without missing a beat; Rosalind Russell's Hildy had as much ink coursing through her veins as every guy not named Archie Leach and she could match barbs, put-downs, and wisecracks with any of them.

Yes, it was fiction, but the audience bought it, because the dedicated woman newshound was not unfamiliar to '40s audiences. That's how the leading female journalists of the era saw themselves. There was, for instance, Martha Gellhorn, today cited as one of the top war correspondents in a time that produced more than its share. Gellhorn went from Bryn Mawr to the Spanish Civil War and on to the D-Day invasion and the liberation of Dachau. She would still be at it at eighty, covering the 1989 invasion of Panama. Gellhorn was married to Ernest Hemingway for four turbulent years, and her name was inevitably linked to his. She hated it. "I was a writer before I met him," she wrote, "and I was a writer after I left him."

To get around restrictions that barred women from the front lines, Gellhorn disguised herself as a nurse and, on D-Day, boarded a ship picking up the wounded. She then produced the following for *Collier's*:

> An LCT drew alongside our ship, pitching in the waves. A boy in a steel helmet shouted up to the crew at the aft rail, and a wooden box looking like a lidless coffin was lowered on a pulley, and with the greatest difficulty, bracing themselves against the movement of their boat, the men on the LCT laid a stretcher inside the box. The box was raised to our deck, and out of it

was lifted a man who was closer to being a child than a man, dead-white and seemingly dying. The first wounded man to be brought to that ship for safety and care was a German prisoner.

Less known but equally intrepid was Sigrid Schultz. Born in Chicago in 1893, Schultz was fluent in five languages and, following World War I, began working for the *Chicago Tribune*'s Berlin bureau; eventually becoming the paper's Berlin correspondent, and, ultimately its bureau chief—the first woman in a major news organization to earn that title. Schultz developed an extraordinary network of contacts and sources in pre-war Germany; she knew Goering well, and interviewed Hitler. Observed William Shirer, who was reporting from Berlin at the same time, "No other correspondent in Berlin knew so much of what was going on behind the scenes as did Sigrid Schultz."

Often employing the pseudonym "John Dickson" and using phony datelines to protect her identify, Schultz gave the *Tribune* one exclusive after another: on the vicious treatment of Germany's Jews; the existence of early concentration camps; the German insincerity on the Munich Agreement; and five weeks before it happened, predicting Germany's breaking its non-aggression pact with the Soviet Union. Throughout her life, she called herself a "newspaperman."

In a 1939 *Time* magazine cover story, Dorothy Thompson was dubbed the second-most influential woman in America after Eleanor Roosevelt. Like Sigrid Schultz, after World War I, Thompson went to Berlin, where the action was, joining the staff of the *New York Evening Post*, and eventually rising to head the bureau. In 1934 she became the first American correspondent to be thrown out of Germany—on Hitler's personal order—after dismissing him in print as "inconsequent and voluble, ill poised and insecure. He is the very prototype of the little man." Thompson later wrote:

> I was really put out of Germany for the crime of blasphemy. My offense was to think that Hitler was just an ordinary man, after all. That is a crime in the

reigning cult in Germany... To question this mystic mission is so heinous that, if you are German, you can be sent to jail. I, fortunately, am an American, so I was merely sent to Paris. Worse things can happen.

Returning to the United States, Thompson wrote a thrice-weekly column for the *New York Herald Tribune* that was ultimately syndicated to more than one 170 papers. Simultaneously, she was a commentator for NBC radio; she was also the inspiration for the classic 1942 Hepburn-Tracy rom-com *Woman of the Year*. Only incidentally, Sinclair Lewis was the second of her three husbands.

That was then, when men were men and women were women, but being a good newspaperman transcended sex. Like so much else, that began to change in the '60s, and would only pick up speed from there.

Future researchers seeking the precise moment when women journalists abandoned even the guise of objectivity—journalism's patient zero—might point to December 1971 and the debut of *Ms.* magazine. Given that in coming years liberal male journalists would cravenly surrender to the new sensibility, it is telling that *Ms.* was birthed by star editor Clay Felker, as an insert to his *New York* magazine. Co-edited by Gloria Steinem, the first stand-alone issue featured Wonder Woman on the cover, and made a splash with a feature called, "Abortion Now, Abortion Tomorrow, Abortion Forever."

Well, no, it was really called, "We Have Had Abortions," listing various titans of womanhood, including Billie Jean King, Judy Collins, Nora Ephron, and, of course, Steinem. Also on offer were "I Want a Wife" (identified as "satire"), "De-Sexing the English Language," and "Rate the Candidates" (McGovern v. Nixon, take a guess!).

It was thrilling and cutting-edge at the time, a bearded-Spock universe version of the *Ladies' Home Journal*, substituting "click moments," consciousness raising, and, yes, abortion horror stories, for household hints and recipes. Young women journalists (and by now, journalism schools, were turning out as many women as men, everyone with the same late-'60s, left-of-center pedigree) wanted in; maybe at *Ms.* itself, but certainly within the newspaper, magazine, and broadcast outlets where they eventually landed. And while plenty of veteran male journalists initially resisted overt attempts to undermine traditional standards of objectivity—*The New York Times*'s Abe Rosenthal was notable in this regard—soon enough they were gone, and with them would go even the pretense of mainstream even-handedness.

Speaking of facts: Has any individual wreaked more cultural havoc than the embittered feminist—sorry, beloved Founding Mother—Steinem? As the intrepid iconoclast Cathy Young observed in a 2013 piece titled "Gloria Steinem Represents the Worst of Modern Feminism," "Steinem is practically a poster girl for the gender-war paranoia and the ideological dogmatism that have led the women's movement down such a destructive path." Young went on to count the ways that Steinem embodied feminism's worst features: a denial of sex differences so dogmatic and unhinged she insisted it was "sexist" that female would-be firefighters be required to pass upper-body strength tests; her endless fixation on male villainy and female victimhood; her deeply divisive political partisanship; and her contempt for free speech that presaged today's crackdown on "disinformation."

For post-Steinem journalists, it was all but assumed that the only legitimate way to regard the world, and especially every issue of purported interest to women, was through a feminist squint. As a Steinem maxim had it: "A woman has two choices—either she's a feminist or a masochist." Steinem famously dismissed Texas Republican Kay Bailey Hutchison—a pro-choice moderate!—as "a female impersonator." Alas, the occasion for Young's all-too-accurate assessment of the feminist icon was Steinem's being awarded a Presidential Medal of Freedom by Barack Obama; which is to say that by then her views had long since been widely embraced as correct and forward thinking.

Through it all, Steinem never ceased identifying as a journalist, and remained on call to pound out words in an emergency. Most notably, when Bill Clinton's presidency was facing multiple accusations of sexual misconduct in 1998 (including Juanita Broaddrick's credible account of rape) she'd rushed out a *New York Times* op-ed in Clinton's defense. This was a signal, to the extent that one was needed, for others to rally around the president. Soon after, *Time* magazine's Nina Burleigh went on the record to *The Washington Post*'s Howard Kurtz with what surely almost every woman in her circle (and more than a few men) seconded in private: "I'd be happy to give [Clinton] a blow job just to thank him for keeping abortion legal. I think American women should be lining up with their presidential kneepads on to show their gratitude for keeping the theocracy off our backs."

Not so long before, that would have ended anyone's journalism career. In the world we now lived in, Burleigh went on to write for *People*, *The New York Observer*, *The New York Times*, *The Washington Post*, and *The New Yorker*, capping off her career with an adjunct journalism professorship at Columbia.

Liberal men in the media, if not outright corrupted, knew to be compliant, which of course amounted to the same thing. Among the earliest collaborationists was then-big deal Alan Alda, beloved from television as *M.A.S.H.*'s Hawkeye Pierce, who in a 1974 "humor piece" for *Ms.* wrote: "Until recently it has been thought that the level of testosterone in men is normal simply because they have it. But if you consider how abnormal their behavior is, then you are led to the hypothesis that almost all men are suffering from testosterone poisoning." It is the first recorded reference to the imagined male disorder.

Soon enough, men's magazines followed the sisterhood in the rush to de-toxify themselves. As Tucker Carlson later noted of *Esquire*, for which he'd written earlier in his career, it "was then a real magazine and now it's this kind of weird, self-hating, 'I'm sorry, I'm a man.'" Male boo-hooing really hit its stride with *The New York Times*'s "About Men" column in the 1980s. No matter the subject—manhood, war, dirty diapers—it always devolved to the same thing: "the general inferiority of men," observed the journalist Michael Kelly, who was killed in Baghdad in 2003 covering the Iraq War.

If male journalists' default position has long been to nod, if not grovel, before strident female colleagues—and since #MeToo, *all* female colleagues, for safety's sake—they know to be especially circumspect on the issue of abortion. For modern feminists the subject is non-negotiable: for those with even marginally differing views, a potential career-ending third rail to be avoided at all costs. This is true at all times and under all circumstances, but it has never been truer than during the bloody battles over Republican nominees to the Supreme Court.

For women journalists, the media *generalissima* of these titanic fights, NPR's Nina Totenberg, stands as nearly formidable a heroine as Totenberg's own longtime pal (never mind the conflict of interest), the late Supreme Court Justice Ruth Bader Ginsberg, officiant at her second wedding. Totenberg skyrocketed to fame with the leaked-to-her scoop that Clarence Thomas had been accused of sexual harassment by Anita Hill, prompting the Senate Judiciary Committee to re-open its 1991 hearings, culminating in Thomas's "high-tech lynching" defense. The Left just missed getting another scalp to go with Robert Bork's—but a superstar had been born.

Nor was Totenberg one to be bullied by a man. When Senator Alan Simpson, a Republican from Wyoming, confronted her on *Nightline* with her self-evident bias, saying, "Let's not pretend your reporting is objective here. That would be absurd," Totenberg famously confronted him post-taping. "You are evil, bitter, nasty and all your colleagues hate you. So fuck you."

For a time, news consumers seeking refuge from the feminist furies could at least find it in the sports section. But that quickly ended. It was one thing to know that there were more aspiring women sports writers—sure, if they could hack it—and it was more interesting than concerning to learn of their forays into the former preserve of the locker room when, in 1978, a federal judge ruled it illegal to ban female reporters. (The not-so-good-for-the-gander department: Different rules still applied for women athletes.)

In an episode that almost seems quaint by contemporary standards, *Boston Herald* reporter Lisa Olson complained about sexual harassment by several naked New England Patriot football players, one of whom reportedly fondled his genitals and asked, "Is this what you want?" Successful lawsuits followed because, we were led to understand, a woman journalist must never be made to feel uncomfortable or disrespected when intruding on the privacy of a yahoo boob. Very soon sports coverage itself changed, with more attention devoted to sports purportedly of interest to women, such as the WNBA—though for some reason, that was never evident in attendance and viewership numbers—and a *great* deal more attention given to issues of race and gender.

A notorious case in point was the Duke lacrosse team rape hoax, which dominated the sports (and news) pages for months in 2006 and 2007. Reporters of both sexes were complicit in pushing Emmett Till-levels of false accusations, but no one was more aggressive than *The New York Times*'s Salena Roberts. "Roberts wrote commentary seething with hatred for 'a group of privileged players of fine pedigree entangled in a night that threatens to belie their social standing as human beings,'" wrote legal analyst Stuart Taylor, who meticulously covered the travesty. Even after the accused were completely exonerated and the *Times*'s sports editor expressed regret over the paper's coverage, Roberts refused to admit that she got it wrong. The real story, she claimed, was the athletes' "culture of affluence and entitlement" that she dared to expose. Roberts went on to *Sports Illustrated* and lucrative book contracts. The Roberts journalism standard was the Steinem standard: "Who?" was the only question of the profession's famous Four W's that mattered, particularly for women.

So it goes, too, with political coverage.

"I was always taught that journalists were charged with writing the first rough draft of history," wrote Bari Weiss, in her famous 2020 resignation letter to *New York Times* publisher A.G. Sulzberger. "Now, history itself is one more ephemeral thing molded to fit the needs of a predetermined narrative."

And in post-feminist America, the narrative is as clear as a 36-point headline. Though it's a fierce competition, arguably no one in the political realm has gotten off more scot-free than either of the Clintons.

Hard to know the female equivalent of blow jobs for Bill, but the usual suspects were all in when Hillary went for the brass ring in 2016. True enough, it had been a harder call in 2008, when Obama was going for it, too. The book *Who Should Be First? Feminists Speak Out on the 2008 Presidential Campaign*, which includes essays by journalists Maureen Dowd, Katha Pollitt, and Robin Morgan, captures the anguished handwringing over "the choice of an African American man or a white woman as the next Democratic candidate for U.S. President." Melanin or chromosomes? Hard choices (ironically, the title of one of Hillary's many memoirs), indeed.

But fast-forward eight years. Now it really was Her Turn, especially once Bernie and his sexist Bernie Bros were dispatched. So, it was all hands on deck for chromosomes! Madeleine Albright perfectly captured the *Zeitgeist* with a reminder at a Hillary event: "Just remember, there's a special place in hell for women who don't help each other." Of course, for media babes, helping Hillary meant dispatching the likes of Broaddrick, Paula Jones, and Gennifer Flowers down the memory hole.

"No one can say for sure how Clinton ended up with a traveling press pool made up almost entirely of women," begins a *Vogue* profile of Hillary's estrogen-heavy press scrum titled "Have Female Journalists Ended the Boys-on-the-Bus Era of Campaign Reporting?" The May 19, 2016 piece features this observation by PBS's Gwen Ifill (whose regard for fairness had been established eight years before in her pro-Biden moderation of the vice presidential debate): "Bias is the absence of a point of view. Women aren't going to favor women, but if you don't have a woman in the room you might not see the whole story." Apparently, this was meant to be taken at face value; with no one noticing that it's impossible to imagine *anyone* defending an all-male press pool covering a male candidate. *Vogue* itself, citing "the profound stakes," would go on to give its first political endorsement ever to Hillary in its October 2016 edition.

Among Hillary's press pack featured in the article were *BuzzFeed*'s Ruby Cramer, *Politico*'s Anni Karni, the AP's Beth Harpaz, and *The*

New York Times's Amy Chozick. Chozick went on to write a memoir of the campaign—*Chasing Hillary*—cover-blurbed thusly: "This insanely readable book manages to bring humor and a fresh inside perspective to the saddest event in history." Chozick's book *is* extraordinarily revealing, but perhaps in ways not intended, starting with her overt contempt for Hillary's rival. In Little Rock to cover a Hillary fundraising speech, Chozick, who acknowledged she'd been a fan of *The Apprentice* but hadn't seen Donald Trump "as a candidate yet," decided to take a peek when he serendipitously turned up as the key speaker at an Arkansas GOP dinner:

> Trump walked into the drab conference room soaked in sweat... "Ah, it's nice and cool in here," Trump said, dabbing his drenched forehead with crinkled Kleenexes he'd pulled out from his suit pocket. A couple of dandruff-size white dots stuck to his forehead and temples like snowflakes on orange AstroTurf. I couldn't believe it. Not only did Hillary never sweat...

Chozick did a great job of capturing the highs, the lows, the unremitting drudgery of being a beat political reporter following a campaign, but the constant, Hamlet-like ruminations: *Does she hate me? Does she like me? Does she think I'm being fair? Am I being fair?* were as far from the Hildy Johnson prototype as it's possible for a woman to go. Chozick had "a hard time" watching while Trump and his minions tried to "Swift boat" Hillary and "chip away at Hillary's biggest advantage—her standing among women voters. 'She's not a victim. She was an enabler,' Trump told Fox News."

And, in the wake of "Pussygate," what about younger women, who were muddying the ideological waters with "the mantra that every woman who accuses a man of sexual assault deserved to be believed"? Surely that didn't apply to Hillary's husband! Writes Chozick: "I didn't know what to think. It had been a different era in 1992 when Clinton campaign aides used words like 'bimbo' and 'floozy' and 'stalker' to describe Bill's accusers... But blaming a wife for her husband's trans-gressions also seemed like the ultimate act of sexism."

Chozick prided herself on her in-depth knowledge of the candi-date, often doing a deep dive into her past to find an interesting tit-bit that she could expand into a quirky piece. Yet somehow it never occurred to her to interview Paula Jones or Juanita Broaddrick or Kathleen Willey about their treatment by *both* Clintons. For Hillary's girls on the bus, the former president's bimbos and floozies were so 1998—in 2016, the "ultimate sexism" was daring to hold Hillary Clinton accountable for her *own* deeds.

Election night left Hillary's all-female press corps as spent and life-less as a deflated "I'm with Her" balloon. Chozick writes that those who made it into the New Yorker hotel the next morning to cover her concession speech "were all in some stage of a breakdown. Glasses on, no makeup, hair pulled back in tangly bird's nests. We comforted each other with pats on the shoulder. Hugs would've been too conspicu-ous." Of course, there were tears. Chozick's husband, Robert Ennis, would have made Alan Alda proud: "[He] had tears in his eyes, his posture slumped over in his white T-shirt and boxer shorts..."

Tears that might have been: back at the *Times*, "a color piece that had been envisioned as capturing the white patrons at a dive bar in a Pennsylvania steel town 'crying in their beers' was quickly repurposed into a front-page story on how white men had delivered for Trump." And the bitterest tears of all: "I sat down at my cubicle to write the 'How She Lost' story. Then I finally cried." Weeping men and cursing women (who, of course, can cry if they want to) is media feminism's end game. As Gloria Steinem said in 2017, "I'm glad we've begun to raise our daughters more like our sons, but it will never work until we raise out sons more like our daughters."

And yet no mainstream journalist of either sex dare suggest that a greater threat to the common good than the yang of toxic masculinity might be its yin, venomous estrogen. "What I really wanted to do was draw young women in through the things they had been taught most to care about—fashion and celebrity and stuff—and politicize them that way, kind of in a sneaky way," bragged Moe Tkacik, a founding editor and star writer for the feminist blogsite *Jezebel*. Launched in 2007 as part of the *Gawker* website empire (now defunct) to cater to young women, *Jezebel*, which itself subsequently folded, traded in sneering contempt for difference of political opinion, and its writers further prided themselves on going *mano-a-mano* with construction workers in their swaggering vulgarity. Tellingly, the online magazine served as a launching pad into the legacy media for some of its most aggressively political "reporters," bringing their brand to an ever-larger audience. Nor do they have to be sneaky about it; one-time fringe Jacobins are standard-issue faces and bylines these days in the Corporate Media.

Exhibit A in what has been termed today's "toxic cesspit of performative feminism" is of course, *The View*. This Agony Column come to life is, never forget, part of ABC's news division. Exhibit B might be Taylor Lorenz, *New York Times* alumna and, at this writing, of *The Washington Post*, who alternates between doxxing and otherwise seeking to destroy ideological foes, and weeping when anyone fights back. Feeling victimized by a (female) reporter when being interviewed for an MSNBC segment on cyberbullying, Lorenz afterward tweeted: "No bigger regret in my career than making the mistake of thinking @MorganRadford knew how to accurately report on abuse/harassment… I cannot warn women loudly enough to stay away from her/MSNBC… She produced an insane garbage segment months ago that misgendered a colleague." You've come a long way, baby.

However, the *ne plus ultra*, the cherry on top of the sundae, the nadir, the height—you pick it—of feminist dicta was #MeToo, which sprang to life in 2017, like Athena leaping from Zeus's skull. Amplified by the press in the hope that it would further undermine the despised Trump, the most devious male chauvinist couldn't have done more to infantilize women. Even the name—MeToo!!—evokes a second-grader demanding a goody bag at a birthday party. The following year, the estimable Heather Mac Donald noted:

> There are likely no major newspapers that are not tallying reporter and op-ed bylines, as well as the

topics they cover, by gender and race... In response to the #MeToo movement, the *New York Times* created a "gender editor" who presides over a "gender initiative" to infuse questions of gender throughout all the *Times'* coverage. A recent front-page product of this #MeToo initiative covered the earth-shattering problem facing NFL cheerleaders: to wit, they have a dress code and are forbidden from fraternizing with the players. Despite these allegedly patriarchal conditions, females are still lining up to be hired, to the puzzlement of the *Times*.

That same year, 2018, NPR conducted a survey that produced worrying results to the question, "Has Me Too Gone 'Too Far'?" As *Vox* news reported, "The survey did not define 'too far,' but NPR reports that respondents cited worries about a rush to judgment, unproven accusations that could destroy lives, and a bandwagon effect that could encourage people to overstate claims of sexual misconduct."

Oh, well, as Pulitzer Prize-winning Timesman Walter Duranty famously pointed out during the Stalinist era in the former Soviet Union, "You have to break a few eggs to make an omelet."

Ida Tarbell would be appalled, but she wouldn't be surprised. Why did she oppose women's suffrage? Formerly a radical feminist herself, she had come to regard most women as fundamentally frivolous, and was convinced that if the feminists succeeded in attaining enough power, the eventual result would be the feminization of men, and the resultant weakening of the nation itself.

Cancel that Cassandra!

LETTERS TO AN ACCLIMATISED BEAUTY

BY JENNY KENNEDY

Dear Jenny,

With your recent cover appearance on Paris Match, *you've become known as the bug hostess in elite circles despite rumors that you can't swallow the crunchy critters yourself. Are we heading for a society without meat and how will you cope if you, too, are forced to eat bugs?*

Hungry in Hounslow

Dear Hungry:

You have to understand this is bigger than just you and me, it's about engineering a sustainable planet, and feeding developing nations. Ordinary farmers and people used to eating traditional meat sources don't understand the larger impact. Thankfully this is an organised scheme and the press has a responsibility to help us save the planet and feed those whose survival is threatened by global warming. Who eventually gets to eat traditional meat and who will make the switch to bugs is not going to be decided by you or me. We're all in this together!

******

Dear Jenny,

I'm so impressed by your success with the Green Movement which I follow closely. Despite the fact that we're still largely living on fossil fuels, how have you been able to remain so popular with the media?

Puzzled in Poughkeepsie

Dear Puzzled:

Haven't you heard? First impressions are lasting and headlines rule the day. Truth is, no one really reads the whole story if they even read at all! And who's got time to pore over data? These days it's all about the scroll. The average viewer will scroll through twenty headlines and maybe only read one full piece. So what are the chances they choose to read up on carbon capture? Whether it be sea levels, or weather, or algae bloom, everyone knows neglect of our planet is to blame. So with each quick click we are reinforcing the only thing that matters—rescuing our beloved planet. Heck, it's my love of the planet that's allowed me to employ such artful tools to move the needle on the national conversation.

And if you think readers are busy, think of the poor journalists—their whole life is reading! And some typing. Trust is key in any relationship, and when journalists know they can trust you to provide content, you know you can trust them to sell that content with a juicy headline. But success requires money, and money on this scale requires consensus. So the first thing I had to do was bring everyone round to our side, and headlines provided that consensus.

******

Dear Jenny,

How do you manage to get and keep the media on your side? You seem to manage it so gracefully and with such elan and éclat!

Admiring in Albuquerque

Dear Admiring:

I'd like to think that the media is on the side of right, at least from where I stand they are. But as with everything, it's important to have someone on the inside, not as a cheat mind you, but because in this way they can fact check ongoing progress and be up to date on new projects. It's the computer age and even tech-professionals have to continually be kept up, so why would legacy media be any different? As you know, everyone has good intentions, and journalists all want to do their best. So it stands to reason that they want to be as close to the source as possible. It's a perfect relationship really.

Separately, journalists also tend to be insecure, and who can blame them really? Living in fear that their every error and omission might be called out for the world to see? Remember that whereas they were once trained to question everything they were told, they've advanced to the point that they now know consensus is key. It's an evolution really—evolution by natural selection. Journalists have a job to do, and that job is not to confuse people. We call this 'narrative reinforcement', but I like to think of it as reassurance—something that is needed now more than ever. Previous generations didn't have to worry about CO2 levels, or living on the hottest planet ever. Luckily, the internet culture by its very design, forces us to be concerned with group affirmation—and I'm just happy to help!

******

Dear Jenny,

What behind-the-scenes tool do you employ for maximum effectiveness as an eco-warrior and what can you share with fellow environmentalists to help us be better represented in the media?

Committed in Cincinnati

Dear Committed:

One word: LEXICON. As I've often said, readers today don't have time to read through both morning and evening papers as they once did, let alone keep up with ever-changing terms. *Who's got time for that?* And when the subject is something as important as the environment, we must constantly strive to provide the right words to explain things in easily digestible bites. Take the term 'global warming'. This has confused many. Especially when we had people like NASA publishing studies that showed more than enough Antarctic snow accumulation to outweigh the losses.

Not helpful! By changing the term to the all-purpose' 'climate change' we are able to push on. Most people aren't rocket scientists any more than they are brain surgeons. Adapting the lexicon to suit the needs of the planet has been an invaluable tool in saving it.

******

Dear Jenny,

In your many television appearances, you've often been highly critical of focus groups. Why is that? And if so, why do you still use them?

Confused in Calgary

Dear Confused:

Focus groups are a necessary evil. Why? Because the media needs facts. And where do we get facts? From studies and experts. Focus groups are a study, the results of which are given to experts who then provide the facts. While I'm always concerned with getting it right, the public's obsession with 'validation' forces us to dig down and draw out the facts. Let me explain. At this particular time, we find ourselves unable to form an opinion of our own, lest we be proven wrong. Or worse—cancelled. I mean, how embarrassing is that? Hence the boon in focus groups. If other people think it, well then it must be true, and there's safety in numbers. Sometimes rather than taking the temperature of a group, studies end up *telling* the group exactly how they feel, but they still provide value because experts whom people disagree with... are discounted. Thus, making this process necessary.

Let me walk you through the down and dirty. People assume an arm's length guarantees fairness, but you can't be naive enough to think that people are just conducting random focus groups with no direction whatsoever. I mean, what would that look like and who would you even bring in? So, clearly, you're culling from a group of selected individuals. And to be fair, you have to ask a headache sufferer if you want an opinion on migraine tablets. But it gets stickier. Participants are paid handsomely and I'm sure they ask themselves what's the harm in saying they suffer from the occasional migraine vs. the occasional headache and who can tell the difference anyway? Especially if it means five hundred quid for an hour's work.

On top of that, everyone wants to be heard. Believe me, you've never heard more diverse or fantastical opinions on say, Sainsbury's Butter (a square of butter wrapped in foil), until you've heard the passionate opinion of a bona fide focus group participant. Unsurprisingly, the very-animated participants get invited back. Next there's the person conducting the group—usually something between a Mary Poppins and a Bernie Madoff. They have the job of bringing out the very best in these individuals to prove to the clients that they are getting their money's worth. Then the client (which is usually an ad agency or law firm), goes back to the company to tell them what the people want to hear.

In short—a mess. A manufactured and expensive mess, but a necessary one. And through it, everyone is served.

******

Dear Jenny,

How is it you seem to manage a love affair with the media?

Impressed in Ingrams Green

Dear Impressed:

Far from a love affair, it is anything but! We spend months planning an agenda only to be asked for ongoing proof—which is maddening, and takes time and resources away from the important work we do. Luckily, there are enough decent outlets, whose commitment to saving the planet really shines through. Still, it's important to manage the message. One such way we do that is by press conferences. Here we can focus on the facts that matter and bring in dedicated experts. Notice I said experts, which is what journalists need to get the story up and provide the credibility it deserves.

The smart media get it. I provide a well-orchestrated event, and they have access to the story—free! Chasing down witnesses and facts is exhausting, but in a live event every journalist gets the scoop. So, you see everyone benefits from a press conference. Plus, now you've established relationships, which are critical in any business.

Next, have a back-up story ready. And by ready, I mean produced down to the last comma splice. Journalists don't like being left without content to meet a deadline. Being a dependable resource only strengthens your liaison and in return you can usually count on them to run non-important stories that day to make sure your event gets the coverage it deserves. We call it "access journalism" for a reason!

******

Dear Jenny,

Green technology is so new, there are bound to be mistakes along the way. In the event of embarrassing details leaking, or a project gone horribly wrong, how do you do damage control?

Baffled in Buffalo

Dear Baffled:

Leaking *is* damage control! There's always some good news, and even when you find a hurdle, you must do what you can to save the planet. Other avenues to manage the message are polls and studies. These will always yield some information you can find useful and when all else fails, arrange a public inquiry. The mere fact of questioning a person or situation under the lights lessens the damage. It also has the added benefit of timing. You can drip, drip, drip the facts out in any manner that best suits. It can also give you time to assemble additional details, and in this way every media outlet winds up on the same page. It's something I'm sure you've noticed whenever a big story breaks over the course of many weeks, and inexplicably every news outlet is disseminating the same new details on the same day—a win-win-win!

******

Dear Jenny,

Given that some of your clients have promised to be carbon neutral by 2050 in order to save the planet, how do you get the media to continue to promote your efforts even though you have no evidence on which to base that claim, and even EV charging stations are powered by fossil fuels?

Skeptical in Schenectady

Dear Skeptical:

I appreciate your question. My clients and I have never strayed from our commitment to carbon neutrality and have always recognised that this is a process, as do our friends in the media. Of course, you're free to decide for yourself, but you do understand that respectable news and opinion outlets like *The New York Times* provide both sides of every story, without fear or favour; that's why it is widely recognised as the gold standard of journalistic integrity. Likewise, the *Times* understands our trajectory and has verified our findings. I gather that some significant portion of the public feels that powerful people can use the media to push their own political or economic interests, but these feelings are most strongly held by the least educated. Most people surveyed feel that journalists do a first-rate job in checking sources, verifying facts, and providing evidence to back up claims.

While it's easy to be critical of things one doesn't understand, all the mainstream media works with a global community of reporters, editors, and outlets to improve the quality, understanding, and impact of climate coverage around the world. Consistency provides trust, and to ensure that trust, this global alliance works together like a well-oiled machine. So, you see, we are always working hand in hand to expand coverage of climate change, to improve understanding, and to help readers like yourself.

******

Dear Jenny,

Most people get their news from screens these days as opposed to printed pages. Does this change the way we see stories?

Wondering in Walla Walla

Dear Wondering:

Absolutely! And it's all for the good. I previously explained the benefit of headlines, and how reading only headlines becomes an exercise similar to flashcards. The reader is drilled on select points that are rapidly reinforced. The reader is then more likely to retain the point of the headline but none of the additional content. This is not a bad thing. The news source is serving the reader by both saving him time, and providing him with the talking points he needs most. Repetition of particular themes and branded terms provides a type of Pavlovian conditioning. Thus, readers are able to make connections more quickly and expand on these in their own conversations.

Well, that's all the space we have for today. Now that you have your marching orders, go out there and save the world!

ALL GAY, ALL THE TIME

BY AUSTIN RUSE

In 1971, one of America's greatest essayists published a lengthy article in *Harper's Magazine* that caused an enormous stink among New York's literati. Joseph Epstein's *Homo/Hetero: The Struggle for Sexual Identity* triggered a reaction that, bit by bit, forever changed the way the Corporate Media wrote about homosexuality. So enormous has been the change in the interim that Epstein's piece would never run in the *Harper's* of today. It's doubtful that even the Family Research Council would touch it.

Epstein, an extremely thoughtful writer, hit some notes that jar contemporary ears. He began, accurately enough, with the observation that Americans in 1971 "despise homosexuality without equivocation." But, he said, homosexuality was an anathema, a curse of "sexual inversion" that was downright medieval. Epstein said that homosexuality makes a man "hostage to a passion…that can distort a man, can twist him, and always leave him defined by his sexual condition." Epstein said he wished homosexuality would cease to exist altogether and that "nothing would make me sadder than if [any of his children] were to become homosexual."

You can't even *think* such things today. You'd land immediately on the Southern Poverty Law Center hate list, and GLAAD's Accountability Project would take your words down.

In this chapter, I examine how the media culture has changed exponentially on the question of "gay." No longer are homosexuals held up to disdain. Now they are practically heroes, and it is the Christians for whom their sexual proclivities are sinful who come in for media opprobrium. There has been a 180-degree turn. LGBTs now dominate the Corporate Press.

Epstein's views on homosexuality were not remotely fringy fifty years ago. There was no more important and influential magazine in those days than *Time* magazine. Congressmen, CEOs, small bank presidents, and your third-grade teacher took their cues from *Time*. In January 1966, *Time* published a long think piece called "The Homosexual in America" that said homosexuality used to be "the abominable crime not to be mentioned" but had become "not only mentioned; it is freely discussed and widely analyzed." However, the *Time* writer still referred to homosexuals as "deviates," even "respectable deviates" who are out in the open, "particularly in fashion and the arts."

Time helpfully explained that homosexuals were there to help women in many ways, with their hair, picking out curtains, and escorting them to social events because homosexuals are "witty, pretty, catty, and no problem to keep at arm's length." Be warned, however, because "even in ordinary conversation, most homosexuals will sooner or later attack the 'things that normal men take seriously.'" It is remarkable today to read: "This does not mean that homosexuals do not and cannot talk seriously; but there is often a subtle sea change in the conversation: sex (unspoken) pervades the atmosphere." Nineteen-seventies man viewed the homosexual as sex-obsessed.

Three years later, *Time* ran a piece called "Behavior: The Homosexual: Newly Visible, Newly Understood," in which the unbylined writer refers to gays and lesbians as "male and female inverts." Homosexuals are "parlor darlings" and the women they escort are "fag hags." In a section called "The Dark Side of Love," the writer notes that "[h]omosexual taste can fall into a particular kind of self-indulgence as the homosexual revenges himself on a hostile world by writing grotesque exaggerations of straight customs, concentrates on superficial furbelows or develops a 'campy' fetish for old movies."

The writer offers a taxonomy of homosexual types; the Blatant, who may be "limp-wristed" and lisping; the Secret Lifer with "rigid wrists" and no lisping; the Desperate, who haunts public toilets; the Adjusted, who might be married with kids; the Bisexual; the Situational-Experimental, that is, soldiers and prisoners. All in all, read with contemporary eyes, schooled in the newest mores, quite astounding.

Enter Joseph Epstein's *Harper's* essay. It so thoroughly appalled Victor Navasky, then an editor at *The New York Times Magazine*, he immediately commissioned a piece from Merle Miller, later a Harry Truman biographer, called "What It Means to Be a Homosexual." It was the first "coming out" essay ever to appear in *The New York Times*.

Still, even gay Miller pulled his punches. He wrote, "Gay is good. Gay is proud," but said that he would have preferred not to have been that way. He says his mother wanted a girl, and she was disappointed in him. Other kids called him "sissy." He says he was an easy target; "undersized always, the girlish voice, the steel-rimmed glasses, always bent, no doubt limp of wrist, and I habitually carried a music roll." He started hanging around the train yards in his small Iowa town and had his first sexual encounter at twelve with a seventeen-year-old runaway who'd been riding the rails.

Miller used the word "gay" in his piece, a violation of the *Times* manual of style that said "gay" was only to be used in uppercase when naming an organization that used the word. Its occasional use was stopped in 1975 when *Times* owner Iphigene Ochs Sulzberger, then eighty-two, did not appreciate a piece on an "all gay cruise" that included a "sadomasochistic fashion show of leather get-ups, including harnesses and G-strings." The ban on "gay" was not lifted at *The New York Times* until 1986.

At the same time that *Time* magazine was calling homosexuals "inverts" and "deviants," and *The New York Times* had banned the word "gay," a few blocks north at *Esquire*, it was gay pedal to the gay metal. Tom Burke published a piece called "Look, Mack, this is a red-blooded, all-American, with-it faggot you're talking to. Show a little respect." The article condemned gay elders who were swishy, limp-wristed, and Judy-loving. That type of gay man, the piece said, "has expired with a whimper, to make way for the new homosexual of the Seventies, an unfettered, guiltless male child of the new morality in a Zapata mustache and an outlaw hat, who couldn't care less for the Establishment's approval, would as soon sleep with boys and girls, and thinks that 'Over the Rainbow' is a place to fly on 200 micrograms of lysergic acid diethylamide." Out went the gay old maid and in came the "new homosexuals" who, we know now, would be affected one way or another by HIV/AIDS just then coming around the corner in the bathhouses and tearooms.

Several important issues and critical moments advanced the change in the Corporate Media. One of the most important was the AIDS crisis. Among the earliest notices was a 1982 article in *The New York Times* called "New Homosexual Disorder Worries Health Officials."

Only 335 men had been diagnosed at that time, and of those 136 had died. Deeply worried that AIDS would cast a dark shadow over homosexuality and homosexuals, one of the Corporate Media's narrative maneuvers sought to convince readers that everyone, not just homosexuals, could get it, and everyone probably would. A few dozen newsweekly covers along these lines screamed that everyone was at risk, not just active homosexuals and intravenous drug users. The coverage from the newsweeklies was relentless. Recall a 1985 *Newsweek* cover with a clearly AIDS-infected Rock Hudson with the cover line that the disease was moving into all populations.

Thirty years before, however, had come sex-research titan Alfred Kinsey and his sometimes-criminal studies. His researchers masturbated babies in the crib to count the number of times the babies could achieve orgasm in an hour. His 1947 report on male sexuality told America that almost everyone committed adultery, and nearly half (47 percent) would eventually have at least one homosexual experience. He reported that 7 percent of the population was more or less permanently homosexual and that these sexual feelings fell along a normal sexual continuum. It should be noted that homosexual activists eventually settled on the 10 percent figure for homosexuality, something Kinsey never claimed, but that has by now become "common knowledge." What's more, under the Corporate Media onslaught, the number has blossomed in the minds of younger generations who now believe the percentage of homosexuals in the population is upwards of 25 percent. If such a vast percentage of people are gay, their thinking ran, then how could the Corporate Press continue to treat them with disdain?

And then there was the toppling of the psychiatric totem, the longtime belief and practice among mental health professionals that homosexuality was a mental disorder, generally stemming from a remote father and a suffocating mother, a condition that could be treated with talk therapy. Getting this notion out of the official *Diagnostic and Statistical Manual of Mental Disorders* was the most critical moment in the shift of opinion in the American populace and the Corporate Media.

Dr. Jeffrey Satinover, a clinal psychiatrist educated at MIT, Harvard, Yale, and the C.G. Jung Institute in Zurich, best describes how this happened: It was not based on science, but on politics and coercion. Satinover's 2007 paper *The Trojan Couch*, explains how activists inside and outside the American Psychiatric Association laid siege to the governing body, advancing highly questionable studies about the frequency of homosexuality, invading meetings, and threatening participants. It turns out that persuading the governing board to change the DSM II was like pushing on an open door since it included closeted homosexuals and homosexual allies.So significant was this change to the narrative that even highly credentialed opposing views became no longer acceptable. In fact, psychiatrists today who treat unwanted same-sex attractions and behaviors are shunned and sanctioned. The psychiatric guild eventually condemned talk therapy for unwanted same-sex attractions and behaviors, and it is now illegal in many states. There is a great deal of misinformation about "reparative therapy," but it is now routinely referred to as "discredited" and even "torture" in the Corporate Press.

Dovetailing with the change in psychiatric practices came the debate about whether homosexuality was innate and, therefore, unchangeable. This was a central part of the marriage debate leading up to the Supreme Court's *Obergefell* decision imposing same-sex marriage in a country in which thirty-four states had voted to codify man-woman marriage into law. The search for the elusive "gay gene" became paramount. That such a gene was never found has never been important. The permutations of this search are not as important as the fact that most people now believe that homosexuality is connected either to a gene, the hypothalamus, or the flooding of the embryo by too much estrogen for boys or too much testosterone for girls; anything but a choice. The argument thus became that if it is inborn and unchangeable, it is monstrous to try, and even more monstrous to limit its expression legally.

And then came hate and bullying.

They found Matthew Shepard strung up on a fence on a dirt road outside Laramie, Wyoming, in 1998. His death was immediately exploited by homosexual activists, the media, and national politicians in order to advance local, state, and federal hate crimes legislation. They said total strangers murdered Shepard because he was homosexual. *Newsweek* compared him to Jesus Christ. Years later, Stephen Jiminez, a gay reporter, went to Laramie to make a sympathetic documentary about Shepard that would fit the narrative. What he found was quite different. He published a book that demonstrated that Shepard knew his killers quite well, was a regular sex partner with one of them, and he had done drugs with them. It was not a homophobic murder; it was a drug deal gone bad. Yet Shepard's faux narrative is still retailed by the Corporate Media. He is a national hero buried in a crypt at Washington's National Cathedral.

To this day, the corporate narrative is that homosexuals are stalked and killed because of "who they are" and "who they love." Consider the 2016 Pulse nightclub massacre in Orlando, Florida. The story is still told that the Muslim killer deliberately chose Pulse because he knew it was frequented by gays. In fact, he had no idea that the club was gay. He was out hunting with his GPS looking for any nightclub to attack. He just happened to find a gay one.

Every "trans" murder is now suspected of being a hate crime. In September 2019, *The New York Times* reported on eighteen "transgender" murders so far that year and the American Medical Association proclaimed it an "epidemic," particularly among "transgender women of color."

In 2003 had come the Supreme Court case *Lawrence v. Texas*, which made homosexual sodomy a constitutional right, which led inexorably to the 2015 *Obergefell* decision that made gay marriage the law of the land.

Thus it was that AIDS, the "gay gene," "born that way," "hate," and the criminalization of talk therapy for same-sex desires and behaviors became the hinges upon which the Corporate Media changed from disparaging homosexuals fifty years earlier to championing them and denigrating those who still criticize homosexuality—generally conservative Christians. Where homosexuality was something to be treated in the twentieth century, "homophobia" became at least an unofficial mental illness in the twenty-first. *The New York Times* reported in April 2012 that if you were "homophobic," there was a good chance you were actually gay. Somehow, the one-time playground slur, "you're so gay!" had suddenly become acceptable to the Corporate Media.

Besides all gay all the time, the Corporate Press also became all trans all the time. In the entire year of 1995, *The New York Times* printed the word "transgender" only twice, of which one was in a letter to the editor. Five years later, there were twenty-four mentions. By 2005, there were fifty-four stories. In 2016, the year after *Obergefell*, the *Times* ran 1,166 stories about "transgender" issues, about three a day, a 26,000 percent increase in twenty years.

Christians became the sworn enemy of the LGBT movement. Because of their adherence to the tenets of their 2,000-year-old faith, they suddenly became "haters" and "bigots." *The New York Times*, the house organ of gay America, assailed Florida's 2022 Parental Rights in Education bill—H.B. 1557, instantly slurred by its enemies in the Corporate Media as the "don't say gay" bill—as likely to "weaponize" parental rights to "marginalize LGBTQ people." *The New York Times* perceived an "anti-gay agenda," and wondered, "why can't straight men stop obsessing about gay people? Maybe they should interrogate their own prurient interests in other people's love, get at the root and figure out why the idea of male intimacy riles them."

Anti-Christian bigotry has a long history at the *Times*. During the Matthew Shepard brouhaha, columnist Frank Rich, an early gay-rights champion at the paper, referred to the "anti-gay crusade of the religious right." He said Christian conservatives "demonize gay people as subhuman." One 2023 story mocked a Christian prayer service as a "right-wing political movement powered by divine purpose." Also, in 2023, the *Times* said that Montana had taken a hard right turn toward "Christian nationalism."

One could go on and on with how *The New York Times* has come to disdain believing Christians, especially what they believe about human sexuality; the *Times*, however, continues to set the agenda for every news outlet in the country. It has not only become anti-Christian, it has also become all gay all the time.

PART EIGHT: THE RISE— AND FALL—OF THE INTERNET

THE BIRTH OF THE BLOGOSPHERE

BY GLENN HARLAN REYNOLDS

We live today in a post-blogospheric media age. The blogosphere hasn't disappeared by any means, but it no longer plays the central role that it played from roughly 2002 to 2008. This is partly the result of natural media evolution but also the result of very deliberate action on the part of some big players in government and tech. The blogosphere's successors, such as Facebook and Twitter, lack its independence, its decentralization, and its free-flowing nature. On the other hand—very much against the wishes of their creators—those entities have nonetheless empowered ordinary citizens to push back against government- and media-initiated disinformation (to the extent that there's a difference anymore) in a way that remains within the finest tradition of the classical blogosphere.

I'll talk about that, and about where we go from here, later on. But first, how it started, or at least how it started for me.

I was lucky enough to be an early player in the blogosphere's development. I'd call my blog, *InstaPundit*, which started on August 8, 2001, a "late first-wave" blog. I came after people like Mickey Kaus (whose *Kausfiles* was the first blog I ever read), Andrew Sullivan, Josh Marshall, Virginia Postrel, Joanne Jacobs, and Rebecca Blood. But not much after. At the time, the term "weblog," later shortened to "blog," had not yet achieved wide popularity. *Slate* magazine used the term "me-zine," comparing them to the celebrated 1990s indie "zine" phenomenon (independent, quirky magazines published on actual paper).

I taught internet law, which meant I was always looking for ways to keep my hand in online. By the summer of 2001, I had decided to do something new. I had been active with music sites, including a chain of internet "radio stations" on the late, lamented, MP3.com site, and also produced some online bands. For a while, my brother Jonathan and I played a sort of game in which we'd come up with a band name, decide what genre the band went with, then write and record some songs and release an album on the MP3.com site, which made that very easy. (They even made it easy to sell CDs.) So, for example, the Nebraska Guitar Militia, which we decided was an alt-country band. We gave it a fictional backstory of being from Whiteclay, Nebraska, a tiny town that revolves around selling beer to the Indians at the reservation just across the line in South Dakota, and wrote some songs ("The Town that Booze Built," "Waves of Grain"—a lot of alcohol references. Though another song, "Reckoning," predicted a Hillary Clinton/ Donald Trump confrontation, which wasn't bad for 2000). Another band was Mobius Dick, which came from an old math joke ("What's non-orientable and lives under the sea? Mobius Dick!"). That name naturally meant a techno/EDM band, and the Dick actually did tolerably well, with our *Embrace the Machine* becoming the best-selling CD on the MP3.com site for three weeks in 2000. The title track even got written up in *Salon*, back when that outlet was readable. Other Mobius Dick albums included *Got Dick?*, *Indistinguishable from Magic?*, and *Upload Your Mind*.

I had also run a site, RaveRights.com, aimed at defending electronic music promoters from the Drug Enforcement Agency (DEA), which was prosecuting rave promoters under the federal so-called crack house law, which criminalizes owning or operating a building for the purpose of taking drugs. (The DEA took the position that *no one* would go to raves for the music, so they *must* be there for the drugs.) That site was quickly replaced by the Electronic Music Defense Fund, a nonprofit funded by musician Moby, but I did work with the ACLU on a friend-of-the-court brief in a New Orleans case, where I explained the nature and background and audience of electronic music.

But, in part because of teaching internet law, I was always looking for something new to do. I still remember following a link from *Slate* to Mickey Kaus's then-new blog *Kausfiles*. I was struck by how seamless it was—one second you were on an expensive site funded by Microsoft (back when Microsoft was still cool!), then with a single click you were on an independent journalism site funded by an individual—and it looked every bit as slick and professional. Still, my RaveRights experience involved web design and maintenance using a program called DreamWeaver, which wasn't very user-friendly, to put it mildly, and that didn't make me want to start a new site.

Then *Slate* was taken in by a minor hoax involving "monkey-fishing," in which Cajuns allegedly caught wild monkeys living on an island in the Mississippi Delta using baited hooks cast into the trees. That lead to the creation of a short-lived blog of journalistic criticism called *Monkeyfishing*, and when I followed a link to the blog it was "powered by Blogger" and hosted on Blogger's own site, Blogspot. An ad invited me to start my own blog in fifteen minutes, and that's literally how long it took to set up the initial version of *InstaPundit*. Instead of composing stuff in an unfriendly piece of software and then uploading to a server, the Blogger/Blogspot combination meant I could compose and publish on the web. At the time, in the summer of 2001, that was revolutionary.

I had been a regular and prominent commentator on *Slate*'s then-excellent discussion board, *The Fray*, for quite some time, and the *Slate* editors were quick to include *InstaPundit* in their "Me-Zine Central" directory, at which time I thought I had really made it. I remember by late August I was talking with a colleague about my traffic, at the time around two- to three-hundred visits per day, and we both thought that was a lot.

Links from *Slate*, Virginia Postrel, and James Taranto's *Best of the Web* feature at *The Wall Street Journal* boosted traffic, and by September 10, 2001, I had reached the heady heights of more than

1,500 visits per day. The next day was September 11, 2001, and everything changed.

I was at the doctor's for a nasty sinus infection when the towers collapsed. I got to my office shortly afterward and posted the following:

> **TOM CLANCY WAS RIGHT:** And we're living one of his scenarios right now. Not much is known for sure, but it's obvious that the United States is the target of a major terrorist assault. There's a lot of bloviation on the cable news channels, most of which will turn out to be wrong or misleading later. Here, for your consideration, are a few points to be taken from past experience:
>
> **The Fog of War:** Nobody knows much right now. Many things that we think we know are likely to be wrong.
>
> **Overreaction Is the Terrorist's Friend:** Even in major cases like this, the terrorist's real weapon is fear and hysteria. Overreacting will play into their hands.
>
> **It's Not Just Terrorists Who Take Advantage:** Someone will propose new "Antiterrorism" legislation. It will be full of things off of bureaucrats' wish lists. They will be things that wouldn't have prevented these attacks even if they had been in place yesterday. Many of them will be civil-liberties disasters. Some of them will actually promote the kind of ill-feeling that breeds terrorism. That's what happened in 1996. Let's not let it happen again.
>
> **Only One Antiterrorism Method Works:** That's punishing those behind it. The actual terrorists are hard to reach. But terrorism of this scale is always backed by governments. If they're punished severely—and that means **severely**, not a bombed

aspirin-factory but something that puts those behind it in the crosshairs—this kind of thing won't happen again. That was the lesson of the Libyan bombing.

"Increased Security" Won't Work. When you try to defend everything, you defend nothing. Airport security is a joke because it's spread so thin that it can't possibly stop people who are really serious. You can't prevent terrorism by defensive measures; at most you can stop a few amateurs who can barely function. Note that the increased measures after TWA 800 (which wasn't terrorism anyway, we're told) didn't prevent what appear to be coordinated hijackings. (Archie Bunker's plan, in which each passenger is issued a gun on embarking, would have worked better). Deterrence works here, just as everywhere else. But you have to be serious about it.

I think these observations have held up pretty well, alas, but they came at a time when most regular media was paralyzed. Many media sites actually dropped off the internet due to traffic, while the cable TV channels simply ran the same footage of airplanes hitting the towers over and over again while "experts" bleated nonsense. (As in every crisis, a major theme was that Americans would have to "grow up" and surrender freedoms to government.) I then started posting news as I could find it, along with correspondence from knowledgeable readers. I had intended to maintain as much normality as possible and still teach my afternoon constitutional law class, but it soon became apparent that that would be pointless, so I just kept blogging.

James Taranto of *The Wall Street Journal* linked my site again that day as a good place to go for news and information, and my traffic jumped to a then-inconceivable 5,500+ visits. And the post-9/11 era saw a very real, and not entirely welcome, change in the blog. In its first month or so it had been much more of a tech and pop culture blog. Afterward, it became what was known as a "warblog," one devoting much attention to the war in Afghanistan, and later in Iraq, among other places. And it paid more attention to politics than I had in the early days. If you look at my archives, you can see a horizontal line that I drew across the page at 10:57 a.m. that morning, to mark my post World Trade Center-attack writings. The line was more significant than I knew. Before that line were items on conservatives opposing the drug war, Greenpeace opposing biotech corn, another biotech piece by China blogger Andrea See, and Andrew Sullivan on the Left's PC opposition to a genomic-diversity research project in Britain. Afterward it was about bombs falling in Kabul, people who had friends and family at the World Trade Center, a report from Flight 93 by journalist Dennis Roddy, and some great (blogged) words by Virginia Postrel:

> Get these "greatest generation" pundits off TV, starting with David McCullough. Maybe it's nostalgia for the days of internment and rationing, but these guys are way too ready to concede defeat by handing over our liberties in pursuit of an impossible level of safety. Resilience and basic bravery, not a rush to precaution, are called for. The way ordinary Americans can stand up to terrorism is by making sure we retain the right to live normally and by continuing to value the products of normal life.

She was right, and the blogosphere was mostly sounding the same tone in general. Don't get carried away, and don't turn it into a national security war on ordinary people. Sadly, that's not how things went, as we created a massive and—at best—useless "Homeland Security" apparatus.

Not everything was about warblogging, of course. There were posts featuring recipes—my Thanksgiving Leg of Lamb and Lamb and Guinness Stew were popular, as was my cold poached salmon recipe, which I reverse-engineered from a meal at a great little bistro on the Upper West Side. And I increasingly blogged about fitness, tracking my growing interest in lifting heavy as I discovered the work of Mark Rippetoe. And I wrote a lot about longevity research and nanotechnology. In the earliest days of *InstaPundit*, posts tended to be longer—multiple-paragraph takes like mini op-eds. (I think my subconscious model was the "Notebook" section at the front of *The New Republic*, which back then was still an interesting and eclectic magazine of opinion.) Later on, there were more short and pithy one-line posts: a link and an observation, in some ways anticipating Twitter style. My favorite posts, in the days before the blog had comments, were where I updated repeatedly, integrating and responding to reader comments in a long series of updates. Now that there are comments (added during my PJ Media affiliation because they were then thought to boost traffic and search-engine interest), I don't do that as often.

My trademark "Heh" and "Indeed" lines appeared for a purely aesthetic reason. I hate to leave a hanging block quote. But sometimes I'd have a quote where I didn't really want to add anything significant of my own, either because it said everything already, or because I didn't want to detract from its impact. Thus, the one-word "heh," or "indeed"—or, occasionally, the double-barreled "heh, indeed." It fit a surprisingly large range of subjects.

After September 11, traffic skyrocketed, and I was soon at 25,000 then 50,000 visits a day—so many, that at one point, since I didn't have a public counter, I gave the password to *National Review*'s Jonah Goldberg so that he could independently verify my then-hard-to-believe numbers. (In recent years I've averaged roughly ten times that many.)

But it was 2002 that was, as I declared in a column for the late, lamented, TechCentralStation site, "the year of the blog." Blogs were suddenly everywhere, sparking articles in the *Columbia Journalism Review*, the *American Journalism Review*, and news and business publications everywhere. There were blog conferences and programs at Yale, UCLA, the National Press Club, and elsewhere.

For me, 2002 was the best, or at least the most enjoyable, of the glory years. Though blogs tended to lean right then, lots of lefty blogs came into the scene, and everyone was friendly and collegial to a degree that's inconceivable today. (I remember Dave Kopel and I having a civil discussion of "assault weapon" bans with folks in the comment section of *The Daily Kos*. Like I said, inconceivable today.) What used to be called "netiquette," back when the internet was a fairly small and genteel club, still ruled. That changed after the 2002 election, when the Democrats, who thought they were sure to recapture the Senate, didn't do so; by mid-2003, when things started gearing up for the 2004 election, the first beginnings of today's polarized and decidedly non-genteel internet started to appear in earnest.

If 2002 was my best year, 2004 was probably the blogosphere's most influential year. The CBS show *60 Minutes* broadcast a claim that leaked documents from George W. Bush's Vietnam-era Air National Guard days demonstrated that he'd used that service to avoid being sent to Vietnam. Bloggers, however, quickly demonstrated that these documents, allegedly from the IBM Selectric typewriter era, had been created using default fonts from Microsoft Word. Though the Big Media didn't want to cover that, bloggers shamed its members into it—that was back when Big Media was still capable of shame—and John Kerry's bid to Vietnam-vet his way into the White House failed.

This was the blogosphere's peak of influence. (Though in 2002, bloggers on the Left and Right had combined to force Trent Lott to resign as Senate majority leader.) But in 2005, the Corporate Press realized that if it agreed to a story and stuck to it regardless of people pointing out its errors, it could make it largely stick with the public. The story was that President Bush had bungled his handling of Hurricane Katrina. Though even Democrat Donna Brazile later admitted that Bush had done everything anyone could have expected (and journalism professor W. Joseph Campbell put the Katrina narrative in his collection of "Media Myths"), the storyline of Bush being disconnected and incompetent stuck. From that time on, the prospect of *shaming* the press into changing a story, or covering one it was determined to ignore, became increasingly dim.

I also made a change. In 2005, I became affiliated with *PJ Media*, then known as *Pajamas Media*, in response to a remark by CNN President Jonathan Klein disparaging "bloggers in their pajamas." I had some equity, and the original business model was an ad network for independent bloggers tied together with a central website and original reporting. The original plan was to combine the best of left and right bloggers, but that proved unsustainable as things became more polarized. While at *Pajamas*, my wife Helen Smith and I did a podcast, *The Glenn and Helen Show*, which was highly successful by the standards of the day, with heavy traffic and high-profile guests. Later *Pajamas* started PJTV, and I hosted a TV show, mostly from a rather expensive TV studio they put in my basement, for quite a few years. In the mid-2010s, *InstaPundit* became a group blog, as I noticed that I really enjoyed the work of the guest bloggers I brought in when I was on vacation, and started asking them to stay around. *PJ Media* was sold to Salem Media, and I no longer own any of it, though Salem still handles my advertising.

Meanwhile, in the background, the blogosphere's true undoing was arising. Mark Zuckerberg's FaceMash changed its name to The Facebook, later shortened to Facebook, in February 2004. Over the next several years, the walled gardens of the likes of Facebook and Twitter drew in many people who had previously read and published blogs. The allure was seductive: less hassle and overhead, easier access to an audience, improved ability to actually connect with people you knew. And for a while, there wasn't much of a downside. Unsurprisingly, plenty of people left the blogosphere behind.

Then, starting in the mid-2010s, these walled gardens started slamming the gates shut. From being free-speech zones, they became increasingly Orwellian patches overseen by "fact checkers" who made up facts, and "Trust and Safety Councils" whom no reasonable person could trust, and from whom no criticism of the dominant narrative was safe. I strongly suspect that this was not an accident, but a recognition by what hippies used to call The Establishment that uncontrolled media were a threat to their hegemony. There were other things going on, too, including changes in the digital ad market, but even those changes, I suspect, were meant to play a role.

This trend accelerated after the 2016 election, and then again in the wake of the Covid narrative, when all sorts of entirely truthful information was suppressed in the name of "safety." Likewise, the Hunter Biden laptop story was shut down, even though it was true, to the point that Twitter was blocking the sharing of URLs linking to the story even in direct messages. (I left my weekly column at *USA Today*, and switched to writing one at the *New York Post*, after my column on Hunter Biden's laptop was spiked.)

But now there's some pushback. Elon Musk bought Twitter, now X, and although its politicized staff has tried to fight a rear-guard action against his free-speech campaign, the platform is much different than it was. This has forced Facebook and other platforms to relax the censorship somewhat. Substack, a free-speech platform that functions almost like a blog-hosting site, but with subscription and revenue features, has attracted a large number of independent writers, including some old-time bloggers—Andrew Sullivan and Virginia Postrel have moved there, and I have a Substack site where I publish a lengthy essay every week—and people like Bari Weiss who have left Big Media platforms to escape censorship and groupthink.

And, of course, blogs are still around. I'm still there after more than twenty years. Old-time blogs like *Powerline*, *The Volokh Conspiracy*, and even James Lileks's *The Bleat* are still publishing regularly. Joanne Jacobs is still publishing daily about education. Mickey Kaus still runs *Kausfiles*, though he's mostly tweeting. And science fiction author and long-time blogger Bill Quick—who coined the term "blogosphere"—is still blogging at his *Daily Pundit* site.

So, which lessons do I draw from all of this? I mean besides, *what a long, strange trip it's been*?

First, the rise of a new technology can really shake things up. People say that the internet reshaped journalism, but journalism on the web in 2001 looked a lot like journalism everywhere else in 1991. It was mostly institutional news outlets ranging from traditional newspaper sites to webzines like *Slate* and *Salon*. Other than Matt Drudge's *Drudge Report*, and maybe *Slashdot*, there weren't many major non-institutional news sites. It was the invention of blogging platforms, which made self-publishing much, much easier than it was before, that really brought forth the masses.

Second, it flourished because it was *fun*. One of the reasons why left- and right-leaning bloggers got along in the early days was because our mutual joy in being involved in this new thing created a camaraderie that dwarfed our differences, at least for a while. And many people got involved because being a publisher, or a reporter, or a pundit—previously available only to those with powerful institutional resources behind them—was now within the reach of pretty much anybody. A.J. Liebling said that freedom of the press belongs to the man who owns one. Once the blog revolution struck, that was everybody.

Third, the empire always strikes back. The response to all this freedom, much of which was used to point out Establishment lies and spin, was for the Establishment to push back in numerous ways. The rise of platforms that kept people away from the independent blogosphere and within the walls of "curated" content overseen by corporate censors (censors who often operated directly at government behest) was one way. The rise of various campaigns against "misinformation" was another.

But fourth, you can't stop the signal. Despite all the efforts to censor unwelcome messages, the truth gets out. Things that were derided as Russian propaganda, censored, and even led their propounders to face career-ending consequences, are now accepted as truth.

That doesn't mean that the censorship was futile, exactly. It almost certainly swung the 2020 election, for example. It was expensive, though, and the fallout has been an enormous loss of trust in institutions that were previously highly regarded. Over time, it's a losing game for the Establishment, and the cracks are already beginning to show.

So, what's next? Well, as I said, you can't stop the signal. And I aim to misbehave.

CITIZEN JOURNALISM AND THE BREITBART LEGACY

BY HANNAH GILES

"I'm going to treat her like she's my daughter." When sources come to me, instead of going to The New York Times *that have vast resources, they're coming to this goofball who works out of a basement most of the time in West Los Angeles and all I can do is tell my sources or the parents of my sources that I'm going to march with them and whatever their peril is will be my peril. And if I have to act like a rodeo clown to divert attention from them so that they're protected, I'll do it. And I think that's one of the reasons people come to me. They know I'm not just using and abusing them. I'm putting my money where my mouth is. I'm going to fight with them, next to them, and protect them as much as humanly possible.*
—Andrew Breitbart

That's how Andrew Breitbart's short retelling goes of a conversation he had with my father Doug Giles in September 2009. The conversation lasted about four hours. It happened the night after he launched his Big Government.com website with James O'Keefe's and my first ACORN Housing video. The one in which I went undercover as a "prostitute" who wanted a mortgage for a house. The pitch was: I would use a dozen or so underage girls who were smuggled in from El Salvador to not only pay my mortgage but also fund my boyfriend's future congressional campaign.

As Breitbart and my father were having their come-to-Jesus moment about my life, I was having a mini panic attack. Not because of anything that had to do with their conversation or the fact that I was just dropped off at a stranger's home for the night by my friend Jason Mattera, or because I had just been on national news for the first time, but because I could feel what felt like toxic makeup chemicals seeping into my bloodstream through my face pores.

To be clear, I am a libertarian hippy athlete. I have been for most of my life. That day, September 9, 2009, I went from being an introverted college junior, surfer girl, jiu-jitsu fighter, and personal trainer to the symbol of a resistance movement. I was thrust into the national spotlight literally overnight. I had never worn makeup until going on Fox News's *Glenn Beck* show that day, and I was freaking out.

How would I get this suffocating poison powder off my face so my skin could breathe? I tried washing it off with soap, but that didn't put a dent in it. Oh, the turmoil and embarrassment my twenty-year-old self felt at that second. In that same moment, I realized how technically unlikely a candidate, and seemingly unprepared, for this era-defining moment in history I was.

Meanwhile: The men fought, cried, and brainstormed together. Eventually, I found some baby wipes and got the makeup off. Maybe I could figure out life in the fast lane.

In May 2009, I was driving from Miami to Southeast D.C., with my mother, for an internship with the National Journalism Center, while at the same time aspiring to be an operations officer for the CIA. In the wake of a heated election and the subprime mortgage crisis, my political research for my college newspaper was intensely focused on ACORN, the Association of Community Organizations for Reform Now, an organization that had helped to get Barack Obama elected as president. It was a membership-based, taxpayer-funded, leftist agitation group instrumental in the controlled demolition of the housing market while fronting as an advocate for low-income housing.

Dissuading me from applying to the CIA, my mom asked me, "Why don't you do an investigation into that ACORN group you're so obsessed with? Merge your undercover aspirations with journalism." I said, "Mom, there is no way I will have a chance to investigate ACORN. I am an intern. A nobody. It will never happen."

The conversation ended. But like all good parental advice, it stayed with me.

After just a few days in Washington, I remember calling out to God in front of the Supreme Court and asking for guidance and direction. "How would I change a city this far gone?" I wanted a clear sign from the Lord on what I was supposed to do with my time in D.C., how I could be useful for His plans. And like all prayers, it was answered in its own due course. Specifically, on a late afternoon run the next day. I had felt hopeless and lost, but my youthful angst was quickly turned into peace and finally, into resolve.

On that run around Capitol Hill, I saw all the federal offices, the bustling departments, filled with bureaucrats lording over America with their rules, regulations, and dictates. I saw young professionals busying themselves, to-and-fro, with the operations of the federal state. But just a few blocks away, in every direction, was abject poverty.

In these places just outside the orbit of Washington's view, there was an ACORN Housing office. It was the national headquarters. I stopped and looked through the window. There were stacks of mortgage applications everywhere. From my research I knew that ACORN was not just helping people with paperwork; the group was doing that public work in order to fund and finance the private political work of building power. ACORN was using public tactics, a public face, in order to build an army of effective and trained leftwing operatives who could have a tremendous political impact.

Its most prominent alumni was now the president of the United States.

ACORN had been credibly accused of massive voter fraud. It had been accused of diverting millions in donations to the family members of its board of directors. It presented itself as solving the problems of poverty, but in reality, it was often just another abuser of the vulnerable who pretended to care while perpetrating the abuse.

Continuing on my run, a few blocks past the office the enormity of the problems of poverty hit me like a wave washing over me. The homelessness, the drugs, prostitution, and the number of children who were caught in this system weighed on me. There had to be something that could be done to help these fellow Americans, but every possible solution was co-opted by ACORN. Every bit of political will to help was steered into funding for its organization and efforts.

The nearby church could have saved this neighborhood, but it was likely partnering with ACORN. Probably with the best of intentions, the church felt as though it should coordinate with the community organization. Every solution was being bottlenecked by this one entity, and this one entity wasn't interested in solving the problem.

If ACORN actually did eradicate or reduce poverty, if it uplifted the poor and built a society of self-sufficient citizens, it would be putting itself out of business. The interests were not just misaligned, they were completely at odds with ACORN's stated goals.

My brain was ablaze with so many follow-on thoughts and then it was like a lightning bolt hit and made everything clear. I needed to go undercover, into ACORN Housing as a prostitute running a brothel with underaged girls I was smuggling in from El Salvador. I needed to show this disconnect. I had to show the public how the morals of this organization had become completely detached from reality. I could take what I knew of the organization and its desire for money and power, and showcase it through effective undercover video journalism.

I didn't want to hurt the ACORN office staff, and I didn't want to hurt the people who were in need of their services. I wanted to expose a corrupt system. I wanted to capture on camera the moral evil of an organization that sought power instead of trying to help people. I wanted to make it clear that the organization was presenting itself as something it wasn't, which was no fault of the low-level staff. If ACORN was on the up and up, then my sting operation would be a bust, but as a twenty-year-old college student I had nothing to lose.

Like Ida Tarbell, Upton Sinclair, or Nellie Bly, I could present truth to the public through demonstrative journalism, through the kind of undercover journalism that had been missing from America for a century. All of this got worked out in my head before I arrived back at my apartment that night.

A few weeks later I was describing this revelation to a friend, while on another run. I told him all about my idea to go undercover as a prostitute. He said, "You want to go undercover and turn it into news? I know just the guy." The friend re-introduced me to someone I had run across before, the kind of fearless warrior who would expose this truth and would be willing to take the risks necessary to make it happen: James O'Keefe.

James had already suffered for his journalism, losing a job because a conservative employer didn't appreciate "activism in the form of video journalism." In those days, not only did the political Right misunderstand the future of journalism, it still misunderstood journalism itself. The Right thought that that policy papers and studies and sound positions on the issues of the day were the recipe for change. The "white paper industrial complex" putting a PowerPoint deck on obscure policies was the height of political technology.

James knew better, and had a history at Rutgers of doing things that were ahead of their time. He was figuring out how to take ideas and concepts and visualize them. He and a handful of others were putting the pieces in place to start a revolution in journalism. I brought James the research, planning, and thoughts behind the systemic injustice of ACORN and the poverty that it relied on for its own personal riches.

In our videos we captured the callous assistance given to purported human traffickers. We saw the absolute absence of morals or ethics. In almost every office, it turned out that our hypothesis was not just correct, it was chronic.

Capturing that content was only part of the challenge. Now we needed to explain it, and we needed to figure out how to release it. James and I had a wide set of media and movement contacts throughout Washington, so we started innocently asking around. We presented the footage to people, and many were shocked, but unsure of what to do with it. Others warned us of unlimited legal liability and encouraged us to never release it, and to delete it.

We approached one conservative champion in Congress whose staff wanted a special screening of the material. James and I were both excited by how we were being treated. It felt validating to have the attention of powerful people and their respect for the work, risk, and investigation we had completed. James only brought in the audio recordings from our time inside a few ACORN offices. After they listened, this congressional team immediately demanded that we give them all the tapes and agree to never release them without their permission. We both instantly understood what was going on, and we promptly left with our recordings and never looked back.

A few days later James was connected directly to the man who would see this project for its full potential and had the courage and insanity to do something about it: Andrew Breitbart.

Breitbart had an energy level that no one could keep up with. He buzzed and crackled with action at all times. He had an existing soapbox—Breitbart TV and his behind-the-scenes role as the other half of the *Drudge Report*. But he wanted more, and he had the social connections across Hollywood, New York, and Washington to make magical things happen. He was everywhere and he was engaging and inspiring. He personified the "happy warrior." People wanted to follow him into battle.

Breitbart was going to use our work, my ACORN investigation, to launch his next "big" site, following on the heels of his previous Big Hollywood website, this one to be called Big Government. What he understood was that this was the new model. We had not only developed a great project and delivered the goods in a way that had never been seen before in modern journalism, but this was a new type of content and a new genre of journalism that conservatives were pioneering. This was the opening of the era of citizen journalism.

But we didn't want to just complain about the media, we wanted to *be* the media. I knew we had made it big when we were featured in an episode of the satiric cartoon, *South Park*. We were achieving the kind of penetration into pop culture that the political Right just never gets, especially in a positive way. Watching Jon Stewart on *The Daily Show* condemn the ACORN members involved was another major cultural flashpoint. By March 2010, fifteen of ACORN's thirty state chapters had folded. Congress withdrew financial support. And by November, the national organization filed for liquidation. We had been able to use an investigative project, a type of journalism not used for over a century, to affect real change. We had removed this cancer from the backs of the poor.

Now began the real political and social challenge of using that chaos to build something better in its place, to rebuild on a foundation of honesty, integrity, and love to make something better.

The fame and attention that came with a national media story and sensation had a few positive moments. It has always been wonderful to meet truth-tellers around the country, the best people in America from all walks of life with whom I immediately felt a kinship. But the threats and the prejudice that comes with even fifteen minutes of fame is exhausting. You start to realize that you can't ever go back to a quiet non-public life. Trying to manage fame is a completely different skill from journalism and I didn't want that for myself, my family, or my kids.

I wanted to do the stories. I was excited to break apart stubbornly hidden truths that protect the powerful. I wasn't thirsty for social media likes. The aftermath of the project was exhilarating and exhausting. The constant death threats became a major source of anxiety. The way in which the work was understood and often misunderstood was also frustrating. My thinking matured and evolved, and I started to understand that my motives had to be fundamentally different than those of progressives. I shouldn't seek to change the world in the ways I wanted it changed, I shouldn't be engaging with sensitive topics with an activist agenda to impose. Instead, I needed to have a laser focus on injustice, especially systemic injustice, and bring those issues into public view.

That distinction might seem small but the change in mindset ultimately differentiates the activist from the journalist, the partisan from the truth-teller. I didn't want to lie on behalf of libertarians and Republicans, I didn't want to hurt Democrats or liberal billionaires; rather, I wanted to address the injustices in America and help to highlight the ways in which they might be fixed by people of all tribes and factions.

Many of the major failings and crises that we are dealing with exist because the institutional media covered up and papered over problems to get short-term solutions rather than confronting obvious injustices in our midst.

After Andrew died in March 2012, everything changed. All of a sudden, the captain of our motley crew of dissidents was gone. We had lost the glue that held so many strong egos in check. But his parting gift to us all was the leadership and charisma he bestowed on us in his every step. Andrew showed us the path forward but alas wouldn't live to see the end of the journey.

Since then, the powers that be have sought to contain the Breitbart revolution by outright deplatforming and un-personing people via social media. They cancel bank accounts. They attack funders and advertisers to dry up donations. They use endless lawfare through proxies to bankrupt the courageous. Members of the Left have learned that few courts care to apply defamation law to them, but will strictly scrutinize even the most minor of mistakes by truth-tellers.

I'm a longtime practitioner of jiu-jitsu, and one of the core principles of jiu-jitsu is using your enemies' strengths as weaknesses against them. I believe we can apply that basic principle to the current oppressive media landscape to upend the entire propaganda complex. But "journalists" have to be laser focused on revealing untold truths to as many people as possible, despite the consequences.

I am wary of being called a "conservative journalist" because all I want to be is an effective journalist who is focused solely on the truth, wherever that takes me.

PRESENT AT
THE CREATION
BY LARRY O'CONNOR

There was a moment during Andrew Breitbart's funeral when I purposefully scanned those sitting around me and soaked their faces into my memory banks. I wanted to remember who was there. I wanted to remember the faces of the men and women Andrew had chosen to help to develop and build his new media empire all while fulfilling his vision of a revolutionary new media paradigm. I wanted to remember who was left to carry his torch.

I'm sad to say that nearly twelve years after his sudden and devastating death at the age of forty-three, I'm not sure if the faces I now see in my mind's eye were really there, or whether I've placed them there because I *know* they were part of our team and have continued Andrew's astounding and enduring legacy.

Greg Gutfeld was there. So was Ben Shapiro. Andrew Klavan, Dana Loesch, Michael Flynn (not the three-star general), Michael Walsh, Matt Drudge, and Dennis Miller. I also saw a couple of congressmen and possibly a senator. I saw a few recognizable actors from film and television plus a good handful of media types from the traditional, corporate "mainstream media." The very mainstream media Andrew wanted to single-handedly destroy.

While listening to Andrew's father-in-law, legendary actor and raconteur Orson Bean, eulogize Andrew with a dirty joke about a prostitute and a homeless man, I desperately wanted to remember every fun, hilarious, and outrageous moment I had with Andrew over the previous three years when he built an upstart, single-page blog called *Big Hollywood* into the multimedia goliath you know today as Breitbart News.

There were plenty of hilarious moments to ponder. The Breitbart team laughed more than any group of co-workers I've ever seen. Mostly, because Andrew was always trying to make us laugh. He'd text me a cryptic and urgent "call me" as if there was a *huge* story for which he needed me to drop everything, immediately. When I called, he'd read me a tweet he was about to send out to the world to see if I thought it was as funny as he did (I always did). Once he asked me for a synonym for "sphincter." Another time he asked if everyone knew what "taint" meant. I naively responded with the definition of taint, the adjective. He meant the noun. It's slang. You might not want to look it up at the office.

Andrew was refining these one 140-character missives on Twitter and delivering his sphincter-laden, taint-infused one-liners to Anderson Cooper, or to Jake Tapper, or the attorney general of the United States. You see, Andrew needing to know if his tweet was funny and whether there was a more effective word than sphincter to communicate to a network anchor *was* urgent.

I tried to remember all of those "busting my gut from laughing" moments, but all I could focus on was the fight—and the future.

Andrew was a visionary, no doubt. He saw a new media world where the gatekeepers, poised to determine what counted as information worthy of consumption for the American people, would be irrelevant, if not extinct. He saw this new media world emerge firsthand, at the moment when Matt Drudge broke the Monica Lewinsky scandal on his rudimentary, single-page, monochromatic *Drudge Report* website. With that one story, he saw the networks and *The New York Times* with their billion-dollar combined budgets reduced to mere spectators to the biggest political scandal since Watergate. If it happened with Lewinsky, he thought, why can't it happen again? Why can't it happen in perpetuity? Why must the American people wait for a handful of editors in a corner office in midtown Manhattan to determine what was "fit to print" or broadcast?

Why, indeed.

As Drudge's primary editor, Andrew learned the rhythmic nature of the news cycle. He saw the rhythm increase from the courtly, restrained waltz of the mid-1990s to the hyper-driven, hip-hop street performance a decade and a half later when he launched his "big" sites: *Big Hollywood, Big Government, Big Journalism,* and *Big Peace.* Breitbart understood the flow of the cycle and how news stories ebbed and flowed with the newspaper and nightly news deadlines. He saw them the way a champion surfer watches a series of waves developing on their way to shore. He harnessed those waves and rode them like no one else.

But then, in 2011, something extraordinary happened. Andrew didn't just deliver news items and original reporting into the news cycle waves—he personally got caught in the center of a whirlpool of events that would either end with his destruction (and perhaps even his arrest on federal criminal charges), or he would be single-handedly instrumental in the downfall of a powerful member of Congress with connections to the Clinton dynasty. This was the Anthony Weiner scandal.

It was the evening of May 27, 2011, when Andrew called an emergency conference call of all his editors. I jumped on and Andrew informed us that in the past hour a tweet had been sent from the account of Representative Anthony Weiner, Democrat of New York, that included a picture of an erection barely contained within the confines of a pair of snug, cloth underpants. There was no doubt the picture was sent from the congressman's account. By the time we were on the phone discussing it, the tweet had been deleted. Andrew had taken a screenshot of it and several of us (me included) had seen the tweet and could verify that the screenshot was not doctored, the tweet had definitely originated from Weiner's verified account.

But how to handle this as a news story? What, exactly, had happened? We couldn't claim the picture was sent by Weiner because it could have been someone in his office with access to his account. Or, he could have been hacked. Was this newsworthy, and if it was, what was the actual story here?

During the conference call, we observed Weiner's tweets disappearing before our eyes as well as the Twitter and Facebook page of the intended recipient of the tawdry image. Weiner than claimed on his account that he had been hacked. "We're watching the cover-up," Andrew said to all of us. As usual, he was right.

"Of course, we have a story here," he said. "We have a huge story. A sitting congressman's Twitter account has been hacked with a pornographic image. It may very well be an attempt to frame him." It was either that, or that Weiner was guilty of some pretty tawdry stuff, and now he was engaged in covering it up and lying about it. Andrew personally wrote the headline: "Weinergate: Congressman Claims 'Facebook Hacked' as Lewd Photo Hits Twitter." Yes, Andrew himself coined the phrase: "Weinergate."

The original post was published late in the evening of May 27, Pacific time, as all articles on the sites were time-stamped from Los Angeles since this was Andrew's home and base. Social media exploded. By the time the East Coast woke up the next morning, it was already a sensation.

It was Memorial Day weekend, and the usually dormant news cycle was perfectly poised for a story like this. We were tracking how mainstream outlets would cover it, and before long it was clear that the main focus was not on Weiner but on Breitbart.

Weiner continued to stick with his denial and his claim that he had been hacked. Suddenly, reporters started pointing the finger at Andrew. The narrative evolved and before Memorial Day rolled around Andrew found himself on phone call after phone call (while he was supposed to be spending quality beach time with his devoted wife and children) denying that he had hacked the social media accounts of a sitting congressman.

After all, who are you going to believe—a leftwing Democratic politician married to Hillary Clinton's personal assistant, Huma

Abedin, or a "rightwing blogger" like Andrew Breitbart? Weiner was a darling of the liberal press in Manhattan and Washington, a protégé of New York Senator Chuck Schumer. Former President Bill Clinton, of all people, had officiated at Weiner and Abedin's wedding. Whereas Breitbart was a pariah, and the mainstream media treated him as such.

Cable news became obsessed with the story, but not because a famous and powerfully connected congressman was embroiled in a sexting scandal. The cable news outlets were obsessed because they thought they could destroy Breitbart. This was their way of finally being rid of the rightwing upstart who made his name defying their rules and barging into their private club like Rodney Dangerfield in the movie *Caddyshack*.

CNN had Andrew on to discuss our story (which was really an exercise in the CNN host attacking him and our coverage of the story). Breitbart factually noted that the media should be scrutinizing Weiner and digging into his apparent interest in sharing lewd, lascivious material with very young women. House legal analyst Jeffrey Toobin was then brought on the air to analyze the legal trouble that Weiner or Breitbart might be in, depending on whom one believed.

"What Andrew Breitbart was insinuating about [Weiner] with young girls and stuff is outrageous. And frankly, it's too bad that he got to say that stuff on CNN," Toobin said. "Look, this is a light-hearted story. This is a silly little thing that happened; it's not a big deal." (Toobin's "not a big deal" is just delicious in light of what led to his career downfall a decade later.)

Over on MSNBC, it was *Salon*'s Joan Walsh who piled on Breitbart and turned him (and those of us who worked on the sites) into the villains of the story. Joan had come to the conclusion that Weinergate was the product of a "rightwing smear machine," and Andrew Breitbart was the creator and operator of the machine. On Twitter, she dialogued with *New York Times* columnist Charles Blow and said, "If the story is false, we only know about it because of the Breitbart empire." Corporate journalists at the major, established institutions were spending their energy and effort blaming the messenger, Breitbart, instead of pursuing the truth: that their liberal hero, Anthony Weiner, actually did this awful, self-destructive thing.

The pressure on Andrew was tremendous as Weiner stuck to his story. But cracks were starting to show. By mid-week, some reporters noted that Weiner had not contacted the FBI or even the Capitol Hill Police about the alleged cyber-intrusion. He had lawyered up, however. CNN's Dana Bash confronted Weiner on the steps of the Capitol and his performance was less "noble victim" and more "obfuscating perp." It was clear that he was hiding something. Weiner's original, unequivocal denial that the photo didn't belong to him and wasn't taken by him, had morphed into a weasel-y admission that he could not say "with certitude" that it wasn't him.

We had him. Despite how gut-wrenching and frustrating and, frankly, terrifying it was for Andrew to combat the accusations that he had committed a federal crime and had endangered his business with such a reckless stunt, we all knew something that the rest of the world didn't. From an anonymous tip, we knew that Weiner had done this before, and we knew he was lying, even if the entirety of traditional media had already determined that its golden boy couldn't possibly have done such a thing. By the time Andrew infamously took the podium and hijacked Weiner's own press conference in midtown Manhattan on June 6, 2011, the day our tipster's story was published, Andrew had been fully vindicated, even if Toobin, Joan Walsh, and the rest of his detractors refused to acknowledge it.

The Weinergate affair best exemplifies the revolution that Andrew fought and won in his three short years in the public eye. Like the Lewinsky scandal fifteen years before, the Weiner story broke online and outside of the self-appointed news gatekeepers. If they had been in charge still, they would have shelved the story. It would have died. No, it would have been killed. But Andrew's new-media revolution created the environment where *The New York Times*, *The Washington Post*, and the broadcast networks were irrelevant bystanders. They were left to play catch-up and when they finally got to the story, rather that reporting on it and investigating it, they decided to participate in the cover-up.

And once Andrew took the stage and pointed his finger at those very reporters who had assembled to hear Weiner's *mea culpa*, the real story had been revealed. The partisan frauds that had ruled the information monopoly in our country for decades had been exposed and they were as culpable as the lascivious congressman.

Ultimately, the Weinergate story was a media story. About how the media missed the news. Ignored the news because its members didn't like what they saw. Distorted the news so it could fit their preconceived narrative. And finally, how the members of the media memory-holed the news, evidenced by their willingness to celebrate Weiner's triumphant return to public life in 2013 when a "rehabilitated" Weiner came a whisker away from becoming mayor of New York City. He would have easily won the election if it weren't for yet another sexting scandal.

Since the Weinergate affair, things have never been the same for the legacy media. The landscape has been changed forever. The stories that the members of the media care about are consumed by an ever-dwindling audience. Americans are now skeptical of their narrative, and what animates the producers at ABC News or the editorial board at *The Washington Post* is irrelevant to the majority of Americans who follow the news.

The revolution was complete when in 2016 a man who was rejected by the editorial boards of ninety-eight of the one hundred largest newspapers in America won the presidential election. Andrew would have loved how thoroughly the media was humiliated, ignored, and dismissed by the American people on election night, 2016. And without a doubt he would have relished Trump's no-holds-barred war with the media throughout his presidency.

CENSORSHIP: THE FIRST REFUGE OF COWARDS

BY BILL WHITTLE

In late 2008, I was hired by PJTV, an internet start-up whose goal was to provide conservative-leaning news and commentary through online video content. The idea of video commentary was fairly revolutionary at the time. YouTube—launched on Valentine's Day of 2005—had been an online oddity for its first year of existence; I have some vague recollection of it as being some kind of video storage site. But in 2006, YouTube was purchased by a still-nascent company called Google, and by the time I first stepped into the chroma-key green cube at the PJTV studio in Hawthorne, California, online video political content was beginning to gain some traction.

I had first been hired by PJTV to do the work I had been doing for the previous eight years: editing video documentaries for venues such as *The History Channel*, *The Discovery Channel*, and *The Learning Channel* (this being back in ancient times when they were about history, discovery, and learning). In 2003, I struck show-business, gig-based gold by landing what would turn out to be regular work when I was hired for a five-year run as editor for *Shootout*, a movie-industry talk show hosted by film producer Peter Guber and former editor of *Variety*, Peter Bart.

During this age of regular paychecks, I began writing essays about the good things I saw in America. My editing bay had a window with an excellent view of the by-God Hollywood sign, and as the cadre of leftwing elitists camped below, those letters continued to undermine that fundamental love of country, my desire to defend it grew proportionally. I'd been a theater major, which meant that I had spent my college years surrounded by people very much like the person I used to be: filled with self-importance, in awe of my own intellectual majesty, absolutely incapable of error, and with a total and passionate belief in things I knew absolutely nothing about. Many decades later, when hosting a conservative talk show, I was asked by a young member of the panel why it was that conservatives were so old. "Because it takes a while for life to beat the stupid out of you," I replied. That change of heart is what inspired me to name my blog *Eject! Eject! Eject!* My belief in liberalism had taken a direct hit from a surface-to-reality missile; the jet was on fire, headed for the mud, and it was time to pull the loud handle and punch out.

After some experimentation, my friend and PJTV colleague Andrew Klavan had been the first to hit paydirt with a video he did called *Shut Up*, which was about censorship. It soon pulled hundreds of thousands of views. I followed shortly thereafter with "The True Story of the Atomic Bombs," the first in my series of video commentary I called *Afterburner*. That got millions of views. And right around then—2009—social media, primarily YouTube and Facebook, suddenly provided people like me with a platform capable of reaching really astonishing numbers of people. And, so, many of us sold our little, privately owned farms—our blogs—and moved to the big cities where the eyeballs were. And everything just seemed peachy—for six or seven years.

It took that long to realize that something was wrong. It took several more years to realize what it was. You might want to write this down:

> *The reason that modern censorship is so overwhelmingly pervasive and powerful is because conservatives moved from their own private property onto someone else's private property.*

Our government was designed by a once-in-human-history collection of philosophers, historians, and thinkers; practical men of unparalleled education and experience who spent a great deal of their lives studying the nature of tyranny in order to try to find a way to prevent it. They devised a document, a blueprint to make a government, that had layers upon layers of engineering fail-safes with the sole aim of preventing other people from telling you or me what to do, what to say, or what to think. Up until the birth of the Information Age, censorship had been enforced by coercive violence: in other words, sending goons to smash printing presses, kick in the teeth of uppity writers of conscience, and usually both. America's Founding Fathers feared and understood this so clearly that they dedicated the first item in the Bill of Rights to freedom of speech, and the second item to the means of defending freedom of speech. And in this they were, and remain, spectacularly—indeed, unimaginably—successful. No one in America today is being censored by coercive violence. No one.

In the years immediately following the end of the Great War—World War I—a number of communist intellectuals gathered in Germany, looked out at the smoldering ruins and asked themselves, "what the hell just happened?"

There it was: the long-promised, global conflagration that would, with scientific certainty, lead to the worldwide socialist revolution that would free the proletariat from that capitalist-driven bloodbath and into the sunny heights of the inevitable communist utopia. One cannot overstate the shock and amazement among these Marxists when this did not occur. To their dying day, neither Lenin, nor Trotsky, nor any of the other True Believers could comprehend how a German worker would side with Germany while French workers sided with France and British workers sided with Britain. Marxism was not politics. Marxism was not theory. Marxism was science. And like loyal collectivists everywhere, then and now, they had followed the science. And nothing happened.

This group of Marxist intellectuals decided to form what we would today call a think tank in order to study this dismaying problem. They named it the Institute for Social Research, and since it was based in Frankfurt, Germany, the teachings and theories to emerge from the Institute would come to be known as products of the Frankfurt School.

Now, if you are a rational person—and because you are reading this the chances for that are excellent—you might take issue with the aims of the Frankfurt School. You see, its members quickly realized that the reason the worldwide workers revolution did not, in fact, occur was because by the 1920s those capitalist bastards were improving the workers' standard of living to such a degree that there was no longer any incentive for revolutions in general, and Marxism in particular. They had indoor plumbing! They had luxury items! In America, individual, common working men owned their own cars! How could Marxism compete with that?

Well, it couldn't, and they knew it.

Now, as a rational person, you might draw the conclusion that whatever legitimate grievances that might have led to Marxist theory had for the most part been corrected. Everyone was living better. Hooray!

But Marxists are not rational people. They are religious zealots of a godless faith, and so whether Marxism was still needed or not was completely irrelevant. Marxism. Must. Be. And if the workers would not be the vanguard of the revolution, then the big brains at the Frankfurt School would have to find some other group to raise the Red Banner. And that's exactly what they did. If the revolution would not come through the *economy* then it would come through the *culture*, and if the heavy lifting would not be done by working people then it would be done by the dispossessed.

We now turn to the mechanism that these so-called progressives used to control information.

The internet cannot be censored, and it cannot be controlled, and, in fact, it cannot even be destroyed. That's why it was built. In the late 1960s, DARPA—that would be the Defense Advanced Research Projects Agency—decided that it would be handy to have a communications system capable of withstanding a full-scale thermonuclear attack on the United States. That's a thorny problem. It would require a network with virtually limitless redundancy. Messages would be broken into multiple identical fragments, and these fragments would travel through a near-limitless number of independent pathways to be assembled by into an intact message at the destination. You could cut a cable of such a system and the message would get through. You could cut hundreds, or thousands, or even millions of individual cables and the message would still get through. You cannot control that, or censor it, and ironically enough, that is precisely the case today as well. No one can silence my conservative commentary once it reaches the internet. But! Those in control of the information gateways do not have to erase my commentary. All they have to do is to make sure that no one can find it.

Which brings us to a fully twenty-first-century term: shadow banning. From Wikipedia, the free encyclopedia:

> Shadow banning, also called stealth banning, hellbanning, ghost banning, and comment ghosting, is the practice of blocking or partially blocking a user or the user's content from some areas of an online community in such a way that the ban is not readily apparent to the user, regardless of whether the action is taken by an individual or an algorithm. For example, shadow-banned comments posted to a blog or media website would be visible to the sender, but not to other users accessing the site.

As I mentioned earlier, in our sweet-summer-child golden naiveté, we bloggers—endless numbers of privately owned information sources—gave up the self-distributing networks that drew people to our own websites and hopped wide-eyed onto the bus to the Big City: YouTube and Facebook, where millions of information-starved viewers sat waiting, conveniently aggregated by someone else.

Ten years ago, one of my *Afterburner* segments (or its re-skinned, PJTV-independent counterpart called *Firewall*) would be considered a terrible failure if it did not break 500,000 views in the first week or so. My latest *Firewall*, which was posted seven months ago, currently sits at 18,000 views. My YouTube channel still shows one 187,000 subscribers—these are people who pushed a button specifically telling YouTube that they wanted to be notified when any new content of mine was posted. You would think that number of viewers or so would be the absolute floor when it came to the number of views. This is shadow banning in action.

When Prager University, an online site, sued YouTube several years ago about this same issue, it provided evidence that less than 5 percent of the people who subscribed in order to receive content from Prager U actually received the notification they had specifically requested. This is an import point: We are not talking about YouTube *failing to promote* Prager's, or my, or anyone else's, content. This is YouTube actively, aggressively denying notification to people who assume that being subscribed to a YouTube channel actually means being subscribed to a YouTube channel.

Now if you are in the opinion business and you hope to reach the gates of Heaven upon your demise rather than the gates of Hell, then you have a moral obligation to make an effort to be factually correct. And, so, I have asked myself, many times, if this decline in viewership was due not to nefarious dial-turning on the part of flabby, green-haired, twenty-something hysterics but rather to lack of interest in what I have to say, or declining quality of content, or the fact that styles and audiences change over time, or all three. In other words, is this precipitous decline in my viewership no one's fault but my own?

Here's the thing: In addition to the long-format *Afterburners* and *Firewalls*, which routinely topped 1 million views and often got three or four times that number (a video I did on gun control got 30 million views on Facebook seven years ago), I also do smaller, less widely popular daily commentary with my fellow old-school bloggers Steve Green and Scott Ott. The show is called *Right Angle*.

When we started *Right Angle*, it was pulling anywhere from 25,000 to 40,000 views, on average. And then, overnight, right in front of our eyes, those numbers dropped to somewhere between 12,000 and 15,000. Overnight. We'd build the viewership back up again, and then, again, an overnight drop to between 6,000 and 9,000 views. Why, if I didn't know better, that data pattern would seem to indicate that someone had turned an enormous electronic monkey wrench while I was sound asleep, comfortable in the knowledge that my AR-15 in the closet and my 1911 Colt .45 under my bed were keep me safe from harm. And they have kept me safe from harm. But they have not kept me safe from censorship.

When I cut and pasted the Wikipedia definition of shadow banning, I was struck by a term I had not heard used in this context before, and that term was "hellbanning." It's an excellent term, and I'll tell you why. This process deprives you of your audience without providing an explanation, and the go-to conclusion that every writer comes to is that your work no longer matters, is no longer relevant, and therefore no longer wanted. It is soul-destroying in a way that having scribbled pieces of paper secreted out of a dungeon through bribery and subterfuge is not. The Russian dissidents fighting coercive violence suffered terribly under the Soviets, but they never doubted that what they were doing mattered enough to possibly cost them their lives.

On April 7, 1775, Samuel Johnson wrote that "patriotism is the last refuge of a scoundrel." April 7 happens to be my birthday, although I was just a kid at the time and have no recollection of him saying it. He was referring to *false* patriotism, by the way.

In this essay I decided to call this shadow banning, this passive-aggressive, gutless, faceless, nameless, arbitrary and stupid form of censorship as "the first refuge of cowards" because that's what it is. Every time I see a message suppressed, I ask myself, "what are you so afraid of?" If your vaccine is safe and effective, then what are you so afraid of? If your electoral system is airtight and fraud-proof, then what are you so afraid of? If there is no biological distinction between men and women, then what are you so afraid of?

If you're right about Marxism, human nature, history, climate change, gun control, abortion, Hillary's emails, and Hunter Biden's laptop, then what are you so afraid of?

Well, that's easy. Truth. That's what they're afraid of. That's what they've always been afraid of. And this is why we will win.

THE END

CONTRIBUTORS

Peter Berkowitz is the Tad and Dianne Taube senior fellow at the Hoover Institution, Stanford University. He has written four books, edited six volumes, published hundreds of articles on a diversity of topics, and contributes regularly to *RealClearPolitics*. From 2019 to 2021, he served as director of the U.S. State Department's Policy Planning Staff.

Monica Crowley is a news analyst on multiple television, radio, digital, and print platforms, a *New York Times*-bestselling author, and host of the *Monica Crowley Podcast*. Previously, she served as assistant secretary of the Treasury for Public Affairs in the Trump administration and as foreign policy assistant to former President Richard Nixon in his final years.

Jack Dunphy (a pseudonym) was an officer with the Los Angeles Police Department for more than thirty years. Now retired from the LAPD, he works for a smaller (and better managed) police agency in Southern California.

Clarice Feldman is a retired litigation lawyer living in Washington, D.C. She represented Jock Yablonski and the Miners for Democracy in multiple suits to reform the United Mine Workers of America and also served as an attorney with the Department of Justice's Office of Special Investigation, assisting in the denaturalization and deportation of those who assisted the Nazis in World War II. She is a regular contributor to *American Thinker* and *The Pipeline*.

Tom Finnerty is the deputy editor of *The Pipeline*, an online publication devoted to energy issues, and in particular to exposing the environmentalist movements' war on freedom and prosperity throughout the world. A New Yorker by birth, Finnerty divides his time between New England and Ontario.

John Fund is a columnist for *National Review* and a former member of *The Wall Street Journal*'s editorial board.

Jon Gabriel is editor-in-chief of Ricochet.com, and an opinion contributor to the *Arizona Republic*, CNN.com, and *Discourse* magazine. He was formerly director of marketing for the Goldwater Institute, and served as a submarine reactor operator in the U.S. Navy.

Hannah Giles is the mother of three young children, an award-winning journalist, Valente Brothers Jujutsu Black Belt and former CEO of Project Veritas. She enjoys sustainable farming, gardening, painting, drawing, raising packs of Livestock Guardian Dogs and training with her Personal Protection K9s.

Sebastian Gorka, Ph.D., served as President Trump's Strategist in the White House and is presidential appointee to the Defense Department's National Security Education Board. He hosts the daily radio show *America First* on the Salem Radio Network. His latest book is *The War for America's Soul*.

Ian Gregory assisted Margaret Thatcher with the preparation of Prime Minister's Questions when he was eighteen, later attending Oxford University on an open scholarship to study philosophy, politics, and economics. He spent seven years at the BBC as a TV news producer. He now runs Abzed.com, a political and media relations agency.

Steven F. Hayward is the Gaylord Distinguished Visiting Professor at Pepperdine University's School of Public Policy and a fellow of the Public Law and Policy Program at Berkeley Law. He is the author or co-author of nine books, most recently *M. Stanton Evans: Conservative Wit, Apostle of Freedom*.

Mark Hemingway is a senior writer for *RealClearInvestigations* and the books editor at *The Federalist* and has written for outlets as diverse as *The Wall Street Journal*, *The Weekly Standard*, and MTV.com. Born in Bend, Oregon, he now resides in Alexandria, Virginia, with his wife and two children.

Andrew Klavan is the author of such internationally bestselling crime novels as *True Crime*, filmed by Clint Eastwood, *Don't Say a Word*, filmed starring Michael Douglas, *Empire of Lies*, and *When Christmas Comes*. He has been nominated for the Mystery Writers of America's Edgar Award five times and has won twice. He currently hosts a popular podcast, *The Andrew Klavan Show* at the *Daily Wire*.

Charlie Kirk is the founder of Turning Point USA and host of *The Charlie Kirk Show* podcast.

Mark Krikorian has been executive director of the Center for Immigration Studies in Washington, D.C., since 1995. His books include *The New Case Against Immigration, Both Legal and Illegal*, and *How Obama Is Transforming America Through Immigration*. He holds a master's degree from the Fletcher School of Law and Diplomacy and a bachelor's degree from Georgetown University, and spent two years at Yerevan State University in then-Soviet Armenia.

Jenny Kennedy is *The Pipeline*'s sustainable-lifestyle columnist. Born in British Hong Kong, she grew up in London and attended Cheltenham before completing her studies at the University of Southern California. A three-day eventer on the British Olympic equestrian team, Jenny has worked as a dressage coach in Hampshire, Findlay, Southampton, Palm Beach, and Hoboken.

Thomas H. Lipscomb has been the editor and publisher of numerous bestsellers, having served as publisher and CEO of three book publishing companies, most recently as founder of Times Books. His reporting and commentary have been published in many newspapers, including *The New York Times*, *The Washington Post*, *The Wall Street Journal*, and the *Chicago Sun-Times*.

Lance Morrow is the Henry Grunwald Senior Fellow at the Ethics and Public Policy Center. The son of an editor of the *Saturday Evening Post* and of a Washington columnist for the Knight syndicate, Morrow grew up in Washington, attended Gonzaga High School, and graduated magna cum laude from Harvard University. Morrow's award-winning essays have appeared in *Time*, *Smithsonian*, *The New York Times*, *The Atlantic*, and other publications.

Arthur Milikh is the executive director of the Claremont Institute's Center for the American Way of Life. He specializes in American political thought.

John J. Miller is director of the Dow Journalism Program at Hillsdale College, a writer and podcaster for *National Review*, and the founder and executive director of the Student Free Press Association, best known for its news website, *The College Fix*.

Elizabeth Nickson was trained at *Time* magazine, became European bureau chief at *Life* magazine, and went on to write for many major publishers in the U.S., the U.K., and Canada. She is a senior fellow at the Frontier Centre for Public Policy in Winnipeg, Canada, and writes *Welcome to Absurdistan* on Substack.

Larry O'Connor is a radio talk show host on Washington, D.C.'s WMAL, and a senior columnist and creative director at Townhall Media. He was a general manager and producer for Broadway musicals before Andrew Breitbart plucked him from obscurity and launched his career in journalism and conservative commentary.

John O'Sullivan is the founding editor of *The Pipeline*, editor-at-large of *National Review*, editor of Australia's *Quadrant*, and president of the Danube Institute in Budapest, Hungary. He has served as associate editor of the *Times* of London, as editorial and op-ed editor for Canada's *National Post*, and as special adviser to Margaret Thatcher. He is the author of *The President, the Pope, and the Prime Minister: Three Who Changed the World*.

Peter Prichard was the top editor of *USA Today* from 1988 to 1995, when it reached a daily sales of 2.3 million and became the largest-circulation newspaper in the nation. He helped to develop two versions of the Newseum for the Freedom Forum and served as its president and chair. He is the author of *The Making of McPaper: The Inside Story of USA Today* and *Killing Grace: A Vietnam War Mystery*.

Ashley Rindsberg is an investigative journalist and the author of *The Gray Lady Winked: How* The New York Times's *Misreporting, Distortions & Fabrications Radically Alter History*. He lives in London with his family.

David Reaboi is a communications professional who has spent the past two decades focused on American national security and political warfare. He lives in Miami Beach, and his public work appears at *Late Republic Nonsense* on Substack.

Glenn Reynolds, the founder of *Instapundit.com*, is the Beauchamp Brogan Distinguished Professor of Law at the University of Tennessee. He writes regularly for the *New York Post*, and for a decade was a columnist at *Popular Mechanics*. His books include *The Appearance of Impropriety* (with Peter W. Morgan), *An Army of Davids*, *The Judiciary's Class War*, and *The Social Media Upheaval*.

Michael Ramirez is a two-time Pulitzer Prize winner, editorial cartoonist for the *Las Vegas Review-Journal*, a contributor to *The Washington Post*, and is internationally syndicated with Creators Syndicate. He has also received the 2021 Overseas Press Club Award, the 2005 National Journalism Award, and is a five-time National Cartoonists Society Editorial Cartoon division winner.

Austin Ruse is president of C-Fam, a research institute in Special Consultative Status with the U.N. Economic and Social Council. He is the author of four books and hundreds of columns and essays.

Ben Scallan is an Irish journalist and political commentator with Gript Media, a husband, a father, and a convert to Catholicism. He was born and raised in Dublin to an Irish father and Jamaican mother.

Kurt Schlichter is a retired U.S. Army infantry colonel, an attorney, author, and a senior columnist at Townhall.com.

Elizabeth Sheld, Ph.D., is a veteran political strategist and pollster. She writes regularly on liberty issues, including firearm policy at such outlets as *American Greatness, RealClear Policy, Breitbart News*, and *The Federalist*. In her spare time, she shoots sporting clays and watches documentaries.

Kyle Shideler is the director and senior analyst for homeland security and counterterrorism at the Center for Security Policy in Washington, D.C.

Roger L. Simon is an award-winning novelist, Oscar-nominated screenwriter, and editor-at-large of *The Epoch Times*. His latest book is *American Refugees: The Untold Story of the Mass from Blue States to Red States*.

Peter Smith, after a career in economics and banking, now writes for *Quadrant*, Australia's leading conservative online site and magazine, and for *The Pipeline*. He is the author of *Bad Economics: Pestilent Economists, Profligate Governments, Debt, Dependency & Despair*. He lives in Sydney, where he attends an Anglican church.

David Solway is a Canadian essayist, songwriter, and poet. He has authored more than thirty volumes on poetry, travel, translation, education theory, and politics. Solway lives in Vancouver with his wife, author and video content creator Janice Fiamengo.

Priscilla Turner is a former movie executive and writer for network television. After a prior incarnation as a Berkeley leftist, she went on to create one of the earliest conservative online blogs, *Priscilla's Daily News*. She is also the author of seven children's books, including *The War Between the Vowels and the Consonants* and *Among the Odds & Evens: A Tale of Adventure*.

Michael Walsh is the former music critic and foreign correspondent for *Time* magazine, and the author or editor of eighteen books, including *The Devil's Pleasure Palace*, *The Fiery Angel*, *Last Stands*, and *Against the Great Reset*. He is the editor of *The Pipeline*.

George MF Washington is a thirty-year veteran of the movie business, analyzing Hollywood through a conservative lens. He can also quote movies better than you can. His work can be found at *The Continental Congress* on Substack.

Armond White is an American film and music critic who writes for *National Review* and *Out*. He was previously the editor of *CityArts* (2011–2014), the lead film critic for the alternative weekly *New York Press* (1997–2011), and the arts editor and critic for *The City Sun* (1984–1996). Other publications that have carried his work include *Film Comment*, *Variety*, *The Nation*, *The New York Times*, *Slate*, the *Columbia Journalism Review*, and *First Things*.

Bill Whittle is an amateur historian, a computer graphics artist, a screenwriter and director, and a thousand-hour, instrument-rated owner and pilot of experimental aircraft. His thousands of political videos have been viewed about 100 million times. He lives in Los Angeles.

J. Peder Zane is a columnist for *RealClearPolitics* and an editor at *RealClearInvestigations*. His writing has won the Distinguished Writing Award for Commentary from the American Society of Newspaper Editors. He was a news assistant at *The New York Times* during the early 1990s.